SHORENSTEIN APARC STANFORD

THE WALTER H. SHORENSTEIN
ASIA-PACIFIC RESEARCH CENTER

Studies of the Walter H. Shorenstein Asia-Pacific Research Center

Andrew G. Walder, General Editor

The Walter H. Shorenstein Asia-Pacific Research Center in the Freeman Spogli Institute for International Studies at Stanford University sponsors interdisciplinary research on the politics, economies, and societies of contemporary Asia. This monograph series features academic and policy-oriented research by Stanford faculty and other scholars associated with the Center.

Dynasties and Democracy

THE INHERITED INCUMBENCY

ADVANTAGE IN JAPAN

Daniel M. Smith

Stanford University Press

Stanford, California

Stanford University Press

Stanford, California

Printed in the United States of America on acid-free, archival-quality paper

Library of Congress Cataloging-in-Publication Data

Names: Smith, Daniel M., 1982– author.
Title: Dynasties and democracy : the inherited incumbency advantage in Japan / Daniel M. Smith.
Description: Stanford, California : Stanford University Press, 2018. | Series: Studies of the Walter H. Shorenstein Asia-Pacific Research Center | Includes bibliographical references and index.
Identifiers: LCCN 2017050717 (print) | LCCN 2017055065 (e-book) | ISBN 9781503606401 (e-book) | ISBN 9781503605053 | ISBN 9781503605053 (cloth : alk. paper) | ISBN 9781503606401 (e-book)
Subjects: LCSH: Politicians—Family relationships—Japan. | Families—Political aspects—Japan. | Incumbency (Public officers)—Japan. | Political parties—Japan. | Democracy—Japan. | Japan—Politics and government—1945–
Classification: LCC JQ1681 (e-book) | LCC JQ1681 .S6895 2018 (print) | DDC 328.52/073—dc23
LC record available at https://lccn.loc.gov/2017050717

Typeset by Newgen in 11/14 Garamond

Cover design: Christian Fuenfhausen

To my mother and father.

Contents

Figures

Tables

Preface and Acknowledgments

Democracy is supposed to be the antithesis of hereditary rule by family dynasties. And yet, looking around the world, one sees that "democratic dynasties" continue to persist. They have been conspicuously prevalent in Japan, where more than a third of all legislators and two-thirds of all cabinet ministers in recent years have come from families with a history in parliament. Such a high proportion of dynasties is comparatively unusual and has sparked serious concerns over whether democracy in Japan is functioning properly.

In this book, I introduce a comparative theory based on a framework of supply and demand to explain the causes and consequences of dynasties in democracies like Japan. I argue that members of dynasties enjoy an "inherited incumbency advantage" in all three stages of a typical political career: selection, election, and promotion. However, I argue that the nature and extent of this advantage, as well as its consequences for elections and representation, varies by the institutional context of electoral rules and candidate selection methods within parties. In the late 1980s, roughly half of all new candidates in Japan's long-ruling Liberal Democratic Party (LDP) were political legacies. However, electoral system reform in 1994 and subsequent party reforms have changed the incentives for party leaders to rely on dynastic politics in candidate selection. A new pattern of party-based competition is slowly replacing the old pattern of competition based on localized family fiefdoms. Nevertheless, path dependence and a continue supply of legacy hopefuls impedes more dramatic change.

This book is the end product of several years of feedback from countless individuals. I owe a debt of gratitude to the many mentors and friends who helped me develop the project and see it through to completion. My first introduction to Japanese politics was at the University of California, Los Angeles, where an undergraduate course taught by Michael Thies and Linda Hasunuma set me on a path of inquiry that has become the main focus of my research. My undergraduate thesis adviser, Miriam Golden, deserves credit for pushing me to pursue graduate study at the University of California, San Diego, after first going to Tokyo to study Japanese politics with Steve Reed at Chuo University on a Ministry of Education, Culture, Sports, Science, and Technology (MEXT) research fellowship. Over the course of nearly two years, Steve patiently imparted his vast knowledge of Japanese politics and prepared me for graduate school better than anyone else possibly could have. The idea to study the causes and consequences of Japan's political dynasties from a comparative perspective sprang forth in 2006 during one of our many conversations.

At UCSD, I was fortunate to be trained and mentored by many others, including the members of my dissertation committee: Kaare Strøm (chair), Matt Shugart, Ellis Krauss, Gary Cox, Gary Jacobson, and Krislert Samphantharak. Kaare Strøm thoughtfully guided me through graduate school and has created more opportunities for me than I can ever repay. Matt Shugart, Ellis Krauss, and Gary Cox also played integral roles in shaping my ideas, improving the direction of my research, and helping me to learn and grow as a scholar. Countless other faculty mentors and peers at UCSD aided me to slowly, but purposefully, build this project, including Yasu-hiko Tohsaku, Eiko Ushida, Takeo Hoshi, Ulrike Schaede, and Megumi Naoi.

Later, my ideas benefited from the feedback and support of colleagues at the Walter H. Shorenstein Asia-Pacific Research Center (Shorenstein APARC) at Stanford University and in the Department of Government at Harvard University. At Stanford, I thank Phillip Lipscy, Kenji Kushida, Takeo Hoshi, Dan Sneider, Gi-Wook Shin, and the administrative staff at APARC. At Stanford University Press, I thank especially Geoffrey Burn, Kate Wahl, Marcela Maxfield, Anne Fuzellier, Stephanie Adams, and Olivia Bartz. At Harvard, I am grateful to my friends and colleagues in the Department of Government, the Reischauer Institute of Japanese Studies, the Weatherhead Center for International Affairs and its Program on US-Japan Relations, the Minda de Gunzburg Center for European Studies, and the Institute for Quantitative Social Science for their support and encouragement. I especially want to thank Susan Pharr and Torben Iversen, who have served as invaluable faculty mentors, and Mark Ramseyer, Ezra Vogel, Stephen Ansolabehere, Jeff Frieden, Kenneth Shepsle, Jim Snyder, Peter Hall, Daniel Ziblatt, Dustin Tingley, Arthur Spirling, Eric Beerbohm, Ryan Enos, Horacio Larreguy, Gwyneth McClendon, Josh Kertzer, Jon Rogowski, Matt Blackwell, Yuhua Wang, and Shin Fujihira for feedback and conversations that helped sharpen my ideas and improve my analysis.

Several scholars in Japan have provided helpful comments, support, or insight, including Steve Reed, Masataka Harada, Yukio Maeda, Michio Muramatsu, Naoto Nonaka, John Campbell, Kenneth McElwain, Kuniaki Nemoto, Hiroshi Ishida, Kaori Shoji, Kentaro Fukumoto, Hidenori Tsutsumi, Naofumi Fujimura, Greg Noble, and participants in workshops at the Institute of Social Science at the University of Tokyo. Outside of Japan, I thank Shane Martin, Jon Fiva, Benny Geys, Olle Folke, Johanna Rickne, Pablo Querubín, Kanchan Chandra, Brenda van Coppenolle, Carlos Velasco Rivera, Amy Catalinac, Len Schoppa, Frances Rosenbluth, Mike Tomz, Juan Pablo Micozzi, Kiyoteru Tsutsui and countless others in audiences at conferences and workshops at Harvard, Yale, the Instituto Tecnológico Autónomo de México (ITAM), Princeton, Stanford, the University of Michigan, and the Norwegian Business School (BI), for conversations and critiques that have moved this project along. Steve Reed, Susan Pharr, Mark Ramseyer, Robert Pekkanen, Jon Fiva, Masataka Harada, Gary Cox, Torben Iversen, Max Goplerud, Shiro Kuriwaki, José Ramón Enríquez, Brandon Martinez, Griffin Gonzalez, graduate students in my seminar on political institutions in fall 2016, and anonymous reviewers read and commented on all or large parts of the manuscript. Their feedback was crucial in the final stretch.

This project has been supported financially by several generous programs. Field research in Tokyo in 2010–2011 was made possible by the generous support of the Japan-US Educational Commission (JUSEC, Fulbright Program Japan). I thank JUSEC director David Satterwhite, and especially Jinko Brinkman and Mizuho Iwata, for facilitating my research in Tokyo and helping to arrange interviews with politicians. Thanks are also owed to Yukio Maeda and the Institute of Social Science at the University of Tokyo for hosting me during this year of field research. Additional field research in Ireland was made possible with the help of Shane Martin, and financial assistance from the UCSD Friends of the International Center. Other aspects of the project, including follow-up interviews in Japan, were financially supported by the Reischauer Institute of Japanese Studies. The Weatherhead Center for International Affairs generously supported a workshop for an earlier draft of the book. I thank the participants of that workshop for sharing their time and expertise with me in Cambridge: Ethan Scheiner, Frances Rosenbluth, Yusaku Horiuchi, Susan Pharr, Torben Iversen, Jim Snyder, Shane Martin, Naofumi Fujimura, and Shin Fujihira.

This book could not have been possible without the dedicated work of a team of student research assistants and their efforts in data collection. Special thanks are owed to graduate students Colleen Driscoll, José Ramón Enríquez, Max Goplerud, Shiro Kuriwaki, and Mafalda Pratas Fernandes, as well as undergraduates Mark Daley, Ross Friedman, Anna Gomez, Griffin Gonzalez, Brandon Martinez, Anna Menzel, Megan Mers, Andrew Miner, Darragh Nolan, Anthony Ramicone, Aaron Roper, Carlos Schmidt-Padilla, Isabel Vasquez, Anthony Volk, and Eric Xiao. Joan Cho and Danny Crichton helped me to locate and code data on South Korean dynasties, and Naoko Taniguchi, Nathan Batto, Pablo Querubín, Brenda van Coppenolle, and Kanchan Chandra kindly shared their own data or statistics on dynasties. Koji Sonoda helped me locate the data on Japanese politicians' assets. Harvard librarians Kazuko Sakaguchi and Kuniko McVey also pointed me in various helpful directions. Alex Storer, Ista Zahn, and Kareem Carr at the Institute for Quantitative Social Science helped immensely with data collection issues. Additional methodological feedback from Simo Goshev, Ista Zahn, Matt Blackwell, Jon Fiva, Horacio Larreguy, Masataka Harada, and Gary Cox helped move the project along. Shiro Kuriwaki helped to create the map featured in Chapter 2. Teppei Yamamoto created the original figure for the conjoint analysis results that appear in Chapter 5. Amy Catalinac provided the Hellinger distance measure used in Chapter 7. I am also grateful to the many politicians and party staff members in Japan who shared their experiences and viewpoints with me in personal interviews.

Collaborations and conversations with my coauthors have shaped this project in numerous ways. I thank Robert Pekkanen, Ellis Krauss, Hidenori Tsutsumi, Steve Reed, Yusaku Horiuchi, Teppei Yamamoto, Shane Martin, Olle Folke, Johanna Rickne, Ethan Scheiner, Justin Reeves, Amy Catalinac, Gary Cox, Mike Thies, Jon Fiva, Benny Geys, and Masataka Harada for their contributions to related research projects.

This list is exhaustive, but undoubtedly I have left some people out who have made a positive impact on me or this research. Thank *you*, too. Last, and most important, I thank my family for their continuous and patient support, especially John and Annie, who put up with me in the final push to finish this book.

A final note is warranted in light of recent events. In late September 2017, as this book was already in production, Prime Minister Abe Shinzō decided to call a snap election for the House of Representatives. Continuing the trend set in motion after Japan's 1994 electoral reform and accelerated since the LDP's 2005 party reforms, the new legacy candidates who emerged in 2017 were mostly the offspring of longtime incumbents from existing dynasties who were first elected under the pre-1994 electoral system, or of those who had died suddenly in office. These include the sons, grandsons, or brothers of former prime ministers and other cabinet ministers: Hatoyama Tarō, Nakasone Yasutaka, Hiranuma Shōjirō, Kōmura Masahiro, Yasuoka Hirotake, Yosano Makoto, Kimura Jirō, Wakabayashi Kenta, and Kaneko Shunpei.

But it was not smooth sailing for many of these new legacies. Hatoyama and Hiranuma did not get the LDP's nomination and had to run with the label of the newly formed Party of Hope and as an independent, respectively. Nakasone was forced to run on the Kita Kanto proportional representation (PR) list rather than in his grandfather's old district in Gunma prefecture (where the party's nomination had already been granted to another legacy incumbent from the PR tier, Omi Asako). He, along with Kōmura, Kimura, and Kaneko, managed to win seats, but Yasuoka, Hiranuma, and Hatoyama were all rejected by the voters. Yosano was ranked near the bottom of the LDP's Tokyo PR list and narrowly lost out on a seat. Wakabayashi, who previously served in the House of Councillors, narrowly missed winning a seat through the Hokuriku Shinetsu PR list. Another new LDP legacy candidate, Shiraishi Hiroki, whose father, Tōru, had served only two terms before dying suddenly in office, was also defeated. Hokkaido 11th District featured a contest between Nakagawa Yūko (LDP), the incumbent widow of former finance minister Nakagawa Shōichi, and Ishikawa Kaori, a former television announcer and wife of disgraced former Democratic Party of Japan MP Ishikawa Tomohiro. Ishikawa ran with the nomination of the newly formed Constitutional Democratic Party of Japan, and defeated the LDP incumbent.

Thus, although many new legacy candidates ran in 2017, the pattern continues to reflect changes in supply and demand in dynastic candidate selection, as described in the chapters of this book. Legacy candidates are still emerging, and often getting the nomination of the LDP, but these legacies tend to be descendants of powerful existing dynasties with strong supply-side incentives to run. Those who try to succeed weaker incumbents, or who offer less to the party leadership in terms of their other qualities, have a harder time getting nominated and elected. Over time, the changes set in motion by Japan's institutional reforms will continue to reduce the prevalence of dynastic politics in the LDP.

Daniel M. Smith
Cambridge, MA
December 2017

Dynasties and Democracy

ONE

Introduction
Dynasties in Democracies

> At the antipodes of the monarchical principle, in theory, stands
> democracy, denying the right of one over others. *In abstracto,*
> it makes all citizens equal before the law. It gives to each one of
> them the possibility of ascending to the top of the social scale,
> and thus facilitates the way for the rights of the community, an-
> nulling before the law all privileges of birth, and desiring that in
> human society the struggle for preëminence should be decided
> solely in accordance with individual capacity.
>
> —*Robert Michels (1915, p. 1)*

On April 1, 2000, Prime Minister Obuchi Keizō of the long-ruling Liberal Democratic Party (LDP) of Japan suffered a sudden stroke at the age of sixty-two and later died following a monthlong coma.[1] As prime minister, Obuchi had been described as having "all the pizazz of a cold pizza" because of his bland personality and style.[2] However, as a candidate for the House of Representatives, the lower and more powerful chamber of Japan's bicameral parliament, the National Diet, he had been extremely successful. Obuchi's father had been a member of parliament (MP) in the House of Representatives for Gunma Prefecture's 3rd District until his death in 1958. In 1963, at the age of twenty-six, Obuchi ran for his father's old seat and won his first election. He went on to win eleven consecutive reelection victories, and earned more than 70 percent of the vote against two challengers in his final election attempt in 1996.

In the June 25, 2000, general election held shortly after his death, the LDP nominated Obuchi's twenty-six-year-old daughter, Yūko, as his replacement. Yūko had quit her job at the Tokyo Broadcasting System (TBS) television network to become her father's personal secretary when he became prime minister in 1998. In her first election attempt, she defeated three other candidates with 76 percent of the vote. Since then, she has consistently won between 68 percent and 77 percent of the vote in her district and has faced only weak challengers from minor parties. The LDP's main opposition from 1998 to 2016, the Democratic Party of Japan (DPJ), fielded a candidate against her only in the 2005 general election: a thirty-six-year-old party employee with no prior electoral experience.[3] He managed to win only a quarter of the vote in the district.

A young and politically inexperienced woman like Obuchi Yūko would normally be considered a weak candidate in Japan, where the average age of first-time candidates is forty-seven, and female candidates are rare (Obuchi was one of just five women nominated in a district race by the LDP in the 2000 election). Yet by virtue of her family background, and no doubt aided by sympathy votes after her father's death, she enjoyed an incredible electoral advantage in her first election—both in terms of her name recognition with voters and in terms of the lack of high-quality challengers—and this advantage continued in subsequent elections. In 2008, after just three election victories, she became the youngest cabinet minister in postwar Japanese history when she was appointed minister of state in charge of the declining birthrate and gender equality in the cabinet of Prime Minister Asō Tarō. Few other LDP MPs have advanced to positions of power in the cabinet as quickly.

The Puzzle of Dynasties in Democracies

This book is about the causes and political consequences of dynasties in democracies. It examines the factors that contribute to their development over time and across space, and the advantages that members of dynasties, such as Obuchi Yūko, enjoy throughout their political careers—from candidate selection, to election, to promotion into higher offices in cabinet. It also considers the potential consequences of dynastic politics for the functioning of modern representative democracy. More specifically, the research design employed in this book takes advantage of institutional change in the country of Japan to help shed comparative light on the phenomenon of dynasties across democracies more generally. The aim is to improve our understanding about how dynastic politics have evolved over time in Japan, as well as how Japan's experience might provide insight or lessons for understanding dynastic politics in other democracies around the world.

How might we conceptualize "dynasties" in democracies? Dynasties are, of course, common at the executive level in nondemocratic regimes such as monarchies or personal dictatorships. An autocratic ruler can often successfully anoint a family member as his (it is almost always "his") successor when the party system or leadership selection mechanisms are weak, and the extant power distributions among the broader elite are sustained (Brownlee, 2007).[4] An example is North Korea's Kim Jong-un, who came into power in 2011 as the "Great Successor" to his deceased father, Kim Jong-il, who himself became supreme leader following the death of his father, Kim Il-sung, in 1994. Another example is Syrian president Bashar al-Assad, who inherited his position in 2000 from his father, Hafez al-Assad, who had ruled Syria in a personal dictatorship since 1971.

But that similar dynasties should continue to exist in *democracies* seems to run counter to widely held normative visions of democratic opportunity and fairness—even given the fact that members of dynasties must ultimately be popularly elected. The democratic ideal that "all men are created equal" should presumably extend to the equality of opportunity to participate in elective office, such that no individual is more privileged simply by birth to enter into politics. We might therefore expect democratization to catalyze an end to dynasties, as all real democracies eventually provide for the legal equality of all citizens to run for public office, barring minor restrictions based on place of birth, residence, age, or law-abiding conduct. Even before full democratic reform, modernization and the rise of capitalism should contribute to the decay of the traditional patrimonial state, such that historically dominant families should begin to "fade from macropolitics" (Adams, 2005, p. 29).

And yet throughout the modern democratized world, it is still possible to find powerful political dynasties—families who have returned multiple individuals to public office, sometimes consecutively, and sometimes spanning several generations. It is not uncommon for parties and voters to turn to "favored sons," "democratic scions," or the "People's Dukes" for political representation, despite the availability of less "blue-blooded" candidates.[5] Recent prominent examples from outside of Japan include President George W. Bush and Senator Hillary Clinton in the United States, Prime Minister Justin Trudeau in Canada, Prime Minister David Cameron and Labour Party leader Ed Miliband in the United Kingdom, President Park Geun-hye in South Korea, Marine Le Pen and Marion Maréchal-Le Pen in France,

Prime Minister Enda Kenny in Ireland, President Benigno Aquino III in the Philippines, Sonia and Rahul Gandhi in India, Alessandra Mussolini in Italy, and Tzipi Livni in Israel.

Defining what exactly constitutes a dynasty can be complicated given the variety of family relationships and levels of government in which family members might serve. In this book, a *legacy candidate* is defined as any candidate for national office who is related by blood or marriage to a politician who had previously served in national legislative or executive office (presidency or cabinet). If a legacy candidate is elected, he or she becomes a *legacy MP* and creates a *democratic dynasty*, which is defined as any family that has supplied two or more members to national-level political office.[6] This definition of what constitutes a dynasty is more liberal than that used by Stephen Hess (1966, p. 2), who defines a dynasty in the American context as "any family that has had at least four members, in the same name, elected to federal office." The definition used here is not limited to dynasties with continuity in surname. In addition, only two family members are necessary to constitute a dynasty, rather than four members, which would limit the scope of the analysis to countries, such as the United States, with a longer democratic history. The definition also does not require that a legacy candidate be a member of the same party as his or her predecessor, or run in the same electoral district, although both conditions generally tend to be the case. Family members can serve consecutively or simultaneously, with the exception that two family members first elected at the same time would not constitute a democratic dynasty.

By this definition, Japan stands out among democracies for its high proportion of legacy MPs. Figure 1.1 shows the average percentage of legacy MPs among all MPs elected in the past two decades (1995–2016) in twenty-four democracies for which data are available. Since the 1996 general election, more than a quarter of all MPs in the Japanese House of Representatives have been members of a democratic dynasty, a fact that puts Japan, along with Ireland and Iceland, in the company of economically developing and younger democracies like Taiwan, the Philippines, and Thailand (the most dynastic country for which data are available). Greece, Belgium, and India occupy what might be considered the middle stratum of dynastic politics, with between 10 percent and 15 percent of members in recent years coming from democratic dynasties.[7] In most other democracies, legacy MPs tend to account for between 5 percent and 10 percent of parliament. This level of dynas-

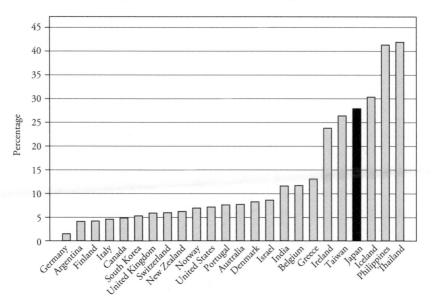

FIGURE 1.1 Prevalence of democratic dynasties around the world

SOURCES: Thailand (2011): Thananithichot and Satidporn (2016); Philippines (1995–2010): Querubín (2016); Iceland (1995–2013): biographical archive of the Althingi; Taiwan (2001–2012): Batto (2015); Greece (2000–2012): Patrikios and Chatzikonstantinou (2015); Belgium (1995–2012): biographical archive of the Chamber of Representatives and online biographies; India (2004–2009): Chandra, Bohlken, and Chauchard (2014); Denmark (2011): *Ekstra Bladet* newspaper; Portugal (2005–2011): compiled from online biographies and local and national newspaper reports; United Kingdom (1997–2010): van Coppenolle (2017) and House of Commons Library; South Korea (1996–2012): National Assembly Museum and website; Argentina (1995 only): Rossi (2017); all other data are part of the Dynasties in Democracies Dataset (see Appendix B).

NOTE: Bar values represent the average percentage of legacy MPs in each country (lower chamber only) elected between 1995 and 2016 (as noted in sources). Observations across elections are pooled, so individuals who served multiple terms are counted multiple times. Data for the Philippines are based on a proxy measure matching names. Data for India do not include relations to members of the upper house (Rajya Sabha). All other data are based on verified biographical information.

tic politics might thus be considered a "normal" level for healthy democracies. Among the democracies for which comparative data are available, Germany appears to be the least prone to dynastic politics, with less than 2 percent of members of the German Bundestag in recent years counting as legacy MPs.

What accounts for this variation across democracies, and for the high level of dynastic politics in Japan? It is perhaps unsurprising that dynasties might abound in nascent and developing democracies, where the economic rents from political office are often greater than the opportunities for riches outside of public office. If access to political decision-making authority enables politicians to live considerably better than their constituents, then this should provide greater incentives for such elites to seek to maintain their grip on power. The pool of elites who are interested, eligible, and qualified for public office may also be shallower in new and developing democracies. Members of the elite ruling class may be among the few with the education, wealth, and other technical skills and resources necessary to be effective candidates and policymakers.

Similarly, a lower supply of high-quality non-legacy candidates might help to explain a high proportion of dynasties in small democracies such as Iceland. The Icelandic Althingi contains just sixty-three seats and represents a population of only about 320,000 people (more than half of whom live in and around the capital of Reykjavík). A smaller-sized parliament also means that even a small increase or decrease in the raw number of legacy MPs can mathematically have a big effect on the overall proportion in parliament.[8] We might expect to find similarly high proportions of dynasties in other small countries, such as the island democracies of the Pacific and Caribbean. For example, President Tommy Remengesau Jr. of Palau is the son of a former president, and Prime Minister Enele Sopoaga of Tuvalu is the brother of a former prime minister.

However, economic development in larger democracies should be expected to eventually lead to a decline in dynasties, in part because it should broaden the structure of political opportunity so that a more diverse range of citizens will be qualified and able to get involved in politics, including through direct participation in elective office. The development of competitive and programmatic political parties should further limit the power of dynasties and increase the opportunities for capable outsiders to enter politics. Indeed, in nearly all established democracies, the trend over time has been a decrease in dynasties since democratization.[9] In the United Kingdom, for example, the proportion of legacy MPs in the House of Commons declined from more than 30 percent in the late 1800s to less than 10 percent in recent decades (van Coppenolle, 2017). The proportion in the Swiss National Council peaked at around 19 percent in 1908, then gradually dropped to less than 6 percent by the 2000s. In Italy, the proportion of legacy MPs in the Chamber of Deputies declined from roughly 13 percent in the immediate postwar period to less than 5 percent today. Dynastic membership in the Canadian House of Commons reached its zenith of 11 percent in 1896, and today is also less than 5 percent.

In the United States, despite several high-profile legacy candidates among presidential hopefuls in recent decades—such as Al Gore, George W. Bush, Mitt Romney, Jeb Bush, Hillary Clinton, and Rand Paul—the general trend in Congress has also been a decline in dynasties.[10] In the early decades of American democracy, over 15 percent of members of the House of Representatives were related to a previous member of Congress (either chamber) or the president. However, in recent decades, members of such dynasties have accounted for only around 6 percent to 8 percent of members (Dal Bó, Dal Bó, and Snyder, 2009; Feinstein, 2010). Dynasties have elicited a considerable amount of attention in the US media in recent years, but their prevalence in Congress is actually comparable to the prevalence of dynasties in most other developed democracies.

In striking contrast, Japan witnessed a steady increase in dynasties for several decades following democratization. After Japan's defeat in World War II, the US Occupation (1945–1952) introduced universal suffrage and equality of eligibility for public office, and enshrined these rights in the postwar Constitution of 1947.[11] Since then, despite rapid economic growth and the legal opportunity for all citizens to participate in politics, the proportion of legacy MPs in the Japanese House of Representatives subsequently crept upward, toward a zenith of over 30 percent by the late 1980s. Dynasties have been particularly prevalent within the conservative LDP, which has been the dominant party in Japan since its formation in 1955. Over time, the proportion of dynasties in the LDP swelled—from less than 20 percent of elected members in 1958, the first election after the party's founding, to over 40 percent by the early 1980s. Moreover, nearly half of all new candidates for the LDP in the 1980s and early 1990s were legacies.

In contrast, the share of legacy MPs in the Japan Socialist Party (JSP), the LDP's main opposition on the left until 1993, rarely exceeded 12 percent. In the third largest party, the religious party Kōmeitō, the average was just 5 percent. In the center-left DPJ, the proportion was initially over 25 percent, owing to the numerous former centrist members of the LDP who joined the party after it was founded in 1996. However, the DPJ subsequently recruited fewer new legacy candidates, and the proportion of legacy MPs in the party declined to around 16 percent. As a result, when the DPJ won a landslide victory over the LDP in 2009, the proportion of legacy MPs in the House of Representatives dropped to 22 percent—still high by comparative standards but the lowest proportion in Japan since the 1960s. In the 2014 House of Representatives election, 156 out of 1,191 candidates were legacy candidates (13 percent); however, 125 of these legacy candidates won, so legacy MPs accounted for 26 percent of the 475 MPs in the chamber. Ninety-eight (78 percent) of these legacy MPs were members of the LDP.

Such a disproportionately large presence of dynasties in a long-established and economically advanced democracy like Japan runs counter to our expectations for how the nature of political representation develops over time in democracies, as well as widely held normative visions of democratic opportunity and participation—particularly when the trend over time is toward more dynasties rather than fewer. Elections in Japan are free and fair, and the country does not suffer from the severe economic inequality or lack of social mobility and access to higher education that may pose barriers to greater participation of non-legacy candidates in developing democracies. With a population of over 120 million people, it is also difficult to believe that there are simply not enough willing or qualified non-legacy candidates available to run for public office.

How have dynasties managed to persist and multiply, particularly within the LDP, despite the lack of formal barriers to candidacy for all eligible citizens? What is it about democratic dynasties like the Obuchi family that allows them to thrive across multiple generations in an advanced industrialized democracy like Japan? Do legacy candidates possess special advantages, such as name recognition, familiarity with politics, or financial resources above and beyond those of other candidates, which make them more capable of "succeeding" in politics (in both senses of the word)? If so, what are the conditions under which these advantages become more or less pronounced? And what are the potential consequences of dynastic politics for the functioning of democracy and the quality of representation in Japan?

These are the kinds of questions that will be tackled in this book. By examining the phenomenon of democratic dynasties through the case of Japan, the goal is to shed comparative light on two broader puzzles: First, what are the underlying causes of dynastic recruitment and selection in democracies? Second, what are the political consequences of dynastic politics for the functioning of elections and representation?

Why Dynasties? The Causes of Dynastic Politics

One explanation for the phenomenon of democratic dynasties points to the dominance of elites in political life more generally. Scholars of political elites and power have long argued that the ruling class of a society can perpetuate its status over the less organized masses, even within a democracy (e.g., Michels, 1915).[12] The wealth, network connections, and other resource advantages of the elite help them to win elections, and these advantages are often easily transferred to their children, either directly or by virtue of increased opportunities for education and career advancement from the environment of their childhood. Gaetano Mosca (1939, pp. 61–62) provides an elaboration of this point:

> The democratic principle of election by broad-based suffrage would seem at first glance to be in conflict with the tendency toward stability which . . . ruling classes show. But it must be noted that candidates who are successful in democratic elections are almost always the ones who possess the political forces above enumerated [resources and connections], which are very often hereditary. In the English, French and Italian parliaments we frequently see the sons, grandsons, brothers, nephews and sons-in-law of members and deputies, ex-members and ex-deputies.

With a few exceptions, such as the Kennedy family, the most prominent dynasties in US history have shared a more or less common background that might be considered the "best butter" in American politics: "old stock, Anglo-Saxon, Protestant, professional, Eastern seaboard, well to do" (Hess, 1966, p. 3). Similarly, it is common for members of Japanese dynasties to have advanced degrees from the finest universities (or to have studied abroad), and many come from wealthy backgrounds. For example, brothers Hatoyama Yukio and Kunio were heirs to the Bridgestone Corporation fortune through their mother.[13] Even in democracies, elite families might continue to dominate the political process simply by virtue of their superior endowments of income, education, and connections. These advantages might arguably give legacy candidates a head start over non-legacy candidates in building a political career.

This type of elite dominance theory for dynastic politics is likely to have the most power in explaining dynasties in developing democracies, where political elites typically enjoy higher standards of living than their constituents and political parties play a smaller role in organizing and financing political competition. In the Philippines, for example, jurisdictions represented by legacy MPs tend to be associated with higher poverty, lower employment, and greater economic inequality (Mendoza et al., 2012; Tusalem and Pe-Aguirre, 2013). A high proportion of dynasties has also been documented in developing democracies in Latin America, such as Mexico (Camp, 1982) and Nicaragua (Vilas, 1992), and in South Asian developing democracies like India (Chhibber, 2013; Chandra, 2016) and Bangladesh (Amundsen, 2016).

If holding political office brings private rents that exceed what might be gained in other professions, elite families might also try to hold on to power through direct manipulation of the electoral or candidate selection processes. For example, Pablo Querubín (2011) finds that term limits in the Philippines do not stop the perpetuation of dynasties—rather, they allow them to spread because politicians tend to seek higher office and get their relatives elected to their previous positions. Pradeep Chhibber (2013) looks at dynastic succession in party leadership in India through a similar lens. He argues that dynastic leadership succession is more likely in parties that lack broader organizational ties to groups in society and have centralized party finances in the top leadership. Such personalized parties might be compared to family firms, with incentives to keep leadership and control of the party within the family (as well as knowledge of any financial malfeasance). Kanchan Chandra (2016) makes a similar argument about access to state resources and weak party control over nominations to explain the Indian case, but she considers all MPs elected to recent parliaments, not just party leaders.

THE INHERITED INCUMBENCY ADVANTAGE

In contrast to prior research on dynasties in developing democracies, the existing research on dynasties in developed democracies has focused more specifically on the electoral and informational advantages of a dynastic background. Legacy candidates enjoy strong name recognition, network connections, ease in raising campaign funds, and familiarity with politics and campaigning through increased exposure to the political life of family members, and this may result in their being favored over non-legacy candidates in the recruitment and selection processes. These advantages are much like the well-known advantages enjoyed by incumbents.

The incumbency advantage in US congressional elections, and its growth over time, has been widely studied since it was first pointed out in the early 1970s (Erikson, 1971; Mayhew, 1974). The source of the incumbency advantage has been divided in the existing literature into three main components: (1) the direct advantages of being in office (e.g., increased name recognition, perquisites of office, and the ability to direct funds to one's district), and indirect advantages owing to (2) the differential quality of incumbents due to on-the-job experience, and (3) the deterrence of high-quality challengers. These components of the incumbency advantage can be a challenge to disentangle, as some might reflect ex ante qualities that helped a candidate win election in the first place, whereas others can be considered the result of the "treatment" of winning office. Recent studies have aimed to estimate the causal effect of incumbency on future election outcomes through the use of regression discontinuity (RD) designs applied to close elections, where the treatment of winning office can be considered "as good as randomized" (Lee, 2008).[14] The conclusion from most of these studies is that marginally elected incumbents tend to enjoy significantly higher probabilities of being renominated and reelected in future races. Comparative studies have identified a similar incumbency advantage in a wide range of countries and contexts.

It is not difficult to imagine how a legacy candidate, particularly one who immediately succeeds his or her family member as a candidate in the same electoral district, might "inherit" part of a predecessor's incumbency advantage, both in terms of concrete electoral advantages (name recognition, connections, and resources) and—because of those perceived electoral advantages—in terms of candidate selection. The advantages enjoyed by a new legacy candidate as a result of his or her family ties to a previous politician can be regarded as an *inherited incumbency advantage.*

In a seminal study of dynasties in the US Congress, Ernesto Dal Bó, Pedro Dal Bó, and Jason Snyder (2009) reject the idea that dynastic persistence reflects differences in innate family characteristics (what we might call the "best butter" argument for elite dominance) and argue that the probability of a dynasty forming increases with the length of time a founding member holds office—suggesting a "power-treatment effect" acting on the ability of dynasties to self-perpetuate. In other words, dynasties become more likely to form as a (potential) founding member builds up what is likely to be a greater incumbency advantage. Although holding office for several terms should not necessarily affect the innate personal characteristics of a politician's child or other close relative, it most certainly increases his or her political connections, familiarity with election campaigns and the policymaking process, and name recognition. These positive effects of officeholding may thus help perpetuate an elite family's status in politics. The implication, as Dal Bó, Dal Bó, and Snyder (2009, p. 115) put it, is that "power begets power."

In most cases of dynastic succession in politics, the aspect of the incumbency advantage that is most easily heritable is name recognition. Similar to affiliation with a party label, family names can function as "brands" that convey information to voters at a low cost, helping to cue the established reputation of the family (Clubok, Wilensky, and Berghorn, 1969; Feinstein, 2010). They can be especially valuable when party labels are a weak source of information. If personal reputation is important to garnering votes, candidates whose relatives had served in politics can capitalize on the name recognition and established support inherited from their relatives. Name recognition can help a legacy candidate get selected, and elected, even if he or she enters the political scene several years after a predecessor's exit from politics. It can also play a role in the selection of a legacy candidate following the sudden death of an incumbent, with party elites hoping to capitalize on any possible sympathy vote in the resulting by-election. Nominating a relative in such cases may even be viewed as closely approximating the wishes of the electorate that had previously given a mandate to the now-deceased politician.

Previous studies of dynastic politics in Japan have also emphasized the importance of name recognition in elections that are centered more on candidates' personal characteristics and local ties than on their party labels or policies (e.g., Ishibashi and Reed, 1992; Taniguchi, 2008).[15] Michihiro Ishibashi and Steven R. Reed (1992) note that a legacy candidate in Japan benefits not only from name recognition but also from the connections his or her predecessor built to influential people in the party hierarchy, and to financial backers, which may help secure a party nomination. Even when a legacy candidate does not share the same name—for instance, in the case of a son-in-law, or a daughter who has married and taken a new surname—he or she might still benefit from the political capital (e.g., connections, financial resources) built up by a predecessor over the years.

At the most basic level, the persistence of dynasties in Japan and other democracies might therefore be explained by the inherited incumbency advantage enjoyed by legacy candidates and the effect that this advantage has on voters and party elites involved in candidate selection. However, the fact that there is variation across countries and parties, as well as variation over time, suggests that something is missing in the "power begets power" theory of dynasties. First, why do dynasties seem to be so much more prevalent in Japan than in other developed democracies? In other words, if there is a power-treatment effect of incumbency, why has it apparently been so much stronger in Japan than elsewhere? Second, why is there so much variation in the proportion of legacy candidates in different parties in Japan? Party differences within democracies cast doubt on the simplicity of the power-begets-power theory, as well as any explanation for dynasties that rests solely on country-level explanations, including ones that might point to history or culture as determinants of dynastic politics. A complete understanding of the causes of dynastic politics in democracies like Japan must account for differences at several levels of analysis, including country, party, district, and individual politician.

A further limitation of existing studies of democratic dynasties is that they often only analyze winning candidates (i.e., congresspersons or MPs) or measure trends in dynastic recruitment within a single institutional context. The problem with analyzing winning candidates is the inability to disentangle the attractiveness of legacy ties in the candidate selection stage from the electoral advantages enjoyed by legacy candidates once they are chosen (i.e., the roles of party elites versus voters in the perpetuation of dynasties). The problem with analyzing a single institutional context is the difficulty in evaluating the external validity of the theory and empirical findings. This is especially true given that much of the previous theoretical research on dynasties has focused on the candidate-centered US context, where candidates are chosen in primary elections by voters (thus removing the direct influence of party elites from the equation).[16] In most other democracies, parties exercise control over candidate selection.

Comparative models of candidate selection suggest that within a given institutional context, there are supply and demand reasons behind the emergence of individual candidates for office (e.g., Norris, 1997; Siavelis and Morgenstern, 2008). Why, then, might some countries feature a higher supply of legacy candidates? On the flip side, why might there be greater demand for such legacies in the candidate recruitment and selection processes of some parties? If the supply of legacy candidates were related only to the existence of capable offspring of incumbent politicians, then we would expect to see such legacy hopefuls in ample supply across all democracies. After all, politicians in all democracies are capable of producing or adopting children who could potentially succeed them as candidates, and most also have more distant relatives such as nephews and nieces. Likewise, if being a legacy candidate offered the same electoral advantages across all democracies, then we should expect to see equal demand for such candidates from the actors involved in the candidate recruitment process. The comparative empirical record suggests that neither is the case.

A COMPARATIVE INSTITUTIONALIST APPROACH

This book offers an explanation for variation in dynastic politics across democracies and parties that focuses attention on the institutional factors affecting the supply and demand incentives in candidate selection. In brief, the argument is that dynastic candidate selection will be encouraged in institutional contexts that increase the perceived value of a potential candidate's inherited incumbency advantage, and decrease the ability or desire of national party leaders to control the selection process. While all democracies are likely to feature some amount of dynastic politics, particularly in the early years following democratization, certain institutional features can facilitate and even encourage the formation of dynasties by increasing the electoral value of the inherited incumbency advantage. At its core, this explanation rests upon assumptions about the role that institutions play in structuring political behavior. It is useful, therefore, to provide a brief overview of this theoretical framework.

Institutions are humanly devised constraints, rules, or standard operating procedures that structure the behavior of political actors such as voters, candidates, and party leaders (North, 1990; March and Olsen, 1984). Formal institutions are laws or written codes governing political behavior, and they include the constitutional structure of the state (e.g., separation of powers), electoral rules, and sometimes the candidate selection procedures within parties. Informal institutions, in contrast, encompass the norms, conventions, and other unwritten rules that are routinely practiced and expected by political actors. Examples of informal institutions include the routine renomination of incumbent politicians, the seniority system for promotion to higher office, and the proportional allocation of cabinet portfolios to factions or parties in a coalition government.

Institutions are generally regarded as "sticky," meaning that they are relatively stable and resilient to changes in the individual actors operating under their constraint. One of the advantages of this stickiness is that institutions can be useful for predicting the equilibrium behavior of political actors operating within those systems. The analytical use of institutions to explain and predict equilibrium behavior has been a key feature of the rational choice approach within the so-called new institutionalism perspectives in political science (Hall and Taylor, 1996). In short, the rational choice approach assumes that individual actors—be they voters, candidates, or party leaders—have clear and transitive preferences over outcomes, and when given the opportunity and agency to make a choice, these actors can be expected to pursue the choice that will maximize the chances of achieving their preferred outcomes. Institutions are critical components of this approach because they serve as coordination mechanisms, helping to structure incentives, constrain choices, and increase certainty about the strategic behavior of other actors in the same system.

However, as with all humanly devised constraints, institutions are sometimes subject to change—either piecemeal, with new layers and conditions being added to old ones, or wholesale, with entirely new arrangements and concomitant behavioral incentives introduced (Streeck and Thelen, 2005). The most dramatic mode of institutional change, complete displacement of one set of rules with another, can be conceived of as either occurring exogenously (i.e., precipitated or imposed by some external source or pressure), or endogenously (i.e., purposefully designed by the actors currently operating in the system).[17] Whether to treat institutional change as exogenous or endogenous is an analytical question that must be considered by the researcher. For rational choice proponents who are interested in formalizing predictions for equilibrium behavior under a set of institutions, it is often useful to view institutional change as an exogenous shock that displaces the prior institutions with new ones and produces incentives for a new behavioral equilibrium. This can often be a useful approach in research that uses quantitative data, as outcomes of interest can be measured and the average effects of institutional changes can be estimated via statistical tools. Several studies based on a rational choice approach have been influential in reshaping conventional wisdom in the study of Japanese politics (e.g., Ramseyer and Rosenbluth, 1993; Cox, 1994). A recent example of a perspective inspired by rational choice is Frances Rosenbluth and Michael Thies's (2010) overview of how electoral reform and other changes of the 1990s have transformed Japan's politics and political economy.

In contrast, proponents of the historical institutionalist approach—a second approach within the "new institutionalism" perspectives—tend to prefer a more nuanced analysis of institutions and behavior that endogenizes their creation and impact. Historical institutionalists often use qualitative methods to evaluate the temporal sequence and process through which institutions evolve and change. When institutional change does occur, behavioral patterns from a previous institutional regime can linger or persist, often with adaptation, as a reflection of path dependence (Pierson, 2004). In other words, institutional change does not necessarily create a tabula rasa for political behavior—often the very actors who effected the change continue to exist and operate under the new rules, and the historical legacy of the past cannot be easily discarded. Moreover, the institutions that precede any kind of institutional change are likely to influence the nature and components of the new institutions. A recent application of the historical institutionalist approach to understand Japanese politics is Ellis Krauss and Robert Pekkanen's (2011) examination of how the LDP adapted its existing internal party structures to suit new pressures and challenges following electoral reform in 1994.

The rational choice approach and the historical institutionalist approach both tend to view institutional change as rare moments, or "critical junctures," where the existing stickiness of the system is opened up to both agency and choice (Mahoney and Thelen, 2009, p. 7). The difference in the approaches often boils down to the objectives of the researcher. What are the outcomes of interest, and how can we measure them? Do we want to understand what sorts of behavior we might expect to observe in equilibrium under a given set of institutions, even if this comes with the cost of some level of abstraction? Or do we want to understand the more detailed nuances of how certain behaviors persist or evolve over time following an institutional change?

The examination of dynastic politics in this book includes elements of both the rational choice and the historical institutionalist approaches, and draws on both quantitative and qualitative data—in other words, it is a mixed-methods or multimethod approach (Seawright, 2016). Many of the conceptual terms just introduced are relevant later in the book in interpreting how Japan's dynastic politics have evolved in response to institutional change. The comparative theory introduced for understanding the causes of dynastic politics is more in the tradition of a rational choice approach to predicting the expected equilibrium behavior under different institutions (although the formal language of many rational choice models is avoided). However, the analysis takes an approach more in the tradition of historical institutionalism when evaluating the adoption of institutional reforms and the adaptation of political actors over time in Japan. This combined approach lends itself to the use of quantitative and qualitative data and methods. In addition to extensive quantitative data on candidate characteristics, election results, and legislative behavior, the analysis in each chapter draws on personal interviews with politicians and party organization staff from the major parties in Japan. The hope is that such a combination of data and approaches will paint a more complete picture of how institutions influence the practice of dynastic politics, as well as the impact of key institutional reforms in Japan.

THE ARGUMENT IN BRIEF

The theory proposed in this book for understanding democratic dynasties is based on a supply-and-demand framework of candidate selection. On the supply side, potential legacy candidates will be more likely to want to run for office if their predecessors had served longer tenures in office, allowing them greater time to be socialized into a life of politics. In addition, potential legacy candidates will be more likely to want to run if the family already has a history of multiple generations in politics. However, these supply-side incentives can be assumed to be relatively universal across countries and parties. To explain the observed variation across country and party cases, the theory posits a demand-side interaction between the inherited incumbency advantage of a potential legacy candidate and factors that increase or decrease what can be thought of conceptually as a dynastic bias in candidate selection.

Of these demand-side factors, the argument of this book is that the institutions of the electoral system and candidate selection process within parties are key contributors to the observed patterns in dynastic recruitment in democracies. This is not to say that other factors, such as population size, age of the democracy or party, level of economic development, political culture, or other variables, do not play some role in dynastic politics. The nature of a party's organizational base, and idiosyncratic events like a politician's death in office, can also play an important part in determining the supply and demand for legacy candidates. However, the influence of these factors can be significantly constrained or enhanced by the institutional context of elections and candidate selection.

The electoral system is the set of rules that determines how votes are cast and counted to determine the winner(s) of elections for public office. It is therefore the key institution for aggregating voter preferences in modern representative democracies. However, the ways in which votes are cast and counted across different electoral systems can have profound impacts on the nature and functioning of representation. Most important, electoral systems that require voters to choose a candidate, rather than a party, tend to generate incentives for voters to focus on the personal attributes and behavior of candidates (Carey and Shugart, 1995). The personal vote is a "candidate's electoral support which originates in his or her personal qualities, qualifications, activities, and record" (Cain, Ferejohn, and Fiorina, 1987, p. 9). It stands in contrast to a vote cast strictly for a party and the policies it represents. The implication of the personal vote for representation is that in candidate-centered systems (where the personal vote matters more than the party vote), the individual candidate, rather than the collective party, is perceived to be the primary agent of representation for voters. Candidate-centered electoral systems thus tend to emphasize direct accountability and responsiveness of individual candidates to voters, in contrast to accountability based on voters' evaluation of the programmatic goals and performance of parties (Carey, 2009).

Under candidate-centered systems, party leaders face a potential trade-off in candidate selection decisions. Leaders must balance the utility they can get from each potential candidate in terms of three main party priorities: vote seeking, policy seeking, and office seeking (Strøm, 1990). Although a candidate with a strong personal vote may be more likely to earn an extra seat for the party, that individual strength might allow him or her to dissent from the party's preferred legislative policy priorities with greater impunity. A party may sometimes prefer to nominate a candidate who has a weaker personal vote but who contributes to the party's image or policy goals as a loyal agent of the party. But doing so also comes with the risk of losing the seat. The outcome of these competing incentives in candidate nomination decisions will depend on the relative electoral value of the personal vote. The implication for dynastic politics is that electoral systems that generate stronger incentives for candidate-centered (rather than party-centered) vote choice will increase the relative value of the inherited incumbency advantage as a personal-vote-earning attribute, both for voters and for party actors involved in candidate selection. Thus, the demand for legacy candidates will be higher, on average, under candidate-centered electoral systems than under party-centered electoral systems.

However, even within the same electoral system context, the candidate selection process within parties can also have an influence on the practice of dynastic politics. Candidate selection can be defined as the "process by which a political party decides which of the persons legally eligible to hold an elective office will be designated on the ballot and in election communications as its recommended and supported candidate or list of candidates" (Ranney, 1981, p. 75). In practice, the structure and process of candidate selection can vary across parties, even under the same electoral system. Reuven Hazan and Gideon Rahat (2010) identify four dimensions in candidate selection institutions: candidacy (i.e., who is eligible to run), the selectorate (i.e., who decides the nomination), the appointment or voting system (i.e., through which voting rules nomination decisions are made), and decentralization (i.e., whether the decision is made centrally or locally). Variation on each of these dimensions can produce different outcomes in the types of candidates who are selected and their behavior once in office.

Of the potential institutional dimensions of candidate selection, the argument in this book is that the level of inclusiveness in candidate eligibility and the degree of decentralization in the process are likely to have the greatest influence on dynastic politics. Put simply, a more inclusive candidate pool provides parties with a greater supply of potential non-legacy candidates. Nevertheless, whether or not party leaders make use of those candidates may also depend on the hierarchical level at which selection takes place within the party. All else being equal, in parties where the candidate selection process is decentralized to local party actors, legacy candidates will be more likely than non-legacy candidates to secure the nomination. This is because legacy candidates will possess closer ties to local party actors, but also because the priorities in candidate selection may differ between local and national party actors. Although local actors may prioritize local connections (which legacy candidates frequently enjoy), party leaders at the national level may take a more diverse approach to candidate selection that serves broader goals for policy or party image—such as nominating more women, minorities, or policy experts to balance the party's overall roster of personnel. The extent to which the priorities of the national party leadership are reflected in the attributes of the party's personnel will depend on whether, and to what extent, the leadership exercises control over nominations.

When or if the leadership of a decentralized party attempts to centralize decisions in candidate selection, this effort may be met with resistance from local actors. The implication for dynastic politics is that politicians who want to perpetuate a family grip on politics in their local districts may oppose efforts by national party leaders to centralize control over nominations. Thus, whether the outcome of the candidate selection process results in a legacy candidate being chosen will ultimately depend not only on the relative utility that the party perceives it will get from nominating (or not nominating) a legacy candidate but also on the ability of party leaders to control the decision-making process.[18]

INSTITUTIONAL REFORM IN JAPAN AS A NATURAL EXPERIMENT

The two biggest challenges to comparative research on democratic dynasties are data availability and causal inference. The first is a challenge because historical biographical data on MPs and their relationships to other politicians are scarce for many democracies and may be unreliable in terms of accuracy in others. Finding and coding accurate data on candidates (not just elected MPs) is an even greater challenge. Where verified data on family ties are available, the complex nature of many relationships within dynasties can also make measurement and analysis a messy business.

For example, how do we treat two relatives with partially overlapping terms, or with several years between the final election of the predecessor and the first candidacy of the successor? How about a legacy candidate who runs in a different district from his or her predecessor? Or a pair of relatives where one person preceded the other in local political office, but the other was first to be elected into national office? And for legacy candidates with multiple generations of predecessors in politics, which relationship is the most important: the relationship to the most proximal member or the relationship to the founding member of the dynasty? All of these considerations make it extremely difficult to measure and analyze the true impact of dynastic ties across candidates within a single country, let alone across countries.

The second challenge to comparative research on dynasties, causal inference, arises because dynastic politics may be influenced by myriad country-specific, party-specific, or context-specific confounding variables that are difficult to measure and control in statistical analyses. Caution is warranted in interpreting any cross-sectional variation in a small-n comparative study. For example, it could be that multiple factors—including history, culture, population size, years of experience with democracy, or level of economic development—contribute to a country's patterns in dynastic politics, and these factors may overshadow institutional effects. Similarly, dynastic politics within parties may vary by idiosyncratic differences related to ideology, personalities of leaders, time-specific events, size and age of the party, and so on. Political institutions are not randomly assigned to different countries—

each arrives at its present situation through its own history and course of democratic development. Moreover, selection into a democratic dynasty is not random, much like selection into politics more generally (Dal Bó et al., 2017). This fact makes it difficult to separate the effect of dynastic ties from other traits when evaluating the downstream effects of dynastic politics. All of these factors also make it impossible to pinpoint the causal effects of the electoral system and candidate selection institutions through cross-sectional analyses.

The case of Japan presents a unique opportunity to gain analytical leverage over the effect of institutions on dynasties within a single democracy. From 1947 to 1993, members of the House of Representatives were elected using the single nontransferable vote (SNTV) electoral system in multimember districts (MMD). Under the SNTV system, each voter casts a single vote for a candidate in a district of magnitude M, and the top M candidates in the district are elected. In Japan, the average M was four seats. Any party that aimed to win a majority of seats in the legislature therefore needed to nominate more than one candidate in each district. Such intraparty competition resulted in elections that were "hyper-personalistic" (Shugart, 2001, p. 29), with candidates campaigning predominantly on the basis of their personal attributes or behavior rather than a commitment to their party label or its national policies.

This was particularly true for candidates from the dominant LDP, which almost always nominated multiple candidates in each district, often from competing internal factions within the party. Each candidate would thus work tirelessly to cultivate his or her own personal support base, known as a *jiban* in Japanese, to win elections. Candidates organized and maintained their jiban through personal support organizations called *kōenkai*, which were specific to each candidate and formally separate from the party organization.[19]

From its foundation in 1955 until 1993, the candidate selection process in the LDP was largely decentralized to local actors and subleaders. When an LDP candidate retired or died, his or her faction and the interest groups associated with the candidate—especially the kōenkai—often sought out family members of the outgoing candidate to run as successors. A candidate who immediately succeeds a family member in the same district after inheriting a jiban and its kōenkai organization can be defined as a *hereditary candidate*.[20] Hereditary candidates constitute a special subset of legacy candidates, where the connection to the previous candidate is particularly close. The SNTV system meant that new candidates often had to challenge multiple incumbents in a district, so for factions and kōenkai members hoping to maintain control of a seat, a hereditary candidate with an inherited support base was the next best thing to having the previous incumbent run again. By the late 1980s and early 1990s, roughly a quarter of all LDP candidates were hereditary candidates who inherited their predecessors' kōenkai and directly succeeded them into candidacy.

Candidate selection within the JSP and the more moderate Democratic Socialist Party (DSP) was also decentralized, but with greater influence exercised by the two parties' main support networks of labor unions. In contrast, the Kōmeitō and the Japanese Communist Party (JCP) did not regularly nominate multiple candidates in a district, and both used a highly centralized candidate selection process. As a result, candidates from these parties could rely more heavily on their party labels in campaigning, and leaders had fewer incentives to seek out legacy candidates as successors. Indeed, neither the Kōmeitō nor the JCP exhibited anything near the same patterns in dynastic candidate selection as the larger, decentralized parties.

The rising trend in hereditary succession within the LDP might have been expected to continue well into the 1990s and 2000s. However, a series of corruption scandals and voter dissatisfaction with long-term LDP dominance, money in politics, and the collapse of Japan's bubble economy led to several major party defections prior to the 1993 House of Representatives election. Many in the political and academic worlds saw the SNTV system as a key institutional cause of the problems plaguing the country. The end of the Cold War also deflated the importance of the LDP as the country's political defense against communism and opened the way for new parties to enter the electoral arena. As a result of the election, the LDP narrowly lost its majority but remained the largest party. Eight other parties (excluding the JCP) formed a coalition government, which made electoral reform of the House of Representatives its top priority.

Reformers debated several variations on a mixed-member majoritarian (MMM) system (Shugart and Wattenberg, 2001) that would combine two parallel tiers of electoral competition: one a British-style first-past-the-post (FPTP) system in single-member districts (SMDs), the other a closed-list proportional representation (PR) system in regional MMDs. The MMM system that was ultimately adopted in 1994 and went into effect in 1996 was a compromise between reformers who hoped to create Westminster-style politics in Japan—party-centered election campaigns, with two strong, cohesive parties that alternate regularly in government—and smaller parties whose leaders knew that a pure FPTP system would spell their certain demise (Otake, 1996; Kawato, 2000).

The electoral reform eliminated intraparty competition, which dramatically reduced the candidate-centered nature of elections while simultaneously increasing the importance of party image and national policy platforms in campaigning and voting (e.g., Reed, Scheiner, and Thies, 2012; McElwain, 2012; Catalinac, 2016). In addition, the traditionally decentralized process for candidate selection in the LDP and other parties began to change. Since the 2000s, the LDP and other parties have experimented with a new method in candidate selection, open recruitment (*kōbo*), which expands the pool of potential candidates and places greater control in the hands of party leaders. This innovation was used most effectively by the DPJ, which replaced the JSP as the main opposition party in the postreform period. The process has been far from smooth in the LDP, with a key factor in the resistance to change being the continued desire among members of existing dynasties to continue their family business in politics. Nevertheless, since the first election under the new electoral system in 1996, and especially after reforms to the candidate selection process in the mid-2000s, the proportion of legacy candidates and MPs has begun to decrease. In the 2012 general election, the share of legacy candidates in the LDP dropped below 30 percent for the first time since 1972.

Meanwhile, the adoption of the new MMM electoral system has coincided with an increase in the percentage of legacy MPs appointed to the cabinet. Shortly after the electoral reform was adopted in 1994, the LDP regained control of government and ruled in coalition until 2009—when it was swept out of office by the DPJ's landslide victory in that election. The LDP's second period out of government ended with a reciprocal landslide victory over the DPJ in the 2012 election. Although the proportion of legacy MPs in the LDP has been decreasing steadily since the first election under MMM in 1996, the proportion of legacy MPs appointed to LDP cabinets has increased, to roughly 60 percent of cabinet ministers, on average, in recent cabinets. Moreover, seven of the ten prime ministers to have served since 1996—Hashimoto Ryūtarō, Obuchi Keizō, Koizumi Junichirō, Abe Shinzō, Fukuda Yasuo, Asō Tarō, and Hatoyama Yukio—have been members of powerful dynasties.

What has been the true impact of Japan's institutional reforms on the importance of the inherited incumbency advantage and the practice of dynastic politics in candidate selection? And why has there been a decrease in new LDP legacy candidates since reform but an increase in their membership in cabinet? The electoral reform and subsequent party reforms in Japan might be considered a "natural experiment" of institutional change in an otherwise constant environment, which helps to resolve some of the challenges to causal inference that pose a barrier to comparative research on dynasties. Nothing about the reforms drastically changed Japanese history, culture, or other country-level variables that might affect the supply of legacy candidates. Moreover, the 1994 electoral reform was not directly motivated by the problem of dynasties,[21] and references to dynastic politics did not noticeably appear in the media until several years after reform (Figure 1.2), in large part due to the prevalence of legacy MPs in the cabinet. Beginning in 2000, there were small upswings in coverage during election years for the House

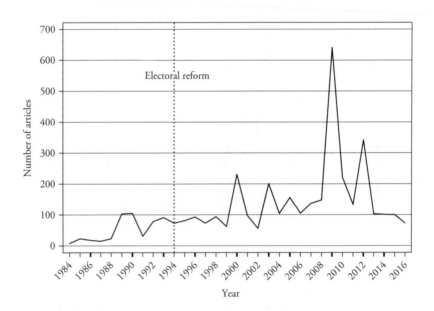

FIGURE 1.2 Media coverage of dynastic politics in Japan

SOURCE: *Asahi Shimbun* Kikuzo II Visual Database.

NOTE: The figure shows the number of articles in the *Asahi Shimbun*, by year, where the word *seshū* (hereditary) appears in the text. This word is often used in reference to hereditary succession in politics, but also captures unrelated articles—thus, the figure should be interpreted only as giving a relative sense of the importance of the issue. The dashed vertical line indicates the year of electoral reform (1994). Election years for the House of Representatives are highlighted with bold ticks on the x-axis (year). Elections for the House of Councillors are held every three years, with 1986 being the first in the sample (there was a double election that year).

of Representatives, culminating in a huge spike in coverage around the time of the 2009 election, when the DPJ made an issue out of dynastic politics to attack the LDP. But by that time, the LDP had already changed its recruitment behavior in important ways, as this book documents.

In terms of dynastic politics, the electoral reform can therefore be treated analytically as an exogenous shock to the system, and we can apply rational choice theory to make predictions about how Japan's new institutions should begin to structure behavior in new and different ways. In contrast, the party reforms to candidate selection within the LDP and DPJ can be considered endogenous responses to the new electoral environment. The case of Japan thus illuminates the dynamic and piecemeal nature of party responses to institutional change over time. When electoral systems and candidate selection procedures undergo institutional reforms, how, and to what extent, do voters, candidates, and party leaders respond to the new incentive structure? How many elections does it take for reforms to bear fruit? How do incumbents respond to new incentives, in contrast to newly recruited candidates? And how do incumbents and party leaders solve differences when new institutional rules put their priorities at odds—for example, when a retiring incumbent wants his or her child to take over as the next candidate, but party leaders prefer a non-legacy replacement?

The postreform MMM system also creates an opportunity to observe how parties' candidate selection strategies differ across electoral system contexts (in Japan's case, FPTP versus closed-list PR), even within the same country and election year. This type of "controlled comparison" using mixed-member systems has previously been used to shed light on parties' nomination strategies with regard to women and minorities (e.g., Kostadinova, 2007; Moser and Scheiner, 2012; Manow, 2015) and can similarly help to rule out alternative country-level or time-specific explanations for dynastic politics across electoral institutions in Japan.

Finally, the concept of a jiban in Japanese electoral politics, and the prevalence of direct hereditary succession within the LDP, help to alleviate some of the methodological difficulties in measuring the electoral advantages enjoyed by legacy candidates. For example, direct hereditary succession removes the complexities of concurrent service by two members of the same family, or time gaps between predecessors and successors. The fact that some jiban are inherited by a non-kin successor, such as a political secretary, also provides an opportunity to assess how much of the inherited incumbency advantage can be attributed to family ties versus other types of ties, and how much of the inherited incumbency advantage can be attributed to name recognition versus simply the kōenkai organization and resources.

So What? The Consequences of Dynastic Politics

A separate question to "Why dynasties?" is whether dynastic politics actually generate any major consequences for the functioning of democracy in a country like Japan. In other words, so what? Do legacy candidates represent the most qualified among all potential candidates, or is the structure of the democratic system in places like Japan biased in favor of those privileged by birth with better connections or simply a more recognizable name? What are the potential problems arising from dynastic politics for the functioning of democracy, including the quality of representation and accountability?

Electoral systems and candidate selection methods are fundamental links in the chain of delegation and accountability that constitutes the core relationship between voters and their political agents in modern representative democracies (Strøm, 2000). The quality of representation can depend on who is elected and how responsive they are to the electorate's interests. In most democracies, parties shape the nature of representation by determining whom among potential candidates the voters will evaluate at election time. In general, candidates and elected representatives chosen through these processes can be thought of as either "standing for" their constituents (descriptive representation) or "acting for" their constituents (substantive representation) through legislation or articulation of positions that serve the interests of those who (s)elect them (Pitkin, 1967). In the case of dynasties, it would be unsurprising that a legacy candidate, much like any elite politician, does not descriptively represent the electorate—most come from very privileged backgrounds and a narrow range of occupations. It is not obvious, however, that a legacy MP would do objectively worse at representing his or her constituents in the "acting for" capacity. Whether dynasties have positive or negative effects for the functioning of democracy is an open question in the existing literature.

NEGATIVE EFFECTS?

One might argue that democratic dynasties are simply a benign fact of political life. Just as the offspring of doctors, lawyers, business owners, and even academics may want to follow in their parents' footsteps, why should we be surprised or concerned if similar levels of occupational path dependence exist in politics as well? For a start, evidence from the United States suggests that occupational path dependence is significantly higher in politics than in other occupations, controlling for the prevalence of individuals in those occupations (Blau and Duncan, 1967; Laband and Lentz, 1983, 1985; Dal Bó, Dal Bó, and Snyder, 2009). This suggests that families might derive higher value from maintaining their status in the political elite than maintaining other occupational traditions. More generally, the prevalence of dynasties in a democracy may be symptomatic of the democratic process being "captured" by a small cadre of elites and a potential narrowing of the interests and voices being represented. Public opinion surveys in Japan routinely report that voters do not like the idea of dynasties in the abstract, even as individual legacy candidates continue to get elected to the Diet.

Dynastic politics might also lower the quality of representation. For example, if there is any regression to the mean with regard to political quality within a family, we should not expect legacy candidates to be as high in quality as their predecessors. Yet the inherited incumbency advantage enjoyed by legacy candidates may insulate them from competition or deter the entry of other, possibly more qualified, candidates. Once in office, electorally insulated legacy MPs might shirk their responsibilities and do a poor job representing their constituents. Much like how female candidates in the United States must outperform their male counterparts to overcome higher barriers to entry (Anzia and Berry, 2011), non-legacy candidates who run against legacy candidates might need to be of higher quality and exhibit higher legislative performance if elected. This means that when compared to non-legacy candidates, legacy candidates might paradoxically be of lower quality from the perspective of citizens seeking effective representation, even if they are of higher quality from the perspective of party actors in terms of electoral strength.

There is some evidence to support these concerns. For example, voters' perceptions of political representation in India are much lower in areas represented by parties with dynastic leaders (Chhibber, 2013, p. 290). Similarly, members of dynasties in local Italian politics tend to have lower levels of education—a potential marker of quality—than nondynastic local politicians (Geys, 2017). Journalistic accounts in Japan frequently claim that legacy MPs are poor leaders and lack innovative policy ideas because of their sheltered, privileged backgrounds (e.g., Yazaki, 2010). Legacy MPs seem to enjoy an advantage when it comes to reaching the highest positions of power; yet at the same time, they may be less qualified to handle the difficult policy issues facing them once in office. Apart from Koizumi and Abe (in his second stint as prime minister after 2012), each of the recent legacy prime ministers in Japan failed to adequately confront political problems before stepping down within a year. This has resulted in a great deal of criticism of dynastic politics by the media, scholars, and opposition parties. Dynasties have been condemned as one of the factors contributing to political stagnation and public dissatisfaction with democracy.

Hideo Otake (1996, p. 277) notes that many legacy candidates in Japan had little serious interest in politics when they were pulled into candidacy by the kōenkai of their predecessors:

> Their desire to be politicians had never been strong. Compared to Diet members who clawed their way up to national politics from the local level, these [legacy] Diet members did not see much point in becoming Diet members. Many inherited large fortunes and could afford comfortable living without working as Diet members. They shared an "I can always quit" easy-going attitude.

This "I can always quit" attitude may lead to poor outcomes when it comes to effective policymaking and representation. In 2009, DPJ party leader Okada Katsuya argued that the overabundance of dynasties in Japan "weakens the vitality of politics. Political parties need to recruit candidates from a wider field if they are to select the individuals most suited for the job."[22]

Similar critiques of dynasties are made in the popular presses of the United States, Ireland, Italy, and elsewhere. For example, when Jeb Bush ran for the Republican nomination for president of the United States in 2016, the failures of his brother George W. Bush were regularly pointed to as reason enough to avoid putting another Bush in the White House. Jeb at first seemed to eschew association with his family name by using the simple slogan "Jeb!" before ultimately embracing his family legacy when his poll numbers floundered. On the Democratic side, former Maryland governor Martin O'Malley criticized Bush, as well as his own party's front-runner, Hillary Clinton, by stating that the presidency "is not some crown to be passed between two families . . . new perspective and new leadership is needed."[23]

In Ireland, W. T. Cosgrave and his son, Liam, were the first father-son pair to have both served as prime minister (*Taoiseach*). But the third generation of the Cosgrave line, Liam T. Cosgrave, fell rapidly from grace in 2003 after illegally failing to disclose political donations (Fallon, 2011). Renzo Bossi, the son of Lega Nord party leader Umberto Bossi, was thought to have a promising future career in Italian politics until it was discovered that he had been embezzling party funds and possessed a fake degree from a university in Albania that he had never once attended; he was forced to resign from his local seat in the Regional Council of Lombardy.[24] David N. Laband and Bernard F. Lentz (1985, p. 402) equate legacy MPs who do a poor job in office to students who enter college on a parental "free ride," only to flunk out after partying too much.

Legacy candidates might also pose problems for their parties if their personal electoral advantages allow them to buck the party line with greater impunity. The "I can always quit" mentality could apply not only to participation in politics but also to membership in the party. When legacy candidates have outside electoral options in other parties or as independents, it may become harder for party leaders to maintain discipline and party unity. Moreover, a potential legacy candidate who is denied the party nomination can create an electoral headache for the party if he or she runs against the party's preferred candidate. There is thus a risk that parties might become captive to legacy candidates whose personal qualifications and policy priorities are at odds with the interests of the party as a whole. Of course, this risk applies with regard to any candidate with a strong personal vote; however, unlike non-legacy candidates with a strong personal vote, legacy candidates might be able to free ride on the reputations of their predecessors, reducing the connection between their own personal quality and their personal vote.

POSITIVE EFFECTS?

Critics of dynastic politics often overlook the potential positive effects of dynasties on democracy. For example, electing a legacy candidate may bring continuity in the quality or style of representation for voters in a district, much in the same way as reelecting an incumbent. In considering members of dynasties versus "amateurs" in the US Congress, Glenn R. Parker (1996, p. 88) argues that members of dynasties may be beneficial to the functioning of the legislature, since "family members who have served in Congress can act in a tutorial capacity: knowledge is transmitted about the legislative processes (e.g., logrolling) and norms in the legislature (e.g., universalism)." Legacy candidates may be comparatively more comfortable and familiar with the policymaking process and able to commence political life with minimal training or socialization. To put a different spin on the previous analogy to college students, the experiences of non-legacy candidates and legacy candidates might instead be compared to first-generation college students (i.e., students whose parents did not go to university) and students whose families have a history of sending their children to university. First-generation college students tend to underperform relative to other students, at least initially, even controlling for IQ and secondary school grades (Terenzini et al., 1996).

The electoral advantages that legacy politicians possess may also translate into downstream distributive advantages for their districts. Legislator efforts to bring distributive benefits (commonly known as "pork") to their constituencies tend to be lower where party identification among voters is stronger (Keefer and Khemani, 2009). In other words, legacy candidates elected on their personal reputation might be more motivated to provide benefits, or other forms of active representation, to their districts than politicians who owe their election to their party label alone. In addition, if legacy candidates tend to enjoy more election victories, their seniority status in their parties may help them to obtain important committee and cabinet positions with influence over distributive policy decisions—although this might not always result in better economic outcomes for their districts if the resources are directed only to favored support groups (Asako et al., 2015).

Anticipation of bequeathing one's political resources to a family member in the future may also affect the behavior of incumbents. For example, it has frequently been hypothesized that incumbents in their final term may be more prone to shirking, or worse yet, personal rent-seeking behavior, since they no longer have to concern themselves with the accountability mechanism of reelection (for a review, see Fearon, 1999). Such concerns have sparked a large amount of research on the effect of term limits on incumbent behavior, with potential impacts on everything from legislative responsiveness to fiscal policy outcomes and political malfeasance (e.g., Besley and Case, 1995; Carey, 1996; Alt, Bueno de Mesquita, and Rose, 2011; Ferraz and Finan, 2011). Incumbents who expect their offspring to succeed them in office may have a longer time horizon to consider, and thus a greater incentive to maintain a positive reputation for their successors to inherit (e.g., Olson, 1993; Besley and Reynal-Querol, 2017). That said, strong parties with control over individual members' behavior and a concern for the party's reputation could achieve similar outcomes.

Finally, dynastic candidate selection might sometimes result in positive effects for gender representation, as the inherited incumbency advantage may help female candidates overcome informational inequalities or gender biases among party leaders or voters (Jalalzai, 2013; Folke, Rickne, and Smith, 2017). Dynastic succession may be one of the few ways for female candidates to break into politics in a system where women are generally disadvantaged electorally. Indeed, many female politicians in the United States and elsewhere first entered politics when their husbands died in office, a process sometimes referred to as a "widow's succession" (Kincaid, 1978). At the same time, the institutional structures that contribute to dynastic politics are also likely to be impediments to greater gender representation—in other words, although women may fare best as legacy candidates, doing away with the institutions that encourage dynastic candidate selection would likely help level the playing field for more women to get elected without dynastic ties.

Road Map of the Book

The book proceeds as follows: The first part of Chapter 2 puts the case of Japan into comparative context with an overview of the empirical record across time, countries, and parties. This examination relies on an original panel dataset of the family ties of elected legislators (MPs) in twelve advanced industrialized democracies: the Dynasties in Democracies Dataset. The dataset covers the following countries and time periods: Australia (1901–2013), Canada (1867–2015), Finland (1907–2011), (West) Germany (1949–2013), Ireland (1918–2016), Israel (1949–2015), Italy (1946–2013), Japan (1947–2014), New Zealand (1853–2014), Norway (1945–2013), Switzerland (1848–2011), and the United States (1788–2016). The sources for these MP-level data vary by country, with most based on official biographies published by parliamentary libraries, and others based on careful archival research of additional biographies and newspaper reports.

The second part of Chapter 2 provides a descriptive account of the empirical record in Japan. The dataset used here, and in the remainder of the analyses for Japan, is the Japanese House of Representatives Elections Dataset (JHRED). This panel dataset includes all candidates who ran in any general election or by-election for the House of Representatives from 1947 to 2014. The dataset spans twenty-five general elections, seven of which occurred after electoral reform in 1994. It does not cover elections for the

House of Councillors, the upper chamber of the Diet, although it does code whether a candidate previously served in that chamber, as well as family relations to members of that chamber.[25] The House of Representatives is the larger and more important of the two chambers, with sole responsibility for the drafting and approval of the budget, the ratification of treaties, and the designation of the prime minister. In addition, although the House of Councillors has enacted minor reforms to its electoral system over time, the 1994 House of Representatives electoral reform has been the major institutional change affecting the evolution of Japanese politics in the past two decades. Throughout the book, the general term "MP" refers to members of the House of Representatives unless otherwise indicated. Details of both datasets can be found in Appendix B.

The empirical record illustrates several motivating patterns. First, even though democratic dynasties exist throughout the world, there is considerable variation across countries, parties, and time. Second, Japan stands out as one of the most dynastic countries among the comparative cases—with the level of dynastic politics initially growing over time, in stark contrast to the pattern in most other democracies. The high level of dynasticism is largely accounted for by candidates associated with the LDP. Legacy candidates in the LDP and other parties tend to be more successful than non-legacy candidates, yet the empirical record suggests that there are few differences between legacy candidates and non-legacy candidates in terms of personal characteristics, experience, education, or background—apart from their legacy ties—that might explain this greater electoral success.

Chapter 3 lays out the core theoretical argument for the causes of dynastic politics based on supply and demand incentives in candidate selection. Regardless of institutional context, incumbents who serve longer terms in office, and who are themselves already part of an existing dynasty, will be more likely to have family members who select into a political career. These factors constitute the general supply-side rationale for dynasties but are also reflective of the potential inherited incumbency advantage of a legacy candidate, which should increase demand for such a candidate by party actors. However, the relative demand will be higher where electoral institutions generate candidate-centered elections, and in parties where candidate recruitment and selection processes are exclusive and decentralized, leaving much of the selection decision up to local party actors—in Japan's case, primarily the kōenkai of exiting candidates. Demand for legacy candidates should also be higher in parties with weak organizational linkages to groups in civil society, and when the previous incumbent dies in office. When demand for dynasties is higher, even the family members of incumbents with shorter tenures or a weaker incumbency advantage might be recruited into a political career.

Following the introduction of the theory, the subsequent three chapters make use of the detailed candidate-level data in JHRED to examine the advantages enjoyed by legacy candidates in three stages of a political career: selection, election, and promotion. The first part of Chapter 4 examines the patterns in candidate selection in Japan that prevailed from 1947 to 1993, under the SNTV system. Dynasties under SNTV were more common in the larger, decentralized parties—especially the LDP, where intraparty competition was common. LDP candidates with longer tenures in office were more likely to be succeeded by a family member, although simply being an incumbent had a positive effect. The second part of Chapter 4 describes how the MMM system adopted in 1994 has changed the dynamics of dynastic politics by shifting much of the focus of elections from candidates to parties. Subsequent party reforms within the LDP, such as the introduction of open recruitment in 2004, have expanded the pool of candidates and placed relatively greater control over nominations in the hands of national-level party leaders, who have responded by selecting a more diverse range of candidates. Legacy candidates are still getting nominated, but in recent years, only the most powerful and longest-serving incumbents are likely to be succeeded in politics by a family member. This suggests that the demand-side incentives have changed, leaving mainly the supply-side incentives to explain the continued persistence of dynastic politics. A major consequence of this shift is that the pattern of dynastic politics in Japan is slowly converging toward the pattern commonly found in other democracies. In other words, Japan is becoming "normal."

Chapter 5 shifts attention from the selection stage of a political career to the election stage and examines the inherited incumbency advantage in terms of votes and election outcomes. Do legacy candidates actually perform better in elections? And what is the source of this advantage? In the prereform SNTV period, legacy candidates did indeed enjoy an advantage in terms of election but did not tend to enjoy a vote advantage, nor did they scare away challengers. This is in part because the MMDs of the SNTV system encouraged the entry of new challengers when an incumbent stopped running. Legacy candidates most often succeeded powerful incumbents, whose exit freed up considerable votes in a district and attracted political entrepreneurs into the race. In the postreform FPTP races, legacy candidates tend to enjoy a larger vote advantage, in part due to a stronger "scare-off" effect. This change may be because the SMDs in the new system are not as permissive to challengers as the prereform MMDs, but it may also reflect the fact that the legacy candidates who emerge since reform, as documented in Chapter 4, tend to come from more powerful, long-serving dynasties. Nevertheless, the most important factor for electoral success in the FPTP system is the strength of party support in the district. Original survey data using two approaches—one based on traditional questions and one based on a conjoint survey experiment—indicate that voters do not like the idea of dynasties in the abstract but are indifferent once dynastic ties are grouped with other attributes, such as party label, that they consider more important.

Chapter 6 turns to the promotion stage of a political career to examine the overrepresentation of dynasties in Japan's cabinets and the patterns in ministerial selection over time. In terms of cabinet selection, two institutional contexts are important. In addition to the formal institution of the electoral system, we must also consider the informal institution of seniority rule, introduced to LDP cabinets in the late 1960s and kept in place until the postreform period. The analysis of this chapter reveals that legacy MPs whose predecessors served in cabinet, who can be thought of as *cabinet legacies*, enjoyed a slight advantage in the early years of postwar democracy, before the LDP adopted the informal institution of seniority rule for promotion. Since that time, legacy MPs have enjoyed fewer direct advantages in terms of cabinet promotion. However, the large overrepresentation of legacy MPs in cabinet following electoral reform in 1994 can only be explained in part by seniority in the party—cabinet legacies in recent years enjoy an advantage in cabinet selection even after controlling for seniority. This suggests that cabinet legacies may enjoy informational or network advantages above and beyond the electoral advantages enjoyed by legacy candidates whose predecessors never served in cabinet. The apparent advantage of cabinet legacies in ministerial promotion is also evident in several of the comparative country cases, suggesting a general phenomenon that extends beyond Japan.

After this examination of the advantages of legacy candidates in selection, election, and promotion, Chapter 7 considers several potential downstream effects of dynastic politics on the functioning of democracy and the quality of representation, including effects on gender representation, the representational style of candidates, and legislative behavior. In terms of gender representation, there is a clear pattern across democracies, including Japan, of a gender bias in dynastic politics: women are much more likely to enter politics through a dynastic channel. However, this bias tends to decrease over time. In terms of representational style, an analysis of the textual content of candidate manifestos indicates that dynastic successors (hereditary candidates) present themselves to voters in a way that is more similar to their predecessors, compared to non-kin successors. This suggests that dynasties provide some continuity in representation for voters, which may be part of their appeal. There is less evidence, however, that legacy MPs are any more active in the legislature than non-legacy MPs. Although cabinet legacies tend to speak more in plenary sessions of the Diet since electoral reform, there are no other obvious differences in the legislative activity of legacy and non-legacy MPs. In other words, the empirical evidence paints a complex picture of the impact of dynasties on democracy. The good news for Japan is that the types of legacy candidates who are most likely to get selected into politics since the institutional reforms, namely cabinet legacies, also tend to be more active legislatively than their peers. This suggests that parties in Japan are now selecting on the right "type" of dynasties.

The final chapter concludes with some reflections on lessons that Japan's experience with political dynasties might hold for other democracies, such as Ireland, India, and the Philippines, which continue to be dominated by a seemingly entrenched set of elite political families. What can we learn from Japan's electoral and party reforms? Can we expect similar outcomes in other contexts? How can diversity in representation be encouraged and facilitated without compromising the freedom for all eligible and motivated citizens, including those who come from political dynasties, to seek office? The transformation of democracy in Japan, from competing family fiefdoms to party politics, illustrates how institutional rules can help to determine how dynastic a country's politics will be.

TWO

Putting Japan into Comparative Perspective

> It is often assumed that the Glorious Revolution settled these crucial questions in favor of a sovereign and effectively "modern" Parliament. Dynasticism, if it figures into the picture at all, is supposed to have disappeared as a meaningful political principle then or shortly thereafter.
>
> —*Julia Adams (2005, p. 181)*

How common are democratic dynasties around the world, and how does Japan compare? The main purpose of this chapter is to give a descriptive overview of the empirical record using the two original quantitative datasets that will be used throughout the book. In so doing, the chapter has three aims. The first is to situate the case of Japan in a broader comparative context and highlight some of the puzzles in the aggregate variation in dynastic politics across countries, parties, and time. The second aim is to explore the empirical patterns in Japan, particularly with regard to the demographic qualities and backgrounds of legacy versus non-legacy candidates, to establish that these patterns provide insufficient insight into the sources of Japan's high level of dynastic politics. Finally, the third aim is to demonstrate that alternative theories based on history or culture do not provide credible explanations for the empirical differences between Japan and other democracies.

The first dataset is the MP-level comparative panel dataset covering twelve democracies: Australia, Canada, Finland, Germany, Ireland, Israel, Italy, Japan, New Zealand, Norway, Switzerland, and the United States (Dynasties in Democracies Dataset). Some of the country cases include observations beginning with the first crop of MPs elected following democratization. Others include only MPs elected in recent decades but nevertheless measure dynastic family ties to MPs from prior years. Where relevant, relationships to members of earlier parliamentary bodies, such as the US

Continental Congress and other such constituent assemblies, are included. This dataset will be used primarily in this chapter to highlight patterns in the cross-national, cross-party, and cross-temporal prevalence of democratic dynasties, and to put the case of Japan in comparative perspective.

The second dataset is the candidate-level panel dataset for Japan (JHRED) that covers all candidates for the House of Representatives from 1947 to 2014, and includes their electoral records, personal backgrounds and family relations, and postelectoral appointments to cabinet. This more detailed dataset forms the backbone of the main analyses in the remainder of the book. The data presentations in this chapter highlight some of the aggregate patterns over time and space, and across parties. In addition, this chapter provides the basic descriptive information on the types of family relationships and number of generations within dynasties in Japan.

Measuring the Dynastic Ties of Politicians

One of the greatest obstacles to comparative research on dynastic politics is the scarcity of reliable data on family ties between politicians. In part, this is because obtaining individual-level data on candidates and MPs in general has been a challenge for researchers. However, historical MP-level data for an increasing number of democracies are becoming available, often in the form of freshly digitized records of parliamentary libraries. A few such data sources also code family relations between members. For example, the websites of the Israeli Knesset (parliament) and Canadian House of Commons include family ties to previous MPs among other background and career information in online biographical profiles of current and former MPs— and these records are available in English (as well as Hebrew in the Israeli case and French in the Canadian case). Similar information is available in the online biographies of historical MPs in Finland and Norway, but only in the local language.

Where official biographical information on family ties is not already digitally available, data measurement is a greater challenge because legacy candidates and MPs must be intensively coded by hand using archival material from newspapers, candidate websites, historical biographical dictionaries, census records, and other sources. In contrast to more common variables related to a candidate's background (e.g., gender, date of birth, electoral constituency, prior experience), dynastic family ties can be difficult to find and verify, and are not consistently recorded by the governments or parties of all countries. This is especially true for candidates who are not successful in getting elected. The lack of availability of reliable data may thus introduce some selection bias into any sample of countries used for comparative research on dynasties. For example, if it is difficult to find any information on family ties among politicians in a given country, it could be because the data are poor, or because such ties are simply uncommon. Thus, when the data sample is limited to countries where information on family ties of MPs is obtainable, the patterns that emerge may overlook some important cross-national variation.

A few previous studies have cleverly attempted to get around the scarcity of verified information on family ties by matching politicians based on common surnames within a constituency or party in order to estimate a proxy measure of dynastic ties (e.g., Querubín, 2016; Geys, 2017). However, this method inevitably introduces some amount of measurement error. On the one hand, it may produce some false positives—that is, two or more individuals who share a name but are not related. Common surnames must often therefore be thrown out so as not to overestimate the number of dynasties. On the other hand, the proxy method may also produce false negatives. A legacy candidate might not always share the same name or run in the same district or from the same party. Moreover, unless the entire time span of a country's democratic experience is included in the sample, some anterior relatives will not be observable. Nevertheless, even verified family ties from official biographies may overlook less obvious relationships, so few comparative datasets are likely to be completely free of such measurement error.

Keeping these data limitations in mind, a comparative cross-national look at democratic dynasties is still useful as a starting point for investigating the phenomenon, and to put the case of Japan in perspective. For the purpose of cross-national comparison, the focus here is on legacy MPs in the lower chamber of each country. Each of the countries in the dataset either is coded on the basis of official biographical data provided by the respective parliamentary libraries or intensive coding by hand based on verifiable ties in archival records, biographical dictionaries, and any other credible source that could be obtained.

Recall that a legacy MP is any individual who is related by blood or marriage to a national-level politician (an elected or appointed MP in either legislative chamber in bicameral systems, as well as presidents, vice presidents, or non-MP cabinet ministers, if applicable) who preceded him or her in office. This definition does not count individuals related only to local-level politicians, although such individuals are also common across most cases, including Japan. In part, this definitional restriction is because obtaining complete information on local-level family ties is even more of a challenge than obtaining information on ties between national-level politicians.[1] The measurement of who counts as a legacy MP also excludes relations to deputy or substitute MPs (which are common in list-based systems such as Norway and Italy) unless they actually served in parliament. Finally, the measure does not count members who were related to each other but who were both elected for the first time in the same year (as sometimes occurs with married couples or siblings). Each MP in the comparative dataset is coded to indicate whether he or she preceded a family member into national-level political office (a "senior") and whether he or she succeeded a family member into national-level political office (a "junior"). In addition, the comparative data include information on number of terms served, gender, age, party, district, and cabinet service, but these variables are not available for all cases.

The Comparative Empirical Record

The "snapshot" cross-sectional differences presented in the previous chapter are illuminating but mask some of the variation that can be present within countries across time, as well as across parties. Aggregate variation across democracies can be affected by a number of factors, including population size, economic inequality, occupational mobility, legislator turnover, age of democracy, or institutional variation across districts. For example, the supply of qualified non-legacy candidates will likely be higher in an economically developed country with a large population than in very small or poor countries. The nature of dynastic politics in younger democracies like Israel may also look different if observed several decades from now. A few countries in the sample, including Japan, but also Italy and New Zealand, have experienced electoral reforms, and many others have experienced changes in the party system. The impact of such changes cannot be identified in cross-sectional comparisons of aggregate data. It is thus informative to look at how dynastic politics have developed over time in these different democracies, as well as whether there are notable differences across parties.

COMPARATIVE PATTERNS ACROSS TIME

Figure 2.1 illustrates the longitudinal patterns in the proportion of dynasties in the lower chamber of the twelve democracies in the comparative dataset. The oldest democracy in the world, the United States, is also the oldest democracy in the dataset; and dynasties have long captured the attention of scholars and observers of American politics.[2] America's first dynasty, the Adams family, spanned four generations—including President John Adams and his son President John Quincy Adams—and played a leading role in American politics for nearly two centuries. Other dynasties, such as the Roosevelts and Kennedys, are also well known. Some high-profile legacy politicians have served in executive office in recent decades, including President George W. Bush (whose father, George H. W. Bush, had served in the House of Representatives prior to serving as president himself, and whose grandfather, Prescott Bush, served in the Senate) and Vice President Al Gore (who succeeded his father, Albert Gore Sr., in the same district for the House of Representatives as well as the Senate). As Stephen Hess (1966, p. 1)

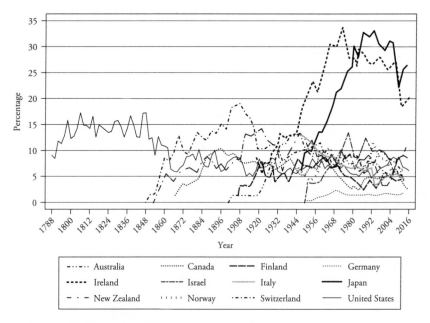

FIGURE 2.1 Country-level variation across time
SOURCE: Dynasties in Democracies Dataset.
NOTE: By-election winners are included where available, grouped with the previous general election.

notes, despite the US Constitution's declaration that "no title of nobility shall be granted by the United States," Americans have consistently returned members of democratic dynasties to office.

Nevertheless, the general pattern in Congress has been a decrease in dynasties over time. In the House of Representatives, dynastic membership reached a peak of just over 17 percent after the 1848 election. In the past two decades, however, only 7 percent of members, on average, have been part of a dynasty.[3] The 115th House of Representatives elected in 2016 included twenty-seven legacy members (6 percent). The decline in dynasties occurred more slowly in the South than in other regions (Dal Bó, Dal Bó, and Snyder, 2009), but today there is not much of a regional difference in the phenomenon. Alfred B. Clubok, Norman M. Wilensky, and Forrest J. Berghorn (1969, p. 1062) conclude that the decline in American dynasties over time was likely the result of "political modernization" rather than factors such as population growth or social change.

For six other countries in the comparative dataset, long-term longitudinal data going back to the first legislative session after democratization or independence are also available. The second oldest democracy in the dataset is Switzerland, with observations commencing with the members of the National Council elected at the 1848 federal election. For the New Zealand House of Representatives, the data begin with members of the first parliament, elected in 1853. The data for the Canadian House of Commons similarly go back to the first federal elections, held in 1867. The data for Finland go back to 1907, the first parliamentary election with universal suffrage following the establishment of the Eduskunta (parliament). For Australia, the data cover all MPs since the inaugural House of Representatives, elected in 1901. Finally, in the case of Ireland, the data commence with the MPs elected from Ireland to the House of Commons of the United Kingdom in 1918. In that election, MPs from the nationalist Sinn Féin (SF) party refused to take their seats, and instead established the first Dáil (parliament) of what would eventually become an independent Republic of Ireland.

As in the United States, the general pattern in most of these democracies is an initial increase in the proportion of legacy MPs as some of the first generation of MPs leave the political scene and are succeeded in politics by family members. This initial increase is then followed by a gradual decrease in the proportion of legacy MPs over time. However, these seven cases differ from one another in the level at which dynasties peak (what we might call the "ceiling" of dynastic politics), as well as the level at which they eventually stabilize (what we might call the "floor"). For the United States, the ceiling was 17 percent. This is slightly higher than the ceilings for Australia (13 percent in the 1940s) and New Zealand (14 percent in 1922), and much higher than in Canada (11 percent in 1896) and Finland (9 percent in 1962). However, it is slightly lower than the ceiling in Switzerland (19 percent in 1908) and much lower than the ceiling in Ireland (34 percent in 1973).

There is also notable variation in the floor for each of these countries. The proportion of legacy MPs in Australia has not exceeded 10 percent since 1963. It has been at 6 percent or less since 1968 in Canada, and since 1972 in Finland. New Zealand witnessed a brief drop in the proportion of legacy MPs in the late 1990s and early 2000s—possibly as a result of electoral reform in 1993—but has since rebounded to its postwar "norm" of roughly 8–10 percent. The decline in dynasties in Switzerland began to pick up pace around the time that the country adopted a PR system (for most elections) in 1918. The proportion of legacy MPs has not exceeded 10 percent since 1963 and has fluctuated between 5 percent and 7 percent since the 1980s. In contrast, Ireland maintained a relatively stable floor of between 25 percent and 30 percent of members until the 2011 general election, when the dominant Fianna Fáil (FF) party was decimated at the polls following the world financial crisis. Even so, at 20 percent, the proportion of dynasties in the Irish Dáil after the most recent election in 2016 exceeds the ceiling proportions for the six other cases.

Although not included in the comparative dataset, similar patterns have been documented in the development of dynastic politics over time in the United Kingdom (van Coppenolle, 2017). The proportion of legacy MPs in the House of Commons was well over 30 percent in the late 1880s, two hundred years after the Glorious Revolution brought an end to the absolute political power of the monarchy. However, the proportion steadily declined over time and has been less than 10 percent since the 1950s. In the 55th House of Commons, elected in 2010, roughly 8 percent of MPs were political legacies.[4] Some notable legacy MPs include former Labour Party leader Ed Miliband, who followed his brother David Miliband into parliament; the former Conservative prime minister David Cameron, whose great-grandfather was Sir William Arthur Mount, a Conservative MP in the early 1900s; and Conservative MP Nicholas Soames, who is the grandson of Sir Winston Churchill. Another Labour MP, Stephen Kinnock, is the son of former Labour leader Neil Kinnock and also the husband of former Danish prime minister Helle Thorning-Schmidt. There has been some media speculation that Euan Blair, the son of former Labour prime minister Tony Blair, might also run for parliament in the future.[5]

Thus, with the exception of Ireland, the general pattern in the democracies for which long-term data are available is a gradual decline over time in the prevalence of dynasties, but with varying ceilings and floors. For the remainder of the country cases in the comparative dataset, observations are available only for MPs elected since 1945, so we cannot paint as complete of a picture of each country's development, except for the case of Israel, where this time period covers the complete history of the Knesset. For all other cases, relationships to pre-1945 MPs are included in the measurement of legacy MPs, but the pre-1945 MPs themselves are not included as observations. For the case of Germany, only MPs from West Germany are included prior to reunification, but relationships to former East German politicians are counted for the purpose of coding legacy MPs in the post-reunification period.

For four of these countries, the proportion of legacy MPs does not exceed 15 percent in any legislature for which data are available. In Germany, the proportion of legacy MPs in the Bundestag (parliament) has never exceeded 2 percent, and many of those who have served came from long-active noble families. One recent example is Carl-Eduard von Bismarck, who is the great-great-grandson of Otto von Bismarck, the first German chancellor, and grandson of Prince Otto Christian Archibald von Bismarck, a member of the Nazi Party in the prewar period and an MP for the Christian Democratic Union (CDU) after the war.

In Israel, the percentage of legacy MPs in the Knesset peaked at 13 percent in 1977, and has since dropped to less than 10 percent throughout the 2000s. The 20th Knesset, elected in 2015, contained eleven legacy MPs (9 percent). One example is Tzipi Livni, leader of Kadima until 2012, who is the daughter of three-term former MP Eitan Livni. She later became leader of Hatnuah and formed the Zionist Union (ZU) together with Labor Party leader Isaac Herzog. Herzog is the son of Chaim Herzog, the sixth president of Israel and a former MP. In addition, Chaim Herzog was a brother-in-law to former MP Abba Eban. The son of former prime minister Ariel Sharon, Omri Sharon, served in the Knesset from 2003 to 2006, until he was convicted of fraud and sent to prison.

The proportion of legacy MPs in the Italian Chamber of Deputies has also declined steadily over time, dropping to a low of 3 percent in 1994, after a number of members became embroiled in the Tangentopoli corruption scandal that brought down the long-ruling Christian Democrats (DC) and ushered in electoral system reform. Nevertheless, many political families are still active in Italian politics, with the proportion in recent parliaments at roughly 5 percent. For example, Bobo and Stefania Craxi (brother and sister) are the children of former prime minister Bettino Craxi of the Italian Socialist Party (PSI). The granddaughter of Benito Mussolini, Alessandra Mussolini, began her career in the neo-fascist Italian Social Movement (MSI) and later affiliated herself with former prime minister Silvio Berlusconi's People of Freedoms (Il Popolo della Libertà, PdL) conservative alliance. Dynasties have been documented in local-level Italian politics as well (Chirico and Lupoli, 2008; Geys, 2017).

In the Norwegian Storting (parliament), the proportion of legacy MPs has fluctuated between 5 percent and 10 percent for most of the period from 1945 to 2013 (Fiva and Smith, 2018). The MPs elected in 2013 included eleven legacies (7 percent), including former Labour Party prime minister Jens Stoltenberg, who is the son of former cabinet minister Thorvald Stoltenberg. Prior to Stoltenberg, the prime minister's office was held by Kjell Magne Bondevik of the Christian Democratic Party (Kristelig Folkeparti, KrF), whose uncle Kjell Bondevik was also a former MP, cabinet minister, and party leader. Of the fourteen prime ministers to serve between 1945 and 2016, four had dynastic family ties to former politicians, and five had family members who followed them into national politics.

How does Japan compare to the other countries in the comparative dataset? One aspect of Japan's experience that immediately stands out is the steep upward trend for most of the period under investigation. Unlike most of the other countries in the comparative dataset, Japan witnessed a steady increase in the proportion of legacy MPs in the House of Representatives over time, with the ceiling to the level of dynastic membership—33 percent in 1993—higher than all other countries except Ireland. Indeed, Ireland appears most similar to Japan in terms of dynastic politics. All other countries' trend lines blend together in the lower part of Figure 2.1, rarely exceeding 10 percent over the entire post-1945 period.

In 1947, the proportion of legacy MPs in Japan was just 6 percent—near the average for most other countries but the absolute lowest level for postwar Japan. However, the proportion of legacy MPs proceeded to grow steadily throughout the following three decades, as incumbents retired or died and were succeeded by family members. The proportion plateaued in the 1980s and 1990s at just above 30 percent, then dropped precipitously in 2009 before making a slight rebound in the 2012 and 2014 general elections. As with Ireland in 2011, the sharp drop in legacy MPs in 2009 can be explained by a shift in the party composition of the legislature following the DPJ's defeat of the LDP in that election. Such drastic swings due to changes in parties' seat shares highlight the need to look more closely at differences across parties within countries.

COMPARATIVE PATTERNS ACROSS PARTIES

The longitudinal trends reveal interesting aggregate patterns in the development of dynasties over time in each of the twelve democracies in the comparative dataset. However, there are also significant differences in the proportion of legacy MPs across parties, and these differences could in part be responsible for fluctuations in the aggregate proportion if the party composition of the legislature changes. Because changes in party systems and changes in specific parties' names over time can quickly become complicated to track longitudinally—especially in the multiparty systems of Israel and Italy—here the presentation will focus only on cross-sectional differences in pooled observations for a sample of the major parties to have held seats in parliament in the past two decades (1996–2016). The purpose is not to provide a systematic account of differences across the parties, or to evaluate the effect of changes in the party composition of the legislature on the aggregate patterns, but to simply document that such differences across parties exist.

Figure 2.2 illustrates the differences across a sample of parties in each country, with the countries arranged in order of maximum level of dynastic membership in a single party. In Germany, although Chancellor Angela Merkel is not herself a legacy MP, her CDU party and its Bavarian counterpart, the Christian Social Union (CSU), have had more legacy MPs in recent years than the Social Democratic Party (SPD), Die Linke (Link), the Greens (G), or the now-dissolved Party of Democratic Socialism (PDS). Many of the CDU and CSU legacy MPs are of noble background, including Carl-Eduard von Bismarck (CDU) noted earlier and Karl-Theodor zu Guttenberg (CSU).

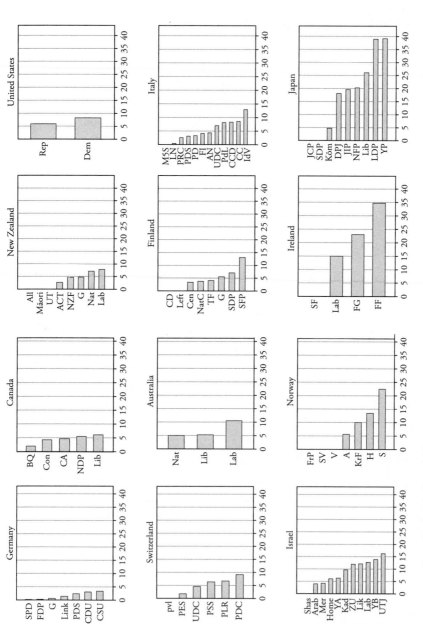

FIGURE 2.2 Party-level variation within countries

SOURCE: Dynasties in Democracies Dataset.

NOTE: Average percentage in sample of major parties, 1996–2016. By-election winners are included where available. Affiliated parties (e.g., cases of name changes but continuation in organization and membership) are grouped together where appropriate. See main text for party abbreviations.

In Canada, legacy MPs have been least common in the Bloc Québécois (BQ) and most common in the Liberal Party (Lib), currently led by Prime Minister Justin Trudeau. Trudeau's father, Pierre Trudeau, previously served as prime minister, and his maternal grandfather, James Sinclair, was an MP. In 2011, there was speculation that Mike Layton, a Toronto city councillor, might run in the by-election following the death of his father, New Democratic Party (NDP) leader Jack Layton, or that Layton's widow, Olivia Chow (already an MP in the party), would seek the top leadership position, but neither ultimately pursued it.[6] The short-lived conservative Reform Party of Canada, which became the Canadian Alliance (CA) in 2000, had just under 5 percent dynastic membership. It merged with the Progressive Conservatives to form the current Conservative Party (Con) in 2003 (Progressive Conservatives are grouped with Con in Figure 2.2). Although there have been fewer Conservative legacy MPs in recent years, at one point in 1962 the proportion exceeded 11 percent. The historical high for the Liberal Party was 13 percent, in 1958.

In New Zealand, the most dynastic party is Labour (Lab). Interestingly, although there have been no legacy MPs elected under the Māori party label, many of the legacy MPs in the Labour and National (Nat) parties— the two largest parties in New Zealand—are of Māori descent, including former cabinet ministers Nanaia Mahuta (Lab) and Tau Henare (Nat). The Green Party (G), ACT, and New Zealand First (NZF) have had fewer legacy MPs—5 percent or less—but this proportion represents a single individual in the former two parties (Kennedy Graham in the Greens and Roger Douglas in ACT), and just three individuals in NZF: Raymond Henare, Ria Bond, and Jim Peters, who is the brother of party leader Winston Peters. All are also of Māori descent. There were no legacy MPs in the Alliance (All) or United Future (UF).

The Democratic Party (Dem) in the United States has had more legacy members than the Republican Party (Rep) in recent years, although this has not always been the case. Up until the Reconstruction era, there were significantly more legacy members among Democrats, largely in the party's stronghold in the South (Dal Bó, Dal Bó, and Snyder, 2009). However, Republicans were more likely to be dynastic from about 1916–1952. Since then, the proportion of legacy Democrats has been 7 percent, on average, compared to 6 percent for Republicans, with the two parties occasionally trading places as the most dynastic.

The four largest parties in Switzerland are the Liberals (Parti Libéral-Radical, PLR), the Swiss Socialist Party (Parti Socialiste Suisse, PSS), the Democratic Union of the Centre (L'Union Démocratique du Centre, UDC), and the Christian Democratic People's Party of Switzerland (Parti Démocrate-Chrétien, PDC), which has had the largest proportion of legacy MPs since 1996. The former president of PSS, Hans-Jürg Fehr, is a legacy MP whose cousin Hermann Fehr served two terms in the 1980s and was mayor of the city of Biel in the canton of Bern. Fewer legacy MPs have served in the Green Party of Switzerland (Parti Écologiste Suisse, PES), which is relatively small by comparison, and no legacy MPs have been elected from the small Green Liberal Party (Parti vert'libéral, pvl).

In Australia, the Labor Party (Lab) appears to be the most likely to engage in dynastic candidate recruitment, with roughly 10 percent of recent MPs counting as members of a dynasty. One such legacy MP is Kim Beazley Jr., who was leader of the party from 1995 to 2001 and again from 2005 to 2006, and later served as ambassador to the United States. His father, Kim Beazley Sr., served for thirty-two years in the House of Representatives and as minister for education under Prime Minister Gough Whitlam in the 1970s. Beazley's successor as Labor Party leader in 2001, Simon Crean, was also a legacy MP. His father, Frank Crean, served in the same Whitlam cabinet as the senior Beazley, and his brother David served in state-level office in Tasmania. Dynasties have been less common in recent years in the Liberal (Lib) and National (Nat) parties.

In four of the remaining countries in the comparative dataset, the aggregate proportion of legacy MPs has been lower than 10 percent but has exceeded 10 percent in some parties. In Finland, the Swedish People's Party (Svenska Folkpartiet i Finland, SFP) appears to be the most dynastic, but this is in large part because it is a small party. The proportion (13 percent) is the effect of just two legacy MPs, Christina Gestrin and Nils-Anders Granvik, serving over this time period. The three largest parties are the Center Party (Cen), the National Coalition (NatC), and the Social Democratic Party (SDP). Among them, the SDP has had the most legacy MPs, including former minister of foreign affairs Erkki Tuomioja and former minister of finance Jutta Urpilainen. The Christian Democrats (CD) and Left Alliance (Left) have not had any legacy MPs in their membership in the past two decades, while there has been one legacy, Merikukka Forsius, elected from the Greens (G), and two, Anne Louhelainen and Ritva Elomaa, elected from the right-wing True Finns (TF). Because the Greens have had fewer members overall, the proportion is higher.

Italy's fluid party system and joint lists also make cross-sectional comparisons of parties difficult. The Christian Democratic Centre (Centro Cristiano Democratico, CCD) and Union of the Centre (L'Unione dei Democratici Cristiani e di Centro, UDC) have had some legacy MPs, as have Italy of Values (Italia dei Valori, IdV) and Civic Choice (Scelta Civica, SC). Because these parties are not very large, the proportion reflects only three to four members. The large People of Freedoms (PdL) party associated with former prime minister Silvio Berlusconi had twenty-one legacy members after the 2008 election (7 percent). Several legacy MPs also hailed from Berlusconi's Forza Italia (FI). Among recent party leaders and prime ministers, there have been a handful of legacy MPs, including former prime ministers Enrico Letta, Romano Prodi, and Massimo D'Alema, who were members of the Democratic Party (PD) and Democratic Party of the Left (Partito Democratico della Sinistra, PDS). The father of former prime minister Matteo Renzi had a career in local politics. Other Italian parties in Figure 2.2 are the National Alliance (AN), the Lega Nord (LN), the Communist Refoundation Party (PRC), and the Five Star Movement (M5S).[7]

Israel's multiparty system is ever-shifting, which makes it especially challenging to track trends in dynastic politics within parties. From the time of Israel's first elections in 1949 until 1977, the dominant part was the Labor Party (abbreviated as "Lab" in Figure 2.2, but known as Mapai until 1968), which has been led by legacy MP Isaac Herzog since 2013. On the right, the largest party since 1973 is Likud (Lik), founded by Menachem Begin in 1973. Although the current leader of Likud, Prime Minister Benjamin Netanyahu, is not a legacy MP, Menachem Begin's son, Ze'ev Binyamin "Benny" Begin, is a member. United Torah Judaism (UTJ) only appears to be heavily dynastic because it is a very small party. A single legacy MP, Meir Porush, serving over the entire time period in the sample, accounts for the large proportion. Yitzak Levy is also singularly responsible for the proportion of legacies in the Jewish Home (Home), as is Yair Lapid in Yesh Atid (YA). There was also only one legacy MP elected through the Joint List of Arab parties (Arab): Haneen Zoabi. The other parties or electoral alliances included in Figure 2.2 are Yisrael Beiteinu (YB), Kadima (Kad), Shinui (Shin), Shas, Meretz (Mer), and Zionist Union (ZU). Of these, only Shas had no legacy members during the time period covered.

The most dynastic Norwegian party in recent years has been the Center Party (Senterpartiet, S). However, the Center Party is also a relatively small party, electing between ten and eleven members to the most recent parliaments, including two to three legacy MPs in each. The two largest parties, the Conservative Party (Høyre, H) and Labour Party (Arbeiderpartiet, A), have had between three and five legacy MPs in each parliament but tend to elect more members overall. The Liberals (Venstre, V), Socialist Left Party (Sosialistisk Venstreparti, SV), and Progress Party (Fremskrittspartiet, FrP) have not elected any legacy MPs to recent parliaments, whereas the small Christian Democratic Party (KrF) elected five individual legacy MPs to the Storting between 1996 and 2013.

Dynasties in Ireland have always been most common in Fianna Fáil (FF); however, the larger proportion in the pooled observations of recent Fianna Fáil MPs is in part the result of the party's devastating loss in the 2011 election. Before the election, the party had seventy-seven MPs, twenty-eight of whom were legacies (36 percent). In the 2011 election, the party lost all but 20 seats, but nine of the survivors were legacies, resulting in a legacy proportion of 45 percent. Legacy MPs in Fine Gael (FG) have made up 20–25 percent of members across all recent elections (between eight and sixteen individuals). A few legacy MPs have also been elected from the Labour Party (Lab), but Sinn Féin (SF) has had none. Prominent legacy MPs in Ireland include recent prime ministers Enda Kenny and Brian Cowen, and a large number of cabinet ministers (Smith and Martin, 2017).

Japan's partywise comparison again places it at the extreme end of dynasticism among the democracies in the comparative dataset, as legacy MPs in three parties—Ozawa Ichirō's now-defunct Liberal Party (Lib), the LDP, and Your Party (YP)—made up more than 25 percent of total party membership between 1996 and 2016. At 39 percent each, the LDP and Your Party were the most dynastic parties out of all major parties during this time period in the twelve democracies of the comparative dataset. Your Party is a conservative breakaway party founded by an LDP defector, so it is not surprising that its level of dynastic politics would be similar to that of the LDP. The now-defunct New Frontier Party (NFP) was roughly 20 percent dynastic, a proportion similar to that in the conservative Japan Innovation Party (JIP, previously the Japan Restoration Party). The center-left DPJ has only been slightly less dynastic. Kōmeitō (Kōm) counted only two individual legacy MPs in its membership during this time period (Ikenobō

Yasuko and Kitagawa Kazuo), but given the smaller size of the party, their presence meant that 5 percent of the party was dynastic. Not a single MP from the Social Democratic Party (SDP) or JCP came from a political dynasty during this time period, although there have been legacy MPs from both parties in the past (particularly in the SDP's predecessor party, the JSP).

SUMMARY OF THE COMPARATIVE EMPIRICAL RECORD

The cross-temporal and cross-party variation in these twelve democracies serves to illustrate three important points that put Japan into comparative perspective. The first point is that Japan is not alone among democracies in terms of the continued presence of democratic dynasties. Dynastic politics are ubiquitous in some form or another across all democracies, and in different parts of the world. In other words, democratic dynasties are by no means a uniquely Japanese phenomenon.

A second point to note is that, even though democratic dynasties exist throughout the world, there is considerable variation in the level of dynastic politics across countries, parties, and time. The most common temporal pattern in the comparative cases is a decrease in dynasties over time, but different countries appear to have different ceilings and floors to the level of dynastic politics. Moreover, within countries, some parties are much more dynastic than others. In many country cases, the level of dynasticism within specific parties exceeds the overall level of dynasticism in the legislature. Thus, the aggregate proportion of legacy MPs in any given country and time may depend on the party composition of parliament. The cross-national and cross-party variation in dynastic politics is a puzzle that has received only limited attention in the existing literature on democratic dynasties.

The third and final point that merits attention is that, even though democratic dynasties are not unique to Japan, Japan is nevertheless among the most dynastic democracies, and its level of dynastic politics has grown over time, in stark contrast to the pattern in most other democracies. Moreover, Japan's LDP has been the most dynastic major party across all of these democracies, in addition to being the most dynastic party in Japan (together with its smaller offshoot, Your Party). These facts are even more startling considering that Japan is an industrialized democracy with a large population and relatively low levels of inequality.

Japan's Empirical Record

We have already seen how the percentage of legacy MPs among all MPs increased over time in Japan. However, it is also informative to compare this trend to the percentage of legacy candidates among all candidates over the same time period. This will give us a general sense of the electoral advantages that legacy candidates may enjoy, keeping in mind that differences in party, district, and other contextual factors play an obviously important role in determining which candidates are elected. Figure 2.3 shows that the percentage of legacies among all candidates in general elections (by-elections excluded) closely tracked the percentage among elected MPs until around the early 1990s, when the gap between the percentage of legacy candidates and percentage of legacy MPs began to widen.

Altogether, of the 10,060 individual candidates who ever ran in a House of Representatives general election or by-election between 1947 and 2014, 600 (6 percent) were legacy candidates. However, the total number of individuals includes many fringe candidates and candidates from minor parties

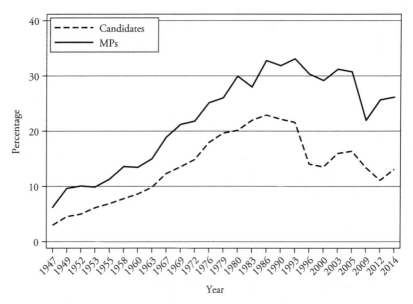

FIGURE 2.3 Legacy candidates and legacy MPs in Japan across time
SOURCE: JHRED.
NOTE: By-elections excluded.

who never had any chance at election. Only 3,065 of the individual candidates who attempted to get elected to the House of Representatives were ever successful in actually becoming an MP, and of these, 477 (16 percent) were legacies. In other words, nearly 80 percent of all legacy candidates in postwar Japan were successful at getting elected at least once. In comparison, just 27 percent of non-legacy candidates were ever elected to the House of Representatives.

We have also already seen that the LDP has had more legacy MPs in its membership in recent parliaments than most of the other parties. But overall, which parties recruited the greatest proportion of legacy candidates into running over the entire postwar period? The left-side panel in Figure 2.4 uses a mosaic plot to illustrate two pieces of information.[8] First, the plot illustrates the distribution of candidates' parties in JHRED for the entire

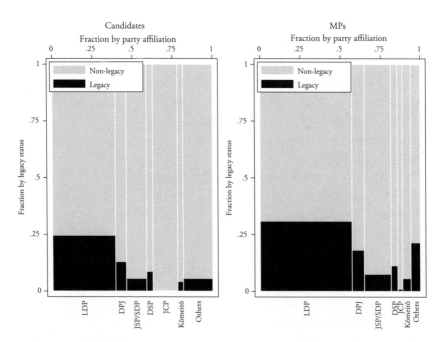

FIGURE 2.4 Party affiliation and legacy status of candidates and MPs in Japan
SOURCE: JHRED.

NOTE: By-elections included. The mosaic plots show the fraction of non-legacy and legacy (x-axis) within each party group, and the fraction of those party groups (y-axis) among all candidates (left panel) and MPs (right panel). All party groups include affiliated independents. LDP group includes all precursor parties (i.e., the Liberal Party, Democratic Party, and variants). JSP/SDP group includes Leftist Socialists. DSP group includes Rightist Socialists. A more complete breakdown is given in Table A.1 and Table A.2 in Appendix A.

time period, which gives us a sense of the prevalence of different parties overall in Japan. Second, the plot shows the distribution of legacy candidates within those parties. The x-axis at the top of the plot gives the fraction of candidate-level observations in the dataset for each major party, whereas the y-axis at the left of the plot indicates the fraction of legacy candidates within each party's total observations.

The actual JHRED party variable contains distinct identification codes for all parties, including separate codes to identify candidates who ran as independents but were in truth affiliated with a party and were either denied the official nomination or chose to eschew it for other reasons. To make the mosaic plot easier to visualize, party-affiliated independents are grouped with their respective parties. The LDP group includes the party's precursors (i.e., conservative parties that fielded candidates from 1947 to 1955 and then merged to form the LDP). The JSP/SDP group includes the Leftist Socialists (1951–1955), and the DSP group includes the Rightist Socialists (1951–1955). Finally, nonaffiliated independents and candidates nominated by minor or short-lived parties are grouped into a single "Others" category.

The mosaic plot allows us to rule out straight away that the LDP's high proportion of legacy candidates has anything to do mathematically with its size—as might explain the high proportions in some of the other small parties in the comparative cases we have seen. Almost 40 percent of all candidates in the dataset are affiliated with the LDP or its precursor parties. Within the LDP group, roughly a quarter of all candidates in the dataset are legacy candidates. The second largest party in terms of the fraction of affiliated candidates is the JCP (15 percent of all candidates), yet it has so few legacy candidates (just 12 observations; less than half a percent of all JCP candidacies) that the fraction is not even visible in the plot.

Among the small and ephemeral parties grouped together with independents as "Others," the largest party is the fringe Happiness Realization Party (affiliated with the Happy Science religious movement), which fielded more than four hundred candidates between 2009 and 2014. Larger nonfringe parties in the "Others" group include the NFP, which was the second-largest party in 1996 (but disbanded shortly after), Renewal Party, Liberal Alliance, Ozawa's Liberal Party, Your Party, Japan Restoration/Innovation Party, and Tomorrow Party of Japan (TPJ). Legacy candidates are most common in these larger, nonfringe parties, all of which were formed by defectors from the LDP—indeed, four of these parties (NFP, Renewal,

Liberal, and TPJ) were all formed by legacy MP and perennial party creator (and destroyer) Ozawa Ichirō.

The right-side panel in Figure 2.4 shows the same type of mosaic plot for elected MPs. Here again, we can see the overwhelming size of the LDP—more than half of all seats between 1947 and 2014 went to candidates affiliated with either the LDP or its precursor parties. The fraction of legacy MPs within the LDP group (31 percent), as with all other party groups, is higher than in the full sample of candidates. This again hints at the electoral advantages that legacy candidates enjoy. Despite being the second largest party in terms of candidates, the JCP was far less successful at electing those candidates. However, among the JCP's elected MPs, the fraction of legacy MPs (1 percent) is now just barely visible. Among the parties grouped into the "Others" category, the most dynastic is the New Liberal Club (NLC), which was a short-lived splinter party of LDP defectors led by several legacy MPs. Of the 49 seats held by the party between 1976 and 1986, 24 (49 percent) were held by legacy MPs.[9] Most of the NLC members rejoined the LDP after 1986.

THE BEST BUTTER?

In his reflections on what might set members of dynasties apart from other politicians in the United States, Stephen Hess (1966, p. 3) hypothesized that legacy politicians might represent the "best butter" in politics: "Old stock, Anglo-Saxon, Protestant, professional, Eastern seaboard, well to do." These characteristics are obviously not all applicable to Japan, but other patterns may stand out. What are some of the background characteristics of legacy MPs in Japan, and do they differ noticeably from those of non-legacy MPs?

It may be useful to first look at the types of family relationships between legacy MPs and their predecessors. The top part of Table 2.1 gives the number and percentage of legacy candidates (one observation per individual) with different types of relationships to the elected politician who preceded their candidacy. Relationships are also split by the gender of the legacy candidate. For legacy candidates with more than one prior relative, the table gives only the most recent relative to have served prior to the legacy candidate's first time running. For example, if an MP had two sons who served one after the other, the second son would be coded as following his brother into politics, not his father. The table also gives the same statistics for the sample of legacy candidates who were successful in getting elected at least

TABLE 2.1
Relationships and generations of legacy candidates and MPs in Japan

	CANDIDATES		MPS		SUCCESSFUL
	(N)	(%)	(N)	(%)	(%)
Predecessor (successor)					
Father (son)	335	55.83	261	54.72	77.91
Father (daughter)	17	2.83	13	2.73	76.47
Father-in-law (son-in-law)	60	10.00	52	10.90	86.67
Father-in-law (daughter-in-law)	2	0.33	2	0.42	100.00
Mother (son)	3	0.50	2	0.42	66.67
Grandfather (grandson)	28	4.67	24	5.03	85.71
Grandfather (granddaughter)	3	0.50	3	0.63	100.00
Uncle (nephew)	37	6.17	33	6.92	89.19
Uncle (niece)	1	0.17	0	0.00	0.00
Brother (brother)	40	6.67	32	6.71	80.00
Brother (sister)	1	0.17	1	0.21	100.00
Sister (brother)	1	0.17	1	0.21	100.00
Wife (husband)	4	0.67	1	0.21	25.00
Husband (wife)	30	5.00	19	3.98	63.33
Cousin (cousin)	3	0.50	3	0.63	100.00
Other male relative (male successor)	34	5.67	29	6.08	85.29
Other male relative (female successor)	1	0.17	1	0.21	100.00
Generation					
Second	392	65.33	300	62.89	76.73
Third	126	21.00	105	22.01	83.33
Fourth	53	8.83	44	9.22	83.02
Fifth	16	2.67	15	3.14	93.75
Sixth or higher	13	2.17	13	2.73	100
Total	600	100	477	100	79.50

SOURCE: JHRED.

NOTE: One observation per legacy candidate or MP. *Father-in-law* includes adoptive fathers. *Grandfather* includes great grandfathers. *Uncle* includes great uncles and uncles who adopted their biological nephews as sons. *Other male relative* includes second cousins, younger relatives (e.g., nephews), and other in-law relationships, as well as any case in which the exact relationship could not be determined. For generation, sixth or higher includes five seventh-generation candidates and two ninth-generation candidates (all successful). Not all generations are present as observations in the data, since some members served only in the prewar period or in the House of Councillors. Coding of generation may not account for all family members in very large families with multiple branches and intermarriage.

once. The final column in the table gives the percentage of individual legacy candidates who were ever successful in getting elected (in other words, the ratio of MPs to candidates in each category).

Not surprisingly, the most common family predecessor among all legacy candidates and MPs is a father. Nearly 59 percent of all legacy MPs followed in their father's immediate footsteps. This is actually higher than in the United States and the United Kingdom, where approximately 30 percent of relationships within dynasties have been parent-child (Dal Bó, Dal Bó, and Snyder, 2009; van Coppenolle, 2017), but comparable to the pattern in Ireland, where 55 percent of predecessors have been fathers (Smith and Martin, 2017). Many of the candidates and MPs in the other relationship categories also had fathers who served before them but with a different family relative serving in between. The second most common type of predecessor is a father-in-law (including adoptive fathers), followed by other common male relatives: brothers, uncles, and grandfathers.

For wives of politicians, the path goes through widowhood in roughly half of the cases (fourteen of the candidates and ten of the MPs). There have been only four husbands who were preceded by their wives. One such husband, Tokano Takeshi, actually ran unsuccessfully as a candidate for the Tōhōkai party in the 1942 general election, but was purged by order of the General Headquarters (GHQ) of the US Occupation prior to the 1946 election. His wife, Tokano Satoko, ran in his place as a JSP candidate in 1946 and won. This makes her, not him, the "senior" member of the dynasty. Takeshi ran and lost again in 1949 and 1952 but ultimately was successful as a Rightist JSP candidate to the House of Councillors in 1953 (thus, he is not included in the MP count in Table 2.1). The one husband to be elected to the House of Representatives was Nishikawa Tomoo (NFP), who was elected in 1996 after his wife, Matsu Akira (legal name Nishikawa Reiko), had already been elected to the House of Councillors. The single case of a brother following a sister into office is Momiyama Akira (LDP), who directly succeeded his sister, Momiyama Hide. However, she herself had followed their adoptive father, Momiyama Hiroshi.

An interesting fact to note is that the success rate for legacy candidates who follow a father into politics tends to be lower than the success rates for legacy candidates who follow other common male relatives (fathers-in-law, grandfathers, uncles, and brothers). There are three possible, and not necessarily mutually exclusive, explanations for this difference. One is a regression to the mean in terms of the quality of politician's children. In other words, the father may have been successful because he was exceptional, but the son (or daughter) was just average.[10] In Japan, it is not uncommon to adopt a son-in-law as heir to a family estate or business, especially when the head of the family or founder of the firm lacks a biological male heir. The adopted son then takes the name of the family and continues the patrilineal line. There is even an adage in Japan that relates this practice to quality: "You cannot choose your sons, but you can choose your sons-in-law." Research on family-run firms in Japan has found that businesses inherited by sons-in-law tend to perform better than those inherited by biological heirs (Mehrotra et al., 2013). Similarly, sons-in-law and more distant male relatives may be, on average, of higher political quality than sons.

A second possible explanation is a difference in selection bias for the recruitment of non-consanguineous or distant relatives. No legacy candidacies are randomly assigned. But following a father into politics may seem to be an obvious or "natural" career choice for many political children, just as occupational inheritance from father to child is common among doctors, lawyers, and other professions. As a result, some children of male politicians may wish to follow in their fathers' footsteps even if he was not particularly popular or successful. In contrast, it could be the case that following a more distant male relative into politics involves more of a calculated decision to select into politics. The male predecessors in such cases may have been more popular, or party actors involved in candidate selection may have had greater reason to recruit a relative as a successor even if there was no son available to nominate. The electoral success of the successors, then, might have more to do with the quality of the predecessors than with the quality of the successors.[11] The third possible explanation is that sons, for whatever reason, may face stiffer competition from other challengers when they attempt to succeed their fathers. If sons also tend to be of lower quality, on average, then they are easier for those challengers to defeat.

The bottom part of Table 2.1 gives the number of generations of politicians within the family for legacy candidates and MPs. For unelected candidates, this is the number of members who would have served from the family if they had been elected. However, if a legacy candidate failed to be elected, the family would not count as having successfully created a democratic dynasty. For those who were ultimately successful, however, the number represents the number of members of the MP's dynasty (including the

MP) to have served in the Diet.[12] About 65 percent of all legacy candidates only had one previous family member serve in national politics before they ran, and 77 percent of these second-generation legacy candidates were successful in getting elected—thus creating a democratic dynasty. The success rate grows with each successive generation in a dynasty. In other words, members of older political dynasties—that is, those with a larger number of previous members—tend to get elected if and when they run. All of the legacy candidates with six or more predecessors were successfully elected to the House of Representatives, which is not surprising if one considers that the incentives for perpetuating a dynasty likely depend on the past success of members of that dynasty. Roughly 83 percent of legacy candidates, and 82 percent of legacy MPs, shared the same family name as their nearest predecessor.

Is there a Japanese equivalent to the American Eastern Seaboard? In other words, have some of Japan's prefectures or regions been more dynastic than others? Although the Eastern Seaboard may have been a common regional setting for some of the most prominent dynasties in the United States, the most dynastic US region historically has actually been the South. For the case of India, in contrast, Kanchan Chandra (2016, pp. 18–20) finds that dynasties are relatively evenly dispersed across districts and regions. Figure 2.5 shows a map of Japan's forty-seven prefectures, shaded to indicate the percentage (range) of legacy MPs among all MPs elected from each prefecture from 1947 to 2014. Because district boundaries change over time, the data are aggregated to the level of prefecture. In addition, MPs elected to the PR tier in the postreform period (in which districts are regions comprising multiple prefectures in most cases) are excluded. Lighter (darker) shaded prefectures indicate a lower (higher) percentage of all seats in the House of Representatives that were held by legacy MPs.

If there is a Japanese equivalent to the American Eastern Seaboard, it is actually the country's *western* seaboard. The two most dynastic prefectures are neighboring prefectures in the Chugoku region of western Japan: Yamaguchi (47 percent), which is home to Prime Minister Abe Shinzō (Yamaguchi 4th District), and Shimane (53 percent), home to former prime minister Takeshita Noboru. The Abe dynasty accounts for the large share of the dynasties in Yamaguchi. Abe is a sixth-generation legacy MP. He succeeded his father, Abe Shintarō, whose father-in-law, former prime minister Kishi Nobusuke, also came from Yamaguchi. In addition, Abe Shintarō's

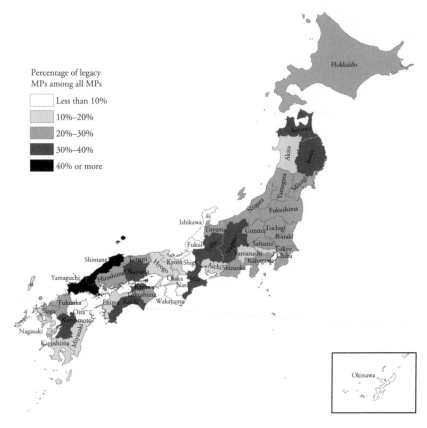

FIGURE 2.5 Geographic dispersion of Japan's dynasties

SOURCE: Map created by Shiro Kuriwaki with author's calculations from JHRED.

NOTE: Observations pooled over all MPs who served from each prefecture. Excludes MPs elected in the PR tier of the postreform electoral system. By-election winners are included.

father (Shinzō's paternal grandfather), Abe Kan, served prior to 1947. Kishi's brother, former prime minister Satō Eisaku, served from Yamaguchi, as did his son Satō Shinji. Finally, Abe Shinzō's younger brother Kishi Nobuo has been an MP for Yamaguchi 2nd District since 2012. No other prefecture has been so consistently dominated by one family.

The high proportion of dynasties in Shimane may in part be because it is a relatively small prefecture in terms of population and parliamentary seats, with only a single five-seat district from 1947 to 1993, and just two single-seat districts from 1996 to 2014. For much of the prereform period, competition in the LDP revolved around Takeshita, Sakurauchi Yoshio, and

Hosoda Kichizō. In postreform Shimane 1st District, Hosoda's son, Hosoda Hiroyuki, has consistently held the seat (he was first elected in 1990). Since 2000, the seat in Shimane 2nd District has been held by Takeshita's brother, Takeshita Wataru (Noboru himself won the seat in 1996).

The least dynastic prefecture is Shiga, where less than 1 percent of all elected MPs since 1947 have been legacy MPs. Shiga is also a relatively small prefecture—like Shimane, it returned just five MPs in a single prefecture-wide district from 1947 to 1993. Since electoral reform, it has had four single-seat districts. One of Shiga's longtime MPs was Uno Sōsuke, who served as prime minister for just two months in 1989 before resigning amid a sex scandal involving a geisha.[13] His son-in-law Uno Osamu later won a seat in the PR tier (so does not contribute to the percentage indicated in the map). The only legacy MP to ever hold a non-PR seat in Shiga Prefecture is Konishi Osamu in Shiga 2nd District, who was elected in a by-election in 2001. He lost his race in the general election in 2003 but was elected to the PR tier.

Six other prefectures—Okinawa, Wakayama, Fukui, Oita, Nara, and Ishikawa—have been represented by legacy MPs less than 10 percent of the time. All other prefectures fall in the range of 10–40 percent dynastic. There are no clear patterns in the geographic distribution of dynasties unless one reads into the white-shaded belt running from Ishikawa on the western coast to Wakayama on the Pacific coast. However, the small percentage of dynasties in each of these prefectures likely has more to do with the smaller number of seats in each, and the occupation of these seats for many decades by first-generation MPs. For example, it was widely expected that former prime minister Mori Yoshirō of Ishikawa Prefecture—who served fourteen terms from 1969 to 2012—would be succeeded by his son, Yūki, who was a local prefectural assembly member. However, Yūki died suddenly in 2011. Okinawa may have fewer legacy MPs in its record simply because it has only been a prefecture since 1972, when the United States returned sovereignty over the islands to Japan.

Gender and age are also relevant demographic background characteristics to consider. Previous studies in diverse contexts have noted that women have often entered politics on the heels of a close male relative (e.g., Jalalzai, 2013; Basu, 2016; Folke, Rickne, and Smith, 2017), often in the form of a so-called widow's succession. Japan is not different from other democracies in this regard. While women have made up just over 5 percent of all non-legacy MPs, they account for 8 percent of all legacy MPs (Table 2.2). Or considering the

TABLE 2.2

Demographic and occupational backgrounds of non-legacy and legacy MPs in Japan

	Non-legacy	Legacy
Age at first election (median)	48	42
Female	5.49	8.18
Born in prefecture	72.98	72.25
Local politician (mayor, governor, assembly member)	36.32	17.40
Member of the House of Councillors	3.28	5.45
National bureaucrat	14.72	20.13
MP's personal secretary	11.67	40.25
Business executive	9.51	16.77
Labor union activist	10.32	2.73

SOURCE: JHRED.

NOTE: One observation per MP (non-legacy N = 2,588; legacy N = 477). Entries are percentages except for age, which is the median. The sample for calculating the median age for first-term MPs excludes individuals who were first elected before 1947 or who first served in the House of Councillors. The sample is reduced for place of birth due to missing data (non-legacy N = 1,673; legacy N = 436). Occupational backgrounds are not mutually exclusive. All group differences are statistically significant except for birth in prefecture.

relationship from a different angle, legacy MPs represent roughly 22 percent of all female MPs but just 15 percent of all male MPs. Chapter 7 explores the relationship between gender and dynastic recruitment in more detail, but these patterns indicate that one characteristic that sets legacy MPs apart from other MPs is that they are significantly more likely to be women. In addition to the gender difference, legacy MPs in Japan also tend to get elected at a younger age than non-legacy MPs. The median age for first-term legacy MPs in the House of Representatives is forty-two years old, compared to forty-eight for non-legacy MPs. Legacy MPs in the United States and Ireland have similarly been shown to enter politics at a younger age (Dal Bó, Dal Bó, and Snyder, 2009; Smith and Martin, 2017).

The difference in age at entry suggests that legacy MPs might be able to bypass some of the traditional pathways to a career in national politics, such as first gaining experience in local politics (e.g., municipal or prefectural assembly member, municipal mayor, or prefectural governor). Prior local political experience is often viewed as an important stepping-stone to national office and a key measure of candidate quality (Jacobson, 1989). In bicameral systems, serving in the other chamber (i.e., the House of Councillors in Japan) is also an obvious indicator of experience. In addition to these traditional ways to gain political experience, candidates in Japan often gain experience and connections through careers in the national bureaucracy or by serving as a personal secretary to an incumbent MP (Scheiner, 2006).

Table 2.2 shows the percentage of non-legacy MPs and legacy MPs who had a background in each of these common pathways into politics. Legacy MPs are indeed significantly less likely to have progressed through local politics on their way to national office than non-legacy MPs. This is again consistent with previous findings in the United States and Ireland, as well as in India (Bohlken, 2016). In contrast, legacy MPs in Japan more often gain political experience through serving as a personal secretary to an incumbent MP (most often their relative). Prior experience in the House of Councillors or the national bureaucracy is also slightly more common among legacy MPs, but this is because these pathways are more common in the LDP. The difference between non-legacy and legacy MPs for these two pathways is not significant if only LDP and LDP-affiliated MPs are compared.

Recall that sons-in-law tend to perform better in elections than biological sons. It is difficult to determine whether this is because they are of higher quality, given the challenges in accurately measuring the quality of individuals. However, if political experience can be considered an indication of quality, then sons-in-law are slightly more likely than sons to have experience in prior elective office in local politics or the House of Councillors (25 percent compared to 20 percent), and much more likely to have had a career in the national bureaucracy (58 percent compared to 11 percent). This makes sense given that bureaucrats are an obvious set of eligible bachelors who might come into contact with politicians and their daughters. Sons-in-law are less likely to have served as a politician's personal secretary (27 percent compared to 51 percent).

Information on place of birth is only available for 2,109 of the 3,065 individual MPs in JHRED, but for this sample there is no significant difference between non-legacy and legacy MPs in terms of whether they were first elected in the prefecture of their birth (roughly three-quarters of MPs regardless of legacy status). In other words, legacy MPs are no more likely to be "local" than non-legacy MPs. Among the other occupational backgrounds coded in JHRED (law, medicine, education, agriculture, business, news media, labor union, and religion), only business and labor union backgrounds are significantly different across non-legacy and legacy MPs. A business background includes major experience as a company executive (such as president or director, not simply employee). About 17 percent of legacy MPs had some such experience, compared to less than 10 percent of non-legacy MPs, and the difference is significant even if the sample is restricted to the LDP, which has historically had stronger ties to business interests. It is impossible to say whether dynastic succession in politics for these MPs might be encouraged by patterns of dynastic succession in business leadership. The difference between non-legacy and legacy MPs in terms of labor union background is entirely driven by party differences. About 10 percent of non-legacy MPs had a background in the labor movement, compared to just 3 percent of legacy MPs. However, a labor union background is common only among MPs from the JSP, DSP, and JCP. The difference between non-legacy and legacy MPs is not significant when comparing within these parties.

Finally, it is worth investigating whether legacy MPs tend to have higher levels of education or wealth than non-legacy MPs. Such human capital resources might help explain why legacy candidates do better in elections than non-legacy candidates, although existing research has reported inconsistent patterns. Benny Geys (2017), for example, finds that legacies in local Italian politics tend to have lower levels of education than their non-legacy peers. In contrast, legacy MPs in India tend to be slightly more educated than their non-legacy peers (Bohlken, 2016), and most legacy MPs in Ireland do not have significantly higher or lower levels of education (Smith and Martin, 2017).[14] Unfortunately, JHRED does not contain complete information on the educational backgrounds of all MPs from 1947 to 2014. However, we can get a sense of whether there are any differences by looking at the group of MPs elected in 2014, for which complete information is available.[15]

Figure 2.6 again uses mosaic plots to show the distribution of level of education and place of education by legacy status for the 475 MPs elected in 2014. For level of education, displayed in the left panel, the "postgraduate degree" category includes any degree (master's or doctorate) above a bachelor's degree. "Some university" includes university dropouts and graduates of junior colleges. For place of education, displayed in the right panel, MPs are grouped according to the place where they earned a junior college or bachelor's degree (or "secondary school" if they did not attend university or

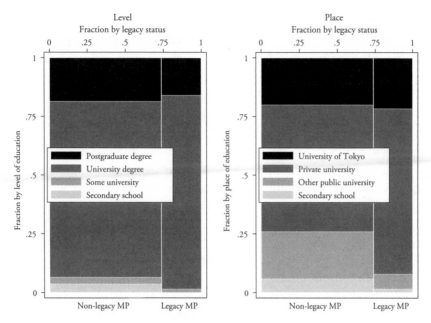

FIGURE 2.6 Level and place of education of non-legacy and legacy MPs in Japan
SOURCE: JHRED.
NOTE: Data for MPs elected in the 2014 general election. The mosaic plots show the fraction of non-legacy MPs and legacy MPs (x-axis) and the fraction within each group (y-axis) with each level of education (left panel) and place of education for undergraduate degree, if applicable (right panel). Foreign universities are grouped with private universities.

dropped out). Universities and colleges are grouped into three categories: the prestigious University of Tokyo (the country's top public university), "private university" (including all private universities, as well as foreign universities), and "other public university" (all other local public universities in Japan).

A bachelor's degree from the University of Tokyo, which has very competitive and merit-based admissions, might be viewed as an indication of an MP's quality of intellect or knowledge. While many private universities are prestigious, a degree from one may also be viewed as a measure of wealth (although tuition is still lower than private universities in the United States). Other public universities, apart from Kyoto University, are generally considered less prestigious than the University of Tokyo. The mosaic plots indicate that although there is not much of a difference between non-legacy and legacy MPs in terms of having earned a postgraduate degree, legacy MPs (about a quarter of all MPs in 2014) are more likely to have earned at least a university degree (left panel). In contrast, the fraction of MPs who attended a private university for their undergraduate degree is much higher among legacy MPs than non-legacy MPs (right panel). This may be an indication of greater wealth in the families of legacy MPs.

The wealth of non-legacy MPs and legacy MPs can be directly compared by using public declarations of income and assets (*shotoku-shisan kōkai*). These yearly reports have been published in the *Asahi Shimbun* newspaper since 1993. The box-and-whisker plots in Figure 2.7 show the distribution of MPs' declared wealth for all non-legacy and legacy MPs (top panels), and for just the members of the LDP (bottom panels), from 1993 to 2014. Each MP's total worth can vary from year to year, depending on sales of assets, capital gains and losses, and so on, so the observations have been pooled across all twenty-two years of available data.

If we compare the total assets of non-legacy MPs and legacy MPs (left panels), legacy MPs are by far richer. However, this sample includes several

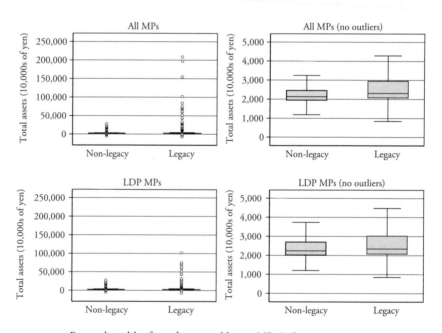

FIGURE 2.7 Personal wealth of non-legacy and legacy MPs in Japan
SOURCE: Based on yearly reports published in the *Asahi Shimbun*.
NOTE: Data for MPs elected between 1993 and 2014. The box-and-whisker plots show the distribution of combined income and assets (minus losses) for non-legacy MPs and legacy MPs. The top panels include all MPs; the bottom panels include only LDP MPs. The left panels include outliers; the right panels exclude outliers.

outliers of extremely rich legacy MPs like Sasagawa Takashi—son of Sa-sakawa Ryōichi, the Class-A accused war criminal who went on to make a fortune in motorboat racing and later founded the Nippon Foundation—whose total assets were as high as ¥2 billion in 2000. Other extremely wealthy legacy MPs include Nakamura Shōzaburō, president of Nittō Kōtsū bus transportation company, and Asō Tarō, whose family owns a mining company. If we exclude these outliers (right panels), the wealth difference between non-legacy and legacy MPs is largely erased, and it is revealed that some legacy MPs have among the lowest wealth. The median declared yearly assets of non-legacy MPs in the LDP is ¥22,410,000, just slightly lower than the ¥23,470,000 of their legacy peers.

SUMMARY OF THE EMPIRICAL RECORD IN JAPAN

The overall empirical record from Japan suggests a number of general patterns. First, the proportion of legacy MPs exceeds the proportion of legacy candidates, both in the aggregate and in specific parties, which suggests that legacy candidates in Japan do indeed enjoy an electoral advantage. The difference between the percentage of legacy candidates and the percentage of legacy MPs cannot simply be attributed to the fact that most legacy candidates are fielded by the LDP and that LDP candidates, in general, tend to enjoy an electoral advantage. Second, the electoral advantage appears to increase with each successive generation within a dynasty. This may indicate a selection effect at the heart of predicting which dynasties will persist beyond a handful of generations. The more generations in a dynasty, the more indication that voters have responded well to members of that dynasty in the past, and the better the response of voters, the more likely a dynasty will continue for another generation.

The overall empirical record does not indicate an obvious geographic pattern to dynastic politics in Japan, much like in the Indian experience. Yamaguchi and Shimane prefectures happen to have had more legacy MPs than other prefectures, but the reasons behind this pattern appear to be largely idiosyncratic. However, it is important to keep in mind that the aggregate prefectural-level patterns presented in this chapter may overlook district-level differences within prefectures, as well as changes over time.

It also appears unlikely that the electoral advantage enjoyed by legacy candidates can be explained by differences in their personal characteristics. Legacy candidates are more likely to be women, and women do not normally do well in Japanese elections. Legacy candidates are also more likely to be younger than non-legacy candidates and less likely to have had previous political experience in elective office at the local level. These patterns suggest that the inherited incumbency advantage enjoyed by legacy candidates may help them to overcome obstacles that might prevent other young, inexperienced, or female candidates from getting selected and elected. However, it does not appear to be the case that the inherited incumbency advantage operates through greater access to education or wealth. Legacy candidates are not considerably more likely to have a degree from the prestigious University of Tokyo or to have a postgraduate degree. They do appear to be more likely to attend private universities than public universities, but apart from a handful of extremely wealthy families, legacy candidates are not uniformly wealthier than their non-legacy counterparts.

These patterns in the characteristics of legacy candidates and MPs in Japan largely correspond to patterns in other countries where comparative data have been explored. As in the United States, India, Ireland, and elsewhere, legacy MPs tend to be younger, less experienced in terms of previous public service in local office, and more likely to be women. However, the average legacy MP is not significantly more educated, nor does he or she possess more wealth, two attributes related to human capital that might be hypothesized as forming part of the inherited incumbency advantage. We must look beyond the "best butter" argument to explain the pattern of dynastic politics in Japan.

History or Culture?

The argument advanced in this book is that institutions, namely the electoral system and candidate selection process in the LDP, helped to foster the emergence and rampant spread of dynastic politics in Japan. However, an alternative explanation is that Japanese politicians—or Japanese people more generally—are historically or culturally predisposed to dynastic politics. After all, Japan had a long history of feudalism and a highly hierarchical social system. Could Japan's postwar experience with dynastic politics simply be a cultural legacy of its past? The party-level differences in all the comparative cases presented thus far already undermine the credibility of such historical or cultural explanations—after all, presumably politicians across different parties in the same country share a common history and culture. Nevertheless, it is useful to briefly explore and definitively rule out this alternative explanation for the case of Japan before proceeding to the main theoretical argument in the next chapter.

Japan has indeed had a long history of hereditary succession in politics, as well as in other occupations. Hereditary rule under the Yamato clan was established in much of Japan by AD 500 and formalized as an imperial system by the mid-600s (Totman, 1981, pp. 21–25). This early imperial rule descended into chaos in the twelfth century, with hereditary military dictators (*shōgun*) warring over the archipelago, until the Tokugawa clan finally solidified control in 1600. Under Tokugawa rule from 1600 to 1868, Japanese society was highly stratified, and hereditary roles were maintained and enforced through strict rules. The feudal lords (*daimyō*) were at the top of this hierarchy, followed by the samurai warrior class, who eventually began to take on more of a bureaucratic role in the state. Farmers, artisans, and merchants ranked below, and each man's status was fixed by inheritance. Some class mobility was possible in the later years of the Tokugawa period through marriages of mutual convenience between merchant and farming families whose wealth was increasing, and lower ranking samurai families who were on the decline (Isoda, 1998). However, male children were generally expected to inherit the same class and occupation of their fathers.[16]

Following the Meiji Restoration in 1868, the Tokugawa caste system was abolished, and greater political participation was allowed. In the 1870s, the government allowed all non-samurai to take on surnames and granted the freedom to intermarry between classes, purchase land, and choose one's own profession. The samurai's stipend was abolished in 1876, effectively eliminating the samurai as a class and ushering in greater political opportunities for rural elites, wealthy businessmen, and landlords, many of whom became active in the Popular Rights Movement in the late 1800s to establish a constitution and an elective assembly (Pratt, 1999, pp. 32–40). Such an assembly, the National Diet, was ultimately established in 1890. The upper chamber, the House of Peers, was modeled after the British House of Lords and restricted to hereditary peers from noble families (*kazoku*) and appointees chosen by the emperor with consultation from the Privy Council.[17] Princes of the blood (who were related to the imperial family but were not in the direct line of succession) were entitled to sit by hereditary right, but they did not exercise this right, nor did they contest elections for the lower chamber, the House of Representatives, which was designed to be closer to the people, like the British House of Commons. Nevertheless, participation in House of Representatives elections was initially open only to wealthy male citizens who could meet the high tax requirement for voting rights and eligibility for public office. In the first Diet election in 1890, about one-third of those who were elected came from the former samurai class (Mason, 1969). The rest were local notables who were both "locally secure and securely local" (Gluck, 1985, p. 69).[18]

The electoral system for the House of Representatives changed multiple times as a consequence of compromises between the oligarchs who controlled the House of Peers and the Privy Council, and party politicians active in the House of Representatives, all of whom had their own preferences. The first electoral law employed a plurality system in small districts, with district magnitude being only one or two seats, with one or two votes given to voters. This system was opposed by oligarchs such as Yamagata Aritomo, who feared the development of strong parties, as well as party advocates like Itō Hirobumi, who disliked the cost and localism of the small district system, and believed (perhaps erroneously) that larger-sized districts would shift the focus to candidates with a more national base, would lower costs, and would strengthen the foundations of parties (Ramseyer and Rosenbluth, 1995; Kawato, 2002). Thus, the electoral system was changed in 1900 to feature larger districts (M greater than six) and the SNTV voting method. The "large-sized" district system was again replaced with a small-sized district system in 1919, with M ranging from one to three seats, but SNTV was retained. Finally, in 1925, universal male suffrage was adopted, and the electoral system again changed to a "medium-sized" (M ranging from three to five) system that would be used for the remainder of the prewar period and again after 1947.

Despite the expansion in suffrage, candidates with local prestige or connections continued to be heavily favored in candidate selection and elections, as did candidates from the former samurai class. Partly, this was due to the imposition in 1925 of a steep election deposit system, with the requirement that a candidate overcome a threshold of one-tenth of the total vote in the district divided by district magnitude to have the deposit reimbursed. The deposit amount was set at a steep ¥2,000, which would have been roughly $1,000 at the time, or roughly $15,800 if adjusted to today's prices (Harada and Smith, 2014). Naturally, this meant that only wealthy or well-supported candidates could afford to run. Harold Quigley (1932, pp. 264–265) notes that candidates from powerful local families were the most successful at getting elected during the prewar years of so-called Taishō Democracy:

> Personal prestige appears to be the essential quality in a candidate. A connection to a formerly powerful clan, relationship to a locally respected family, reputation for cleverness as a journalist or speaker—these attributes are highly regarded by the voters. Party platforms are too indefinite and the speeches of politicians too vague to afford even the well-educated voter a hold on reality. The respect felt for officials contributes to the success of candidates who hold, or have held, prefectural or municipal offices.

In these respects, the historical evolution of dynastic politics in Japan does not differ dramatically from that of many developing democracies or Western European democracies, where political rights were gradually increased through democratic reforms that lessened the influence of the previous aristocratic elite. In many European countries, the introduction of parliamentary democracy at first failed to undermine the power of the noble classes, who came to occupy powerful positions in both elective office and the military. For example, in the late 1890s to early 1900s, the share of elected politicians who were descendants of the aristocratic noble classes remained as high as 20 percent in the United Kingdom, Germany, Italy, and the Netherlands. However, by the end of World War II, only in the United Kingdom did members of the nobility comprise more than 5 percent (but less than 10 percent) of MPs (Rush, 2000, p. 30). Similarly, we have seen how (nonaristocratic) political dynasties have declined over time in most other countries following democratization. However, Japan's democratic reforms in the Taishō and post–World War II periods, while easing restrictions on political participation, actually preceded the dramatic rise in dynasties. Few legacy MPs in the postwar period come from prewar aristocratic families; most come from dynasties that were newly created after full democratization in 1946 (Ichikawa, 1990).

It may also be tempting to ascribe Japan's seeming predisposition to dynastic politics to a cultural norm of filial piety and intergenerational occupational succession that has continued since the Tokugawa times. For example, anthropologist Ruth Benedict (1946, pp. 72–73) argues that, unlike developments in Europe following industrialization and modernization, Japanese tendencies toward feudalism and hierarchy were retained in society, partly because of mechanisms for social mobility that undercut motivations for an even playing field. Indeed, many scholars of postwar Japanese politics and society have commented on the continuing hierarchical nature of social groups, modeled after a traditional family system. Some have also argued that this vertical hierarchy helps to explain patterns of succession in both business and politics (e.g., Ike, 1957; Yoshino, 1968; Nakane, 1970). When a leader retires, he is expected to designate a successor who is suitable to his group or subordinates. Oftentimes, this is a son (usually the firstborn) or, as noted, an adopted son-in-law. Other times, it is a nonrelated successor, such as a personal secretary or close associate. Dynastic succession persists in this form in many businesses—from fish-market stalls (Bestor, 2004) to publicly traded firms (Saito, 2008). This type of "successor designation" was also clearly evident in the patterns of jiban transfer during Japan's SNTV period. Conservative candidates and voters who support the LDP might be especially predisposed to preserving these traditional views of family and obligation.

Historical or cultural explanations are thus common in popular references to dynasties in Japan. For example, a 2008 *Los Angeles Times* newspaper article about Japan's political dynasties quoted a university professor of public management who hypothesized that "the reliance on family succession is historical, a sort of underground current that still flows through Japan, whether in business or in politics. The old ways are changing in business because globalization is forcing companies to compete abroad and make profits. But politics is strictly domestic. In politics, there is no pressure to change."[19]

On the contrary, subsequent chapters of this book demonstrate that dynastic politics in Japan have evolved considerably since institutional reform in the 1990s, which provided the needed pressure to change. The 1994 electoral reform placed greater emphasis on parties and their national platforms. Parties have responded in kind by recruiting fewer candidates from traditional local channels, including legacy candidates, and more candidates who suit their national image or policy goals, such as women, popular celebrities, and policy experts.

If dynastic politics were simply a result of unique aspects of Japan's history or culture, we would not expect to observe much variation across Japanese parties. Yet the data presented in this chapter illustrate that there are considerable differences across parties when it comes to dynastic politics. Since culture and historical patterns are often resilient, we would also not expect to observe much change following institutional reforms to electoral rules or candidate recruitment. Even if dynastic politics were more closely tied to the conservative values of the LDP, we should not expect these values to change dramatically simply because of institutional reform. Yet the nature of dynastic politics in Japan has changed considerably since the 1994 electoral reform, even as elements of path dependence have conditioned the effects of this institutional change.

Additional evidence against a historical or cultural argument for dynastic politics in Japan can be found by looking at patterns in occupational inheritance in other professions. In general, Japan has enjoyed a relatively high level of intergenerational social mobility since the end of World War II (Ishida, 1993), although descendants of the samurai and kazoku peers are still overrepresented among the highly educated and professional elites (Clark, 2014). Figure 2.8 shows the percentage of male respondents who reported having the same occupation and occupational field as their fathers (based on

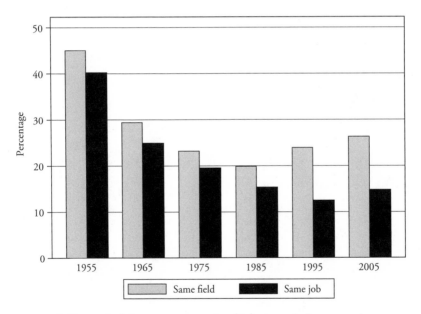

FIGURE 2.8 Changes in father-to-son occupational inheritance in Japan over time

SOURCE: National survey of Social Stratification and Social Mobility (SSM), 1955–2005. Data for the 2015 wave of the survey were not yet available. Women were not sampled in the earliest surveys, and are excluded from the sample for later surveys.

NOTE: Bars give the percentage of male respondents whose reported occupation and occupational field is identical to those reported as their fathers' main occupation and field.

their fathers' main occupation) in the Social Stratification and Social Mobility (SSM) survey, a nationally representative survey that has been conducted once every ten years since 1955. Naturally, there will be some reduction in occupational inheritance over time due to the introduction of new types of technologies and their concomitant professions, as well as the decline in agricultural workers. In addition, some professions, such as Shintō priest, continue to exhibit high levels of occupational inheritance.[20]

Nevertheless, the general pattern in Japan over the past several decades has been a decrease in occupational inheritance from father to son in most professions, even as occupational inheritance in politics was increasing. Moreover, as dynastic politics began to decrease in the 1990s and 2000s, occupational inheritance in other fields experienced a slight increase. In other words, the pattern in occupational inheritance across all professions is the opposite of that observed in the political realm. This suggests that changes in dynastic politics in Japan cannot be explained as part of a broader pattern in the labor market or a generational shift in Japanese society.

In sum, historical or cultural arguments are largely inadequate for explaining Japan's dynastic politics. Each type of explanation lacks sufficient evidence in its favor and cannot explain the change in dynastic politics that we observe over time and across parties.

THREE

A Comparative Theory of Dynastic Candidate Selection

> If democracy can be compared to a restaurant where customers
> (voters) order from a menu of parties and candidates, the pro-
> cess of choosing which candidates will be on the ballot is like
> that of devising the menu itself—*and it all happens before even a*
> *single vote is cast in a general election.*
>
> —*Gideon Rahat (2007, p. 157)*

What explains the growth and decline of political dynasties in a democracy like Japan, and why is it that the selection of legacy candidates seems to be more prevalent in some parties, such as Japan's LDP, than in others? More generally, how can we explain variation in dynastic politics across time, countries, parties, districts, and even individual families?

As illustrated by the case of Iceland—where in recent decades more than 30 percent of parliament has been dynastic—the size of a democracy's population may be one factor that contributes to the prevalence of dynasties. In the case of new or developing democracies, an additional factor may be the economic incentives to enter politics. Public office provides considerable private rents, which may exceed what politicians might otherwise hope to earn in other professions. It should not be surprising if they or their relatives want to continue to enjoy those rents.[1] At the same time, the pool of potential non-legacy candidates who are interested, eligible, and qualified for political office may also be shallower in new and developing democracies. Members of the elite ruling class, including legacy candidates, may be among the few who possess the education, wealth, and other technical skills to be successful as politicians and policymakers. As a general trend, we might therefore expect to find a relatively greater proportion of dynasties in new or developing democracies than in established, developed democracies. The historical pattern of decreasing shares of dynasties over time in most democracies, as documented in the previous chapter, supports this conjecture.

However, the comparative theory introduced here focuses primarily on explaining variation in the level of dynastic politics in the political parties of larger, developed democracies, where institutions are relatively stable, democratic norms are well established, and a sufficient number of qualified non-legacy candidates can be reasonably expected to exist within the population of citizens eligible to run for office. Indeed, it is in economically developed and large democracies like Japan that a persistence of dynastic politics is the most puzzling.

The existing literature aimed at explaining the formation of dynasties in democracies has stressed the value of the electoral and resource advantages of legacy candidates—the inherited incumbency advantage. However, the focus has largely been on country-specific explanations that take the institutional context of the electoral and candidate selection processes as given. Thus, existing explanations tend to emphasize the micro-level dynamics involved in the emergence of dynasties—such as the strength of a founding member's incumbency advantage (most often operationalized as length of tenure in office)—rather than also considering the macro-level institutional sources of dynastic politics in the system as a whole.

The comparative theory presented here is more expansive and considers how both micro-level differences between individual candidates and macro-level differences between parties and countries might explain how incumbency—and hence the potential inherited incumbency advantage—relates to the formation and perpetuation of dynasties in democracies. The hope is that such a comparative theory will help us to better understand not only the evolution of dynastic politics over time in Japan but also, more generally, the observed variation in the prevalence of dynasties across other democracies.

Supply and Demand in Dynastic Candidate Selection

To understand the phenomenon of democratic dynasties, we must first consider the institutions of candidate selection in a given party. We can think of candidate selection decisions as the outcome of supply and demand factors that operate within, and are influenced by, the context of political institutions (Norris, 1997; Siavelis and Morgenstern, 2008). More concretely, understanding the candidate selection process may involve four levels of analysis: (1) the political system (including the legal system, electoral system, and party system), (2) the actual rules and processes for recruitment and selection within party organizations, (3) the supply of candidates, and (4) the demand from gatekeepers, such as local or national party organizations. The latter two levels of analysis, involving supply and demand, operate at the same stage of the recruitment process and can be understood as "nested" within the broader context of the party recruitment process and the institutional structure of the political system as a whole, such that individual candidate selection decisions take place in what Pippa Norris (1997, p. 1) describes as a "funnel of causality." In other words, whether or not a dynasty will form (or continue to the next generation) depends on the supply of potential legacy candidates and the demand for such candidates by actors involved in the candidate selection process. Importantly, supply and demand will be shaped by the institutions at the system and party levels above them.

Notably absent from this theoretical framework of candidate selection is the role of voters. However, voters' preferences can be incorporated conceptually into the demand-side considerations of gatekeepers. In systems with primary elections, such as the United States, voters—or more precisely, voters who turn out in primary elections—are the gatekeepers, so their preferences for certain types of candidates are directly reflected in the outcomes of candidate selection. In other systems, party actors involved in candidate selection can be assumed to make nomination decisions in part based on the perceived or expected preferences of general election voters for certain types of candidates. Although voters' preferences and the attributes of the actual candidates who are selected may not always perfectly align, it is reasonable to assume that party leaders involved in candidate selection care about winning elections, and accordingly will nominate candidates that they expect to be most effective at earning votes and seats for the party.

FACTORS AFFECTING THE SUPPLY OF LEGACY CANDIDATES

It is impossible to measure and evaluate all the factors that might contribute to a citizen's decision to seek nomination as a party's candidate (or run as an independent where possible) because most potential candidates remain "unseen" until they actually declare their candidacy (Fowler and McClure, 1989). Nevertheless, on the supply side, we can imagine that both political capital and motivation play a role in determining the pool of candidates

(Norris, 1997, p. 13). Political capital might include political connections, education, previous experience, the financial resources necessary for waging a successful campaign, and sponsorship by particular interest groups in society seeking representation. Motivation, in contrast, could include family tradition, political ambition, or a sincere desire to advance certain policy changes. It is important to note that, in addition to providing a motivation to run, a family tradition in politics might also be highly correlated with some of the political capital endowments enumerated earlier (though not all, as documented in the previous chapter). In addition, a potential candidate's preexisting political capital should also be attractive to the gatekeepers involved on the demand side of candidate selection.

In one of the most ambitious attempts to date to measure the factors that determine whether a potential ("unseen") candidate will decide to run for office, Jennifer Lawless and Richard Fox (2010) surveyed nearly four thousand individuals in the United States with successful careers in business, law, education, and political activism—four backgrounds commonly associated with a future career in politics—and asked about their personal ambitions to run for office in the future. Respondents whose parents had previously run for elective office (at any level) were up to 10 percentage points more likely to envision a future in politics for themselves—strong evidence that a family tradition in politics can influence political ambition (Lawless, 2012, p. 85).

The children and other close relatives of long-serving incumbent politicians may be especially drawn to a political career of their own, since they will have been exposed to politics and socialized into political life from an early age.[2] Perhaps more practically, longer-serving incumbents will be more likely to have children who are old enough to appreciate political life and want to follow in their parent's footsteps. As a general supply-side hypothesis, we might therefore expect the following:

Hypothesis 1: Incumbents with longer tenures in office will be more likely to have a family member who wants to follow them into politics as a candidate.

A natural extension of this hypothesis is that the supply of potential legacy candidates will be greater in countries and parties where incumbent turnover is lower.

Given that family tradition may play a role in influencing political ambition, a second supply-side hypothesis follows:

Hypothesis 2: Incumbents who are part of an existing dynasty will be more likely to have a family member who wants to follow them into politics as a candidate.

For example, suppose a potential male candidate's father was a politician. He may choose to follow in his father's footsteps, or he may choose to forge a different career path, branching out to create his own name and identity. In contrast, if his father and grandfather were both politicians, he may be more socialized to believe that politics is the family vocation, much like a son in a family-run business (think of business firms that include "& Sons" in the name, and the pressure this might exert on the next generation). Such a person may feel it is his destiny, or at the very least his obligation, to take over the reins (or the reign, as it were) after his father steps down.

Of course, the decision of whether, and more important, when to run can also be influenced by the context of the race at hand, especially one's perceived chances of electoral success. Many would-be candidates who might otherwise desire to run for office will forgo the cost of running if they do not believe they can win—for example, against a powerful incumbent or in a district or election in which their party is unpopular (e.g., Jacobson and Kernell, 1983). Other potential candidates will prefer to wait until they have gained more experience or until they have raised their children beyond a certain age. Jennifer Lawless (2012, p. 2) notes how Robert F. Kennedy Jr., a potential legacy candidate who might have easily won New York's attorney general election in 2006, decided against a run:

> Despite a competitive field of Democratic candidates, party insiders and political analysts agreed that Kennedy's name recognition, political family ties, and reputation as an environmental crusader would have positioned him as the front-runner. Kennedy opted not to seek the Democratic nomination, though, explaining that he did not want to sacrifice time with his wife and six children. He left the door open for a future run, however, stating that his political ambition would likely grow as his family circumstances changed.

It is also possible that some incumbents who want to pass the baton to their child or other relative will strategically retire before an election that they expect their successors will be able to win. In some cases, a retiring incumbent might even try to shelter his or her successor from competition for the nomination. For example, in 2004, Bill Lipinski, an incumbent Democrat for the US House of Representatives serving Illinois' 3rd District, easily won his party's primary election and was renominated. However, Lipinski withdrew his name from the ballot less than three months before the general election and convinced local party leaders to instead nominate his thirty-eight-year-old son, Dan Lipinski, a political science professor at the University of Tennessee. The younger Lipinski moved home and easily won the election, facing only weak opposition from a Republican newcomer in the heavily Democratic district. Critics argued that the elder Lipinski knew for months that he would retire and planned his exit strategically in order to place his son in the seat without a primary fight or high-quality Republican challenger.[3]

In the context of elections in the United States, it is natural for the most part to focus on the supply-side factors of would-be legacy candidates who can propel themselves into electoral competition if they have the political capital and motivation to do so. As Alan Ehrenhalt (1991, p. 19) quips: "Who sent us the political leaders we have? There is a simple answer to that question. They sent themselves." Indeed, despite increased involvement of national party organizations in more recent years, US congressional candidates have often been thought of as individual political entrepreneurs competing for power in a decentralized political marketplace (e.g., Jacobson, 2001, p. 57). Primary elections provide easy access for hopeful political entrepreneurs, as well as political legacies, to enter politics. But what about the demand-side factors influencing their recruitment, selection, and election?

In the United States—apart from exceptions like the Lipinski example—voters in primary elections exercise the demand-side choice of who will stand for election under a party label. Unfortunately, existing studies on the inherited incumbency advantage in the United States do not include data on primary election candidates, so it is not clear whether legacy candidates in that context benefit more from name recognition or from political capital in their campaigns to win the nomination for the general election. However, for general elections, Brian D. Feinstein (2010) finds that legacy candidates in open-seat contests tend to enjoy more positive ratings on feeling thermometers used in the American National Election Studies (ANES) voter surveys, and a positive, though statistically insignificant, advantage in name recall. In contrast, he finds no significant differences between legacy and non-legacy candidates in terms of past political experience at the local level, or in terms of campaign fundraising, which suggests that the roughly 4-percentage-point electoral advantage that US legacy candidates enjoy is more likely attributable to differences in name recognition than differences in political capital. It is probable that the name recognition of a legacy candidate also helps secure the nomination in primary elections and may scare off intraparty challengers (these considerations and their measurement are evaluated in Chapter 5).

However, in the vast majority of democracies outside of the United States, parties—not voters—are the crucial actors in candidate selection, and they take nomination decisions and candidate characteristics seriously, both because the right combination of candidate characteristics can help optimize the party's voter mobilization efforts and because the candidates they recruit and nominate will ultimately determine the makeup and character of the party itself. Not only must they nominate candidates who can help win seats in the legislature; they must also consider how those elected MPs will perform once in office, particularly with regard to their ability to govern and their willingness to pursue the policy goals and interests of the party. In the terminology of rational choice theory, party leaders can be assumed to want to nominate candidates who will maximize the expected utility of the party, not only in terms of earning votes, but also in terms of holding office and making policy (Strøm, 1990; Strøm and Müller, 1999).

Thus, when we want to understand the emergence of dynasties, it is not sufficient just to explain why children of politicians might also want to become politicians (the supply side); we must also consider why parties might want to nominate them (the demand side). Unless there is considerable variation in the length of tenure or the preexistence of family dynasties, the two supply-side hypotheses just presented cannot adequately explain the observed variation in the presence of dynasties across parties and countries. We must consider how and why the demand-side incentives to nominate a legacy candidate might differ depending on the system-level and party-level institutions that structure candidate selection.

THE DEMAND-SIDE RATIONALE FOR DYNASTIES

To understand the demand for legacy candidates by parties, we need to consider the potential electoral utility a party expects to get from their nomination, as well as the potential trade-offs with other party goals, such as maintaining the party's national image and managing discipline and cohesion in the legislature. For the moment, assume that the supply of different types of candidates is fixed but not overly limited, that the cost of finding different types of candidates is not prohibitively high, and that we are only concerned with evaluating the demand for these different types of candidates by parties. Let us also assume that when a party is choosing which candidate(s) to nominate in an election, the party leaders involved in the process are rational actors who aim to maximize the party's collective goals of earning votes, attaining and keeping control of government offices, and crafting and implementing their preferred set of policies.

Each potential candidate has a set of personal attributes, policy positions, and other characteristics that will provide varying levels of utility to the party in achieving its goals. When it comes to candidate selection, party leaders can be assumed to favor the potential candidate whose attributes will maximize the party's overall expected utility. This overall expected utility will be a function of not only the probability that the candidate will win the election given his or her set of attributes but also the value to the party of that candidate, given that he or she has those attributes.[4] We can think of this value as encompassing the candidate's potential contributions to the postelectoral policymaking and officeholding goals of the party, as well as the value a candidate brings to the overall party image or brand. Quite obviously, many attributes will simultaneously increase the probability of winning as well as the postelectoral value a candidate brings to the party. For example, the same leadership qualities or policy expertise that will help a party pursue its officeholding or policymaking goals may also help win votes in elections.

However, some combinations of attributes may require party leaders to consider trade-offs in balancing their various party goals. This might occur when, for example, an electorally popular candidate disagrees with the party leadership over policy. Such a candidate may have a greater probability of winning but would also bring a lower value to the party leadership in terms of legislative cohesion. Another candidate might make an effective steward of the government but is an ineffective campaigner. Such a candidate would represent a potentially high value to the party leadership but, at the same time, would be less likely to get elected, making that value moot. The combination of candidate attributes that will provide the greatest overall utility to the party might also vary depending on time and context. For example, if a new policy issue arises, the value of a candidate with expertise in that policy area may increase.

Keeping this simple theoretical framework in mind, let us first consider a scenario in which a party leader (or group of leaders) is choosing between two potential candidates—one legacy and one non-legacy—to nominate in an FPTP contest and the leadership's priority is to maximize votes in the immediate general election, that is, in the short term. In other words, we will assume that the party leaders are focused only on maximizing the probability of winning. Within each potential candidate's total set of attributes are a number of potential vote-earning attributes that may influence the party leadership's decision, including measures of candidate quality and personality (e.g., experience, level of education, charisma, good looks, name recognition). Importantly, each of these attributes may have a different value to different parties, and even to the same party over time or across space depending on the party's priorities in a given election context. For example, the marginal effect on the expected utility of one attribute (e.g., "insider" experience in the national bureaucracy) might be positive in one election or for one party but may be negative in a different context (e.g., when voters are unhappy with the national bureaucracy). In the most basic sense, the leadership of the purely vote-seeking party can be expected to choose the candidate whose overall combination of attributes represents the greatest positive utility to the party in achieving its short-term vote-related goals.

Now let us consider dynastic family ties as one such vote-earning attribute. The potential vote-earning value of the inherited incumbency advantage encompasses all of the resource and informational advantages of coming from a political dynasty and will vary depending on the *actual* incumbency advantage of the candidate's predecessor. It will also vary over time, across space, and within family relationships—for example, its value may decrease the longer the amount of time between the predecessor's exit and the legacy candidate's entry, if the legacy candidate is running in a different district from his or her predecessor, or if the candidate is related by marriage rather than blood or has a different surname from that of the predecessor. Thus, for non-legacy candidates, the inherited incumbency advantage is zero; but for legacy candidates, it takes some positive value that increases with the name recognition, length in office, and other resources of the legacy candidate's predecessor.[5]

It could be possible in some contexts for a candidate's status in a long-term political dynasty to be an electoral liability, such that his or her family record becomes an inherited incumbency disadvantage. This might occur when a candidate's predecessor was unpopular, or if there is a backlash against dynastic politics. In such cases, the non-legacy candidate will be selected unless his or her other attributes are still of lower vote-earning utility to the party than the remainder of the legacy candidate's other attributes, or unless the legacy candidate can manipulate conditions so as to decrease his or her association with the dynasty (in short, decreasing the value of his or her inherited incumbency advantage). An example of the latter might be how Jeb Bush distanced himself from his family name during the 2016 US Republican presidential primaries by simply using "Jeb!" in his campaign materials. In most cases, however, increasing values of the inherited incumbency advantage should increase the probability of election in an FPTP contest, all else equal, such that its marginal effect on the party's overall expected utility from nominating the legacy candidate will be positive.

Thus, if two potential candidates—one legacy and one non-legacy—are being considered for nomination, and all other attributes are held constant—that is, the two candidates are otherwise equivalent in terms of talent, experience, education, and so on—then the legacy candidate can be expected to provide a higher vote-earning utility to the party than the non-legacy candidate. This means that if a legacy candidate wants to run (i.e., there is a supply-side availability of a legacy candidate), the party leadership has an incentive to nominate him or her unless the vote-earning value of the other potential candidate's attributes exceeds that of the legacy candidate, even with his or her inherited incumbency advantage (this might be the case, for example, if the non-legacy is a well-known celebrity). This also implies that for a non-legacy candidate to win a nomination over a legacy candidate, he or she must be of higher quality (i.e., possess some other valuable attributes that increase his or her probability of election).

If a party's nomination strategy is strictly vote seeking in nature, then the above logic should hold regardless of the attributes of the parties' competitors in the general election. The candidate with the greatest vote-earning utility to the party will get nominated. However, suppose that the leadership, quite reasonably, wants to balance the party's vote-earning priorities with its policymaking priorities (e.g., Wittman, 1973; Schlesinger, 1975). Some candidates may be terrific at earning votes but less ideologically aligned with the party's policy goals and more likely to break with the party in legislative voting. If these other goals are brought back into the party's utility calculus, then party leaders may face a nonnegligible trade-off in candidate selection. A candidate with the highest vote-earning utility may also bring costs in terms of the party's other priorities. For a governing party, for example, a lack of party cohesion can threaten its ability to maintain its status in office.

Suppose that the potential legacy candidate is ideologically more distant from party leaders than the non-legacy candidate, such that the value of having that candidate in the party's legislative membership would be lower, from the perspective of party leaders. Depending on the degree to which the probability of election is influenced by the inherited incumbency advantage, at a certain point the policy cost of the legacy candidate may exceed his or her electoral value to the party, making the overall utility of the non-legacy candidate higher. In this case, the vote-and-policy-maximizing party will need to consider, or try to anticipate, the vote-earning attributes and electability of challengers from other parties. If the nearest challenger has many vote-earning attributes, and the election is expected to be close, then the party may sacrifice its policymaking priorities in order to focus on maximizing its vote. The party will nominate the non-legacy candidate only if that candidate's vote-earning ability is expected to be comfortably higher than the vote-earning ability of his or her closest competitor, or if the policy costs of nominating the legacy candidate are so high that the party is willing to sacrifice its short-term goal of winning the election.

Uncertainty may arise if the party cannot prevent the potential legacy candidate from running in the election without the nomination—for example, as an independent or as the nominee of another party. If the party denies the nomination to the legacy candidate but he or she runs anyway, then it may face a situation in which the closest competitor to its nominated non-legacy candidate is the rejected legacy candidate (running as an independent or under a different party label) whose vote-earning utility was already higher than that of the non-legacy candidate the leadership decided to nominate. Thus, all else equal, the party leadership has an incentive to nominate the legacy candidate over the non-legacy candidate unless the policy costs posed by a potential legacy candidate are especially high, and the party can control access to the ballot or be reasonably sure that the rejected legacy candidate will not get the nomination of another party. The downside of this political calculation is that in situations where vote-earning priorities trump policymaking priorities, a party may potentially end up disunited and prone to low party discipline or party splits.

What about the value of a potential candidate to a party's officehold-ing goals? In addition to party leadership's desire to maximize its control over government offices overall (e.g., Riker, 1962; Leiserson, 1968), it may also want to recruit individuals who would be capable of serving effectively in those offices—those who Michael Laver and Kenneth Shepsle (1994, p. 302) describe as "ministerable." The popularity of the party (or parties) in government is often linked to the performance and individual popularity of ministers, so appointing the right (or wrong) ministers can have conse-quences for a governing party's ability to win votes and seats at election time (Strøm and Müller, 1999). The same may be true for party leaders and other important positions within parties in the opposition.

Consider two potential legacy candidates who are equivalent in all other respects, except that one candidate's predecessor had previously served in a party leadership position or government office, such as cabinet minister, while the other candidate's predecessor had not. For our purposes, we can define the former type of legacy candidate as a *cabinet legacy*, although the logic should apply to other important parliamentary or party offices, such as committee chairmanships or party leadership positions. A predecessor's cabinet experience is likely to increase the electoral value of the inherited incumbency advantage (because of, for example, higher name recognition), and thus may increase the probability of election; but suppose that it does not, and the two potential candidates are equal in terms of their probability of winning. In this scenario, the candidate who is a cabinet legacy may still have greater knowledge of the party organization or leadership style that he or she has observed over time through the experiences of his or her prede-cessor, and this should increase the expected value of that candidate to the party leadership.[6] Notably, the offspring of longer-serving incumbents may also be expected to provide more postelectoral value to the party leadership if it can be assumed that the long-term loyalty of their predecessors will be continued.

In short, not all potential legacy candidates are created equal. It is reason-able to expect that party leaders will have more demand for a legacy candi-date whose expected probability of winning is higher. This will depend on the perceived vote-earning value of his or her inherited incumbency advan-tage, which may be related to such factors as the predecessor's incumbency status at the time of his or her exit, the number of previous terms he or she served, the margin of victory in recent elections, previous cabinet experience, and so on. Some of these factors may also contribute positively to the expected policymaking and officeholding value of the candidate to the party leadership as well. The value of the inherited incumbency advantage will also depend, as noted, on the time between candidacies, the degree of familial closeness between the two candidates, and whether or not they share a common name, party, and electoral district. Nevertheless, as a general demand-side hypothesis, we can expect the following:

> *Hypothesis 3: The demand for a legacy candidate will increase with his or her potential inherited incumbency advantage.*

An important implication of this hypothesis and the preceding discussion is that a legacy candidate with a weaker perceived inherited incumbency advantage may get passed over by party actors involved in candidate selection if some other non-legacy candidate provides more value to the party leadership while still being likely to get elected.

We can now begin to consider the institutional and situational factors—at the system level, party level, and individual level—that might condition the relationship between the inherited incumbency advantage and either the probability of winning election or the expected value of a candidate to party leaders involved in candidate selection. Let us begin with the highest level of potential institutional factors (the system level) and work our way down to the individual-level factors.

THE SYSTEM LEVEL: CANDIDATE-CENTERED ELECTIONS

At the system level, there are very few democracies where legal rules explicitly specify criteria for candidate selection beyond central guidelines (Müller and Sieberer, 2006; Rahat, 2007), and obviously no real democracy should explicitly forbid legacy candidates, so the legal system is not likely to affect dynastic recruitment. The party system may contribute to the overall proportion of dynasties in some countries if the distribution of legislative seats favors parties that tend to recruit more legacy candidates. But the party system alone tells us little about the actual nomination decisions surrounding individual legacy candidates within parties. The system-level institutional factor that might contribute most to the relative demand for dynastic politics in candidate selection is therefore the electoral system.

Certain electoral rules may increase the demand for legacy candidates by increasing the electoral value of the personal vote, which is a "candidate's electoral support which originates in his or her personal qualities, qualifications, activities, and record" (Cain, Ferejohn, and Fiorina, 1987, p. 9). In a seminal study, John Carey and Matthew Shugart (1995) argue that the incentives for a candidate to cultivate a personal vote depend upon three distinct criteria: (1) the degree of party leadership control over access to and rank on ballots, (2) the degree to which candidates are elected on individual votes independent of copartisans, and (3) whether voters cast a single intraparty vote instead of multiple votes or a party-level vote.

According to this typology, the value of the personal vote should be higher in a country like the United States, where ballot access is determined by primaries and voters cast their vote for an individual candidate by name in an FPTP system with SMDs, as in our hypothetical case, than it is in a country like Norway or Israel, where voters instead cast their votes for a party list, seats are allocated to parties in MMDs in proportion to their share of the vote, and candidates are awarded those seats in order of their predetermined ranking on the list—that is, a closed-list PR system. In addition, district magnitude (M) has a contrasting effect on the incentives to cultivate a personal vote depending on the nature of the electoral system. The value of the personal vote decreases with larger M under closed-list PR but increases with larger M in candidate-centered systems. At the same time, increases in M also decrease the relative share of the vote that a candidate needs in order to secure election in candidate-centered systems.

So, while the personal vote will be of some value to candidates in the SMDs of the FPTP system in the United States, it will be of even greater value in the MMDs of the SNTV system used in Japan from 1947 to 1993, especially when intraparty competition occurs. When two candidates from the same party are competing for votes, it is not enough to campaign solely on party labels. Each candidate must distinguish him or herself from copartisans, in addition to candidates from other parties. Similarly, the personal vote will have more value under open-list PR systems, such as in Finland, Belgium, or pre-1993 Italy, where voters are allowed to express a preference for one or more candidates on a party list. In open-list PR systems, seats are allocated to parties, but candidates are elected in order of who gets the most preference votes. Under closed-list PR, in contrast, candidates are elected according to the party's ranking, so the best way for a Norwegian or Israeli candidate who is not at the top of his or her party's list to ensure personal victory is to campaign hard to increase the party's overall vote, and this effort might make a difference only for marginal candidates.

There are two main components of the personal vote. The first component involves the ex post behavior of elected politicians in office, predominantly constituency service or pork-barrel politicking (e.g., Lancaster and Patterson, 1990; Stratmann and Baur, 2002). The electoral incentives to engage in such personal-vote-earning behavior (PVEB) can also result in a legislator defecting from the party's ideal policy positions when those positions diverge from the interests of his or her constituents. Thus, a legislator with a strong personal vote may often be less likely to toe the party line (e.g., Faas, 2003; Hix, 2004; Sieberer, 2010). A second component to the personal vote instead involves the ex ante, preelectoral attributes of candidates. A candidate's personal-vote-earning attributes (PVEA) can include high name recognition, a "quality" background (e.g., previous political experience or training), and local ties to the community or district where the candidate is running (Shugart, Valdini, and Suominen, 2005). While the incentives to cultivate a personal vote may result in greater observed PVEB among incumbents, the same incentives might operate on a party's incentives to nominate new candidates with strong PVEA.

The importance of PVEA for winning votes in candidate-centered elections can increase the perceived value of the inherited incumbency advantage, and thus influence the demand for legacy candidates, either from voters (in primary elections) or from parties (in anticipation of voter preferences in the general election). When the personal reputation of a candidate (or a candidate's "brand name") is more dominant in framing campaigns and voter decisions than the reputation of the party (the party label), a recognized family name and reputation in the electoral district can be especially valuable. Stephen Hess (1966, pp. 7–8) recounts an example from the United States in which name recognition owing to a candidate's legacy status was clearly of importance, especially given the electoral rules employed (emphasis in the original):

> A deadlock over reapportionment in 1964 necessitated the at-large election of the entire Illinois House of Representatives. The ballot of 236 names resembled an orange bath towel. On the Democratic list was Adlai E. Stevenson III, thirty-three, son of the 1952 and 1956 Democratic presidential nominee; on the Republican list was Earl Eisenhower, sixty-six, brother of the 1952 and 1956 Republican

presidential nominee. *Neither legislative candidate had ever sought office before.* When the votes were counted, first among the 118 Democrats was Adlai E. Stevenson III; first among the 118 Republicans was Earl Eisenhower.

It is possible that candidate-centered electoral systems might encourage a larger supply of legacy candidates who hope that their name recognition will help to get them elected. More important, however, is that if political actors involved in the candidate recruitment process are aware of the greater potential marginal effect of personal reputation on the probability of electoral success, there will be greater demand for such legacy candidates.

Compare this logic to the case of incumbents. Incumbent candidates in candidate-centered elections enjoy a significant electoral advantage over challengers because of greater name recognition and experience. For the same reason, parties will typically renominate incumbents, since they usually represent the party's best chance to win the seat again. When an incumbent politician retires or dies, parties might expect to capitalize on some of those advantages by nominating a relative of that politician. But these electoral advantages should be less heritable when elections are not based around voters' evaluations of individual candidates.

Studies on the PVEA of candidates tend to focus on evaluating whether different types of individuals appear in greater frequencies as candidates and legislators in different electoral contexts. A few notable studies also link the preelectoral PVEA to postelectoral PVEB (e.g., Tavits, 2009, 2010; Marangoni and Tronconi, 2011). A general conclusion of these studies is that local ties and candidate quality tend to be more important for gaining votes in candidate-centered electoral systems but that legislators with a strong personal vote are less loyal to the party when their constituencies' interests are at stake. Thus, as illustrated in the theoretical logic presented earlier, parties may face a trade-off in candidate selection between maximizing votes and maximizing party cohesion and discipline in the legislature. In contrast, the PVEA of candidates matter less in party-centered contexts, where party actors involved in candidate selection care more about what those candidates might contribute to the party and its image as a whole. Will they pursue the party's goals in terms of policy? Do they bring policy expertise or other skills to the party? Do they help the party diversify in terms of gender, age, geography, and so on, to serve a wider constituency?

Returning to the party's calculus of a potential candidate's expected utility, let us imagine that we move from the two-person contest for a nomination in an FPTP election to a scenario where a party must choose multiple candidates to nominate on a party list under closed-list PR. In this scenario, the probability of any particular candidate winning has less to do with any of his or her personal attributes, and more to do with his or her position on the list. Party leaders still care about the attributes of nominated candidates, however, as popular candidates may contribute to the party's overall popularity, and hence to the probability of *the party* winning more votes and seats. Nevertheless, as the number of candidates that must be nominated increases, a party will need to consider not only the individual utility of each candidate but also the collective utility of all candidates on the party's list.

As a result, the expected utility of nominating a legacy candidate may still be positive (in terms of name recognition and familiarity to voters, but also in terms of postelectoral value to the party); however, each additional legacy candidate may provide diminishing marginal utility. In contrast, the party may derive increasing marginal utility from nominating a more diverse slate of candidates—in terms of gender, age, policy expertise, and geographic diversity—who improve the overall image of the party and attract votes from different subsets of the electorate. Considered from a voter's perspective, it may seem unproblematic to support a legacy candidate in the local SMD under FPTP; and voters in other SMDs might have similar feelings. But if those SMD candidates were aggregated into a single party list under closed-list PR, the inclusion of so many political dynasties might raise more eyebrows and decrease support for the party. Hence, under closed-list PR, the demand for legacy candidates should be expected to decrease relative to FPTP.

These incentives will be moderated under open-list PR. Under common variants of open-list PR, voters may cast a party-level vote for the entire list or a preference vote for a specific candidate. The personal preference votes earned by candidates first accrue to the party's overall tally to determine the number of seats the party wins; then, the candidates' personal votes determine the order in which they are elected off the list to fill those seats. This means that for a party contesting elections under open-list PR, the marginal utility of another legacy candidate may be higher than under closed-list PR, since each legacy candidate will help bring in personal votes and improve the party's overall chances of winning seats. Party leaders under open-list PR will thus have incentives to strike a balance between candidates with strong PVEA, and candidates who help improve the party's overall appeal, but may not necessarily be huge vote getters.

Importantly, under both types of PR, a party can more easily pass over a candidate who poses policy costs to the party, since he or she will not typically be able to run as an independent. The rejected candidate would have to form his or her own party in order to gain access to the ballot and, depending on the country, the barriers to doing so can be quite high. According to the Public Offices Election Law of Japan, for example, for a political organization to qualify as a party eligible to field a list of candidates in the PR tiers of its electoral systems for the House of Representatives and House of Councillors, that organization must meet one of the following requirements: (1) have five or more members in the Diet, (2) have polled at least 2 percent in a recent previous election, or (3) be prepared to field enough candidates to account for at least 20 percent of the seats up for grabs in the district—and the party must pay a deposit of ¥6 million for each candidate (approximately $53,100 in the 2017 exchange rate).

Thus, the electoral system may generate some basic incentives for candidate-centered elections that increase the electoral value of the personal vote. It is important to note, however, that the electoral system may produce different effects on different parties. For instance, district magnitude may have varying effects on the incentives to cultivate a personal vote depending on the size of the party and its electoral constituency (Grofman, 2005; Crisp, Jensen, and Shomer, 2007). During the SNTV era in Japan, parties such as the LDP and JSP often ran more than one candidate in each MMD, creating intraparty competition that increased the value of the personal vote of each candidate. However, smaller parties, such as the Kōmeitō and JCP, did not run multiple candidates in a district, so the value of the party label was greater, both to candidates of those parties who could campaign on the party's platform and to voters who could use the party label as a cue when deciding among the candidates.

Similarly, in a closed-list PR system like that used to elect members of the Israeli Knesset, not all parties run the same number of candidates on their lists in each district, despite a common district magnitude (in Israel's case, a single nationwide district with M = 120). The PVEA of candidates near the bottom of the list for a large party will not be relevant—neither to voters nor to the party in terms of capitalizing on those attributes in order to increase the appeal of the party—but candidates on a shorter party list may potentially get more attention from voters, and many parties elect only a few members from the list. Even though votes are cast for parties under closed-list PR, a popular candidate near the top of the party list may help attract voters to the party as a whole.

Ireland uses a single transferable vote (STV) system in MMDs with district magnitude ranging from three to five. This system is similar to Japan's SNTV system, because parties tend to nominate multiple candidates, who thus face intraparty competition for first-rank preference votes. However, it is slightly more party centered, since candidates often run as a party "team," and voters rank candidates by order of preference. A first-preference vote for a candidate whose vote total is already great enough to secure election, or for a candidate who has no hope of securing a seat, may be transferred to the second-preference candidate, and so on, in a process that continues until all seats are filled. Most often, though not always, second-order preference votes are cast for copartisans. For example, a majority of voters report that their first preference vote is most influenced by individual candidate characteristics, but between 50 percent and 60 percent of voters also tend to give their second-order preference votes to their favorite candidate's copartisans in sequence (Marsh, 2007). In Australia, the electoral system for the House of Representatives is the alternative vote (AV) system, which is similar to STV, except that the contests take place in SMDs. As a result, there is no intraparty competition, and all vote transfers take place between candidates of different parties. If no candidate wins a majority with first-preference votes, the candidate with the fewest votes is eliminated and his or her votes are redistributed to second-preference candidates, and so on, until one candidate has a majority.

The constitutional structure of the political system—namely, the separation or fusion of legislative and executive power that distinguishes parliamentary and presidential regimes—may also temper the importance of the personal vote, regardless of the electoral system used. For example, although both the United States and Canada use the FPTP system, the nature of Westminster-style parliamentary democracy in Canada means that the value of the party label and party leader image is dominant in elections to the House of Commons (Carty and Cross, 2010), and party voting among the electorate is thus much higher in Canada than it is in the United States. For example, in the 2000 House of Commons election, a candidate's personal characteristics were the deciding factor for only 5 percent of Canadian voters (Gidengil, 2010, p. 238). In contrast, the greater attachment among US voters to individual candidates over parties is supported by the high percentage of voters who split their ticket between presidential and congressional races (e.g., Burden and Kimball, 2004).

Because of the limitations stemming from differences across parties and district magnitude, as well as how the constitutional structures of parliamentarism and presidentialism interact with electoral rules, it is challenging to systematically categorize entire countries and parties into a single scale from more candidate centered to more party centered. There have been some valiant efforts to categorize electoral systems along various continuums of personal vote incentives (e.g., Carey and Shugart, 1995; Johnson and Wallack, 2012); however, such categorizations are inevitably blunt measures of personalism at the system level and cannot capture differences across parties, districts of varying magnitude, time, and other contextual factors.

Nevertheless, a general ordering of common electoral systems from more candidate-centered to more party-centered might go something like: SNTV → STV → open-list PR → FPTP/AV → closed-list PR. Notably, the first three systems (SNTV, STV, and open-list PR) are likely to feature some amount of intraparty competition in larger parties—which should increase the value of each candidate's PVEA. We can also say, therefore, that such candidate-centered electoral contexts can generally be expected to increase the value of the inherited incumbency advantage as a PVEA, and thus increase the expected utility, on average, of a legacy candidate to a party. These considerations give rise to a system-level demand-side hypothesis:

Hypothesis 4: The demand for a legacy candidate will be higher in a candidate-centered electoral context than in a party-centered electoral context.

At the most basic level, the demand for legacy candidates thus ought to be higher under candidate-centered electoral contexts, where a legacy candidate's inherited incumbency advantage is a PVEA that is likely to be of greater electoral value to the party. Note, however, that as the importance of PVEA to the probability of election gets larger, the actual value of the legacy candidate's inherited incumbency advantage can get smaller and still contribute positive utility to the party. Parties in such contexts may even have incentives to actively seek out legacy candidates beyond those who put themselves forward, if the costs to doing so (including practical costs involved in the effort) are outweighed by the potential gains from nominating a legacy candidate. This means that the family members of all previous incumbents, not just those who enjoyed a larger incumbency advantage or served longer terms, might be desirable as potential candidates.

THE PARTY LEVEL: ORGANIZATION AND CENTRALIZATION

The considerations just presented provide a basic logic for why legacy candidates will be in higher demand in candidate-centered electoral contexts than in party-centered electoral contexts. However, the level of demand for dynasties in candidate selection may also be influenced by variation in party-level characteristics and institutions, especially the organizational basis of a party and the rules for candidate selection, and these may operate independently from the electoral system context.

One potential source of party-level variation is the nature of a party's organization. Richard Katz and Peter Mair (1995) describe four types of party organization. First, the "elite party" model of party organization, as its name suggests, is a party that is highly restricted in membership and based on interpersonal networks. This type of party is rare, but might obviously be prone to dynastic politics. A second type of party model, the "catch-all" party (Kirchheimer, 1966), places some emphasis on cultivating membership and participation in the party organization among voters, but this membership is generally weak, and party leaders attempt to competitively mobilize a wider group of voters. Candidates and parties behave like political entrepreneurs, seeking to broker benefits and policies between the state and civil society. Throughout much of postwar Japanese history, the LDP conformed largely to this model of party organization. A third type of party model, the "cartel party," entails parties that mutually seek ways to constrain political competition to stay in power. Individual politicians view politics as a profession, and membership among citizens is not important. Over time, the LDP has increasingly moved toward this model of party organization, as its membership and popularity in the electorate, and thus its secure control of the government, has waned.

Each of these party models is in contrast to the traditional "mass party" model (Duverger, 1954), which is a party that is organized around "predefined and well-defined social groups, membership in which is bound up in all aspects of an individual's life" (Katz and Mair, 1995, p. 6). The mass party model is typical of many early Western European class-based and religious parties (Neumann, 1956; Worley, 2009), as well as the Kōmeitō and JCP in Japan (Smith, 2014), and to a lesser extent, the JSP and DSP. In the mass party model, the party is the representative agent of distinct social groups, and responsible for articulating their political demands. To the extent that the extraparliamentary support bases of mass parties are concentrated among these social groups, party leaders can be expected to screen and select candidates with backgrounds in these groups (Müller, 2000).

The extraparliamentary support bases of mass parties should provide a greater supply of potential non-legacy candidates, and this in turn should decrease the demand for legacy candidates by parties (because party leaders have ample access to non-legacy candidates to nominate). For example, mass parties based around labor unions or religious movements can recruit candidates from within those groups. To a mass party, the extraparliamentary support base provides a ready pool of potential candidates, as well as the added advantage that these candidates have, in a sense, already been pre-screened to ensure a match with the goals and ideology of the party. In contrast, for parties that lack such organizational ties to groups in civil society, it may be more difficult to attract a steady supply of non-legacy candidates. In addition, to the extent that extraparliamentary organizations are a stable and reliable source of support for a party, the probability of its candidates winning should have more to do with their connections to those organizations than with their personal attributes, including legacy ties. Thus, we might expect the following:

Hypothesis 5: The demand for a legacy candidate will be higher in parties with weaker organizational linkages to groups in civil society.

Similarly, external shocks to a party's organizational base may result, at least temporarily, in an increase in the demand for dynasties in candidate selection. For example, if a party's traditional support base is weakened, legacy candidates may become an expedient source of "warm bodies" to nominate. Such a situation might occur for labor movement-based parties, for instance, if certain industries are replaced or union membership declines. The imposition of a quota for gender representation is another example of an external shock that may temporarily increase the number of legacy candidates if parties turn to female relatives of male incumbents to help fill the quota (Folke, Rickne, and Smith, 2017). The same effect may result from the introduction of term limits (Querubín, 2011; Labonne, Parsa, and Querubin, 2017). Similarly, when the dual mandate allowing Irish MPs to sit both in parliament and in local councils was abolished in 2003, many of the incumbents who gave up their local seats were conveniently replaced by their family members, who co-opted into the local councils.

An additional source of variation between parties is the set of internal rules governing the candidate selection process. In short, how a party selects its candidates, and who within the party decides the nominations, can have an impact on the types of candidates who are ultimately nominated by the party. Reuven Hazan and Gideon Rahat (2010) describe four dimensions on which candidate selection institutions can vary. The first is *candidacy*, which refers to the eligibility of citizens to become a candidate from a party. This dimension can range from very inclusive (anyone can offer him- or herself up as a candidate, as in the United States) to more exclusive (e.g., only party members or those who collect enough signatures or meet some other such requirement are eligible). The second dimension is the *selectorate*, which refers to the group of actors who decide the nomination. The selectorate can also range from inclusive (the extreme end being that all primary voters get to decide) to more exclusive (the extreme end being a single party leader). The third dimension is the *appointment or voting system*. This is simply the method or voting rule used to determine the nominee. The last dimension is *decentralization*, which refers to the arena in which the decision process is undertaken (e.g., a local arena or a centralized, national arena). Variation on each of these dimensions can produce different outcomes in the types of candidates who are selected, and their behavior once in office.

When it comes to dynastic politics, each of the dimensions may potentially have an effect on the supply and demand of legacy candidates. However, the most important factors are arguably the degree of inclusiveness of the candidate pool and the level of centralization in candidate selection. The reason inclusiveness matters is the same reason that strong connections to extraparliamentary groups in civil society matter. Increasing the inclusiveness of the eligibility requirements for candidacy may invite more outsiders to apply, most of whom will of course be non-legacy candidates. A wider potential pool of candidates should thus be expected to increase the supply of alternative choices for party actors involved in candidate selection, and this should in turn reduce the demand for legacy candidates as an expedient source of new recruits. This leads us to the following:

Hypothesis 6: The demand for a legacy candidate will be higher where the eligibility for candidacy in the candidate selection process is more exclusive.

The reason the level of centralization matters is that the expected utility of any particular candidate will be viewed through the eyes of the selectorate and may differ depending on whether that selectorate is local or national. Party leaders at the national level may be more likely to balance the probability of winning a local seat with other party goals related to policy and office. A selectorate made up of local party actors, in contrast, is likely to care most about maximizing the probability of winning the seat in the short run, even if it comes at the expense of considerations for the broader value of a given candidate to the party. The localized selection process in the FPTP system used in Canada provides a useful example. As Lynda Erickson and R. Kenneth Carty (1991, p. 334) explain:

> Under Canada's single-member plurality system, local control can pose difficulties for national parties when, for example, they attempt to orchestrate a nationally balanced slate of candidates, or where they are reluctant to be associated with particular individuals. In short, what the central party sees to be in its interests can conflict with local choice.

Local selectorates might also be basing their utility calculus on a different set of values. In the most extreme case, if a retiring local incumbent acts as the sole member of the selectorate, he or she may give a particularly high valuation to the attributes that happen to be possessed by his or her offspring! Michael Gallagher (1988*a*, pp. 13–14) elaborates on this point:

> When selection is firmly under the control of local members, more interested in whether aspirants have "paid their dues" with a solid track record at the local level than in their likely parliamentary capacities, the resulting parliamentarians might be older and less well educated, more likely to have local roots and to be long-standing members of the local party organization. . . . It is possible that a locally controlled process will result in a higher proportion of deputies who are related to previous deputies, as locally prominent political families manage to pass a seat on from one generation to another.

If nomination decisions are heavily influenced or controlled by local bosses or powerful political families, then such bossism may prevail in the form of legacy candidates being nominated. As E. E. Schattschneider (1942, p. 64) famously put it, "The nature of the nomination procedure determines the nature of the party; he who can make the nominations is the owner of the party." Even in the absence of strong bossism, if candidate nomination decisions are made locally, then a local notable with name recognition will likely be advantaged over an outsider with no ties to the district. Legacy candidates inherently feature this advantage in name recognition and local ties.

The foregoing consideration of decentralization in the nomination process may seem similar to what Carey and Shugart (1995) indicate in their first criterion for evaluating the level of personalism in electoral systems:

the degree of party leadership control over access to and rank on ballots. However, their conception of this criterion has more to do with voter influence over outcomes through primary elections and preference voting than with variations in the location and identity of who controls access within the party organization. Because parties operate within electoral systems, it is often the case that the structure of party organizations and candidate selection processes are heavily correlated with the electoral system in use, with the direction of causality unclear. For example, the political entrepreneurs and professional politicians of the catch-all and cartel party models are likely to thrive under candidate-centered electoral contexts and may resist attempts at party centralization over nominations. In contrast, the mass party model is likely to flourish in party-centered contexts, but party-centered electoral systems such as closed-list PR may also be chosen precisely because of the preexisting nature of cleavages or divisions in society (Lipset and Rokkan, 1967; Colomer 2005).

Nevertheless, there can be variation in party centralization in the recruitment process not only between countries using different electoral systems, but also between different parties within a single country, and even the same party over time, or across different regions and districts. Some parties exhibit a higher degree of centralized control over the candidate selection process, and this centralization may be unrelated to the context of the electoral rules (Lundell, 2004; Shomer, 2014), even if parties generally try to shape their candidate selection strategies based in part on the electoral incentives they face—both routinely as part of the institutional structure of elections and in response to specific electoral challenges (Epstein, 1980; Mair, Müller, and Plasser, 2004).

The candidate selection process is regulated by law in some democracies, including the United States, Germany, Finland, New Zealand, and Norway (prior to 2002). However, parties in other democracies have more flexibility, and exhibit greater variation in the selection procedures used. For example, in Italy, national leaders of Christian Democracy (DC) did not exercise as much central control over nominations as party leaders in the Italian Socialist Party (PSI) or the neo-fascist Italian Social Movement (MSI). In the Italian Communist Party (PCI), recruitment was carried out by local party organizations, but under very strict directives from the national party headquarters (Wertman, 1988). In Ireland, only Sinn Féin exercises dominant central control over nominations (Gallagher, 1988*b*). The other major parties use a more decentralized procedure involving local nominating conventions. In Israel, Labor has used a more decentralized process (namely, internal party primary elections) than the other parties, although parties such as Likud and Meretz have also experimented with greater use of party primaries in candidate selection (Shomer, 2009; Akirav, 2010).

These differences in the degree of centralization in the recruitment process of parties within the same electoral system context suggest an additional source of institutional variation in the supply and demand for legacy candidates. All else equal, we can expect the following:

Hypothesis 7: The demand for a legacy candidate will be higher where the candidate selection process and decision are decentralized to local actors.

Note, however, that this hypothesis may also be highly correlated with the organizational strength of a party, and that electoral reforms that make elections more party centered may also increase the organizational strength of parties and encourage party leaders to centralize the candidate selection process. Note also that the logic here applies primarily to the selection of rank-and-file candidates—very centralized parties that are personalistic in nature may be more likely to be dynastic at the leadership level (Chhibber, 2013).

Other party-level variables, such as the degree of inclusiveness in the selectorate or specific voting procedures for choosing or ranking candidates, may also play a role; and some parties will have idiosyncratic rules that discourage the formation of dynasties. For example, in pre-1993 Italy, the PCI routinely practiced an internal party rule of replacement of incumbent candidates after two or three terms (Wertman, 1988).[7] If socialization in politics and exposure to the political process contribute to the supply and quality of would-be legacy successors, then the children of PCI incumbents would be at a considerable disadvantage in receiving this exposure.

THE INDIVIDUAL LEVEL: WHO DIED AND MADE YOU CANDIDATE?

Finally, in addition to electoral and party institutions, there may also be a number of factors at the individual level that can affect the demand for legacy candidates. Such factors are likely to vary from country to country, or across different parties, but one is worth noting as a general hypothesis:

Hypothesis 8: The demand for a legacy candidate will be higher following the death of an incumbent in office.

When an incumbent dies in office, a legacy candidate may be viewed by party leaders as an ideal replacement in the ensuing by-election (if by-elections are held), regardless of the institutional context. Party leaders may calculate that voter sympathy would increase the expected probability that the legacy successor would win and retain the seat for the party. Or, faced with the need to find a replacement candidate on short notice, they might simply value a legacy successor as an expedient stand-in for the remainder of the term, one whom might then be replaced later if the party finds a better option.

Many Irish legacy MPs first gained their seats in the by-elections held to replace their deceased relatives (Gallagher, 2003), and many female legislators in the United States and elsewhere first entered politics when their husbands died in office (Werner, 1966; Kincaid, 1978). An example from Japan is the experience of the Sekō dynasty. Sekō Kōichi was an LDP MP for Wakayama Prefecture from 1932 until 1960. After losing his seat, he passed the baton to his son, Sekō Masataka, who was successfully elected in 1967. Masataka lost the next election in 1969 but in 1971 ran successfully for the House of Councillors and represented Wakayama for five terms. On September 25, 1998, Masataka died suddenly in office at the age of seventy-five. His nephew, thirty-five-year-old Sekō Hiroshige, was working in Tokyo as an employee of NTT, Japan's largest telecommunications company. Although Hiroshige had never lived in Wakayama and had no previous aspirations to go into politics, party leaders in the LDP, particularly those belonging to the same intraparty faction as his uncle (the faction of Mori Yoshirō), recruited him to run in the November 8 by-election. It did not matter that Hiroshige had no prior political experience or direct ties to Wakayama; what mattered was that he was a Sekō.[8] He won the three-way by-election race with 50 percent of the vote.

It should be noted that death in office may be highly correlated with an incumbent's age and length of tenure—a popular politician may be more likely to continue running and winning until he or she dies, and conversely, incumbents who die at a young age will be less likely to have children who are old enough to be eligible to run. But if the sudden death of an incumbent increases the demand for a legacy successor, it might mean that even weaker incumbents who die in office will have a higher probability of being succeeded by a family member. It is also important to note that if the mechanism works through the pathway of by-elections, death in office should not be relevant in list-based PR systems, which do not use by-elections to replace incumbents who leave office.

PUTTING IT ALL TOGETHER

In sum, the comparative theory proposed here to explain variation in dynastic candidate selection across time and space encompasses supply and demand factors, which are in turn influenced predominantly by the institutional context of the electoral system and party organizations. On the supply side, we can expect that longer-serving incumbents and incumbents with a family history of supplying candidates to national politics will be more likely to produce potential legacy successors, thanks in part to the political socialization of family members. As a result, all democracies will inevitably exhibit some level of dynastic politics that flows from this supply of legacy candidates.

The key factors for explaining variation in dynastic politics across countries and parties, however, reside in the demand-side calculus of candidate selection within parties. As a general rule, party leaders involved in candidate selection will attempt to balance the expected probability of winning a seat, given a potential candidate's observed attributes, with the expected value that the candidate will bring to the party and its other goals beyond winning the seat. The relative balance of these two priorities, however, will be influenced by the institutional context within which candidate selection takes place. Attention has been focused on a few key hypotheses that can be derived from this theoretical framework, although others are also possible. The most important of these hypotheses for the argument of this book are that the demand for legacy candidates will be higher under candidate-centered elections, when parties are weakly organized, when candidacy requirements are more exclusive, and when candidate selection is decentralized to local party actors. These institutional conditions will either increase the expected utility of a legacy candidate's inherited incumbency advantage to a party or reduce the availability of high-quality non-legacy alternatives. Parties and other actors involved in candidate selection will thus favor legacy candidates when they are available, and possibly even seek them out when they are not. In addition, where the demand for candidates with a personal vote is higher, the actual value of the candidate's inherited incumbency advantage can be lower and still be of significant vote-earning utility to a party.

Of course, candidate-centered elections may also generate conditions for greater incumbency advantage and greater successive wins by the outgoing incumbent. In this respect, the characteristics of incumbents can also be considered an outcome of the institutional context. But in terms of the recruitment of new candidates, the attributes of the outgoing incumbent candidate instead can be thought of as inputs into the next nomination decision, and these inputs are interpreted in the context of the institutional setting within which decisions are taken.

The Comparative Evidence

The main research design and identification strategy employed in this book relies on institutional reform in Japan as a form of natural experiment. However, a brief exploration of the comparative evidence may be informative before presenting the detailed hypotheses, derived from the theory, which can be tested on the empirical data from Japan. How well do the hypotheses laid out in the preceding discussion fit with the empirical record of the set of democracies documented in the previous two chapters?

Unfortunately, testing the theory with cross-national and cross-party data poses two main challenges. First, such comparisons are vulnerable to numerous confounding variables, since unique historical trajectories, culture, and individual political leaders all could potentially mitigate the institutional incentives for dynastic politics in a given party or country. It is even more difficult to determine whether observed differences in dynastic politics can be attributable to the electoral or party institutions in small-N comparative studies where variation on these variables may be limited. As such, the comparative evidence can at most be considered suggestive evidence, not the kind of "smoking gun" evidence we might want in order to make strong causal inferences about the relationship between institutions and dynastic candidate selection.

For example, of the countries for which comparative data are available, only Ireland uses the STV electoral system for its lower chamber. The comparative theory would predict that the intraparty competition under STV, much like under SNTV, should increase the value of the personal vote and thus increase the demand for legacy candidates. Indeed, the empirical record presented in Chapter 2 shows that dynastic politics have been much more prevalent in Ireland than in many other democracies, and similar to the level of dynastic politics in Japan under SNTV. The share of dynasties is also higher in the decentralized Fianna Fáil and Fine Gael parties than in the highly centralized Sinn Féin. Existing empirical research on Ireland has also confirmed that legacy candidates enjoy a significant inherited incumbency advantage in elections and cabinet selection (Smith and Martin, 2017). However, without additional country cases that use STV, it is hard to say whether the observed level of dynastic politics in Ireland is a result of the electoral system rather than some other latent variables unique to Ireland or its main parties.

Similarly, dynastic politics have been comparatively more prevalent in Belgium and Greece, both of which use forms of open-list PR. The intraparty competition inherent under open-list PR should, according to the theory, increase the demand for legacy candidates. However, dynasties have been relatively less prevalent in some other open-list (or "flexible-list") PR cases, including Denmark, Finland, Switzerland, and pre-1993 Italy.[9] Does this mean that intraparty competition under open-list PR does not increase the demand for legacy candidates? Or could there be other factors at the system or party levels in the latter countries (e.g., district magnitude, party size) that mitigate the effect? Dynasties have also been quite prevalent in some Israeli and Norwegian parties, and extremely prevalent in Icelandic parties. All three countries, as well as Italy from 2006 to 2013, use a closed-list PR system.[10] Closed-list PR should, according to the comparative theory, decrease the demand for legacy candidates relative to the other common electoral systems. However, without the availability of a counterfactual "Israel," "Norway," or "Iceland" operating under an alternative electoral system, we cannot hope to isolate the effects of the electoral institutions from other factors, such as the size of the party or population. The same issues apply to Canada, the United States, pre-1993 New Zealand (all FPTP), and Australia (AV).

In addition, the MP-level Dynasties in Democracies Dataset does not distinguish MPs elected in FPTP contests from closed-list PR in the mixed-member systems of Germany, post-1993 New Zealand, and Italy (1994–2001). At the MP level, electoral reforms in Italy, New Zealand, and Japan also complicate cross-national comparisons, since MPs in any given postreform year will have been recruited under completely different institutional contexts (however, using the detailed candidate-level data in JHRED, the mixed-member system and electoral reforms in Japan will prove important to the empirical strategy in later chapters).

The second challenge to cross-national and cross-party tests of the theory is the fact that parties' recruitment methods may vary across time or districts within countries, and are often opaque to outside observers. Only a handful of studies have tried to systematically categorize the recruitment processes of parties (e.g., Lundell, 2004; Shomer, 2014; Poguntke et al., 2016), and most often only at static points in time. In reality, party recruitment processes change occasionally and can even differ across districts in the same election. Thus, static measures of party organizational strength or centralization are likely to introduce bias into any comparative analysis. At the same time, dynamic measures of party-level differences can be difficult to code without access to the internal rules of candidate selection within parties over time. Finally, as with electoral institutions, unless a party experiences some form of exogenous shock to its organization or internal rules and processes, we cannot ascertain the counterfactual level of dynastic politics that such a party might have had under different contexts.

Nevertheless, the comparative MP-level observations in the Dynasties in Democracies Dataset can be used to produce some prima facie evidence in support of a few of the hypotheses just presented. First, we can explore the first supply-side hypothesis (H_1) that longer-serving incumbents will be more likely to have a legacy successor who wants to run. This hypothesis is closely related to Hypothesis 3, the demand-side hypothesis that parties will want to nominate a potential legacy candidate whose predecessor had a strong incumbency advantage (to the extent that this might be indicated by length of time in office). Previous country-specific studies of the United States (Dal Bó, Dal Bó, and Snyder, 2009), the Philippines (Querubín, 2016), the United Kingdom (van Coppenolle, 2017), Norway (Fiva and Smith, 2018), and Argentina (Rossi, 2017) have all found that longer tenures in office are associated with a higher probability of founding or continuing a dynasty.

Figure 3.1 illustrates the overall relationship between increasing lengths of tenure and the probability that an individual lower chamber MP in the comparative dataset will be followed into office by a family member. The predicted probabilities are based on a simple logit regression of *Senior* (a dummy variable equal to one if the MP preceded a relative in office) on *Number of terms* served before leaving office. The sample is restricted to the final term served by MPs who stopped running between 1945 and 2000, to allow some time for future family members to enter the data.[11] Finally, MPs

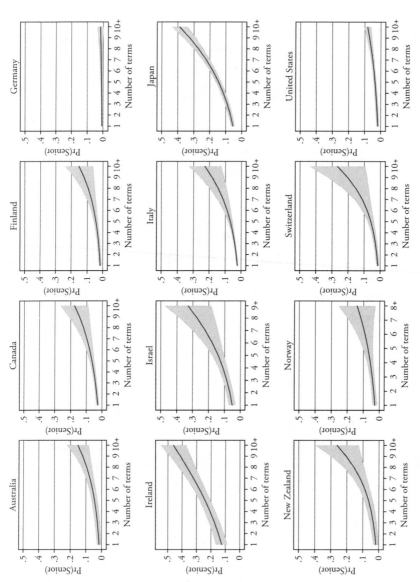

FIGURE 3.1 Length of tenure and dynastic succession in twelve democracies

SOURCE: Dynasties in Democracies Dataset.

NOTE: Data sample restricted to final term in office for MPs who served between 1945–2000. Predicted probabilities estimated separately for each country based on a logit model regressing *Senior* on *Number of terms* served by an MP (without other controls but with robust standard errors). Shaded areas represent 95 percent confidence intervals. MPs with 10 or more terms are grouped together, except for the cases of Norway and Israel (only two Norwegian MPs served more than eight terms; only eight Israeli MPs served more than nine terms).

who served ten or more terms are grouped together, since the number of individuals serving more than that falls dramatically and varies considerably by country (due to fewer MPs with long tenures, those with eight or more terms are grouped together for Norway, and those with nine or more terms for Israel).[12] The basic pattern provides evidence in support of the hypothesis that longer serving MPs will be more likely to have a family member follow them into office. In each country, the probability of preceding a family member increases with the length of time an MP spends in office, and the relationship is statistically significant in all cases except Germany.

The relative contributions of supply (H_1) and demand (H_3) *within* each country cannot be disentangled with the observational data available. However, the differences *across* countries suggest that there is variation in demand for dynasties in different democracies. Most notably, there is a higher probability that an MP will precede a family member in Ireland, Israel, and Japan, even at shorter lengths of tenure in office. For MPs in these countries who serve eight or more terms before leaving office, the predicted probability of a family member following in their political footsteps is over 30 percent. In contrast, the pattern among most of the other countries—Australia, Canada, Finland, Italy, New Zealand, Norway, Switzerland, and the United States—is remarkably similar, despite the fact that the number of years accounted for by each term can vary slightly across countries and time.

Why does this variation suggest differences in demand rather than supply? Suppose the probability of an MP preceding a family member were related *only* to supply. If that were true, then we might expect the relationship to be roughly equivalent across all countries, as it indeed appears to be for most of the countries in the comparative dataset. The logic is that most MPs are capable of having children, and all are likely to have some number of close relatives; the longer an MP serves in office, the more time one or more of these relatives has to be socialized into politics. This socialization process should account for the largest component of the supply of legacy candidates. One might imagine that variation in the supply of legacy candidates might occur if the economic payoffs to political office were significantly different across countries, such that even the children or relatives of MPs who served short terms might have strong economic reasons to seek office themselves. Without data on the economic payoffs to political office across these countries, this possible supply-side explanation for the variation cannot be entirely ruled out. However, there is little reason to expect that the economic payoffs should be significantly higher in Ireland, Israel, and Japan than in the other countries. Rather, the differences across countries are more likely to flow from differences in demand for legacy candidates in the candidate selection processes within parties.

The comparative dataset also allows us to get a sense of the second supply-side hypothesis (H_2), that a legacy MP will be more likely than a non-legacy MP to precede a family member in office, because of his or her existing family history in politics. Figure 3.2 disaggregates the MPs in each of the twelve countries into two categories of legacy status (non-legacy and legacy) and shows the percentage in each category who were followed into office by a family member. In each of the country cases, the share of "junior" legacy MPs who go on to become "senior" to another legacy MP is higher than the share of non-legacy MPs who start a dynasty. This relationship is not simply due to the fact that legacy MPs tend to serve longer terms. In all cases, the predicted probability of having a family member follow in an MP's footsteps is higher within existing dynasties, regardless of the number of terms served (not shown).[13]

In the case of Japan, even legacy MPs who served just a few terms in office have a higher than 20 percent predicted probability of preceding another family member in politics, compared to less than 10 percent for non-legacy MPs. At the mean length of tenure for this sample—four terms—a Japanese legacy MP is roughly 20 percentage points more likely to have a family member follow him or her into office than a non-legacy MP. If the full range of number of terms is used (i.e., not grouping ten or more terms together), it is only after seventeen terms that a non-legacy MP is just as likely to become the founding member of a new dynasty as a legacy MP from an existing dynasty is to extend that dynasty to the next generation.

Finally, for four of the country cases—Canada, Ireland, Japan, and the United States—the comparative dataset contains a sufficient number of recorded deaths to estimate the relationship between death in office and dynastic succession at different lengths of tenure. These cases all happen to be systems where by-elections are held to replace incumbents who leave office midterm. Figure 3.3 illustrates the relationship between length of tenure and the probability of preceding a family member in office, conditional on whether the MP died in office. As predicted by Hypothesis 8, death in

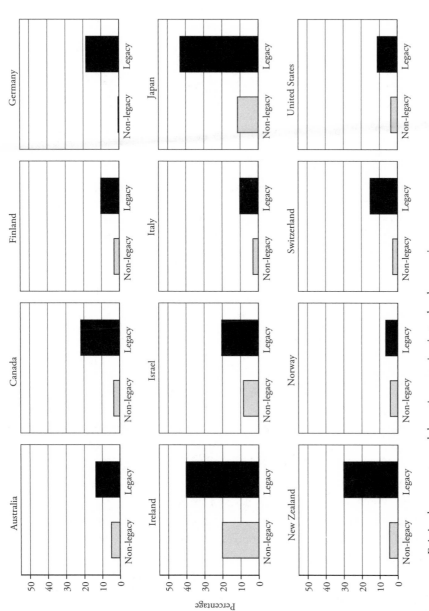

FIGURE 3.2 Existing legacy status and dynastic succession in twelve democracies

SOURCE: Dynasties in Democracies Dataset.

NOTE: Data sample restricted to final term in office for MPs who served between 1945 and 2000.

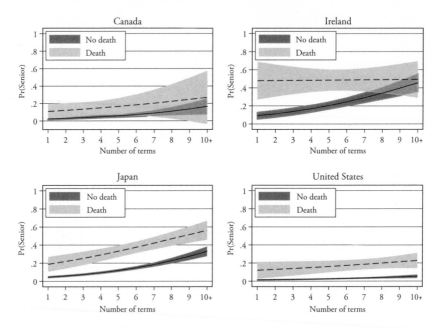

FIGURE 3.3 Death and dynastic succession

SOURCE: Dynasties in Democracies Dataset.

NOTE: Data sample restricted to final term in office for MPs who served between 1945 and 2000. Predicted probabilities for each group estimated separately for each country using a logit model regressing *Senior* on the interaction between *Death* and *Number of terms* served by an MP (without other controls but with robust standard errors). Shaded areas represent 95 percent confidence intervals.

office has a positive relationship with dynastic succession. The relationship is particularly striking in the case of Ireland, where deceased MPs are about as equally likely to be replaced by a family member regardless of how many terms they served in office before their death.

These patterns provide some evidence in support of the supply-side hypotheses and hint at evidence in support of some of the demand-side hypotheses. However, as already noted, the comparative data are likely to mask important confounding variables and are vulnerable to a number of measurement issues. For example, one measurement issue in the preceding analysis is that MPs from the same family with overlapping terms are included, so that *Number of terms* in some instances is measured at a point in time *after* the MP became a *Senior* member of the dynasty. For the remainder of the book, the empirical analysis will focus on testing the implications of the comparative theory with an in-depth examination of the case of Japan. A focused examination of institutional reform within the single country case of Japan provides several analytical advantages over cross-national comparisons, as it helps us to isolate the influence of institutions from other factors at the system level (including history, culture, population size, or level of economic development) and party level (including idiosyncratic differences related to ideology, personalities of leaders, time-specific events, size, and age of the party) that may contribute to a country's patterns in dynastic politics. All of these factors make it difficult to pinpoint the effects of the electoral system and candidate selection institutions in cross-national analyses.

A number of other features of Japan make it an ideal test case for the theory. First, as we have seen, there have been a substantial number of dynasties in Japan, which means that the estimated relationships between variables of interest are less likely to be affected by a handful of observations on particularly "influential" individuals. Second, in addition to the fact that Japan experienced electoral reform, which allows for a before-and-after analysis of dynastic politics, the MMM system it adopted in 1994 combines two systems: FPTP in one tier and closed-list PR in a second tier. Because they operate simultaneously in the same country and same election, mixed-member systems like Japan's provide an opportunity for a "controlled comparison" of electoral system effects (Moser and Scheiner, 2012). Third, unlike in many of the comparative cases, the general pattern in Japan has been one of direct succession between predecessors and successors; MPs from the same family with overlapping tenures are comparatively less common. This situation allows us to make better inferences about the factors that contribute to hereditary succession at the time it occurs.

Predictions for the Case of Japan

The SNTV electoral system used from 1947 to 1993 resulted in intraparty competition in the LDP and JSP, the two largest parties. As a result, candidates campaigned predominantly on the basis of their personal attributes or behavior rather than on a commitment to their party label or its national policies. This was especially true for candidates from the LDP. Candidates in the JSP faced less intraparty competition but faced competition within the socialist camp from the more moderate DSP. Kōmeitō and JCP candidates, in contrast, did not have to face copartisans or competitors from parties with similar ideologies and could therefore campaign less on the basis of their personal-vote-earning attributes, and more on the basis of their party platforms.

In addition, the candidate selection process in the LDP was extremely decentralized. When an LDP candidate retired or died, his or her faction and the candidate's kōenkai played the largest role in finding a successor. Candidate selection within the JSP and DSP was also decentralized, but with greater influence exercised by the two parties' support networks of labor unions, which also provided a steady supply of potential candidates. In contrast, both the Kōmeitō and JCP used highly centralized selection processes. For the prereform period, we can thus make the following predictions:

1. From the supply-side incentives outlined in the theory, we can predict that dynastic candidate selection will be more likely to follow the retirement of long-serving incumbents (H_1), and particularly incumbents who were themselves part of an existing dynasty (H_2).

2. From the demand-side incentives at the system and party levels, we can predict that dynastic candidate selection will be higher in the LDP, JSP, and DSP, where intraparty or intracamp competition made elections and candidate selection more candidate centered (H_4). We can also predict more dynastic politics in the LDP because of its weaker organization than the other parties (H_5) and its more decentralized candidate selection process (H_7), although the relative importance of these factors will be more difficult to assess.

3. Finally, from the demand-side incentives at the individual level, we can predict that candidates who won their last election (H_3) or died in office (H_8) will be more likely to be succeeded by a family member, even holding length of tenure constant.

The 1994 electoral reform to MMM and subsequent party reforms in the 2000s have altered the institutional context in which candidate selection decisions are made, particularly within the LDP. The electoral reform eliminated intraparty competition, which dramatically reduced the candidate-centered nature of elections while simultaneously increasing the importance of party image and policy platforms in voting decisions (Maeda, 2009; Reed, Scheiner, and Thies, 2012). In addition, the traditionally decentralized and exclusive process for candidate selection in the largest parties has undergone a transformation. Since 1999, the DPJ has experimented with an open-recruitment process, allowing would-be candidates from anywhere in the nation to appeal to the party for a nomination in an open district, including those outside of their home turfs. The central party organization plays a dominant role in screening and selecting these candidates. In contrast, although the LDP introduced a similar open-recruitment system beginning in 2004, its process is carried out locally with national oversight rather than nationally. In the LDP system, local party officials thus still wield considerable influence, despite the increased candidate pool and increased scrutiny from the national headquarters. The process of reform in the LDP has been far from smooth, with a key factor in the resistance to changes in candidate selection being the continued desire among existing dynasties to continue their family business in politics.

The comparative theory presented in this chapter would predict a decrease in the demand for legacy candidates, because elections will be less candidate-centered. If name recognition and other PVEA of individual candidates are less important to winning votes, party leaders will be able to focus more on balancing their other policymaking and officeholding goals in candidate selection decisions, and these efforts might also increase the overall image of the party. However, there is no reason the reforms would affect the supply of legacy candidates who follow long-term incumbents. The children and other relatives of long-serving MPs will still have stronger personal motivations for running than their counterparts among MPs with shorter tenures. If and when a legacy candidate wants to run, the LDP may still have a difficult time preventing that candidate from securing the nomination, as the candidate selection process, even with open recruitment, is still partly decentralized. Moreover, according to H_1 and H_2, the legacy candidates who do decide to run will most often be related to long-serving incumbents from existing dynasties, as these individuals are the most likely to have strong supply-side ambitions. Because these supply-side driven legacy candidates are still likely to be of higher quality and vote-earning utility than many non-legacy candidates, the party has even fewer incentives to pass them over, even if national-level politicians are involved in the decision.

In contrast, since the value to the party of name recognition and other aspects of the inherited incumbency advantage will be lower under the new, more party centered, system, party actors involved in candidate selection will have fewer reasons to seek out weaker legacy candidates. Moreover, they will have more opportunities to find credible alternative candidates thanks to the open-recruitment system. The implication is that we should observe fewer legacy candidates who are related to weak incumbents and fewer examples, such as Sekō Hiroshige in Wakayama Prefecture, of legacy candidates who are pulled into running by party actors. This means the realized inherited incumbency advantage and overall quality of new legacy candidates should actually be higher under the new system than under the old system, even though there will be proportionally fewer legacy candidates. For the postreform period, we can thus make the following predictions:

1. From the supply-side incentives, we can predict that dynastic candidate selection will continue to be more likely to follow the retirement of long-serving incumbents (H_1), and particularly incumbents who were themselves part of an existing dynasty (H_2).

2. From the demand-side incentives at the system and party levels, we can predict that dynastic candidate selection will decrease in the LDP and other parties following the exit of weaker incumbents in the FPTP tier of the new mixed system (H_4), and particularly after party reforms increasing the inclusiveness of the candidacy pool (H_6).

3. The transition should be more noticeable in the DPJ, owing to the greater level of centralization in the candidate selection process (H_7).

4. Finally, we can predict that dynastic candidate selection will be lower in the closed-list PR tier of the new mixed system than in the FPTP tier, as name recognition is not important for winning election (H_4).

The next chapter turns to empirically testing these predictions with the quantitative data from JHRED and qualitative data from interviews with politicians and party staff in the main Japanese parties.

FOUR

Selection
From Family Business to Party Priority

> Some American voters will cast their ballot for the Democratic
> ticket or the Republican ticket merely because their fathers
> and grandfathers had voted that way. Compared to the United
> States, attachment to a party label is less strong in Japan; and
> in keeping with the Japanese mode of politics, loyalty seems to
> be focused more on individuals. This is probably the reason a
> jiban can often be transferred from father to son . . . from man
> to widow, or from a political leader to his chief disciple.
>
> —*Nobutaka Ike (1957, p. 203)*

> It used to be that any fool could get the nomination if he
> inherited a jiban. Since the reform, we are paying much more
> attention to candidate selection.
>
> —*Senior staff member in the LDP national headquarters, May 31, 2011*

Tsushima Yūji was born in Tokyo in 1930 as Shima Yūji but grew up us-
ing his mother's surname, Ueno. He graduated with a law degree from the
University of Tokyo and joined the Ministry of Finance as a bureaucrat.
In 1964, he married the daughter of writer Tsushima Shūji, better known
by his pen name, Dazai Osamu. Dazai's father, Tsushima Genemon, was a
member of the prewar House of Peers from Aomori Prefecture in northern
Japan. Dazai's brother, Tsushima Bunji, was the first elected governor of
Aomori from 1947 to 1956, and an LDP MP for Aomori 1st District from
1958 to 1963. When Yūji married into the Tsushima family, he adopted his
wife's famous political surname.

The daughter of Tsushima Bunji was married to Tazawa Kichirō, who
served as an LDP MP for neighboring Aomori 2nd District from 1960 to

1996, thus making Tazawa and Tsushima Yūji cousins by marriage. In 1976, Tazawa and faction leader Ōhira Masayoshi recruited Yūji into running for Bunji's former seat, on the basis of his strong qualifications as a former bureaucrat (Ōhira had previously met him as minister of finance while Yūji was working in the ministry) and his connections to the Tsushima and Tazawa families.[1] He won his first election, and ten consecutive elections after that, eventually rising to the level of leader of his own faction in the LDP and twice serving as minister of health and welfare.

The Tsushima case is one example of the way in which dynastic recruitment was practiced in Japan during the period from 1947 to 1993 when the SNTV electoral system was used to elect members of the House of Representatives. Larger parties, particularly the LDP, routinely nominated multiple candidates in each district, which resulted in elections where candidates campaigned predominantly on their personal-vote-earning attributes and behavior rather than their commitment to the party label or its national policies. A candidate with connections to a previous incumbent thus had a head start in collecting the personal votes needed to win election. In addition, the candidate selection process in the LDP was decentralized and dominated by the factions and kōenkai of the previous incumbents, which reinforced the tendency to recruit candidates with such connections. Over time, legacy candidates like Tsushima became the most common type of candidate nominated by the LDP, and the presence of dynasties in parliament swelled to an unusually high level for a developed democracy.

After electoral reform in 1994, Tsushima won four elections in the new Aomori 1st District in the FPTP tier of the new MMM system. He decided to retire just before the 2009 election, and his eldest son, Tsushima Jun, was selected by the local prefectural party organization to run as his replacement. However, the LDP's central party organization, facing public criticism for its dynastic politics, decided to override the local decision and deny the official nomination to the younger Tsushima.[2] He ran anyway as an independent but ended up losing the election when a second conservative independent decided to enter the race and the conservative vote was split between them. A candidate from the DPJ won the election with a plurality of the votes that was lower than the combined share of the two conservative independents. In the following election, the LDP reversed its decision and gave Jun the party's nomination. This time around, he went on to win the seat.

This chapter examines the practice of dynastic politics in candidate selection under SNTV, particularly within the LDP, and the changes that have occurred since the adoption of MMM. Under the new mixed system, intraparty competition in the LDP has been eliminated, and elections have increasingly become more party-centered. In addition, the LDP and other parties have introduced new innovations in candidate selection that have broadened the pool of candidates and allowed party leaders to exercise greater control over nomination decisions, superseding the previous influence of the kōenkai support organizations, faction leaders, and other local elites. The result of these institutional reforms has been a dramatic decrease in demand for new legacy candidates. Legacy candidates are exceedingly rare in the PR list tier of the new system and have decreased substantially in the FPTP district tier as well, rapidly approaching the level more commonly observed in other developed democracies.

However, the effects in the FPTP tier have been partially mitigated by path dependence and a continued supply of legacy hopefuls. A key factor slowing the predicted effects of reform is the carryover of long-term LDP incumbents elected under the previous electoral rules, many of whom have sons who have been serving as their personal secretaries and who wish to succeed them when they retire. As illustrated by the case of Tsushima Jun, when such a legacy hopeful wants to run, denying him or her the nomination can create electoral costs for the party. Nevertheless, party leaders now have a greater ability to prevent weaker legacy candidates from running—and less of an incentive to seek them out. As a result, the new legacy candidates who do tend to emerge and get nominated represent a qualitatively different breed. They are more likely to come from established, long-serving dynasties, and more likely to have their own personal ambition to run rather than being coaxed into a political career by the party or kōenkai elites.

Elections and Candidate Selection Under SNTV

For the first postwar election in 1946—the first election with suffrage for women—the provisional government used a limited vote system in large districts.[3] This system was very permissive to new candidates from diverse backgrounds, and indeed, over 8 percent of the elected MPs were women. However, the permissiveness of the system also allowed for a proliferation of small and radical parties.[4] In 1947, the GHQ of the US Occupation permitted the reintroduction of the medium-sized district electoral system used prior to the war. From 1947 until 1993, the 466–511 members of the House of Representatives were thus elected by SNTV, with most districts returning between three and five members.[5] The return of smaller-sized districts in 1947 proved a barrier to more diverse representation, and the number of female MPs and minor parties declined rapidly.

From 1947 to 1955, party competition narrowed to a few large, though internally divided, parties in three main ideological camps. On the right, the conservative camp contained two main parties: the Liberal Party, led by Yoshida Shigeru, and the Democratic Party, which by the time of the 1955 election was led by former-Liberal Hatoyama Ichirō. On the left, there was a socialist camp (JSP) and a communist camp (JCP). In 1951, the socialist camp was temporarily divided when the JSP split into the Leftist JSP and the Rightist JSP over disagreement about the San Francisco Peace Treaty. However, the two factions of the JSP reconciled their differences and reunited after the 1955 general election, which resulted in the JSP controlling a third of the seats in the House of Representatives. Faced with what they perceived as a growing threat from the left, the leaders of the Liberal and Democratic parties decided to merge and form the LDP, which would be the dominant party for the next three and a half decades. However, the LDP's divided origins would continue to be reflected in its internal party factions, which competed for control of the party leadership.

In 1960, the socialist camp was divided again when the moderate (rightist) wing of the JSP broke away to form the DSP. The religious party Kōmeitō entered the electoral arena in 1964. Nevertheless, the relatively stable party system from 1955 until 1993, when the LDP lost its majority in the House of Representatives, has often been referred to as the "1955 System" (see Schoppa, 2011). During the 1955 System era, electoral strength across ideological camps was relatively consistent. Meanwhile, intense competition prevailed between candidates within the same party or camp.

ELECTIONS: INTRAPARTY AND INTRACAMP COMPETITION

Any party hoping to win a majority of seats would need to nominate more than one candidate in each district. The LDP nominated multiple candidates in over 80 percent of all districts with more than two seats up for grabs from 1958 (the first election after its founding) to 1993. The second-largest party, the JSP, also nominated multiple candidates in many districts, but intraparty competition declined steadily over time—from more than 80 percent of districts in 1958 to less than 20 percent by 1980—as the party weakened and was faced with competition from both the DSP and the JCP (which gained in popularity in the 1970s), and even from the Kōmeitō.

As the JSP weakened in electoral strength, nominating multiple candidates in a district could risk splitting the party's support in such a way that no candidate would get elected, an outcome known as "falling together" (*tomodaore*). The party's incumbent candidates no doubt also opposed running extra candidates in elections where they felt insecure (Reed and Bolland, 1999). The Kōmeitō, which held a distant third place for party share of the votes and seats from 1969 until 1993, never nominated more than one candidate in a district, whereas the JCP and DSP did so in only a small handful of cases.[6] This fragmentation on the left meant that only the LDP nominated enough candidates to secure a majority in the House of Representatives on its own.

Candidates from the LDP and JSP also faced competition within their respective camps from small splinter parties and independent challengers who did not receive, or chose to eschew, the official party nomination. In the case of the LDP, some established incumbents ran as independents after losing the official nomination due to a scandal or party discipline issue. For example, after being arrested for accepting bribes from the Lockheed Corporation in 1976, former prime minister Tanaka Kakuei resigned from the LDP but continued to run and win as an independent until retiring in 1989. During the same time period, a few other LDP MPs broke with the party and formed the New Liberal Club (NLC), contesting several elections before rejoining the LDP.

Other would-be LDP candidates who did not receive the official nomination would run as LDP-affiliated independents, oftentimes supported unofficially by an LDP faction. Because of the influence of factions in determining the party leader (who, because of the LDP's legislative majority, would become prime minister), faction leaders were constantly seeking to expand their ranks in the Diet. An independent candidate backed by a faction might be able to unseat an LDP incumbent from a rival faction, since the SNTV system meant a candidate could often win with less than 20 percent of the vote (Nemoto, Pekkanen, and Krauss, 2014). LDP-affiliated independents who were successful in getting elected would be given ex post nominations by the party and would then join the LDP's legislative caucus.

From 1958 to 1993, an average of eight successful LDP-affiliated independents were given ex post nominations each election, and in many cases these ex post nominations helped the party maintain their legislative majority.[7]

JSP-affiliated independents also sometimes ran, albeit much less frequently. However, JSP candidates faced further competition from the DSP and DSP-affiliated independents. Although JSP and DSP candidates had separate core bases of support (public-sector and private-sector unions, respectively), they still had to compete for the support of non-union, non-JCP voters on the left. Another splinter party, the Social Democratic League (SDL), entered competition in 1978. All of these parties thus competed for votes within the socialist camp. In addition to the conservative and socialist camps, there were the Kōmeitō and JCP camps (which were coterminous with the respective parties apart from a few affiliated independents and small communist-related parties) and a hodgepodge of other minor parties and independents who did not fit into one of these ideological camps (such as far-right extremist candidates).

Grouped according to ideological camp, there were even fewer districts where candidates from the main two camps did not face competition from other copartisan or co-camp candidates vying for the same pool of voters. While LDP candidates faced intracamp competition in nearly all districts, JSP candidates faced intracamp competition in roughly 60 percent of districts since the 1970s, even while official intraparty competition had declined to around 20 percent of districts. In districts where candidates faced intraparty and intracamp competition, it was not enough to campaign on party label or ideology alone. Indeed, many voters made their decisions on the basis of individual candidate characteristics rather than party label. For example, in voter surveys conducted between the 1950s and early 1990s, roughly 40 percent of respondents reported that the "candidate" was more important than the "party" in making their voting decision.[8]

Three factors, known in Japanese as the "three *ban*" (*sanban*), were especially important for election: *jiban* (support base in the electorate), *kaban* (financial resources), and *kanban* (name recognition or reputation) (Ike, 1957, pp. 192–202). Faced with so much competition, candidates needed to cultivate each of the three ban to build any kind of electoral advantage in their districts. Nathaniel Thayer (1969, pp. 98–102) distinguishes between two types of jiban: vertical jiban were based geographically around a candidate's hometown or main residence; in contrast, horizontal jiban were more spread out and might be based on a particular policy issue, industry, or interest-group network, such as union members. Most conservative politicians built jiban that were of the vertical type (Curtis, 1971; Hirano, 2006), but the use of horizontal jiban developed through policy differentiation was also common, and facilitated by membership on committees of the LDP's internal policymaking organ, the Policy Affairs Research Council (PARC). Most LDP MPs wanted to sit on committees within one of the "big three" PARC divisions with influence over distributive policy (Agriculture and Fisheries, Construction, and Commerce and Industry), but there was less membership overlap between MPs from the same district on committees responsible for other policy sectors (McCubbins and Rosenbluth, 1995; Tatebayashi, 2004). This policy differentiation helped LDP MPs gain expertise and stand out from other copartisans in the district.

Candidates maintained their jiban through their kōenkai, which were formal organizations of supporters dedicated to electoral mobilization in behalf of the candidate. Although some kōenkai existed during the prewar period, conservative politicians started to build them as a general practice beginning in the 1950s, and candidates from other parties soon followed suit (Masumi, 1995, p. 236). Kōenkai helped to institutionalize a candidate's personal vote by facilitating favors, constituency service, and pork-barrel projects that benefited the local residents represented by the candidate. A candidate's kōenkai might comprise multiple overlapping groupings, with membership in each group organized around a personal connection to the candidate, geography, or a specific target of representation, such as women, youth, or various interest groups (Krauss and Pekkanen, 2011, p. 37).

The kōenkai were critical to the organization and mobilization of a candidate's jiban, but building and maintaining strong kōenkai was incredibly expensive. An election could be called at any time, and the campaign period was extremely short (from 1958 to 1992, only twenty days). Politicians thus needed to cultivate close ties with their supporters throughout the inter-election period. They did so by organizing regular parties, informational discussions, and excursions to hot springs and other attractions for kōenkai members. Members would pay nominal fees to belong to the kōenkai, but the fees did not cover the costs of maintaining the organization. Studies in the 1980s estimated the average start-up cost of creating a kōenkai at between $700,000 and $1,000,000, with a similar sum required yearly to maintain them (Kitaoka, 1985; Ishikawa and Hirose, 1989). Moreover, the election deposit requirement meant that a candidate was required to pay roughly $14,000, on average, just to gain access to the ballot, and average campaign expenditures by 1993 had reached $117,900 (Harada and Smith, 2014). Expensive kōenkai and election campaigns are a big reason kaban (financial resources) was a second major factor in a candidate's successful election, and why money politics and corruption were so rampant under the SNTV system in Japan (Curtis, 1988, pp. 157–191). LDP candidates received some funds from the party and their faction, but the high cost of elections often resulted in a search for funds through more illicit means, especially by faction leaders whose rank-and-file members demanded financial support for their loyalty.

Finally, kanban (name recognition) also helped to distinguish a candidate from competitors. Under SNTV, voters needed to select a single candidate, often from among many copartisans, so personal name recognition was key to electoral success. In addition, the actual method through which ballots were (and are still) cast further reinforced the importance of name recognition: when voters cast their ballots, it is obligatory to physically write out the name of a candidate. This means that voter awareness of a candidate's name is crucial. Candidates are aware of this, and it is reflected in campaign practices, even to this day. During the short campaign period before an election, candidates can be heard repeating their names and brief slogans ad nauseam in front of train stations, or from sound trucks that cruise through the neighborhoods of their district. Candidates with complicated or obscure characters (*kanji*) in their name often use a simplified script (*hiragana*) to help voters avoid mistakes that could lead to an invalid vote.

CANDIDATE SELECTION: VARIATION ACROSS PARTIES

The 1950 Public Offices Election Law, which forms the basis for election law to this day, regulates all aspects of election rules and campaigning but imposes few legal constraints on candidate eligibility. A candidate for the House of Representatives must be at least twenty-five years old at the time of the election, whereas a candidate for the House of Councillors must be at least thirty years old. Additional restrictions apply to individuals deemed medically incompetent, anyone who is currently serving a prison sentence, and current public employees of the national, prefectural, or local governments (Fukui, 1997). However, the actual process of candidate selection is at the discretion of parties, and in practice each party used different criteria and methods for screening and selecting its candidates.

The internal party organization of the LDP was highly decentralized, with promotion based on seniority rule and interfactional balancing (Satō and Matsuzaki, 1986). Candidate selection was similarly decentralized. When a candidate retired or died, it was the kōenkai (often with heavy influence of factional leaders) that acted as the selectorate for the new candidate, with the central party leadership and national party only affirming their choice and settling issues of how many candidates would ultimately be given an official party nomination (Reed, 2009). An attempt in 1963 by party leaders to eliminate factions and centralize party control of nominations and campaign activities by replacing kōenkai with local party branches failed, and the LDP candidate selection process remained decentralized (Nonaka, 1995; Krauss and Pekkanen, 2011, pp. 57–58).

The decentralized nature of candidate selection in the LDP resulted in nominations favoring three distinct types of candidates with local ties: the personal secretaries of the previous candidate, local politicians who supported the previous candidate, and legacy candidates (Fukui, 1997). Each of these backgrounds represented between 20 percent and 40 percent of new candidates in any given election year. As documented in Chapter 2, many legacy candidates first served as secretaries to gain experience and position themselves to smoothly inherit the seat. Former bureaucrats, who would sometimes "purchase" the kōenkai of a retiring incumbent, represented a fourth common type of candidate, although candidates with this background gradually declined, and were replaced with ever more legacy candidates (Usui and Colignon, 2004; North, 2005).[9]

The JSP organization resembled the LDP's in its loose structure, factionalism, and decentralized authority (Stockwin, 1992). Candidates for the JSP also developed their own kōenkai but to a lesser degree, and the kōenkai of outgoing incumbents played only a negligible role in recruiting new candidates. A heavier influence in candidate recruitment was exerted by the party's main support organization, the General Council of Trade Unions of Japan (Sōhyō), which predominantly represented the public-sector unions. Prefectural party headquarters also played a role in proposing candidates to the national headquarters for approval. For these reasons, more than half of all candidates from the JSP were active in the labor union movement prior to running for office, while another 30 to 40 percent were members of local or prefectural assemblies (Fukui, 1997). The DSP was supported by the All Japan Labor Federation (Dōmei), which represented mostly private-sector unions that were less militant and more business oriented than those represented in Sōhyō.[10] DSP candidates were also chosen locally, and thus mostly drawn from among local politicians and trade union leaders (between 20 percent and 40 percent of candidates came from each background in any given election year).

In contrast to the conservative and socialist parties, both the JCP and Kōmeitō were (and are still) highly centralized in their organization and candidate recruitment processes, although candidates from both parties also formed kōenkai. The Central Committee of the JCP exercises tight control over all aspects of the party organization, including candidate selection (Shiratori, 1988, pp. 180–181). The JCP generally makes efforts to nominate candidates with some connection to local affairs, but it is not uncommon for its candidates to change districts and run as "parachute" candidates for the party elsewhere. Thus, local ties are not dominant in deciding nominations. The party recruits many of its candidates from among party employees, citizens' group activists, anti-JSP union members (particular a minority faction from the Japan Teachers Union, Nikkyōso), and left-wing lawyers (Curtis, 1979). By 1980, the JCP had formally enforced a party rule that all kōenkai had to be "party kōenkai," in both name and form, rather than candidate-based kōenkai (Lam, 1996).

The Kōmeitō was founded in 1964 as a political offshoot of the Nichiren Buddhist organization Sōka Gakkai, much in the way that many early mass parties in Western European democracies emerged out of class or religious movements (Ehrhardt et al., 2014). Although the party officially severed its formal ties to Sōka Gakkai in 1970, the party's core organization and support base in the electorate is nearly coterminous with the religious organization (Hrebenar, 1992). The party leadership organ, the Central Secretariat, is composed of the party president and several other senior members. Before an election, it consults with the party's Election Strategy Committee and considers which candidates to nominate. The Central Secretariat even exercises control over the final selection of local (municipal and prefectural) candidates recommended by the party's local candidate selection committees. In contrast to the LDP, where new candidates might approach the party directly or run first as independents in the hope of getting an ex post nomination, most Kōmeitō candidates do not have prior ambitions for public office until a party leader or religious leader taps them to run (Smith, 2014). Nearly all Kōmeitō candidates are also members of Sōka Gakkai, and are frequently screened and recommended to the party leadership by influential leaders of the Sōka Gakkai organization.

Table 4.1 summarizes the differences in intraparty and intracamp competition facing candidates from the five main parties that contested elections to the House of Representatives during the bulk of the SNTV period, and the nature of the parties' candidate selection processes. This variation allows for some comparison in terms of dynastic politics based on differing party and electoral contexts, holding country-specific factors (e.g., history, culture, and other system-level variables) constant. However, because the two cases of parties with a centralized candidate selection process (Kōmeitō and JCP) are also the same two parties whose candidates did not face intracamp competition, we do not have much analytical leverage over the relative importance of these two (probably related) variables for the SNTV period.

Following the theory outlined in Chapter 3, we would expect to see a greater percentage of legacy candidates in the LDP and among conservatives than in the JSP and among other socialists, despite similarly decentralized candidate selection processes, owing to the increased intraparty (or intracamp) competition faced by conservative candidates. A greater number of

TABLE 4.1

Party variation in intraparty and intracamp competition and centralization of the candidate selection process in prereform Japan

Party	Intraparty competition?	Intracamp competition?	Decentralized candidate selection?
LDP	Yes (97% of contests)	Yes (99% of contests)	Yes
JSP	Yes (55% of contests)	Yes (78% of contests)	Yes
DSP	No (99% of contests)[a]	Yes (99% of contests)[b]	Yes
Kōmeitō	No	No	No
JCP	No (99% of contests)[c]	No (95% of contests)	No

[a] The DSP ran two candidates in Kanagawa 1st District and Tokyo 6th District in 1960; thereafter they never ran multiple candidates.

[b] The DSP faced one or more intracamp challengers in all but two election contests: Osaka 1st District in 1983 and 1986.

[c] The JCP ran two candidates in Kyoto 1st District and Kyoto 2nd District in several elections between 1972 and 1990.

intracamp competitors should mean that the reputation and name recognition of an individual candidate would have been more important for securing election. The JSP and DSP also benefited from a more concrete support base, labor unions, from which to recruit candidates. Given that candidates from the Kōmeitō and JCP never (or rarely) faced intraparty competition and were selected through highly centralized candidate selection processes, we would expect to observe the lowest percentage of legacy candidates in those parties.

Japan Under SNTV: Land of the Rising Sons

In the first three elections after democratization, less than 5 percent of candidates for the House of Representatives were legacy candidates. Many of these early legacy candidates were actually standing in as proxies for prewar candidates who were purged from office during the US Occupation. When the purge was lifted in 1952, a number of the purged politicians returned to national politics and their relatives stood down. For example, Takaoka Daisuke was a conservative politician who served three terms in the prewar House of Representatives for Niigata 2nd District. After he was purged, his brother Tadahiro ran in his place in 1947 and 1949 (winning a seat in 1947). When the purge was lifted, Daisuke took back control of his jiban and contested an additional six elections, eventually joining the LDP.

To fill the remainder of the candidate vacuum during the purge, conservative party leaders, in particular Yoshida Shigeru of the Liberal Party, actively recruited high-level bureaucrats and other outsiders without any legacy ties. When the purge was lifted, purged politicians like Hatoyama Ichirō returned, yet when Hatoyama's Democratic Party merged with Yoshida's Liberal Party in 1955 to form the LDP, the incumbent former bureaucrats from the Liberal Party remained a major force in the party.

By the time the Occupation-era recruits began to retire and die in the 1960s and 1970s, however, many of them had built up large and successful kōenkai, which were often transferred upon retirement or death to a relative (usually the eldest son), creating a new generation of dynasties. In fact, the founding members of roughly 35 percent of all dynasties active in the late 1980s were first elected during the four elections of the Occupation, from 1946 to 1952 (Ichikawa, 1990, pp. 10–11). Some founding members got their initial starts in the prewar period, particularly in the 1924 election just prior to universal male suffrage, but the majority of dynasties were created in the postwar period.

DIFFERENCES ACROSS PARTIES AND CAMPS

Legacy candidates were most common in the LDP. Of the 6,070 candidates who ran at least once between 1947 and 1993, 428 (7 percent) were legacy candidates (for details, see Table A.3 in Appendix A). Almost half (181) of the legacy candidates were nominated by the LDP (37 percent of LDP candidates), while another seventy-seven were LDP-affiliated independents (21 percent of such independents). The JSP fielded only twenty-nine legacy candidates (7 percent of all JSP candidates), whereas the DSP fielded fourteen (8 percent). Recall that candidates who directly succeed a relative into candidacy in the same district represent a subset of legacy candidates called hereditary candidates. About half of the legacy candidates in the conservative and socialist camps were of this direct hereditary candidate variety—a total of 177 individual candidates who ran between 1947 and 1993 (3 percent of all candidates).

The Kōmeitō and JCP fielded a much smaller number of legacy candidates and not one of them was a hereditary candidate. There were only five Kōmeitō legacy candidates (3 percent of the party's total) in the House of Representatives during this period, including Ishida Kōshirō, Nishinaka Kiyoshi, and Asai Yoshiyuki, all of whom had relatives who had served in the House of Councillors, and Kitagawa Kazuo, whose father had been elected from a different district in the House of Representatives. The fifth legacy candidate, Watanabe Michiko, also ran in a separate district from her husband, Watanabe Ichirō.[11] Although some JCP district successors had the same name as their predecessors, it is not possible in most cases to verify whether they were relatives because of the scarcity of information released by the JCP for candidates who did not win. One JCP legacy candidate, Takada Tomiyuki, was the son of prewar politician Takada Ryōhei. But Tomiyuki ran as a communist for only the first three elections (1947–1952) before joining the JSP. Another JCP candidate, Yonehara Itaru, was the son of prewar House of Peers member Yonehara Shōzō.[12] In total, only three confirmed JCP legacy candidates (less than 1 percent of all JCP candidates) ran between 1947 and 1993.

The percentage of legacy candidates running in elections under the LDP label grew steadily from just over 10 percent of candidates after the party's founding in 1955 to a zenith of nearly 50 percent prior to the 1993 election, the last election to be held under SNTV (Figure 4.1). In contrast, legacy candidates accounted for less than 10 percent of the JSP's candidates in most elections. The DSP nominated over sixty candidates in elections in the 1960s, and only five of these were legacy candidates. However, by the 1970s the party decreased its number of nominations to around forty-five candidates and continued to nominate several of its legacy candidates, which resulted in the share of legacy candidates exceeding 20 percent by the 1990 and 1993 elections. One DSP legacy candidate in 1960 and 1963 was Kikukawa Kimiko, widow of former Rightist JSP MP Kikukawa Tadao, who died in 1954. Kimiko first ran as a Rightist JSP candidate in 1955, then with the JSP in 1958 following the reunification, but later split with the party again to join the DSP in 1960. Other DSP legacy candidates in the 1960s included former Rightist JSP MP Kinoshita Tetsu, who replaced his brother Kaoru when the latter ran for governor of Oita in 1955, and Asō Yoshikata, whose father Hisashi served in the prewar House of Representatives.

The difference in dynastic politics is roughly the same when the parties are grouped into the two main ideological camps. The conservative camp,

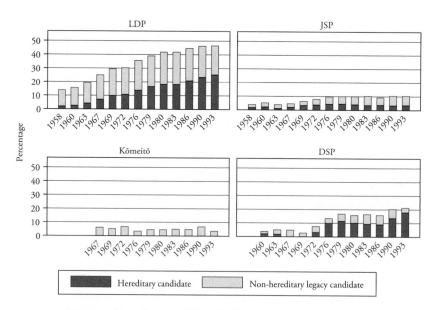

FIGURE 4.1 Legacy and hereditary candidates in the main parties, 1958–1993
SOURCE: JHRED.

NOTE: By-elections not included. The JCP is excluded since legacy candidates were rare. Kōmeitō first ran candidates in 1967; DSP first ran candidates in 1960.

which includes the LDP, its precursor parties, breakaway parties such as the NLC, and LDP-affiliated independent candidates, had many more legacy candidates than the socialist camp, which includes the JSP and the DSP, along with the Leftist and Rightist JSP when the party was split prior to 1955, affiliated independents, and the SDL, which split from the JSP in 1978 (the Kōmeitō and JCP camps are largely coterminous with the parties).

THE IMPORTANCE OF JIBAN, KABAN, AND KANBAN

Previous research on dynastic politics in Japan has attributed the growth in legacy, and especially hereditary, candidates in the LDP to the kōenkai system (e.g., Ichikawa, 1990; Ishibashi and Reed, 1992; Taniguchi, 2008). When an incumbent retired, he or she (most often he) and the kōenkai played the largest role in determining a successor, and incumbents could "transfer" their jiban to a successor through the kōenkai organization and its network of contacts and funds. Sometimes a successor would be a secretary or local politician with close ties to the outgoing incumbent but who was not related by blood or marriage (i.e., a non-kin successor). But often the successor was the outgoing candidate's son or other close relative (i.e., a kin successor or hereditary candidate). The successor to an outgoing incumbent would "inherit" resources that the incumbent had developed over the course of his career in the Diet and that helped contribute to his incumbency advantage in office. Non-kin successors inherited the jiban and kaban resources, but not the kanban, since they did not share the same family name. In contrast, as kin successors, hereditary candidates usually benefited from all three.[13]

A legacy candidate who ran in a separate district or many elections after his or her predecessor had left office might still benefit from kanban, and in many cases jiban and kaban if he or she were a successor to a non-relative. For example, brothers Hatoyama Kunio and Hatoyama Yukio (prime minister from 2009 to 2010) were the grandsons of former prime minister and LDP founder Hatoyama Ichirō, who served in the House of Representatives from 1915 until he was purged in 1946, and again from 1952 until his death in 1959. Their father, Hatoyama Iichirō, served in the House of Councillors (1974–1992), and a great-uncle, Hatoyama Hideo, and two great grandfathers, Hatoyama Kazuo and Terada Sakae, served in the prewar House of Representatives. Kunio was elected first, in 1976. He ran in Tokyo 8th District (currently Tokyo 2nd District), which was the constituency of his grandfather and great grandfather, but he was not able to inherit any jiban. As Mayumi Itoh (2003, pp. 159–160) explains:

> With the death of Ichirō in 1959, Yamada Hisatsugu, former administrative vice minister of foreign affairs and the Hatoyama family's long-time confidante, succeeded to the district. The family's kōenkai (politician's support groups) in the district were disbanded. At that time, the Hatoyama family and Yamada made an agreement that Yamada would return the district to the family should a family member decide to run in the future. However, when Kunio decided to run in 1976, Yamada had already won three terms and did not honor the promise.

Despite this difficulty, Kunio was able to win election with the most votes in the district, no doubt thanks to the strong kanban associated with the Hatoyama family name.[14]

Yukio decided to enter politics in 1986 after earning a PhD in engineering at Stanford University and working as an academic in Tokyo. Since his brother Kunio was already running in the family's old district in Tokyo, Yukio had to look elsewhere for a place to run. Fortunately, a friend of the Hatoyama family, Saegusa Saburō, decided to retire and bequeath his jiban in Hokkaido 4th District to Yukio (Itoh, 2003, p. 164). Thus, Yukio inherited a jiban, whereas Kunio did not, despite running in the same district as the family predecessors. Both brothers would thus be considered legacy candidates but not hereditary candidates.

In the case where an incumbent died suddenly in office without naming a successor, the kōenkai was still very influential in nomination decisions, and often the easiest candidate to unite around was a relative. When an incumbent MP died in office, nominating a relative was not only a convenient way to find a replacement—it could also be viewed as closely approximating the wishes of the electorate, which had previously given a mandate to the deceased candidate. In addition, a relative of a deceased MP may have been more successful in gathering any sympathy vote available. Nominating a relative was also a common way to settle disputes when more than one candidate sought to be the successor.

For example, following the sudden suicide of Hokkaido 5th District's Nakagawa Ichirō in 1983, his son, Shōichi, quit his job in banking to run for the seat in the election that year. However, Ichirō's personal secretary, Suzuki Muneo, also wanted to run, and claimed that Ichirō had been opposed to hereditary succession.[15] The LDP leadership did not want to nominate both Suzuki and Nakagawa, as it already had two other incumbents in the district, Kitamura Yoshikazu and Yasuda Kiroku. Ultimately, Nakagawa was given the official nomination with the support of the kōenkai and was the top vote getter in the district. Suzuki ran and won as an independent, and was given an ex post nomination. But the entry of both Nakagawa and Suzuki resulted in Kitamura and Yasuda both losing their seats.[16]

One hereditary successor faced competition from within his own family. Prior to the 1986 election, Kumamoto 2nd District incumbent Sonoda Sunao passed away. His eldest son from his first marriage, Sonoda Hiroyuki, sought to succeed him, but so did his widow, Sonoda Tenkōkō, who challenged her stepson in the race. Tenkōkō had previously been elected in Tokyo 7th District in 1946 as one of the first female Diet members, and she met her husband when they were both serving in the Diet. She lost four consecutive elections in the 1950s and decided to quit politics. But with the death of her husband, she saw an opportunity to return to the national stage. Kōenkai members were divided over whom to support, and the party avoided taking sides in the family dispute by declining to nominate either candidate. Tenkōkō ran as an independent with the backing of the Nakasone faction, while Hiroyuki had the support of the Fukuda faction (to which his father had belonged). Although the Sonoda jiban in the district was divided, Hiroyuki ultimately won and was given an ex post nomination.[17]

An incumbent who had invested many years of effort into building a strong jiban may have had strong personal reasons to "keep it in the family" (Taniguchi, 2008). In most cases, it was the first-born son who would inherit the jiban—a 1990 *Kyōdō* news survey of thirty-eight hereditary MPs found that 60 percent were the first-born sons; 15 percent were second-born sons, followed by 10 percent each for third-born sons and sons-in-law (Ichikawa, 1990, p. 268). Politicians who did not have a biological son of their own would often adopt a son who could eventually inherit the seat. In Japan, it is common for a powerful man of business or politics who lacks a male heir to adopt a son, especially a nephew or son-in-law, as his legal heir. Sons-in-law adopted in this manner, such as Aichi Kazuo of Miyagi 1st District and Urano Yasuoki of Aichi 4th District, then take the last name of their fathers-in-law and eventually succeed them. Tsushima Yūji, whose story was described at the beginning of this chapter, is a similar case, although he followed his uncle-in-law into office.

Politicians who had amassed large political war chests could also avoid a heavy tax burden on those funds if they were transferred through the kōenkai organization to a successor (Uesugi, 2009, pp. 65–78). Under the

Political Funds Control Law, kōenkai funds are managed by a candidate's political fund organization. If a candidate retires from office and disbands his or her kōenkai, any remaining funds in the accounts of the fund organization are subject to taxation. However, if the money is transferred to another candidate's fund organization (e.g., that of a child running simultaneously) or if the name of the organization is changed to reflect a new candidate taking it over, the funds are not taxed. Political inheritance was thus a useful mechanism for keeping accumulated financial resources in the family without incurring a tax penalty for exiting politics and disbanding the kōenkai accounts. A retiring incumbent might also have felt the need to encourage a relative to act as successor if he or she had acquired a substantial amount of debt to financial supporters that could not be paid off in the near future. Appointing a son or other relative as successor would signal that there was a credible commitment to the continuity of the family "business" and that the successor would repay any political debts when funds became available (Iwai, 1990).

The kōenkai supporters may also have had demand-side financial incentives to recruit a hereditary successor, as doing so could help ensure their continued access to central government resources (Igarashi, 1986; Ichikawa, 1990). The centralized budget allocation process and highly clientelistic operation of LDP politics created incentives for local organizations, candidates, and voters to align with the LDP in order to gain access to redistributive expenditures of the central government. Kōenkai members and local politicians who lent their electoral support to national-level LDP politicians needed to build strong relationships with those politicians to access the central government and maintain an important "pipeline" to pork (Scheiner, 2006). When a politician retired or died, the kōenkai could guarantee its continued access to the central government by nominating a winning successor. Hereditary candidates were ideal to rally behind, since they were familiar to most core supporters and voters. Indeed, of the hereditary MPs surveyed by *Kyōdo* in 1990, 25 percent reported that the main influence on their decision to run was pressure from the kōenkai; another 25 percent reported influence from their father or mother. The most common response, at 45 percent, was "other," but unfortunately the survey did not ask about local or national party influence or factional influence. In a separate question, 32 percent of respondents said that it was the strong push of their predecessor's kōenkai that resulted in the opportunity to run (Ichikawa, 1990, pp. 268–269).

Finally, the LDP organization itself had little reason or power to object to a hereditary successor, because most came well equipped with the funds and support network necessary to win election. In the decentralized LDP, candidates' campaigns were largely self-financed or supported by factions rather than by the party itself. A hereditary candidate with an established kōenkai and ample funds would have been an attractive and expedient choice for the LDP to nominate in order to keep a continued grip on that seat with minimal cost to the party. Moreover, if the party expected the hereditary candidate to win, there was no sense denying him the nomination, even if party leadership favored a different candidate. If a hereditary candidate were denied the nomination, he could run as an independent and threaten to upset the party's ability to elect all of its nominated candidates.

The name recognition of legacy candidates was also clearly valuable. In the candidate-centered electoral context of SNTV elections, a recognizable family name could serve as a "brand name" or cue to voters in a system where party label could not always serve the same function. As Michihiro Ishibashi and Steven R. Reed (1992, p. 369) note, "Voters who have gotten used to voting for Watanabe can continue voting for Watanabe." A few legacy candidates, including Okada Haruo in Hokkaido 4th District and Nakamura Kishirō of Ibaraki 7th District, even went so far as to change their names to be *exactly the same* as their fathers' names prior to succeeding them.[18] Changing one's name may sound extreme, but for a legacy candidate, it could be a good strategy for capitalizing on name recognition without confusing less observant voters.

The experience of legacy MP Kōno Tarō serves as a good illustration. He first ran for the House of Representatives in 1996 from Kanagawa 15th District, a district that included part of the jiban of his father, Kōno Yōhei. After the electoral reform in 1994, the district lines were redrawn, splitting Yōhei's jiban in two, and Tarō and his father ran simultaneously in neighboring districts.[19] Yōhei was leader of the LDP during the brief period from 1994 to 1996 when it did not hold the premiership, and he had inherited his jiban from his father, Kōno Ichirō, after Ichirō's death in 1965. Ichirō's brother, Kenzō, was also a member of the Diet, and their father, Jihei, had been involved in local politics. Tarō explains how voters would sometimes confuse him with his predecessors, despite him having a different given name: "In my first election, there were about a thousand voters who [mistakenly] wrote my grandfather's name. When I showed up to events, elderly ladies would even ask, excitedly, 'Oh, Kōno Ichirō is here?'"[20] Although this anecdote recalls the dynamics of electoral campaigning in the 1996 election, after electoral reform, campaign practices at that time were still very much like in elections held prior to reform (Otake, 1998).

In Kōno's case, being a member of a famous dynasty carried both benefits and liabilities. As the son of Yōhei and grandson of Ichirō, some older voters mistakenly confused him with his predecessors, even though his grandfather had long been deceased. Other voters, even conservative ones, did not like him from the start because there had been bitter intraparty competition prior to electoral reform between his father and other LDP candidates in the district. But, he concludes, in the end his name recognition was an advantage as a first-time candidate:

> Name recognition is very important, and I think I got an advantage. I would be standing at Chigasaki station, and all I would say is "Good morning, my name is Kōno Tarō." I did it from 6 to 8, two hours a day. Several days later, I remember, a guy walked up to me and said, "Hey, you've been here for a while, what's your name?" I was thinking, "That's all I've been saying for days!" But so I said, "My name is Kōno Tarō." And he said, "Oh, be careful, people might mistake you as the son of Kōno Yōhei!" So name recognition is important. Either they like you or they hate you, but at least they will know your name. If you are nobody, it's very hard because people don't even know your name.[21]

The importance of name recognition can also be seen in patterns of marriage in political families. Japanese law requires that a married couple adopt a single surname. In approximately 95 percent of marriages, the wife adopts the husband's surname (White, 2014, p. 245). However, as earlier noted, when the wife's father is powerful or lacks a biological son of his own, the husband will often adopt the wife's surname. LDP MP Suzuki Naoki's father, Naoto, had been elected to both houses of the Diet prior to his death in 1957. Yet when Naoki married Tanaka Makiko, daughter of future prime minister Tanaka Kakuei (1972–1974) in 1969, he took his wife's family name. Even though he ran in the same district as his father (Fukushima 3rd District) in 1983, the national name recognition associated with his father-in-law, who was from neighboring Niigata Prefecture, was arguably more valuable than that of his father, who had died twenty-six years earlier. Tanaka Makiko later ran for her father's seat in Niigata 3rd District in 1993 and topped the poll. Of the sixty legacy sons-in-law who ran between 1947 and 2014, twenty-one (35 percent) had changed their surnames to match those of their political fathers-in-law. That is quite a difference from the 5 percent in the general population.[22]

The inherited resources of jiban, kaban, and kanban that legacy (and especially hereditary) successors enjoyed during the SNTV period were the key ingredients of the inherited incumbency advantage of legacy candidates. Because the kōenkai apparatus generally remained intact following a hereditary succession, hereditary candidates continued to enjoy the resource advantages that their predecessors had acquired during their tenure in office. In the context of intraparty competition and financially expensive elections, this inherited incumbency advantage also made hereditary candidates ideal nomination choices under the kōenkai system of decentralized candidate selection in the LDP.

HOW TO SUCCEED IN POLITICS: PREDICTING HEREDITARY SUCCESSION IN THE LDP UNDER SNTV

Which factors at the individual level were correlated with dynastic candidate selection during the SNTV period? The candidate-level data in JHRED and the prevalence of direct hereditary succession in the LDP make it possible to estimate the degree to which certain characteristics of an exiting candidate are associated with an increased probability that he or she will be succeeded by a relative, without the need to account for variation in time between candidacies (as the passage of time could weaken the jiban or name recognition of the candidate, as well as capture macro-level changes in dynastic politics). Focusing on direct hereditary succession within the LDP also solves the issue of candidates who run simultaneously with their relatives or who run in different districts.[23]

The analysis to follow is restricted to LDP candidates who stopped running after one of the twelve elections between 1958 and 1990 (one observation per candidate, for a repeated cross-sectional data structure). The rationale for beginning the sample in 1958 is that it was the first election held after the formation of the LDP. The sample ends in 1990 to account for the fact that the hereditary successors of candidates exiting after 1990 ran in 1993, the last election held under SNTV. This sample period also has the advantage of party system stability. From 1958 to 1990, there were 625 individual LDP candidates who exited the political scene following an election, an average of fifty-two each year (min. = 26; max. = 74).[24] The sample includes all exiting candidates, not just incumbents.

The baseline model is a simple ordinary least squares (OLS) regression of the following form:

$$Y_{it} = \beta_0 + \beta_1 Incumbent_{it} + \beta_2 Prior\ wins_{it} + \beta_3 Existing\ dynasty_{it} + \beta_4 Death_{it} + \epsilon_{it}, \quad (4.1)$$

where *Incumbent* is a dummy variable equal to one if candidate *i* won a seat in the last election *t* prior to exit (280 candidates); *Prior wins* is the total number of terms served before the final election attempt (min. = 0; max. = 18; mean = 5; standard deviation = 3.9); *Existing dynasty* is a dummy variable for whether the exiting candidate is a legacy candidate (109 candidates); *Death* is a dummy variable for whether the candidate died prior to the following election (129 candidates); and ϵ is an error term.[25] *Incumbent* and *Prior wins* are associated with Hypotheses 1 and 3 derived from the theory laid out in the previous chapter regarding the relationship between the inherited incumbency advantage and dynastic succession. *Existing dynasty* additionally captures the spirit of Hypothesis 2 regarding a family history in politics. *Death* is included to test Hypothesis 8 regarding death in office.

Y represents one of three dependent variables. The first, *Precede candidate*, is a dummy variable coding simply whether the candidate preceded a family member as a candidate in any future election, regardless of that candidate's district, party label, or election outcome. The second, *Precede MP*, is a dummy variable for whether the candidate preceded a successful candidate (i.e., a family member went on to win election and become an MP, in either chamber). Again, this second dependent variable is intended to provide a broad account of dynastic selection and is not limited to candidates whose family members immediately ran in the same jiban in the election after the predecessor exited. Both of these dependent variables also include any family members who might have run for office *after* electoral reform.

The third and main dependent variable, *Bequeath*, is a dummy variable that takes on the value of 1 only if the candidate immediately transferred his or her jiban to a family member in the election following his or her exit; otherwise it equals 0, signaling that no family member directly succeeded the outgoing candidate. The coding of this variable does not discriminate based on whether the successor candidate went on to win the election. The interest is in whether the outgoing candidate was immediately succeeded as a candidate in the same district by a family member. A total of 122 such direct successions occurred between LDP candidates and their family members in the sample, an average of ten each year. This dependent variable is the most restrictive but also most likely to capture the relationship between exiting candidates' attributes and dynastic candidate selection during the SNTV period.[26]

Figure 4.2 plots the coefficients (predicted change in probability) and 95 percent confidence intervals of the main explanatory variables based on separate regressions for each of the three dependent variables. Each regression is estimated as a linear probability model for simplicity and ease of interpretation, but the results are consistent when estimated with probit or logit.[27] All regressions are estimated with robust standard errors. For ease of interpretation, the *Prior wins* variable in Figure 4.2 is standardized so that the mean is 0, and standard deviation is 1. The models include additional controls (not shown in the figure) for gender, age and age-squared, four categories of population density, and district magnitude, as well as fixed effects

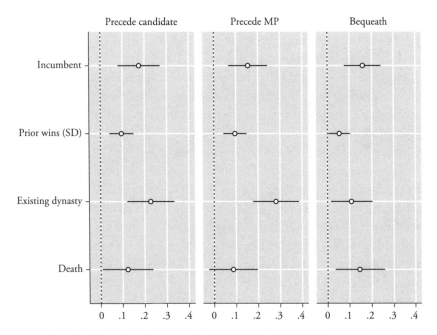

FIGURE 4.2 Predicting dynastic succession in the LDP under SNTV

NOTE: Estimated with OLS using robust standard errors. Points and bars represent the estimated coefficients (predicted change in probability) and 95 percent confidence intervals. Models include controls for gender, age and age-squared, four categories of population density, and district magnitude, as well as fixed effects for region and year. Table A.4 in Appendix A displays the full set of results with and without controls. Estimates in this figure correspond to model 6 in Table A.4, but with *Prior wins* standardized.

for year and region (specifically, the eleven regions used for the postreform PR districts). Table A.4 in Appendix A shows the results with and without these controls, and with each explanatory variable estimated separately.

Not surprisingly, and consistent with existing empirical work in other contexts, LDP candidates with longer tenures in the House of Representatives are associated with a higher probability of dynastic succession. All else held constant, each additional win by an LDP candidate is associated with a roughly 2-percentage-point increase in the probability of preceding a family member in politics. An increase in tenure by four terms (one standard deviation) over the mean number (five terms), increases the probability of succession at any time in the future by about 10 percentage points, and direct hereditary succession by about 5 percentage points. However, winning one's final election is also important. An incumbent who leaves office is between 15 and 17 percentage points more likely than a losing candidate to be followed by a relative. Candidates who come from an existing dynasty (meaning that they are themselves already legacy candidates) are estimated to be roughly 11 percentage points more likely to be directly succeeded, and up to 28 percentage points more likely to have a family member elected as an MP in either chamber at any point in the future. Finally, candidates who die in office (or before the next election, if an unsuccessful candidate) are roughly 15 percentage points more likely to be succeeded, although the estimate for the model using *Precede MP* as the dependent variable suggests that their relatives do not always go on to win.

When it comes to death, a number of factors may be at play. If the death occurs shortly before a scheduled election, a hereditary successor may be a convenient stand-in on short notice. If the death is followed by a by-election to fill the seat, then local leaders may hope to capitalize on any sympathy vote during the by-election by nominating a relative. If a candidate dies too young, however, he or she might not have children who are old enough to directly succeed him or her. For example, when Gunma 3rd District incumbent Obuchi Mitsuhei died in office at the age of fifty-four in 1958, his son, future prime minister Obuchi Keizō, was only twenty-one years old, and thus ineligible for candidacy under Japan's Public Offices Election Law. Because Keizō was too young to succeed his father, the Obuchi jiban was temporarily held by former House of Councillors member Iyoku Yoshio until the 1963 general election, when Keizō was old enough to run. Iyoku lost his race in 1960, but Keizō reclaimed the seat in 1963 and held on to it until he died in 2000.

It is important to consider that, even though these results suggest the importance of incumbency for predicting hereditary succession in the LDP, incumbency is associated with a host of other attributes and qualities beyond simply the fact of getting elected. We can isolate the "local average treatment effect" of incumbency in a candidate's final election attempt by using a regression discontinuity (RD) design (Thistlethwaite and Campbell, 1960). This approach compares the outcomes (*Bequeath* = 0 or 1) for individuals who were only marginally elected to those who were only marginally defeated. Whether or not such marginal candidates were elected can be considered "as good as random," so differences in outcomes can be more credibly attributed to the "treatment" of winning office in their final attempt (rather than, for example quality, effort, or resources). RD designs have been used extensively to measure the incumbency advantage (e.g., Lee, 2008; Caughey and Sekhon, 2011; Eggers et al., 2015; Erikson and Titiunik, 2015), as well as the inherited incumbency advantage for candidates in other contexts (Dal Bó, Dal Bó, and Snyder, 2009; Querubín, 2016; van Coppenolle, 2017; Fiva and Smith, 2018), usually focused on a candidate's first election or first reelection attempt.

Here, the approach is different in that we will focus on the *final* election attempt of LDP candidates in the sample who were within five percentage points of either losing the race (marginal winners) or winning the race (marginal losers). This leaves 440 candidates in the sample. The treatment is whether or not the candidate wins a seat in the district (meaning the candidate was an incumbent at the time of death or retirement). Figure 4.3 plots the predicted probabilities that an exiting LDP candidate would bequeath his or her jiban to a family member given his or her final vote share margin. The vertical line at 0 represents the threshold for electoral victory or defeat. To the left of the threshold are candidates who narrowly lost (vote-share margin is the difference between the candidate's vote share and the vote share of the last-place winner in the district). To the right of the threshold are candidates who narrowly won (vote-share margin is the difference between the candidate's vote share and the vote share of the first runner-up in the district). As in the main regression results, the estimated effect of incumbency on the probability of hereditary succession in the RD results is roughly 15 percentage points. This underscores the importance

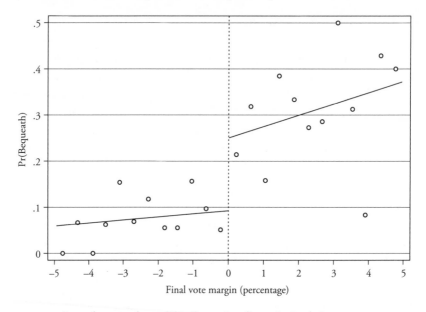

FIGURE 4.3 Incumbency at the margins: Regression discontinuity design

NOTE: Figure shows the predicted probabilities of *Bequeath* = 1 for LDP candidates who ran between 1958 and 1990 whose margin of victory (defeat) in their final election attempt was within 5 percentage points of the loser (winner). Created using the *rdplot* command in Stata (Calonico, Cattaneo, and Titiunik, 2014), with twelve bins for the sample of observations on either side of the cutoff.

of incumbency in predicting hereditary succession in the LDP under SNTV—although it is still important to consider the possibility that strategic politicians who hoped to bequeath their jiban might have waited until they narrowly won before exiting politics.

We can also evaluate whether the predicted probability of succession at each number of additional wins is conditional on the other key variables by including their interactions in the models. The results of this analysis using a logit regression are presented in panels A, B, and C in Figure 4.4. The only interaction that significantly alters the slope of the predicted line relating *Bequeath* and *Prior wins* is *Existing Dynasty*. Exiting LDP candidates who are already themselves part of a dynasty have a roughly 30 percent probability of being succeeded, regardless of length of tenure. In contrast, longer tenures steadily increase the predicted probability of a new dynasty forming. This again illustrates the supply-side effect of an existing multigeneration family history in politics, as posited in Hypothesis 2 and documented with the MP-level data in Chapter 3.

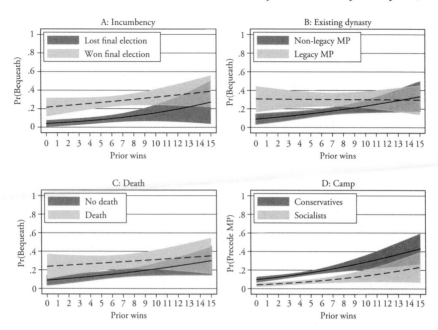

FIGURE 4.4 Effect of length of tenure conditional on other explanatory variables, 1958–1990

NOTE: All models estimated as logit models. For panels A, B, and C, the dependent variable is *Bequeath*, and the plot shows the marginal effects of *Prior wins* interacted with one other explanatory variable, as indicated, holding all other variables constant. As in the main results, the level of observation is each LDP candidate in the final election before no longer running (*N* = 625). For panel D, the sample includes all exiting conservative (*N* = 904) and socialist (*N* = 653) candidates. The dependent variable is *Precede MP* (because direct succession is less common in the socialist camp), and the plot shows the marginal effects of *Prior wins* interacted with ideological camp, holding all other variables constant. All models include controls for gender, age, age-squared, four categorical dummies for population density (rural, semirural, semiurban, urban), categorical dummies for district magnitude, and fixed effects for region and year. Shaded areas represent 95 percent confidence intervals.

Finally, we can evaluate how the relationship between length of tenure and dynastic succession differs across party camps. This is important because it could be that the LDP features more dynasties simply because its members are more likely to have longer tenures—thus increasing the *supply* of legacy hopefuls, as posited in Hypothesis 1. In actuality, plenty of JSP and DSP candidates also served many terms in the House of Representatives (the maximum for the LDP from 1958 to 1990 is nineteen terms, compared to sixteen for the JSP and fourteen for the DSP). Expanding the sample to include all exiting candidates from the conservative and socialist camps (including affiliated independents) and interacting *Camp* with *Prior wins* allows us to rule out this possible explanation (see panel D in Figure 4.4). The predicted probability of having a future family member elected to parliament for an exiting conservative politician who had previously served five terms (which was the average for the LDP) is roughly 16 percent, twice as high as the 8 percent predicted probability for an exiting socialist politician with the same number of wins. This pattern is consistent with the party-level difference predicted by Hypothesis 5 in Chapter 3, given that the socialist parties had stronger organizational ties to groups in society (labor unions). Only after ten wins do the confidence intervals of the predicted probabilities for the two camps begin to overlap.

Electoral Reform and Party Adaptation

The tendency toward dynastic candidate selection within the LDP might have continued unabated were it not for the huge institutional changes that came in the 1990s. When the LDP briefly lost control of government following the 1993 general election, the eight-party coalition that came into power under Prime Minister Hosokawa Morihiro of the Japan New Party (JNP) was united in the sole purpose of reforming the electoral system. Although the reform initiative was not predicated on a perceived need to rid the country of dynastic politics, the prevalence of hereditary succession in the LDP was an outcome that, as with many other aspects of postwar political behavior, had its origins in the nature of competition under the SNTV system. Reformers hoped that the new MMM system would result in a decline in kōenkai, factions, money politics, corruption, and other pathologies of the SNTV system.

Under the new MMM system, candidates can be elected by simple plurality (i.e., FPTP) in one of three hundred SMDs, or as part of a party list for one of 180 seats distributed through closed-list PR in eleven regional districts.[28] The regional districts range in magnitude from M = 6 (Shikoku) to M = 33 (Kinki, reduced to 29 before the 2000 election). Each voter casts one vote for an individual candidate in the FPTP tier (by writing the candidate's name) and one vote for a party list in the PR tier (by writing the party's name). The candidate with a plurality of votes in an FPTP contest is elected to serve that district, whereas seats in the regional PR districts are allocated to parties in proportion to their share of the vote using the D'Hondt formula. Unlike the mixed-member proportional (MMP) systems used in Germany and New Zealand, there is no compensation between the FPTP and PR tiers to produce overall proportionality in the legislature; seats are distributed in parallel within the respective tiers and districts.

A party may list a candidate in both tiers, so that if the candidate fails to win the FPTP contest he or she can still be elected in the PR tier if his or her position on the list is high enough to qualify for a seat given the number of seats the party wins. More than one such "dual-listed" candidate can be ranked at the same position on the party list prior to the election, so that the actual ranking after the election is determined by a "best-loser" calculation (*sekihairitsu*), which is based on how close the candidate came to winning the SMD. The general practice within the LDP and DPJ is for most candidates in SMDs to be "competitively" dual listed in such a manner, although a few have opted to abstain from this electoral safety net (Krauss, Nemoto, and Pekkanen, 2012).[29] In contrast, the Kōmeitō, JCP, and many other small parties tend to use the dual-listing provision less frequently and depend predominantly on the PR list to elect their preferred candidates.[30] Dual-listed candidates who win a seat through the PR tier have sometimes been pejoratively dubbed "zombies," since they "died" in the FPTP tier but were "resurrected" in PR (Pekkanen, Krauss, and Nyblade, 2006).

Some parties will place a few important candidates, such as elder statesmen or high-profile candidates, in "safe" list positions above the competitively ranked dual-listed candidates before filling out the bottom of the list (below the large number of dual-listed candidates) with less important candidates, usually local party staff.[31] For example, in the 2005 election, Prime Minister Koizumi placed former ambassador and political scientist Inoguchi Kuniko in a safe position at the top of the party's list in the Tokyo PR district, ahead of all of the dual-listed SMD candidates. Inoguchi had appeared frequently in the media while in her ambassadorial role, so her nomination as the list leader for the LDP attracted considerable positive attention for the party, as did the nomination of several other high-profile female candidates by the LDP that year. However, when it appeared certain that the LDP would lose the subsequent election in 2009, Inoguchi was refused another safe position at the top of the party list.[32]

Political scientists and reformers expected several interparty and intraparty outcomes to result from the electoral reform (e.g., Ramseyer and Rosenbluth, 1993; Ozawa, 1994; Cowhey and McCubbins, 1995). First, in terms of interparty competition, the introduction of SMDs was designed to shift the electoral focus from candidates to parties and generate more national policy-oriented campaigns centered on two main parties (Duverger, 1954) while still allowing for small parties to gain some representation in the Diet. The rise of two-party competition in SMDs was also expected to produce alternation in government. Second, many observers predicted intraparty changes within the LDP, as the reforms were expected to catalyze the demise of several peculiarities of the LDP organizational structure that thrived under the 1955 System, including kōenkai and factions. For example, Mark Ramseyer and Frances Rosenbluth (1993, p. 197) anticipated that "in its organization and functioning, the LDP would grow to resemble more closely British parties. Personnel, electoral strategy, and policy decisions would be centralized." With more nationally focused campaigns, party leaders would want to exercise greater control over policy, discipline, and candidate selection.

Other scholars were less optimistic that the reforms would drastically change the nature of Japanese parties and elections, owing in part to the fact that campaign laws remained restrictive, so personal support networks should still matter (e.g., Christensen, 1994; Otake, 1998). Thus, despite the electoral reform, little would change in terms of the types of candidates chosen to run with the LDP label. Haruhiro Fukui (1997, p. 112) writes:

> The major parties are likely to remain committed to the same old rules in the selection of their candidates, that is, the acceptance of recommendations made by prefectural and local branches, respect for incumbency, and the importance attached to winnability. It is therefore unlikely that they will choose to sponsor in future elections any types of candidate very different from those they had chosen under the old system.

In terms of dynastic politics specifically, Margaret McKean and Ethan Scheiner (2000, p. 472) predicted that the rampant practice of hereditary succession would continue unless or until the LDP lost its control of government:

> The insistence of major LDP politicians in 1996 that they run in their SMDs, rather than heading up their party's PR list, reflects how important it is to them that they use the new system to continue cultivating district-based support organizations, not just for themselves but as an heritable asset, just as one would try to keep family wealth of other kinds to bequeath to heirs. . . . If the long dominance of the conservative party is what makes inheritance of a seat worthwhile to the heirs, then we would expect to see less bequeathing and inheriting of parliamentary seats only if the new SMD-PR system manages to end one-party dominance.

Indeed, the first election held under the MMM system was largely a disappointment for observers who hoped to witness radical changes in campaign practices or party politics. Campaign practices remained largely unchanged, and even candidates who were newly nominated under the new system chose to create kōenkai. For example, LDP candidate Hirasawa Katsuei, who ran in Tokyo 17th District without any former ties to the district, built his kōenkai with the help of local politicians and by scraping together remnants of the kōenkai of his predecessors, who were no longer running in that district because of redistricting (Park, 1998; Krauss and Pekkanen, 2011, pp. 81–90). New LDP candidate Kōno Tarō inherited part of his father's jiban in Kanagawa 15th District in 1996 after electoral reform split the previous district in two parts. Kōno created his own new kōenkai and worked to build on the existing support base he inherited from his father.[33]

One reason the impact of the reforms was delayed was the disarray of the non-LDP parties. The biggest of these parties was the New Frontier Party (NFP), formed in 1994 by former-LDP heavyweight and reform proponent Ozawa Ichirō from many of the parties that had been in the anti-LDP coalition of 1993–1994. Ozawa had been a rising star in the LDP. He inherited his seat in Iwate 2nd District at the age of twenty-seven, when his father, Ozawa Saeki, died in office prior to the 1969 general election. He quickly became a protégé of Tanaka Kakuei, who was LDP secretary general at the time, and ascended the ranks of the party to become secretary general himself in 1989 (like Tanaka, at just forty-seven years old). In 1993, he orchestrated the vote of no confidence against the cabinet of Prime Minister Miyazawa Kiichi that led to the election, and along with Hata Tsutomu and their followers, formed the Renewal Party, which went on to win fifty-five seats. After the anti-LDP coalition fell to pieces in 1994, the Renewal Party merged with Hosokawa's JNP, the DSP, and part of Kōmeitō to form the NFP. In the 1996 election, the NFP won 156 seats out 500, falling well behind the LDP's 239 seats.

The second largest challenger to the LDP, the DPJ, was founded in 1996 by former-LDP member Hatoyama Yukio, former-SDL member Kan Naoto of the New Party Sakigake, and Yukio's brother Kunio, who left the NFP to form the DPJ but later returned to the LDP.[34] When the NFP broke up in 1998, Ozawa formed the Liberal Party with his followers, but members of six of the other former parties that had been part of NFP merged with the DPJ to become the "new" DPJ. Eventually, Ozawa and the Liberal Party also merged with the DPJ in 2003, and Ozawa began to play a large role in the DPJ leadership, serving as party president from 2006 to 2009, and as secretary general from 2009 to 2010.[35] The early failure of these parties to coordinate or coalesce around a single alternative in SMDs during the first few elections may have helped the LDP win more seats than it would have had it faced a single viable challenger.[36]

A second reason the MMM system did not produce immediate results in terms of party organization and behavior was the dual-listing provision. Since districts could be represented by both the winner of the FPTP contest and a dual-listed PR winner, both might theoretically behave like FPTP candidates in the legislature (McKean and Scheiner, 2000). The practice of dual-listing candidates has created SMDs with effectively two district-focused incumbents, who compete with each other to build and maintain their personal vote in order to be the SMD winner in the following election. This reality has dampened the potential influence of the PR tier on electoral and legislative behavior.

Third, but most important, most of the candidates who ran in the first few elections, and all of their party leaders, had first been recruited and elected under the old SNTV system. They had already invested countless resources into building their kōenkai, had learned certain campaigning styles, and had climbed their way up in the party organization through seniority and factional politics, and thus had little desire to radically alter the established patterns of campaigning and internal politicking that had served them well to this point. This was particularly true for midcareer politicians who had not yet reached the pinnacles of power and therefore had the most to lose by disrupting the old system. Indeed, during the turbulent year of LDP party splits in 1993, junior-level politicians who were electorally weak and senior-level politicians who were electorally secure were the most likely to defect from the LDP (Reed and Scheiner, 2003). Those who stayed in the LDP were less reform minded and more invested in the party's status quo organization.

Eventually, however, the opposition parties coalesced around the DPJ.[37] Despite the initial party system upheaval, two-party competition began to take shape in the FPTP tier by 2003, with the LDP and DPJ capturing over 80 percent of the votes and seats in most districts. Both parties also began to produce preelection manifestos to present their policy goals to the electorate—a practice initiated by the DPJ in 2003 and quickly copied by the LDP (Tsutsumi and Uekami, 2011). Voters, for their part, began to shift their attention in elections from candidates to parties. In the 2000 general election, more voters reported that they placed greater importance on "candidate" than "party" in surveys; but by the 2009 general election, over 60 percent of voters said that "party" was more important (Shinoda, 2013, p. 149). As a result, candidate quality and other personal characteristics have begun to play less of a role in determining election outcomes than party label (Maeda, 2009; Reed, Scheiner, and Thies, 2012).

The LDP managed to regain and retain its control of government thanks to a number of factors, including a coalition agreement with Kōmeitō beginning in 1999, the continued weakness of the opposition at the local level (Scheiner, 2006), and Prime Minister Koizumi Junichirō's electoral popularity and reform image—most importantly in the 2005 general election, which was largely fought over the national policy issue of postal privatization (Machlachlan, 2006; Reed, McElwain, and Shimizu, 2009). But some of Koizumi's most popular reforms undermined the LDP's support in rural areas, and by 2007, the party had lost its control of the House of Councillors. In 2009, the LDP lost control of the House of Representatives in a landslide defeat to the DPJ, temporarily ending five decades of nearly uninterrupted LDP dominance.[38] After fifteen years and five general elections, the reforms had finally produced their intended effects in terms of interparty competition and alternation in power.

But parties had been changing internally as well. Although Ellis Krauss and Robert Pekkanen (2011) correctly note the continued use of kōenkai in mobilizing supporters of individual LDP candidates, the trends they analyze apply mainly to LDP incumbents who were first selected and elected under the old system, or in the tumultuous first election held in 1996, while the party system was still in flux. Such incumbents had little reason to disband their hard-built kōenkai simply because of the reform, especially with such a volatile party system. If we want to evaluate the effect of reform on party personnel decisions, including dynastic candidate selection, we must therefore look at new candidates nominated since reform. Many of the candidates who were newly recruited for nominations in the FPTP and PR tiers of the new system have experienced a much different environment. This is because the two main parties have responded to the new electoral system with internal reforms to their candidate selection processes that have made candidate eligibility more inclusive and strengthened the control of party leaders in nomination decisions.

Once again, the DPJ led the way, largely by necessity owing to its lack of any local organization or local politicians from which to recruit new candidates. In 1999, the party began to experiment with an open-recruitment (*kōbo*) system for selecting candidates in the FPTP tier—a process that proved successful, and one that the LDP began to copy in 2004.[39] The open-recruitment system decreased barriers to entry to attract a more diverse range of candidates while simultaneously undermining the previous influence exercised by outgoing incumbents and their kōenkai in determining a successor candidate. Party leaders have taken a more active role in candidate selection—in some cases, directly recruiting high-profile academics, journalists, and celebrities. The process for determining candidates and their rank order for the PR tier is even more centralized.

A reduction of dynastic politics was not an immediate concern of the reformers. Indeed, many of the reformers in the LDP, including Ozawa Ichirō, Hatoyama Yukio, and Hata Tsutomu, were themselves legacy MPs, and Prime Minister Hosokawa was the grandson of Prince Konoe Fumimaro, the last prime minister before the start of World War II. However, the move toward party-centered campaigns and the increased importance of party image means that the local personal-vote-earning attributes like name recognition and connections to kōenkai that were important under the SNTV system are now in relatively lower demand in the candidate selection process. Moreover, the increased scrutiny on parties after reform resulted in dynastic recruitment becoming something of an embarrassment for the LDP, especially in the run-up to the 2009 election. The party, concerned for its national image, accelerated reforms designed to attract a more diverse range of candidates.

PARTY RESPONSES TO THE NEW ELECTORAL ENVIRONMENT

With the switch to MMM, parties faced new incentives in candidate selection (Asano, 2006). First, since the old MMDs were divided into fewer SMDs than the previous number of seats, nominated candidates needed to have wider appeal beyond the narrow, geographically based jiban that could previously secure election. Candidates could no longer secure a seat with only 10 or 15 percent of the vote, as in the past. As a result, candidate and legislator behavior began to shift toward strategies aimed at attracting a broader range of voters. For example, candidates' campaign manifestos since electoral reform have included a larger percentage of issues related to programmatic policies, including foreign policy issues, in contrast to local or particularistic policies (Catalinac, 2016). LDP MPs are also now active in a wider range of PARC committees than in the past, presumably to cultivate a broader policy expertise to attract diverse voters in the new electoral environment (Fujimura, 2015).

Second, because there is only a single party-nominated candidate in each SMD, party leaders have greater incentive to be concerned with who that candidate is, the extent to which his or her policy preferences align with the party leadership, and whether he or she contributes positively to the party's image. The party-level vote in the PR tier reinforces the need for SMD candidates to represent a single, coherent party message, even if that message does not perfectly coincide with the interests of local party actors in the district.

Third, the party list component in the PR tier encourages parties to present a more diverse range of candidates, especially more women. Since dual-listed candidates fill many of these list positions, this means nominating more diverse candidates in SMD contests as well. In the case of gender, the impact of the electoral reform was dramatic and immediate. From 1958 to 1993, the LDP only nominated seventeen individual female candidates (less than 2 percent of all LDP candidates). Of these, eleven (65 percent) were legacy candidates. In the last seven elections held under SNTV, the LDP nominated just seven female candidates to the House of Representatives.[40] Of these women, only two were not legacy candidates. However, since electoral reform, the LDP and other parties have begun to recruit and nominate many more female candidates, as illustrated in Figure 4.5. In 2014, the LDP nominated forty-two female candidates (12 percent of its candidates) and the DPJ nominated twenty-nine (15 percent of its candidates). Overall, women now make up roughly 17 percent of all parties' candidates. Among first-time LDP candidates, the share of former national bureaucrats has decreased from 22 percent in the last seven elections under SNTV to 13 percent under MMM; the share of MP secretaries has decreased from 40 percent to 27 percent; and the share of those born locally (in the prefecture) has also decreased, from 81 percent to 74 percent. The share of former local assembly members has declined slightly less dramatically, from 34 percent to 29 percent. Meanwhile, the number of first-time LDP candidates with some

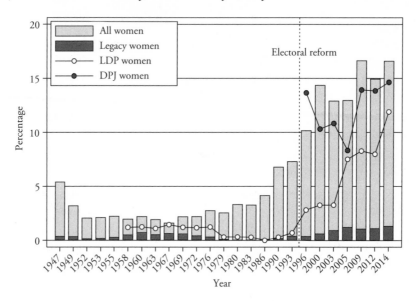

FIGURE 4.5 Female candidates for the House of Representatives, 1947–2014
SOURCE: JHRED.
NOTE: By-elections are excluded. FPTP and PR tiers of the postreform MMM system are grouped together. The vertical dashed line marks electoral reform in 1994.

kind of national celebrity status, such as former Olympic athletes or television "talent," has increased from just two candidates (less than 1 percent) in the last seven elections of the prereform period to thirteen candidates (2.5 percent) since reform.

Several aspects of the new system facilitated these changes in candidates' backgrounds. The dual-listing provision reduces the winner-take-all nature of the SMD system, so that nontraditional candidates such as women still have an opportunity to gain a seat through the PR tier. This is also true for potential "quality" candidates who might otherwise be cautious about challenging an incumbent, making it easier for parties to recruit such candidates. In addition, the Political Party Subsidy Law of 1994 provides public funds to parties.[41] With these funds, party leaders can support their preferred candidates rather than having to default to nominating self-financed candidates (such as those who inherit a kōenkai war chest). Matthew Carlson (2007, pp. 42–44) notes an increasing reliance on the local party branch organizations for funds by new LDP candidates rather than personal fund agents or kōenkai. With fewer hereditary candidates and only weak intraparty "groups" rather than factions, DPJ candidates have been especially dependent on the party for funds. Most candidates now receive more funds from the party than from any other source, and parties have more funds to distribute, which increases the power of party leaders.

With their party image in mind, party leaders have paid more careful attention to the types of candidates they nominate, and as a result, they have increased efforts to centralize decision making in the candidate selection process. The two main parties have also introduced creative new methods for attracting candidates—most notably, the open-recruitment system through which interested and eligible citizens can apply to become candidates for the parties. Although many legacy candidates are still nominated without having to apply through the open-recruitment system, many others have been forced to do so (and in some cases have been passed over for a non-legacy candidate),[42] and the number of districts in which candidates are selected without first competing in the open-recruitment process has been declining. The introduction of open recruitment thus undermines the inevitability of a legacy candidate being nominated, as it provides the party with a greater number of candidate options and gives party leaders more direct control over the recruitment process.

THE ADOPTION AND IMPACT OF OPEN RECRUITMENT

At the time of its founding in 1996, the DPJ consisted of only fifty-two members of the House of Representatives and five members of the House of Councillors. Most of these were former members of the JSP (renamed SDP in 1996) and younger members of Sakigake. It had virtually no organizational base in local prefectures or among local prefectural assembly members, as local elections had been held in 1995, before the party's formation. In contrast, nearly half of all local assembly members were aligned with the LDP (Uekami and Tsutsumi, 2011, pp. 12–13). The main existing alternative to the LDP at the time, the NFP, managed to elect an average of only five assembly members (about 5 percent of assembly seats) in the twenty-seven (of forty-seven) prefectures in which it gained any representation at all. Even when the DPJ was able to run candidates under its banner in the 1999 local elections four years later, it managed to elect an average of only four members in the forty-four prefectures that held elections (about 6 percent of the seats) (Scheiner, 2006, pp. 134–135).

To add to the difficulty of recruiting candidates to run in SMDs without any local politicians, in 1996 the party had to compete for the non-leftist anti-LDP vote with the NFP and with members of Sakigake who opted not to join the DPJ. As a result of the party's weak local presence and inability to attract more party switchers, it was able to field candidates in only 143 SMDs in 1996, with an additional eighteen candidates running purely on the party's PR lists. Even after the NFP broke up in 1998 and many of its ex-members joined the DPJ, the "new" DPJ had a party delegation of less than a hundred incumbents in the House of Representatives (Kato and Kannon, 2008, p. 346) and was still weak at the local level. So the party needed to seek innovative new ways to attract candidates to stand under its label in subsequent elections. The open-recruitment system was an important method it employed.

The first party to hold an open-recruitment contest to attract candidates for a national election was the JNP in advance of the 1993 House of Representatives election. One of the candidates selected in that process was Edano Yukio, who would eventually join the DPJ and serve as chief cabinet secretary under Prime Minister Kan Naoto, and later lead the Constitutional Democratic Party of Japan after its formation in 2017. The JNP dissolved in 1994, and many of its members joined the NFP. For the 1996 general election, the NFP also held an open-recruitment contest to find candidates. According to Asao Keiichirō, who was selected as a candidate in that process, the NFP released a national announcement for applicants, who were interviewed in two rounds—first as a group, then individually. The interview committee in both rounds consisted of an incumbent member of the House of Representatives, Nishikawa Taiichirō, and two outside (nonpolitician) members with well-known credentials in business and society: Fuji Xerox chairman Kobayashi Yōtarō and manga cartoonist Hirokane Kenshi.[43]

In 1999, DPJ party leaders decided to implement a national open-recruitment contest to fill the party's nominations for the upcoming 2000 election, taking a cue from the experiences of the JNP and NFP, whose former members were now in the party.[44] They also held a special round of open recruitment aimed specifically at attracting more female candidates (Gaunder, 2013). Between 1999 and 2012, the party screened over five thousand potential candidates through the open-recruitment process, more than four hundred of whom were approved as potential candidates, and ninety-eight of whom were ultimately nominated to stand for election in an FPTP contest (Smith and Tsutsumi, 2016).[45] The process has generally been used to supply candidates to districts where the prefectural party organization (*ken-ren*) could not find a suitable candidate on its own, or where the national party headquarters did not approve of the local choice. The prefectural party organizations are also primarily responsible for supplying candidates for the party's PR list who are not dual listed in an SMD. These are often local party staff members.

The DPJ's open-recruitment process consists of four main steps (Smith, Pekkanen, and Krauss, 2013). First, interested and eligible applicants submit a two-page form to the party with their personal qualifications, preferred electoral districts, and a recent photograph, as well as a short essay (two thousand characters or less) describing their feelings about a chosen theme, their interest in becoming a candidate for the DPJ, and how they would appeal to voters.[46] Second, successful applicants are then further screened in an interview with members of the party's Election Strategy Committee and ranked. In the third step, candidates who pass this stage are registered as "approved candidates" and can be assigned to a district. Apart from the 2005 open-recruitment process, in which the initial applications were collected locally in each district, the entire application process is carried out nationally, and approved candidates enter into negotiations with party leaders about where to run.

When a district has been decided, the fourth and final step is for potential candidates to meet with local party organization officials for final approval. If the proposed candidate is not acceptable to the local party organization, the national party headquarters will propose someone else. The party has also sometimes forced weak candidates from the previous election to face competition for renomination through an open-recruitment contest or internal party primary. The party has an internal rule that candidates who lose three times consecutively will not be renominated, but most candidates are replaced or opt not to run again before that time. This process of replacing weak candidates has improved the quality of the party's personnel over time (Weiner, 2011; Smith, 2016).

In the first election under MMM, the party only managed to field candidates in 143 of 300 SMDs; however, after party mergers and the introduction of open recruitment, it was able to field candidates in 244 of 300 SMDs in 2000, and 268 SMDs in 2003. The party's increased electoral presence also helped increase its share of the PR vote, which in 2003 surpassed that of the LDP. The DPJ's success in 2003 was a wake-up call to the LDP. According to LDP House of Councillors member Sekō Hiroshige, reformers in the LDP were especially surprised to learn that many of the "fresh" new faces in the DPJ who won seats in 2003 had been recruited through the party's open-recruitment process after being passed over by the LDP for more traditional candidates like legacy candidates or local assemblymen.[47] Reformers like Sekō were concerned: "Our candidate selection process is a mess. If we continue like this, our [negative] image as an "old" party will be indelible. If we do not drastically reform the party, it will die" (Sekō, 2006, p. 12). Ironically, many of the young reformers who headed the party's special committee on internal reforms, including Sekō, Abe Shinzō, and Shiozaki Yasuhisa, were themselves legacy MPs.

At the local level, a few scattered LDP prefectural branch organizations had also experimented with open-recruitment contests in the 2000 election. However, after the 2003 election, national party leaders began to consider a more systematic introduction of the method. A by-election in 2004 provided the perfect testing ground. In January 2004, the LDP incumbent MP in Saitama 8th District, Arai Masanori (whose grandfather had once served as a local mayor), was forced to resign after being arrested (and later convicted) of bribery in the 2003 election. Nine other local LDP politicians from the area were also implicated in the scandal, leaving the local party organization in disarray and unable to come up with a candidate for the by-election that followed. The party's internal reform committee decided to implement open recruitment as the method for selecting the party's new candidate. With just two months before the election, the party hired a public relations consulting company and sent out the open-recruitment announcement for "a candidate fit for the 21st century" (Sekō, 2006, p. 21). The party received applications from eighty-one individuals, which the national-level Election Strategy Committee narrowed down to a pool of roughly twenty credible candidates. In the following stage, an ad hoc committee that included professors and other professionals helped to further narrow the pool to six candidates for an interview stage: five men and one woman.[48] In these early stages, the ranking of potential candidates was done in a blind fashion, so that members did not know the names of the applicants.[49]

In the end, the party chose to nominate Shibayama Masahiko, a thirty-eight-year-old lawyer with roots in the district. The public relations stylist quickly went to work advising Shibayama on his image, swapping eyeglasses for contact lenses, and dressing him in modern suits and colored shirts with the top button unfastened. The public relations company even created a cartoon dog mascot called "Shiba Wan" for campaign materials. Party leaders coached him to stress his local roots in the campaign, the Mori faction lent its support with additional staff, and bigwigs like Prime Minister

Koizumi came to support him at several events (Sekō, 2006, pp. 24–31). Against all odds, and with the LDP image badly damaged from the previous incumbent's money scandal, Shibayama managed to triumph in the election over the DPJ candidate, Kinoshita Atsushi, who had been elected through the PR list in 2003 and resigned his seat for the chance to be elected as the SMD representative.

The success of the first official open-recruitment contest encouraged the party to continue to use the process in subsequent elections. Between 2004 and 2012, more than 2,300 potential candidates applied for the official LDP nomination through the open-recruitment process for over one hundred district races.[50] The main difference between the LDP open-recruitment process and that of the DPJ is that the LDP's is implemented and administered locally, with would-be candidates applying district by district, whereas the DPJ's is a national process, with approved candidates being assigned to specific districts after being selected by the central party organization. The exception is the emergency round of open recruitment that the LDP held just prior to the 2005 election, when Prime Minister Koizumi expelled several "rebels" from his party for voting against his postal privatization reforms and sought out new "assassin" candidates to run against them in the election. The difference in the level of centralization in the process stems from the fact that the DPJ introduced open recruitment before it had local organizations or candidates in many districts, and also reflects the tensions between the LDP party leadership and local party organizations, whose members had previously dominated the process.

In the LDP open-recruitment process, potential candidates submit personal statements and résumés, and are then evaluated by a committee composed of both local party leaders and national party representatives. In a few districts, internal party primaries (*yobi senkyo*) have been held in which all local party members are allowed to vote on the candidate. Although a few of the districts in which local branches have held open-recruitment contests might have been largely for show (a *deki-rēsu*, or "rigged race," where the desired winner had been determined beforehand), most have been sincere contests, and all have at least introduced the potential for outside challengers to gain the nomination. Many legacy candidates have also been forced to participate in open-recruitment contests to secure the nomination. However, the use of open recruitment has in many cases been endogenous to the presence (or absence) of a legacy successor—that is, if a legacy successor was available from the supply-side perspective, and the local party branch organization wanted to nominate him or her, then the local organization might not have opted to hold an open-recruitment contest. Nevertheless, the national party needs to approve the decision even in these cases, and in some cases branch organizations have been required to hold an open-recruitment contest if the party leadership was not satisfied with the preselection nominee.

In some nominations, party leaders of both parties have taken a direct and active role. For example, in the 2005 election, Prime Minister Koizumi's personal staff and the party leadership handpicked several of the "assassin" candidates (Iijima, 2006). Many of these assassins were chosen from among open-recruitment applicants who were not chosen for a district race. Others, such as Inoguchi Kuniko, were contacted directly by Koizumi and given prominent positions on the PR lists.[51] These newly recruited candidates were dubbed "Koizumi's children" by the media. Similarly, when Ozawa Ichirō was secretary general of DPJ prior to the 2009 election, he personally recruited several new candidates, many of them women. The media referred to these female candidates as "Ozawa girls," and many were specifically nominated to run against elderly LDP male incumbents to present a stark contrast between the "fresh" new face of the DPJ and the tired, old, and overwhelmingly male look of the long-ruling LDP.[52]

After the LDP's landslide defeat to the DPJ in the 2009 general election, the party was left with 190 SMDs with no incumbent MP. Party leadership adopted a rule for determining the renomination of SMD candidates who lost their district race and were not elected through the PR list: any candidate whose "best-loser ratio" in 2009 was less than 70 percent (i.e., their vote share was less than 70 percent of the SMD winner's vote share) was forced to compete in an open-recruitment contest for renomination. In addition, losing candidates who were older than sixty-five at the time would also have to compete in an open-recruitment contest to get renominated. These new requirements targeted roughly 110 individuals (losing SMD candidates), although in some districts the "best-loser ratio" threshold was relaxed to 60 percent. The party also continued a rule that first-time candidates had to be younger than sixty-five, and SMD candidates older than seventy could not be dual listed in PR. These reforms were intended to hasten generational turnover in the party.[53] The party's new rules indeed resulted in a large turnover of LDP candidates, many of them in their late sixties and seventies, in favor of much-younger new candidates. In total, the LDP used the open-recruitment system to select 117 of its SMD candidates between 2000 and 2012—43 percent of all of its first-time candidates (Smith and Tsutsumi, 2016). The LDP also used the method to select many of its candidates in the 2010 and 2013 House of Councillors elections (Tsutsumi, 2012) and continues to use the procedure to fill nominations in many districts.

Many new parties have also used a form of the open-recruitment system to find candidates. For example, Your Party, which was founded in 2009 by LDP defector and legacy MP Watanabe Yoshimi of Tochigi 3rd District, first used the system to find candidates for the 2010 House of Councillors election. For the 2012 House of Representatives election, open recruitment became the default method for recruiting new candidates for all of the so-called Third Force parties, including Your Party, the Japan Restoration Party (JRP), and the Tomorrow Party of Japan (TPJ), founded by Ozawa Ichirō after he defected from the DPJ earlier that year.[54] The JRP, founded prior to the 2012 election by Osaka's mayor Hashimoto Tōru, held two rounds of open recruitment—first seeking candidates with prior experience in politics or the bureaucracy, and then seeking candidates with backgrounds in business, law, and academic professions. For the 2013 House of Councillors election, Your Party implemented a live-streaming open-recruitment contest online to fill one of its nominations. Interviews with the applicants were recorded and uploaded to YouTube, and all party members were allowed to vote.

How has the introduction of open recruitment changed the nature of Japanese politics? Recall three of the conceptual dimensions of the methods of candidate selection (Hazan and Rahat, 2010): candidacy (who is eligible?), the selectorate (who decides the nomination?), and decentralization (is the decision made centrally or locally?). Japan's open-recruitment system introduced changes across each of these dimensions. First, and importantly for both the LDP and DPJ, the open-recruitment system opened up the selection process to a wider (more inclusive) pool of candidates. In the case of the DPJ, this candidacy pool includes all citizens of legal eligibility to run for office. For the LDP, the pool of potential candidates has been more limited depending on the prefecture and its requirements. When it comes to the selectorate, there has also been some variation—from extreme exclusivity (the party leader handpicks a candidate) to inclusivity within parties (party member primaries, with various appointment or voting systems used). Last, though also important, there is variation between parties when it comes to the degree of centralization of the selection process. Although open recruitment in the DPJ and smaller parties has been mostly centralized, the LDP has opted for a partly decentralized process, with prefectural party branches retaining influence over the initial recruitment procedures, even as central party leaders exercise more control over the final decision.

Perhaps the most basic impact of the open-recruitment process can be observed in the background occupations and characteristics of the candidates chosen through the process. In the case of the DPJ, candidates recruited through the open-recruitment system are less likely to have been born in the prefectures where they ran, and less likely to be of high "quality" (especially in terms of prior local-level elective experience) than other new candidates (Smith, Pekkanen, and Krauss, 2013). However, open-recruitment candidates have done no worse electorally than their traditional counterparts. Despite the desire to recruit more female candidates being a key reason for the adoption of open recruitment in 1999, the number and proportion of new female candidates selected through the process has not been substantial. In 1999, the DPJ managed to recruit five new female candidates through the process (28 percent of the open-recruitment nominees). However, in subsequent years, more of the DPJ's female candidates have been recruited through traditional methods (with many being recruited directly by party leaders like Ozawa). Tsutsumi Hidenori (2012) examines the background characteristics of new candidates from the DPJ and LDP for the 2010 House of Councillors election, and similarly finds fewer new candidates with local-level experience among open-recruitment candidates in both parties, but a higher percentage of candidates who come from professional backgrounds such as law, medicine, or academia. In contrast to the situation in the House of Representatives, however, open recruitment produced roughly the same percentage of new female candidates as traditional methods (20 percent for the LDP, and 50 percent for the DPJ) in the 2010 House of Councillors election.

In the 2012 House of Representatives election, in which most major parties employed some form of an open-recruitment system for recruiting many of their new candidates, the Third Force parties largely used the system to find candidates with similar backgrounds to those of the established parties' candidates, although both Your Party and the JRP were successful in recruiting many business professionals from outside politics, as well (Smith, 2013). In addition, although the LDP employed open recruitment to select the vast majority of its new candidates in 2012, some of the contests were simply a "show" of reform and ultimately selected the insider favorite. For that reason, many of the LDP's first-time candidates resembled traditional types, with backgrounds as local politicians, political secretaries, or former bureaucrats. Nevertheless, many other contests within the LDP were legitimately contested, and party veterans were dumped in favor of new, younger outsiders. For example, seventy-year-old Yoshida Rokuzaemon, who lost his seat in Niigata 1st District to a DPJ opponent in 2009 with a best-loser ratio of just 54 percent, was forced to compete in an open-recruitment contest for his renomination, and was replaced by twenty-eight-year-old former bureaucrat Ishizaki Tōru, who went on to win the seat in the election. Chūma Kōki, a seventy-four-year-old, nine-term LDP MP from Osaka 1st District who also lost in 2009, was similarly replaced in an open-recruitment contest by former local assemblyman Ōnishi Hiroyuki. Many of these veteran MPs who were forced out by the new open-recruitment system decided to run under the label of one of the new Third Force parties, which were eager for experienced candidates to nominate.

Thus, there is some evidence that the open-recruitment system has shaken up the traditional patterns of recruitment in the LDP and DPJ. In addition, the difference in centralization between the LDP and DPJ open-recruitment processes is reflected in the policy preferences of candidates (Smith and Tsutsumi, 2016). While DPJ candidates selected through open recruitment tend to hold policy preferences that are closer to those of the national median voter than their counterparts, there are less significant differences between LDP candidates selected through open recruitment and traditional methods (both of which are still for the most part initiated at the local level).

Table 4.2 summarizes the changes that have taken place in the arenas of elections and candidate selection following the 1994 electoral reform and subsequent party reforms. In contrast to the prereform SNTV system, elections in the postreform MMM system have gradually become more party centered, thanks in large part to the elimination of intraparty competition. In terms of candidate selection, political parties, especially the LDP and DPJ, have responded by taking a more active, and at least partly centralized, role in recruiting candidates for office, and have introduced innovative new procedures for attracting fresh talent.

But what effect have these changes had on patterns of dynastic candidate selection? To the extent that party label and national, programmatic issues have become more important in elections, the local name recognition of legacy candidates should be less valuable as a personal-vote-earning

TABLE 4.2
Aspects of change in elections and candidate selection in Japan

		Prereform SNTV	Postreform MMM
Elections		Intraparty competition	No intraparty competition
		Candidate centered	More party centered
		Need for strong PVEA	Dual listing limits risk
Candidate selection		Decentralized	More centralized, especially in DPJ
		Kōenkai dominant	Party dominant
		Local elites coopt process	Open recruitment expands choice

attribute relative to the prereform period. According to Hypothesis 4, we should therefore observe a decrease in the demand for legacy candidates. Moreover, party actors who are now in charge of candidate selection have fewer incentives to seek out legacy candidates. Indeed, a party full of legacy candidates could generate a negative image for the party. The dual-listing provision removes some of the risk to nominating candidates with nontraditional backgrounds, and the new open-recruitment system facilitates the recruitment of more diverse candidates, including women, by increasing the inclusivity of the candidate pool. Thus, parties have not only new incentives and safeguards to present a diverse slate of candidates but also a more accessible supply of potential new candidates. In accordance with Hypothesis 6, this increased supply of new non-legacy candidates should further reduce the demand for legacy candidates in both the LDP and DPJ. However, the impact might be relatively dampened by the continued decentralization of the process in the LDP, in accordance with Hypothesis 7.

Dynastic Politics Under MMM

If we look at all the year-by-year percentages of legacy candidates among all candidates for the House of Representatives in the last seven elections prior to electoral reform (1976–1993), and compare them to the first seven elections that followed (1996–2014), there is a clear and immediate drop in the percentage of legacy candidates in the postreform period for all candidates, as well as in the LDP (left panel of Figure 4.6). In the LDP, the proportion of legacy candidates declined from a high of nearly 47 percent in the final election under SNTV in 1993 to just 28 percent in the 2012 and 2014 elections (the prereform average was 42 percent, compared to 34 percent in the postreform period). Because the DPJ's membership consists of several former LDP members, an average of 13 percent of its candidates have also been legacy candidates, roughly mirroring the overall percentage of legacy candidates among all parties and independents.

Yet, just as incumbent candidates had no reason to disband their kōenkai simply because of the reform, parties had no reason to suddenly expel all incumbent legacy candidates. Thus, it makes more sense to look at first-time candidates nominated before and after electoral reform to get a picture of the reform's impact on dynastic candidate selection (right panel of Figure 4.6). If we look only at these newly recruited candidates, the percentage of legacy candidates in the LDP has declined more drastically since reform—from an average of 43 percent in the prereform period to just 14 percent in the postreform period, and less than 10 percent in the 1996, 2009, and 2012 elections.

Grouped by the institutional settings of the electoral system and party reform periods, we can also observe a stark difference between the legacy

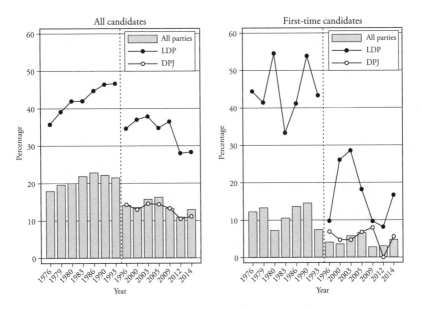

FIGURE 4.6 Legacy candidates for the House of Representatives, 1976–2014
SOURCE: JHRED.
NOTE: Left panel includes all candidates. Right panel includes only first-time candidates, excluding candidates who previously served in the House of Councillors. Vertical dashed line indicates year of electoral system reform. Postreform period includes both FPTP and PR candidates. By-elections are included, grouped with the previous general election. Percentages for LDP and DPJ do not include affiliated independents.

and hereditary candidate nomination patterns that prevailed in the LDP under SNTV, and the situation under the postreform FPTP and PR tiers of the MMM system, including the impact of internal party reforms after 2004 (left panel of Figure 4.7). From 1976 to 1993, 100 of 230 first-time LDP candidates were legacy candidates (43 percent), and 64 of these candidates (28 percent of the total) directly succeeded their predecessors as hereditary candidates. In the FPTP tier of the new system from 1996 to 2003, prior to the introduction of open recruitment (FPTP 1 in Figure 4.7), the share of legacy candidates among 182 new recruits was more than halved, to 20 percent (37 legacy candidates, including 24 hereditary candidates). After party reforms began to take effect in 2005 (FPTP 2 in Figure 4.7), the percentage of legacy candidates, and especially hereditary candidates, continued to decline among new LDP candidates. Since 2005, only 20 out of 185 new candidates (11 percent) have been hereditary candidates. A further thirteen (7 percent of total) were legacy candidates who did not directly succeed

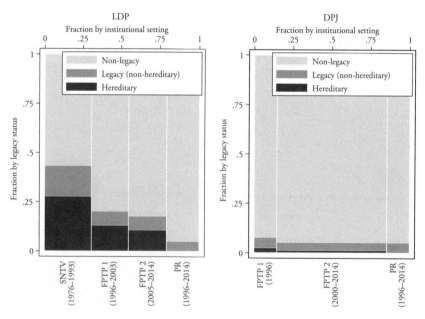

FIGURE 4.7 First-time legacy and hereditary candidates in the LDP and DPJ, by institutional setting

SOURCE: JHRED.

NOTE: The figure is a mosaic plot. FPTP 1 refers to candidates nominated prior to the adoption of open recruitment in 1999 (DPJ) and 2004 (LDP). FPTP 2 are candidates nominated after the reforms to the recruitment system. By-elections are included (the first by-election after LDP recruitment reforms is grouped with FPTP 2 from 2005 to 2014). First-time candidates do not include individuals who previously served in the House of Councillors.

their predecessors. These patterns suggest that the level of dynastic politics in the LDP may be beginning to shift away from the patterns that prevailed under SNTV (and still persist under STV in Ireland), and instead approach the average level in most other democracies, including countries like the United States, the United Kingdom, and Canada that also use an FPTP system for parliamentary elections (see Chapter 2). In the PR tier, the impact of the reform on dynastic recruitment has been even greater. The concept of direct hereditary succession is not applicable for pure PR candidates (i.e., those who are not dual listed in an SMD) because the concept of a jiban does not apply to party lists. Among pure PR candidates, there have been only eight new legacy candidates out of 155 total (5 percent).[55]

In the DPJ, six legacy candidates (8 percent of seventy-seven new candidates) were nominated prior to the introduction of open recruitment (FPTP 1 in right panel of Figure 4.7). These included two hereditary candidates: Okuda Ken, who succeeded his father in Ishikawa 1st District in a by-election in 1998, after the latter's sudden death. The second hereditary candidate, Ōide Akira, ran in Kanagawa 2nd District the 1996 general election, taking over the jiban of his father, former cabinet minister and JSP MP Ōide Shun. After the adoption of open recruitment (FPTP 2), the party nominated an additional twenty legacy candidates (5 percent of 375 candidates), including five more hereditary candidates.[56] Among the seventy-six new candidates who ran only in the PR tier, the DPJ has nominated just four legacy candidates. This also constitutes just 5 percent of all new candidates in that institutional setting. It would be a tenuous assertion to attribute, with any amount of certainty, these observed differences between the LDP and the DPJ to the level of centralization in the open-recruitment system (H_7), which varies somewhat across districts and time in both parties. Nevertheless, the observed patterns do match the theoretical expectations.

HEREDITARY CANDIDATES BECOME A POLITICAL ISSUE

Part of the large drop in dynastic recruitment in the LDP can be attributed to a strategic political response to criticism from the DPJ just prior to the 2009 election. In April 2009, four months before the general election, the DPJ declared that it would no longer nominate any direct hereditary successors, effectively banning the practice within the party, as well as the practice of inheriting an MP's political fund management organization. The party told *Asahi Shimbun* that it hoped the policy would improve its public image, which was tarnished by the arrest of party leader Ozawa Ichirō's personal aide for alleged illegal fundraising.[57]

Because the DPJ had already selected most of its candidates for the upcoming election through the open-recruitment process three years earlier (in 2006), the ban did not directly affect any of its own candidates. Instead, the announcement of the ban was largely an electoral ploy to embarrass the LDP, which had recently come under fire in the media for its dynastic politics, as the three prime ministers who followed Koizumi Junichirō—Abe Shinzō, Fukuda Yasuo, and Asō Tarō—were all hereditary MPs, and each had been criticized for ineffective leadership. Many journalists were questioning whether hereditary MPs were fit to lead, or whether they were simply privileged blue bloods with little real knowledge or experience. Fueling the fire, Koizumi announced his retirement from politics in 2008 and anointed his twenty-seven-year-old son, Shinjirō, as his successor in Kanagawa 11th District (which includes the cities of Kawasaki, Yokosuka, and Kamakura).

The Koizumi family has been active in Japanese politics for over one hundred years, and Shinjirō represents the fourth generation. His great grandfather, Matajirō, represented Kanagawa 2nd District (which became the 11th District after reform) in the House of Representatives from 1908 to 1945, and served in the House of Peers from 1945 until 1946, at which time he was purged from office. Shinjirō's grandfather (Junichirō's father) was born Samejima Junya but changed his name when he married into the Koizumi family. Originally from Kagoshima Prefecture, he served two terms in the prewar House of Representatives from 1937 to 1945 representing Kagoshima 1st District, before he was also purged. When the Occupation ended and the purge was lifted in 1952, Junya returned to the Diet, this time representing Kanagawa 2nd District, as his father-in-law, Matajirō, had died the year before. Junya served seven terms before dying in office in 1969 at the age of sixty-five. At that point, Junichirō took over the jiban and won consecutive elections since, becoming prime minister in 2001.

In the 2005 election, Koizumi (then in his second term as prime minister) won four times as many votes as his DPJ challenger, with 73 percent of the vote. He had hinted that he intended to retire around the age of sixty-five, the same age his father died. True to his word, in September 2008 he announced that he would not seek reelection and that Shinjirō was his chosen successor. Speaking to a crowd of supporters, Koizumi explained: "I asked him if he wanted to be a politician, and he said, 'yes.' Please forgive me for being a doting parent, and I'd be grateful if you would offer generous support to Shinjirō."[58] Shinjirō had worked as his father's secretary since 2007 after returning from the United States, where he earned a master's degree from Columbia University and studied at the Center for Strategic and International Studies in Washington, DC. "He is more mature than I was, when I was around twenty-seven and elected for the first time," Koizumi said.

The Koizumi family is immensely popular in Kanagawa 11th District, and supporters had no trouble throwing their support behind the young and charismatic Shinjirō. However, the DPJ criticized the Koizumi case as a typical example of nepotistic politics in the LDP and adopted its party-level ban on hereditary succession to highlight this perceived weakness. The issue garnered considerable attention in the media, which was already anticipating an LDP defeat in the 2009 election. A *Mainichi Shimbun* survey conducted during the election campaign asked all candidates whether the practice of hereditary succession ought to be restricted (Figure 4.8). Among

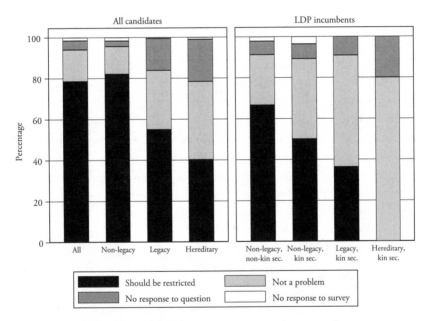

FIGURE 4.8 Candidate survey: Should hereditary succession be restricted?

SOURCE: *Mainichi Shimbun* 2009 preelection candidate survey. Legacy and hereditary coding is from JHRED. Family secretary information is based on whether the incumbent's secretary as listed in the *Seikan Yōran* or *Kokkai Binran* political almanacs had the same family name as the incumbent and supplemented with information from *Kyudan* (http://www.kyudan.com/data/secretary.htm).

NOTE: Number of observations in each group: All candidates = 1,374; non-legacy candidates = 1,194; legacy candidates = 180; hereditary candidates = 97; LDP non-legacy incumbents with non-kin secretary = 138; LDP non-legacy incumbents with kin secretary = 28; LDP legacy incumbents with kin secretary = 11; LDP hereditary incumbents with kin secretary = 5.

the candidates who responded, 82 percent of non-legacy candidates answered that it "should be restricted." Not surprisingly, legacy candidates, and especially hereditary candidates, were more comfortable with the practice—with many answering that it was "not a problem" or choosing to avoid answering the question altogether. However, a surprising 55 percent of all legacy candidates and 41 percent of the subset of hereditary candidates answered that the practice should be restricted.[59]

The LDP waffled. The deputy chairman of the Election Strategy Committee, Suga Yoshihide, and Takebe Tsutomu, the chairman of the Headquarters for Party Reform Implementation, had already advocated a limit on the practice, to begin after the next election. Neither Suga nor Takebe were legacy MPs (although Takebe was later succeeded by his son, Arata, in 2012). Suga personally disliked the practice ever since he had been passed over for a nomination to succeed an incumbent for whom he had worked as a secretary, in favor of the incumbent's son.[60] But the announcement by the DPJ put pressure on the party to speed up its reform process.

At first, party leaders announced that the LDP would also ban hereditary candidates. However, they quickly retreated after intense opposition from other members of the party, many of whom had hopes of being succeeded by their own children.[61] Indeed, among LDP incumbents, opinions differed depending on whether the incumbent currently had a family member serving as their personal secretary.[62] Although 67 percent of non-legacy incumbent MPs favored a restriction of hereditary succession, among LDP incumbents who employed a family member as their personal secretary (perhaps to prime them for succession), opinion was much less in favor: only 50 percent of non-legacy MPs with family secretaries and 36 percent of legacy MPs with family secretaries favored a restriction on hereditary succession. Not one of the five hereditary MPs with a family member serving as secretary was in favor.

Party leaders also knew that Koizumi Shinjirō intended to run whether he had the nomination or not, so denying him the nomination would serve little purpose. As his father's successor, he inherited all of the financial resources (kaban) of his father's political fund agent (*seiji shikin kanri dantai*). In fact, ¥4 million of the funds in the junior Koizumi's fund agent and kōenkai were inherited from his father—roughly 99 percent of all his funds.[63] In the end, the party allowed Koizumi to run, as well as one other hereditary candidate, Usui Shōichi in Chiba 1st District. However, it denied the official nomination in Aomori 1st District to Tsushima Jun, despite him being the son of thirty-three-year veteran and faction leader Tsushima Yūji (whose personal story was detailed at the start of this chapter), because Yūji's decision to retire had been made after the party was already on the defensive.[64] The younger Tsushima ran as an independent with the unofficial support of the LDP and Kōmeitō but faced strong competition from the incumbent DPJ candidate, Yokoyama Hokuto, who had been elected through the PR list after losing in the FPTP contest against Yūji in 2005. Tsushima also faced competition from a conservative independent named Masuta Sekio supported by the Hiranuma Group (a group of former-LDP conservative politicians led by Hiranuma Takeo). In the end, the two conservative candidates divided the vote and Yokoyama won.[65] Tsushima would have to wait until the following election to get the official nomination of the party.[66]

In 2012, the DPJ continued its prohibition on hereditary candidates in its party manifesto. Invoking the popular Japanese manga comic and anime, Lupin III (*Rupan Sansei*), DPJ Prime Minister Noda Yoshihiko stepped up criticism of the LDP's persistent addiction to dynastic candidate selection: "Politics is not a family business! Second generation? Third generation? Politics isn't supposed to be like Lupin!"[67] The LDP tried to shield itself from such criticism with its requirement that all new candidates, including hereditary candidates, be required to compete in an open-recruitment contest to get the nomination. The implementation of this rule prior to the 2012 election further reduced the number of legacy candidates in the party. However, it did not prove to be a difficult hurdle to overcome for several aspiring hereditary candidates.

For example, former prime minister Fukuda Yasuo's son, Fukuda Tatsuo, did not face a single competitor in the open-recruitment contest in Gunma 4th District. In Hokkaido 11th District, the party selected Nakagawa Yūko, the widow of former minister of finance Nakagawa Shōichi, who died shortly after losing his seat in 2009. Shōichi first entered politics in 1983 after the death (by suicide) of his father, Ichirō, as detailed earlier in this chapter. In Saitama 14th District, third-generation legacy candidate Mitsubayashi Takashi was forced to compete in an open-recruitment contest after losing his seat in 2009 with a best-loser ratio of 69 percent. He won the contest but then died suddenly of a heart attack. The party held another contest and chose his brother, Hiromi. Five additional hereditary candidates got the LDP nomination in 2012, including Takebe Arata (Hokkaido 12th District) and Ōno Keitarō (Kagawa 3rd District), son of former minister of state for defense Ōno Yoshinori. Four other LDP candidates with legacy ties to former politicians also ran for the first time (though did not directly succeed their predecessors), and many others had family ties to local politicians.

In some districts, the LDP faced competition from legacy candidates who joined one of the Third Force parties. In Osaka 13th District, for example, five-term LDP incumbent Nishino Akira decided just two weeks before the election not to run again. The JRP, which was formed in Osaka and enjoyed its strongest support there, nominated Nishino's son, Kōichi, who was already serving in the Osaka Prefectural Assembly as a member of the JRP. The LDP held an emergency open-recruitment contest and nominated municipal assemblyman Kamiya Sōhei, but Nishino supporters went largely to Kōichi, who won the seat. In Tokyo 23rd District, Itō Kōsuke, a nine-term MP, lost his seat in 2009 and was forced to compete in an open-recruitment contest, which he lost to former Bank of Japan employee Ogura Masanobu. Itō's son, Shunsuke, took over the kōenkai and ran under the JRP label, but ultimately lost the election to Ogura.[68] In Nagano 3rd District, where former prime minister Hata Tsutomu stepped down, the DPJ at first planned to nominate Hata's son, House of Councillors MP and cabinet minister, Hata Yūichirō. However, this was decided to be a violation of the party's ban on hereditary succession, and Hata's political secretary, Terashima Yoshiyuki, was nominated instead.

In 2014, the LDP nominated only six new legacy candidates. One was in Yamagata 3rd District, where longtime LDP veteran Katō Kōichi was one of the few LDP incumbents to lose his seat in 2012—to an LDP-affiliated independent. The party decided to nominate Katō's thirty-five-year-old daughter, Katō Ayuko, after an open-recruitment contest in which she faced no other challengers. Originally, Katō's successor was intended to be Ayuko's husband, Miyazaki Kensuke, who had even changed his name to Katō Kensuke in anticipation of inheriting the jiban. However, the couple divorced in 2009 and Miyazaki, having changed his surname back again, instead applied to (and won) the LDP's open-recruitment contest for Kyoto 3rd District in 2012.[69]

In Kagoshima 3rd District, the party nominated Miyaji Takuma, the thirty-four-year-old son of eight-term MP Miyaji Kazuaki, who lost his

SMD race in 2012 but nevertheless secured a seat through the PR list. In Osaka 17th District, Okashita Nobuko had been the party's candidate since 2000, after succeeding her husband, Okashita Masahiro. Masahiro was the party's candidate in 1996 but died suddenly in 1998. Nobuko won election in the district twice, in 2000 and 2005, but lost in 2009 and 2012. In 2014, the party replaced her with her thirty-nine-year-old son, Okashita Shōhei, who was already a member of the Osaka Prefectural Assembly. Shōhei lost to incumbent Baba Nobuyuki of the Japan Innovation Party (previously JRP) but secured a seat through the PR list. In Gunma 1st District, the local LDP prefectural branch considered replacing scandal-prone incumbent Sata Genichirō with former prime minister Nakasone Yasuhiro's thirty-two-year-old grandson Nakasone Yasutaka, but ultimately decided to stick with Sata.[70] Yasutaka's father, former cabinet minister Nakasone Hirofumi, is a member of the House of Councillors. After graduating from the same master's program in international and public affairs at Columbia University as Koizumi Shinjirō and Katō Ayuko, and working for some years at JP Morgan, Yasutaka had started working as his father's secretary in preparation for his eventual entry into politics. After 2014, however, it was decided that Sata would be replaced in the following election with Omi Asako, another legacy candidate who was elected in 2014 as a pure PR list candidate but whose father, Omi Kōji, represented Gunma 1st District prior to Sata (Yasutaka was ultimately given a list nomination and won election in 2017).

HOW MUCH REAL CHANGE?

Even though the differences in the percentages of new legacy candidates over time in Figure 4.5 and under each institutional setting in Figure 4.6 appear to confirm the theoretical expectations about the effect of electoral and party institutions on dynastic candidate selection laid out in Chapter 3, it should be clear from the preceding discussion that legacy candidates have by no means disappeared. Indeed, the differences in the percentage of legacy candidates across institutional settings belie the fact that the raw number of legacy candidates before and after electoral reform did not change drastically. The total number of legacy candidates actually increased in 1996 among all candidates, from 206 to 219 candidates, and the number in the LDP dropped only slightly, from 133 to 126 candidates (Table A.7 in Appendix A). Until the LDP's defeat in 2009 flushed out a number of older legacy candidates, the raw number of legacy candidates within the party remained fairly constant (it fell from 120 in 2009 to 95 in 2012). The drop in the percentage of legacy candidates immediately after electoral reform instead partly reflects an influx of new non-legacy candidates. From 1976 to 1993, an average of 891 candidates ran in each election (including by-elections held after the general election). In contrast, the average number of candidates from 1996 to 2014 was 1,345 candidates. In the LDP, there were an average of 319 candidates each election in the prereform period, compared to 346 in the postreform period.

The same explanation helps to account for the decline in the percentage of legacy candidates among new recruits. From 1976 to 2014, a total of 5,486 first-time candidates ran in a general election or by-election for the House of Representatives, including 752 LDP candidates. In the period prior to electoral reform, the LDP nominated 230 new candidates—an average of thirty-three each election (with the exception of 1980, when only six new LDP candidates ran, including one candidate who first ran in a by-election). Of these new candidates, one hundred were legacy candidates—an average of fourteen each election—and sixty-four of them directly inherited their seats as hereditary candidates. In the postreform period from 1996 to 2014, the party nominated seventy-eight new legacy candidates, an average of eleven each election, and forty-four of these legacy candidates were hereditary candidates.

Thus, the raw number of new legacy candidates nominated after electoral reform declined only modestly, even though legacy candidates comprise a significantly smaller share of the party's overall number of candidates. The 2003 election represents the zenith of dynastic candidate selection in the postreform period, with seventeen out of sixty new LDP candidates (28 percent) having family ties to a previous MP. An additional legacy candidate was elected in a by-election shortly after the election. The relatively large percentage in 2014 for the LDP is a result of very few retirements between the 2012 and 2014 elections. Only thirty-six new candidates were nominated, so the six legacy candidates represented 17 percent of new candidates. The difference in the number of new legacy candidates in the LDP and their percentage share within the party begs the question of whether there has actually been a change in the demand incentives for dynastic recruitment at the candidate level as a result of the electoral reform or subsequent party reforms. It would appear that legacy candidates are getting nominated in similar numbers in the postreform period as in the prereform period—the difference is just that there are now many more nominations to go around.

It may therefore be questionable whether the decline in the percentage of new legacy candidates represents a decrease in proportional supply of legacy hopefuls or a decrease in proportional demand for such candidates by the LDP party organization.

If the electoral system and new recruitment methods generate fewer demand-side incentives for parties to recruit legacies, why do they continue to persist at all in recent elections? The reason is that the new institutional environment has reduced the proportional demand for legacy candidates by party actors but has not drastically suppressed the supply of potential legacy candidates. There continues to be a fair number of legacy hopefuls who would like to get the nomination of the party and follow in the footsteps of their predecessors. If these potential legacy candidates are the children of powerful incumbents with high levels of support in the district, the LDP has little incentive to deny them the nomination and risk that they run under a different party label and threaten the party's electoral prospects in the district. The struggles and controversy that have characterized dynastic candidate selection decisions since 2009 would certainly point in this direction. LDP veteran MP and former minister of state for defense Ōno Yoshinori of Kagawa 3rd District (prior to his son Keitarō getting the nomination in 2012) provides some insight into the sometimes tense relationship between the party and strong family dynasties: "When I retire, my son will have to go through an open-recruitment contest to get the nomination. If the party doesn't give it to him, I will not help the party during the election [with my kōenkai]. They will be on their own."[71] In elections where the party's support is uncertain, party leaders might be especially eager to lean on the personal support networks and name recognition of legacy candidates like Ōno.

In contrast, the legacy successors of weaker incumbents provide fewer electoral benefits to the party, and may actually be a liability. If the party is again the subject of criticism for its dynastic politics, party leaders may calculate that they have a better chance with a fresh new face than with a weak legacy candidate. Weaker legacy candidates who seek the nomination can be passed over with the hope that a new non-legacy candidate will improve the party's overall image and still fare well electorally. Since reform, there have been many cases of legacy candidates who have had to run as LDP-affiliated independents after being denied the nomination (see Table A.8 in Appendix A). These independent legacy candidates serve as evidence of the LDP's decreasing affinity for some types of legacy candidates in official nominations.

Most important, in contrast to the SNTV period, party leaders no longer have incentives to actively seek out legacy candidates to nominate. When a nomination opens up, if a high-quality legacy candidate seeks the nomination, the party can go with that legacy candidate. But in the case that there is no obvious legacy candidate, the party now has a mechanism for finding a high-quality non-legacy candidate through the open-recruitment system. Gone are the days of distant nephews in faraway prefectures getting a call from kōenkai members or faction leaders asking them to run.

These changes in party demand for legacy candidates can be observed in the types of legacy candidates who get the nomination since reform. Although the raw number of new legacy candidates in the LDP has not changed dramatically, the types of LDP incumbents who are succeeded has changed. In the final seven elections in the prereform period, 15 percent of exiting LDP candidates who had served fewer than seven terms (the average length of tenure) were succeeded by family members. In the first seven elections in the postreform period, in contrast, just 7 percent of such candidates have been succeeded, and 40 percent of these were candidates who died suddenly in office. In contrast, exiting LDP candidates who have served seven or more terms are actually being succeeded in slightly higher proportions than in the prereform period (41 percent compared to 37 percent of such candidates); however, there are fewer such long-serving MPs.

One plausible interpretation of this change is that the supply-side incentives for children of long-serving incumbents to want to enter politics have remained relatively stable while the demand-side incentives to seek out legacy candidates, even among weaker incumbents, have been reduced. Whereas in the past, the family members of LDP candidates with even relatively short careers were sought out and given the nomination, in the elections since electoral reform, long-serving incumbent candidates have been more likely to be succeeded in office than weaker incumbents. Many of these new LDP legacy candidates come from long-existing dynasties, and most of them succeeded a predecessor who was first elected under the old SNTV electoral rules. This suggests that there may be some path dependence on the supply side, in line with a historical institutionalist explanation for how the reforms have affected MPs differently depending on their familiarity and experiences with the previous institutional context of elections under SNTV.

It is now also seemingly less likely for new dynasties to form. Of the 175 first-time LDP legacy candidates from 1958 to 1993, 113 (65 percent) were second-generation candidates, meaning that their predecessor was the only previous family member to serve in national politics. In contrast, only thirty-nine (50 percent) of the seventy-eight first-time legacy candidates in the LDP from 1996 to 2014 were second-generation candidates, and nearly half of the rest (24 percent) came from families that had supplied four or more members to national office. These trends suggest that the decline in new legacy candidate nominations since reform is the result of a decline in demand for such legacies rather than a decline in proportional supply. Recall from the theory outlined in Chapter 3 that at the candidate level in any given institutional context, the supply of candidates is influenced by political capital and motivation. Children of long-serving incumbents (H_1) and those who come from existing family dynasties (H_2) are still likely to have strong personal ambitions to continue the family business in politics, even under the new electoral and party institutions. The observed change in dynastic politics in Japan is instead the result of a proportional decrease in the party demand for legacy candidates when there is no immediate supply.

This shift is best illustrated with the results of a logit regression of *Bequeath* on the interaction between *Prior wins* and a dummy variable for the postreform period. The data sample is again the seven elections before and after electoral reform for a symmetrical window of time.[72] Between 1972 and 1990, there were 313 incumbent LDP candidates (not necessarily MPs) who exited the political scene after running in an SNTV race (whose potential successors would thus be nominated in the last seven elections of the old institutional rules). Between 1993 and 2012, 335 LDP candidates exited the political scene. Their potential successors would thus be recruited and nominated in the postreform period. Figure 4.9 displays the predicted probability of direct hereditary succession for exiting LDP candidates who had served different lengths of tenure in the prereform and postreform periods (FPTP only).

The results illustrate the decrease in the probability of hereditary succession in the postreform period for exiting candidates with few prior wins. Conversely, the predicted probability of hereditary succession at higher lengths of tenure is actually higher after reform. Because the number of observations (candidates) at each number of prior wins is limited, the confidence intervals of the two periods overlap. However, if we group the number of prior wins into quartiles for the prereform period (zero to two

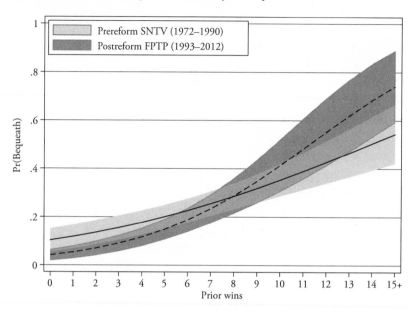

FIGURE 4.9 Length of tenure at exit and hereditary succession, before and after reform

NOTE: Figure shows the predicted probabilities of *Bequeath* = 1 for exiting LDP candidates before (*N* = 313) and after (*N* = 335) electoral reform, at increasing values for *Prior wins*. Excludes pure PR candidates. Candidates with fifteen or more wins are grouped together. Shaded areas represent 95 percent confidence intervals.

terms, three to seven terms, eight to ten terms, eleven to twenty terms) and estimate the predicted probability at these same levels for the postreform period, we do see that LDP candidates who left office after zero to two wins have less than a 5 percent predicted probability of being succeeded in the FPTP era, compared to 13 percent in the final years of SNTV, and this difference is statistically significant.

We can also divide the postreform period into the years before party reforms in 2004 (153 candidates) and after the party reforms (182 candidates). Figure 4.10 displays the predicted probabilities of direct hereditary succession for exiting LDP candidates with different numbers of prior wins (split into quartiles) for the resulting three institutional settings: SNTV, FPTP 1 (prior to 2004), and FPTP 2 (after 2004). Here again, the trend is a decreasing probability of hereditary succession at shorter tenures but less of a change among candidates with longer careers. The most plausible interpretation of these results is that demand for legacy candidates to succeed exiting incumbents with fewer wins has eroded. The legacy candidates who now emerge are the relatives of long-serving incumbents, and these individuals are likely driven by a personal, supply-side motivation to enter politics. The

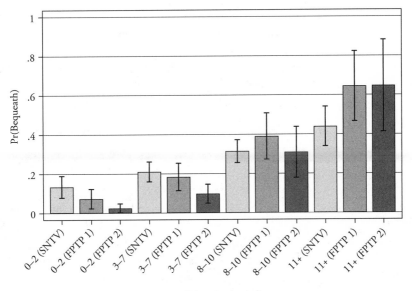

FIGURE 4.10 Length of tenure at exit and hereditary succession, by institutional setting

NOTE: Figure shows the predicted probabilities of *Bequeath* = 1 for exiting LDP candidates before and after electoral and party reform. Number of prior wins is grouped into quartiles. Spikes represent 95 percent confidence intervals.

party has little reason to reject such legacy candidates, but also less reason or need recruit the relatives of weaker incumbents.[73]

Discussion

Electoral institutions are important factors in determining which types of candidates will be attractive to voters and parties in democracies. But candidate recruitment processes within parties can also have an effect on the types of individuals who are selected, either by vesting greater or lesser control in the central party leadership or by opening up the process and range of candidates from which parties can choose.

Many years ago, Austin Ranney (1981, pp. 98–99) reflected on the value of incumbency in candidate selection decisions. In most cases, Ranney noted, parties are predisposed to renominate successful incumbents unless they pose some sort of risk to the unity or policy goals of the party:

> The rationale is obvious. Other things being equal, incumbents are likely to make better candidates than nonincumbents. They are better known to the constituency's voters, it is easier to raise money for their campaigns, and they already

wear the mantle of the elected public official. They are also likely to be better known by the party's selectors and to have served the party for a number of years. And whatever advantages seniority may bring to a legislator and his constituents they will secure by reselecting an incumbent and lose by dropping him in favor of a newcomer. Whatever the reasons may be, the fact is that the greatest single advantage an aspirant for candidacy can have is to hold the office already.

Where the inherited incumbency advantage differs from Ranney's logic is in the phrase "other things being equal." When it comes to the inherited incumbency advantage, the institutional contexts of elections and candidate selection procedures create unequal incentives to recruit and nominate legacy candidates across democracies. The value of a legacy candidate's inherited incumbency advantage will ultimately depend on the institutional context of how candidates are selected and elected. In some cases, this means that, other things being equal, legacy candidates may not be better candidates than non-legacy candidates, at least when it comes to the electoral needs of a party.

The analysis in this chapter demonstrates that Japan's electoral reform and subsequent party reforms in the LDP's candidate recruitment process have decreased the relative attractiveness of legacy candidates to party leaders involved in candidate selection. In Japan's new institutional environment, only the longest-serving or more powerful incumbents are likely to be succeeded by a relative when they exit the political scene. This is mostly a matter of supply rather than demand. Many of the relatives of long-serving incumbents have been planning a political career since before the reforms took effect. The relatives of less important incumbents may also sometimes come forward, but they now face greater competition for a nomination from other contenders, especially when the open-recruitment process is used, and the party may decide that its collective interests in terms of party image, gender diversity, or policy expertise are better served by an outside candidate. Perhaps more important, when a candidate retires without an obvious successor, the party now has a mechanism for finding one, without having to rely on a legacy candidate.

The LDP continues to struggle with the issue of hereditary succession, and political reforms more generally, in part because of path dependence and the continued presence of incumbents in the party who were selected in the previous institutional environment. The reform process in the party continues to be met with the most resistance from these senior members within the party. The tension between younger, reform-minded politicians and the more "old school" of the LDP's leadership can be gleaned from the following anecdote. In 2011, the LDP party reform committee, led by Shiozaki Yasuhisa, drafted a proposal to make the headquarters in Tokyo more modern by installing solar panels, switching to LED lighting, and prohibiting smoking in the building. When members of the reform committee presented the proposal to party vice president Ōshima Tadamori, a heavy chain smoker, he slowly and deliberately lit a cigarette in front of them to show his opposition.[74]

Evidence that dynastic politics in the LDP will continue among senior members can be found by looking at the roster of political secretaries employed by incumbents. Serving as a Diet member's secretary is traditionally one of the important stepping-stones to a political career. Among all members of the House of Representatives elected in 2014, at least 14 percent employed a family member as one of three official secretaries.[75] Most of these members are LDP: of the 292 LDP MPs elected in 2014, 34 of them (12 percent) had male kin relatives serving as secretaries. An additional 13 (4 percent) had female kin secretaries. Although eye-catching in and of itself, this behavior is not simply a reflection of nepotism in doling out taxpayer-funded jobs to family members—many of these family members are being purposefully groomed in preparation to run when the incumbent retires.

A recent example is Wada Yoshiaki, who served as secretary to his father-in-law, eleven-term legacy MP Machimura Nobutaka in Hokkaido 5th District. Machimura was also leader of the intraparty faction within the LDP that included Prime Minister Abe Shinzō. When Machimura died in office at age seventy, Wada was selected to run in the April 2016 by-election, which he won by a bare margin.[76] Kin secretaries like Wada are most common among long-term incumbents who were first elected before the new electoral rules were adopted (i.e., those who have served more than seven terms). While only 11 of the 160 LDP incumbents with three or fewer terms (7 percent) had kin secretaries (perhaps due to their younger age), 9 of the 20 LDP incumbents who served ten or more terms (45 percent) had kin serving as their secretaries, including Machimura and other long-serving legacy MPs like Tanigaki Sadakazu, Ishiba Shigeru, and Nikai Toshihiro. Nikai's son Toshiki ran for mayor of Gobō City in Wakayama Prefecture in 2016, but lost.

Shortly after electoral reform, Margaret McKean and Ethan Scheiner (2000) predicted that dynastic politics in the LDP would continue until the party lost its control of government. The party's 2009 defeat certainly flushed out many existing dynasties, and the new open-recruitment process has prevented several legacy hopefuls from getting the party's nomination. Yet many of the older generation of LDP incumbents and their offspring still want to practice politics like a family vocation. Most of these potential legacy candidates will win the nomination if they seek it. However, the party may decide to pass over others, and if more competitive elections mean that party turnover becomes more regular in the future, fewer and fewer of the new generation of MPs will reach the levels of seniority that have been so heavily associated with the supply of dynasties in Japan. Even so, it is hard not to be pessimistic about whether the LDP will ever fully overcome its predilection for dynastic politics.

The sun appears to be setting on Japan's scions, but it will be twilight for at least a few more elections.

FIVE

Election
The Inherited Incumbency Advantage

> We'd all like to vote for the best man, but he's never
> a candidate.
>
> —*Kin Hubbard*

In this chapter, we shift focus from the advantages that legacy candidates enjoy in candidate selection, to the advantages they enjoy in elections. Just as the incumbency advantage, in terms of votes, can be defined as the additional electoral support that accrues to a candidate by virtue of his or her status as an incumbent, the inherited incumbency advantage in terms of votes can be defined as the additional electoral support enjoyed by a first-time legacy candidate by virtue of his or her family ties to a previous incumbent. The mechanisms behind the inherited incumbency advantage might include better name recognition, financial resources, connections to important political actors or groups that can mobilize votes at election time, an established reputation for service or a particular representational style, differences in prior experience or quality, or differences in the districts in which they choose to run or the number of challengers they face. The inherited incumbency advantage is particularly relevant when candidates directly succeed their predecessors as hereditary candidates, as is often the case in Japan.

In the previous chapter, it was assumed that party actors involved in candidate selection will favor legacy candidates in part because they anticipate that the legacy candidates will win more votes in the election. As a result, under both SNTV and the FPTP tier of MMM, parties like the LDP have few reasons to reject a legacy candidate who wants to run, particularly if his or her inherited incumbency advantage is expected to be substantial. Under SNTV, however, the anticipated electoral advantages of legacy candidates were so great that party actors actively sought them out, even to succeed weaker candidates. But exactly how much better do legacy candidates perform in elections, and what are the sources of this advantage? What makes a legacy candidate electorally valuable to parties, especially the LDP? Do legacy candidates do better in elections simply because of greater name recognition? Or greater financial resources? Or is it something genetic or owing to a privileged upbringing that gives legacy candidates higher ex ante quality? Is it because legacy candidates tend to deter other potential challengers from competition? Or is it because legacy candidates tend to be selected to run in districts or jiban (subdistrict bailiwicks) that are already considered "safe" thanks to the incumbency advantage of their predecessors or the historical strength of the party? Finally, how does the inherited incumbency advantage vary under different institutional contexts?

Two examples help to illustrate the complexities in evaluating the inherited incumbency advantage. The first comes from the Katō dynasty in Yamagata Prefecture. When Katō Kōichi first ran for the House of Representatives in 1972 at the age of thirty-three, there had been a two-election gap since his father, Katō Seizō, died in office. Seizō died in 1965 at the age of sixty-four, two years after finishing first in the four-member Yamagata 2nd District and securing his fifth term in office. In the 1967 and 1969 elections, the jiban was "kept warm" by two other LDP candidates, each of whom failed to win a seat. However, when Kōichi ran, he came in second, less than a percentage point shy of the leading candidate. From 1979 until 1993, he was the first-place winner, often with more than a third of the vote, and served in cabinet on three occasions: twice as minister of state for defense (1984–1986) and once as chief cabinet secretary (1991–1992). In the first two elections after electoral reform in 1994, now in Yamagata 4th District, he faced only weak opposition, and his vote share doubled—to 65.8 percent in 1996 and 72 percent in 2000.

In 2002, Katō had to resign because of a tax law violation committed by his secretary, and the seat was briefly held by political scientist Saitō Jun, who paused his PhD studies at Yale University to run for the seat under the DPJ label. However, Katō won the seat back in 2003, again with nearly 60 percent of the vote. Prior to the 2012 election, the LDP mandated that any candidate older than seventy at the time of the election could not be dual listed in PR. Unfortunately for Katō, he narrowly lost that election (by 1,465 votes, a margin of less than 1 percentage point) to a popular LDP-affiliated former mayor, Abe Jūichi, who ran as an independent after failing to get the party nomination over Katō. In 2014, the LDP held an open-recruitment contest to determine Katō's successor, but his daughter, Ayuko, was the only applicant. Abe, the incumbent, initially expressed interest in getting the official nomination of the party but decided not to enter the contest due to a requirement imposed by the local prefectural branch that each person seeking the nomination pledge to stand down if they did not win a preselection vote of local party members. Katō Ayuko was considered the favorite to win that vote even though Abe had defeated her father in the previous election, so Abe decided to continue running as an independent. Another potential applicant, LDP House of Councillors member Satō Yukari, expressed interest in the nomination, but ultimately decided to run from Osaka 11th District instead.[1]

Katō Ayuko was young (thirty-five years old) and relatively inexperienced compared to Abe, but she was well connected. She had studied for a master's degree in international and public affairs at Columbia University along with another famous legacy candidate, Koizumi Shinjirō, and had worked as a secretary for LDP MP Noda Seiko, as well as for her own father. Moreover, she had chosen to keep her recognizable family name when she married.[2] With the official nomination secured, she went on to win back her "family seat" in 2014 by a margin nearly as thin as her father had lost it in 2012 — just 1,488 votes.

The second example comes from the Ōno dynasty in Kagawa Prefecture. Ōno Yoshinori was born in Taiwan in 1935 during the period of Japanese colonial rule, but he moved to Kagawa Prefecture at the close of World War II. His father served as administrative vice-governor in the prefecture (a bureaucratic post). Ōno graduated from the University of Tokyo with a law degree and began his own successful career as a bureaucrat in the Ministry of Finance, which included a period of study as a Fulbright scholar at the University of Pennsylvania. After marrying the daughter of LDP MP Katō Tsunetarō of Kagawa 2nd District (no relation to the Katō family of Yamagata), he set his sights on a political career. In 1978, he ran and lost in the Kagawa Prefecture gubernatorial election, a loss that he partially attributes to his family connections:

> There was a popular book at the time by Shiba Ryōtarō about stealing the entire country [*Kunitori Monogatari*, 1965]. My father-in-law was doing business in Kagawa and was at the time a member of the House of Representatives. Voters were shouting, "Katō is trying to steal Kagawa Prefecture by making his son-in-law governor!"[3]

Ōno would have to wait until his father-in-law retired in 1986 to get his break. In that election, he inherited the kōenkai of Katō and went on to finish second place in the three-member district, with 25 percent of the vote, and nearly twelve thousand more votes than Katō earned in the previous election in 1983. He consecutively won reelection in the decades to follow, and even served as minister of state in charge of the defense agency (later to become the Ministry of Defense) in the cabinet of Prime Minister Koizumi in 2004. In 2012, he announced his retirement in advance of that year's general election. His son (and secretary), Ōno Keitarō, applied for and won the LDP's open-recruitment contest (in what is now Kagawa 3rd District), and was easily elected to his father's former seat with 63 percent of the vote—facing opposition only from a JCP candidate and an SDP candidate. The DPJ did not bother to field a challenger. In 2014, Keitarō was reelected with 68 percent of the vote, again facing opposition only from the JCP and SDP.

The examples of the Katō and Ōno dynasties illustrate some of the ways in which the inherited incumbency advantage may operate and how it differs across the two electoral system contexts of SNTV and FPTP. Katō Kōichi was able to win his first election, even though he did not directly succeed his father, and even though his father had only won five times and had never served in cabinet. After his first election, Katō's own incumbency advantage grew and became even stronger after electoral reform in 1994. When his daughter Ayuko sought the nomination in 2014, her powerful ties scared off potential challengers in the open-recruitment contest, and she easily won the nomination and went on to defeat the incumbent. At the same time, she had an advantage in terms of her name recognition, close connections to other party leaders, experience working as a political secretary, and opportunities for higher education abroad that were no doubt in part a result of her privileged upbringing.

Ōno Yoshinori did not enjoy the same kind of advantages in name recognition, as he did not adopt his father-in-law's surname. He nevertheless was successful in his first election after inheriting Katō's kōenkai. His son Keitarō, however, benefited from name recognition, the political connections developed during his time as secretary to his father, and the deterrence of challengers in his first election. If a legacy candidate like Ōno is successful in deterring challengers and winning his or her first election, then the inherited incumbency advantage is transformed into an incumbency advantage in subsequent elections. More important, because new legacy candidates in SMDs under the MMM system tend to be the close relatives of powerful incumbents, the inherited incumbency advantage they enjoy may be much higher than the average legacy candidate's advantage under the SNTV system.

Aside from its perceived value to parties in candidate selection decisions, how strong is the actual electoral effect of the inherited incumbency advantage? In this chapter, the candidate-level data from JHRED are used to evaluate whether and how legacy ties function as a form of inherited incumbency advantage in elections, after the decision to run. Do legacy candidates actually perform better in their first election attempt than nonlegacy candidates, controlling for other features of the candidates or district? If so, how large is their inherited incumbency advantage, and what are its most important components—name recognition, higher wealth or campaign resources, deterrence of challengers, or strength of the jiban? Finally, how does the inherited incumbency advantage change when a country like Japan moves toward more party-centered elections?

The existing scholarly literature on the incumbency advantage is based predominantly on models of two-party competition in FPTP races in the United States (e.g., between a Democratic Party candidate and a Republican Party candidate), although some notable attempts have been made to extend the logic of these models to MMD contexts. After briefly reviewing this literature and defining the concept of an inherited incumbency advantage, the first part of this chapter examines whether such an inherited incumbency advantage applies to the SNTV context of Japanese elections up until 1993, looking at the advantage in terms of votes, electoral success, and the deterrence of challengers. The second part of the chapter then examines the changes that have occurred since the introduction of SMDs in the MMM system. Finally, the third part of the chapter explores survey data from recent election years to get a sense of voters' role in the perpetuation of political dynasties in Japan.

Conceptually, the SNTV system can be thought of as an extension of FPTP in which the voting rule is instead first-M-past-the-post (Reed, 1990). Conversely, FPTP is equivalent to using the SNTV voting rule where $M = 1$. Given that the voting rule is conceptually the same, the two systems will be referred to in the remainder of this chapter by the differences in district magnitude: MMD or SMD. In the prereform MMDs, the existence of jiban in the LDP, and the practice of transferring jiban to both hereditary and non-hereditary successors provides an opportunity to analyze the potential mechanisms behind the inherited incumbency advantage of new hereditary candidates. Within the group of hereditary successors, there is also variation in terms of blood relatives (e.g., sons) and nonblood relatives (e.g., sons-in-law, some of whom adopted the family name). The introduction of SMDs has decreased the personalized nature of jiban (due to the elimination of intraparty competition and the increasing development of party-centered voting), but individual districts may still be treated as jiban, even if many have become more like "party" jiban. The postreform SMDs also allow for a more straightforward analysis of the inherited incumbency advantage that can apply many of the same methods used in the American politics literature to study the incumbency advantage.

As revealed in the previous chapter, compared to the prereform period, the legacy candidates who tend to emerge in the postreform period have more often been the relatives of powerful, long-serving incumbents from existing dynasties. As a result, we might expect them to enjoy greater electoral advantages than their prereform counterparts. In contrast, elections under the new SMDs have generated more interparty competition relative to the prereform period, when most competition was between candidates within the same ideological camp. The empirical analysis in this chapter sheds light on how the institutional reforms have affected the nature of the inherited incumbency advantage. New legacy candidates in both institutional environments are decidedly advantaged over non-legacy candidates. However, there is also a selection effect in terms of where legacy candidates emerge, which contributes to the observed advantage. In the postreform period, legacy candidates are most likely to get nominated in party strongholds where any new candidate might have been similarly successful. Evidence from traditional surveys and a conjoint survey experiment suggests that voters in Japan do not like the idea of dynasties in the abstract sense, even as they continue to elect specific legacy candidates in their own local districts.

The Incumbency Advantage as a Heritable Asset

The incumbency advantage has possibly been the most frequently analyzed phenomenon in American electoral politics since Robert Erikson (1971) and David Mayhew (1974) called attention to it in the 1970s. Explanations for why incumbents do better in elections have focused on three possible components: (1) the direct advantages of being in office (e.g., name recognition and other perquisites of office), and indirect advantages owing to (2) the differential quality of incumbents from on-the-job experience and (3) the deterrence of high-quality challengers.

There are two basic approaches to measuring the incumbency advantage: a *vote-denominated* measure (what was the candidate's share of the vote?) and an *outcome-denominated* measure (did the candidate win or lose the race?). A great deal of scholarship in the American context has been devoted to measuring the incumbency advantage in terms of votes (e.g., Gelman and King, 1990; Levitt and Wolfram, 1997; Ansolabehere, Snyder, and Stewart, 2000). These studies of the vote-denominated measure of the incumbency advantage have concluded that, since the 1980s, incumbents in US congressional elections have generally enjoyed a vote advantage of around 7 to 10 percentage points. In contrast, the vote advantage for incumbents tends to be lower (5 to 6 percentage points) in the MMD context of state-level legislative elections (Cox and Morgenstern, 1995; Hirano and Snyder, 2009).

But since the vote-denominated measure of the incumbency advantage may vary over time without having a strong effect on the actual outcome of the race (e.g., Jacobson, 1987; Jewell and Breaux, 1988), an alternative approach to measuring the incumbency advantage is to focus simply on the probability that an incumbent will win his or her first reelection attempt (an outcome-denominated measure of the incumbency advantage). Particularly in the context of MMD elections, this approach may be more appropriate given the variation in the number of copartisan candidates and challengers of multiple parties in a given election, which makes the conventional vote-denominated measure for SMD elections—a candidate's share of the two-party vote—a less relevant measure. Using the probability of reelection as the dependent variable, John Carey, Richard Niemi, and Lynda Powell (2000) find that incumbents in MMD state legislative elections are more vulnerable than their SMD counterparts.

Since the seminal work of David S. Lee (2008), regression discontinuity designs have become popular for evaluating the *causal effect* of winning office on the incumbency advantage. This method helps to separate out some of the ex ante quality effects that make incumbents good candidates in the first place (and hence cannot be attributed to the treatment of winning office). However, these studies often focus on the party incumbency advantage rather than the personal incumbency advantage—with a few notable exceptions (e.g., Fowler and Hall, 2014; Erikson and Titiunik, 2015). In addition, while RD designs are useful for evaluating the effect of incumbency on the future careers of family members (Dal Bó, Dal Bó, and Snyder, 2009; Querubín, 2016; van Coppenolle, 2017; Fiva and Smith, 2018), they are less suited to measuring the inherited incumbency advantage in terms of votes earned in a candidate's first election attempt. Kenichi Ariga (2015) applies an RD design to Japan's pre-1994 MMD elections and finds no evidence that marginal incumbents enjoy an incumbency advantage under MMD. However, the RD results in Chapter 4 demonstrate that marginal winners in their final election attempt were more likely than marginal losers to be succeeded by a relative in the next election. In an RD analysis of close elections in the postreform FPTP tier, Ariga et al. (2016) similarly find no evidence of an incumbency advantage. However, too few of the predecessors to hereditary candidates in the postreform period are close enough to the margins to evaluate the effect of incumbency on dynastic succession using an RD design.

The incumbency advantage is generally believed to be weaker in MMD elections because the vote share required to secure a victory in MMDs is much lower (at most 17 percent in a five-member district, though often much lower when there are many candidates), and individual candidates often must face both interparty and intraparty (or intracamp) challengers. In addition, the lower threshold to victory decreases certainty about each candidate's electoral prospects and may result in an increased number of challengers. Finally, strategic voters may desert top vote earners in favor of the runners-up from the previous election (or the runners-up may actively pursue voters with this appeal), which can cost the election for other marginal candidates.

Studies of the deterrence, or "scare-off," effect in US congressional elections have found that incumbents are often faced with low-quality challengers (e.g., Jacobson and Kernell, 1983; Gordon, Huber, and Landa, 2007). Basically, the story goes that when faced with an incumbent candidate in a district, would-be challengers of higher "quality" (generally defined as having prior elective experience, especially at the local level) will strategically opt to sit out the race and wait until their prospects for victory are higher. The result is that the challengers who do enter the race are of lower quality. These lower-quality challengers pose less of an electoral threat to the incumbent and help to keep him or her in office. In MMDs, the scare-off effect is likely to be lower generally, given the greater permissiveness of the system, greater uncertainty, and increased vulnerability of marginal incumbents. Indeed, Shigeo Hirano and James Snyder (2009, p. 303) find little evidence that an additional incumbent candidate has a scare-off effect on the quality of opposition challengers in MMD contests, although their findings do indicate a slight effect in terms of the number of opposition challengers. The lack of a scare-off effect in MMD elections underscores the importance of the personal-vote-earning ability of candidates in MMD elections, as argued in the comparative theory of dynastic candidate selection from Chapter 3.

How does the well-documented incumbency advantage translate to elections in which a legacy candidate runs for the first time? The aggregate data provide some prima facie support for the existence of an inherited incumbency advantage in both MMD and SMD elections. Table 5.1 gives descriptive statistics on the "success rates" for all non-legacy and legacy candidates, as well as the success rates for the subsample of first-time candidates, split by electoral system period (pure PR candidates are excluded for the postreform period). Among all candidates, legacy candidates won their district races in 80 percent of cases under MMD, compared to a success rate of just 44 percent for non-legacy candidates. Among first-time candidates under MMD, the success rate for non-legacy candidates was only 20 percent. The success rate for first-time legacy candidates was 60 percent. The success rate among the subset of first-time legacy candidates who directly succeeded their predecessor (hereditary candidates) was slightly higher (62 percent). For comparison, the success rate for incumbents under MMD was 77 percent.

In the postreform SMDs, a candidate can either win his or her district race outright, or (if dual listed) might lose the race but still secure a seat through the party's PR list (a "zombie" winner). However, because of the main parties' practice of ranking dual-listed candidates at the same position and using the "best-loser" calculation to determine which SMD losers will get PR seats (as described in Chapter 4), zombies tend to be competitive candidates who only narrowly lost. The district success rate for all non-legacy and legacy candidates in the postreform SMDs resembles the success rates for first-time non-legacy and legacy candidates in the prereform period, and is higher if zombie winners are included. Among first-time candidates in the postreform period, the success rate is just 8 percent for non-legacy candidates, and just 37 percent for legacy candidates. However, for postreform

TABLE 5.1

Success rates of non-legacy and legacy candidates across electoral systems

	ALL CANDIDATES		LDP CANDIDATES	
	Win district	Zombie	Win district	Zombie
Prereform MMD				
All candidates				
Non-legacy	44.23		76.77	
Legacy	79.76		86.71	
Overall	48.61		79.98	
First-time candidates				
Non-legacy	20.02		49.83	
Legacy	59.95		74.03	
(Hereditary)	(61.76)		(76.53)	
Overall	23.11		59.03	
Postreform SMD				
All candidates				
Non-legacy	20.16	8.98	56.08	16.11
Legacy	63.39	10.93	75.99	7.56
Overall	26.63	9.27	63.51	12.92
First-time candidates				
Non-legacy	7.52	5.16	40.32	18.39
Legacy	37.42	14.19	56.94	13.89
(Hereditary)	53.52	7.04	66.67	11.11
Overall	8.91	5.58	43.46	17.54

SOURCE: JHRED.

NOTE: Entries represent the percentage of candidates of each type who won election in a district race (or were elected as "zombies" through the PR list). Sample for all candidates is elections from 1947 to 2014. Sample for LDP is elections from 1958 to 2014. By-election candidates are included. Pure PR list candidates are excluded. Candidates who secured a seat after the election through list promotion (*kuriage tōsen*) are counted as losing. Sample for first-time candidates excludes individuals who ran for the prewar House of Representatives or in 1946 but does not exclude candidates from the House of Councillors.

hereditary candidates, the success rate is still high: 54 percent. If zombie winners are included, new postreform hereditary candidates are almost equally as successful as new hereditary candidates were in the prereform period. For comparison, the success rate (winning the SMD) for the postreform period is 64 percent for SMD incumbents, 32 percent for zombie incumbents, and

30 percent for pure PR incumbents who moved into an SMD. In other words, first-time hereditary candidates have only a 10-percentage-point lower success rate than incumbents but a 20-percentage-point *higher* success rate than incumbents who were elected through the PR list.

Although these aggregate patterns are interesting, it is more informative to look at the changes for LDP candidates across the two institutional contexts. Dynastic politics has been most prevalent within the LDP, so the differential rates of success in the aggregate data could be a result of differential rates of success for LDP candidates generally. For LDP candidates, the difference in success rates in the prereform period is most notable among first-time candidates. Only half of all non-legacy candidates were successful in their first election attempt, in contrast to three quarters of all legacy (and hereditary) candidates. For comparison, the success rate of LDP incumbents during this period was 85 percent. In the postreform SMDs, the success rate for first-time LDP candidates is lower for both non-legacy and legacy candidates relative to the MMD period but is still much higher for legacy candidates (57 percent compared to 40 percent). Moreover, the success rate for new hereditary candidates in the LDP in the SMD period is 67 percent. If zombie winners are included, 78 percent of first-time LDP hereditary candidates were successful. For comparison, the success rate (winning the SMD) for LDP incumbents in the postreform period was 76 percent for SMD incumbents, 45 percent for zombie incumbents, and 50 percent for pure PR incumbents who moved into an SMD. Once again, when it comes to electoral success, first-time hereditary candidates under both MMD and SMD appear to have more in common with incumbents than with other first-time candidates.

The patterns in success rates indicate that legacy candidates tend to enjoy an inherited incumbency advantage, but how large is the advantage in terms of votes, and what are its sources? Legacy candidates, and especially hereditary candidates, are likely to possess many of the direct benefits of incumbency (e.g., name recognition, connections to donors, established campaign organizations), as well as the indirect advantages of higher (ex ante) quality and the deterrence of challengers. Just as high-quality challengers might shy away from running against an incumbent candidate, would-be non-legacy candidates of high quality might also be deterred from running when faced with a legacy candidate if they anticipate that the legacy candidate will do well. In contrast, when a legacy candidate runs, traditional measures of quality involving prior elective experience might have less of an effect—if you are a Kennedy or a Koizumi, does it matter that you have not first served in local office? Indeed, if name recognition is the key to election, then a legacy candidate can have fewer traditional attributes of "quality" and still be expected to perform well in elections. The empirical record in Chapter 2 confirmed that legacy candidates are less likely to have had prior experience in public office than their non-legacy counterparts.

Only a few previous studies have sought to quantify the inherited incumbency advantage in elections, each in the context of stable electoral system conditions. For example, empirical evidence of the advantage has been found in Ireland, where the STV system makes the electoral system context similar to prereform SNTV in Japan (Smith and Martin, 2017). Irish legacy candidates since 1944 have enjoyed a roughly 20-percentage-point higher probability of election than non-legacy copartisans and have tended to capture between 12 and 15 percentage points more of the electoral (Droop) quota required to secure a seat with first-preference votes. The Droop quota, measured as

$$\left(\frac{Total\ valid\ votes}{M+1} \right) + 1,$$

is the absolute minimum number of votes that a candidate must earn to guarantee election in an MMD contest (Droop, 1881). For Ireland's MMDs, a candidate's share of the Droop quota after first-preference votes are tallied serves as a normalized measure of electoral strength across districts with varying magnitude.

In an SMD context, Brian Feinstein (2010) analyzes all open-seat races for the US House of Representatives from 1994 to 2006. Although he finds no evidence that legacy candidates have been of higher quality than non-legacy candidates, legacy candidates nevertheless fared better electorally, earning roughly 59 percent of the vote on average, compared to 48 percent for first-generation candidates. Controlling for differences in experience, campaign expenditures, and the partisanship of the district, he estimates that the inherited incumbency advantage is roughly 3 to 4 percentage points, roughly half the size of the incumbency advantage enjoyed by House members in the 1980s and 1990s. Feinstein attributes the advantage to name recognition, as he is unable to verify any concomitant scare-off effect in terms of the relative quality of non-legacy challengers in open races featuring legacy candidates, nor does he find any significant advantage in terms of fundraising. For SMD races in the Philippines, Pablo Querubín (2016) estimates that first-time congressional and gubernatorial legacy candidates from 1946 to 2007 enjoyed an even larger vote share advantage—up to 15 percentage points. Finally, two recent studies have estimated the inherited incumbency advantage in SMDs in Japan on a limited sample of elections and candidates. Looking only at the advantage of hereditary candidates (not all legacy candidates) in the 2005 general election, Yasushi Asako, Takeshi Iida, Tetsuya Matsubayashi, and Michiko Ueda (2015) find that the average vote share of hereditary candidates is 5 percentage points higher than other candidates, and the probability of winning the SMD race is 22 percentage points higher. In a second study looking only at hereditary candidates, but from 2000 to 2005, Fukumoto Kentarō and Nakagawa Kaoru (2013) find that hereditary candidates perform at least as well as continuing candidates.

Empirical Evidence: How Much Advantage?

The analysis in this chapter builds on these studies to evaluate the inherited incumbency advantage of legacy candidates in Japan using a variety of measures and approaches. The case of Japan presents a challenge because, unlike SMD races with two-party competition, MMD elections featured much greater variation in the number of copartisan and opposition party candidates facing a first-time legacy candidate. Since the switch to MMM, candidates in SMD races still often face multiple opponents, but competition in the majority of districts between 2000 and 2009 converged to the two-party competition predicted by Duverger's Law (Duverger, 1954), with the two largest parties capturing over 80 percent of the votes and over 90 percent of the SMD seats. The remaining SMD seats are usually held by independents who split from one of the two major parties (most often the LDP) or Kōmeitō candidates running in districts as part of a coalition stand-down agreement with the LDP. The emergence of the Third Force parties in 2012 and 2014 complicates the nature of competition in the SMD tier, yet at the same time, few new legacy candidates ran in those elections. The ability for a losing SMD candidate to earn a seat in the House of Representatives through dual listing in the PR tier also alters the calculations of would-be challengers to legacy candidates, such that those who might otherwise be deterred from running will still attempt to compete in hopes of securing a PR seat.

How has the electoral reform and its dual-listing provision altered the electoral dynamics of dynastic politics when it comes to the inherited incumbency advantage? Since the LDP is the only major party to span the entire time period, the focus of the empirical analysis in this chapter is on its candidates, as well as LDP-affiliated independents.

THE INHERITED INCUMBENCY ADVANTAGE IN MMD ELECTIONS

Measuring the inherited incumbency advantage in terms of votes is complicated in MMD elections because each race can vary in terms of the number of competitors, the characteristics of those competitors (e.g., incumbency, quality), and the partisan leanings of the district. In the case of Japan, a candidate from the LDP not only faced competition from the candidates of other parties, such as the JSP, but also faced intraparty competition from other conservatives—indeed, this is where competition was often most fierce. In general, because of the much lower threshold for victory under MMD, as compared to SMD, both the incumbency advantage, and by extension the inherited incumbency advantage, should be lower under MMD than under SMD.

Only a handful of previous studies have analyzed the incumbency advantage in MMD races. Unfortunately, none of the existing studies provides a model that can be easily adapted to analyzing the inherited incumbency advantage in Japan's MMDs. For example, Gary Cox and Scott Morgenstern (1995) extend the logic of the unbiased measure of incumbency advantage first introduced by Andrew Gelman and Gary King (1990) to free-for-all (M nontransferable votes for M seats, or MNTV) MMD races in forty US states from 1970 to 1986, and that find the vote-denominated incumbency advantage (normalized using the Droop quota to account for variations in M) increased at a much lower rate in MMD races over the time period studied than it did in SMD races. Yet they confine their analysis to fully contested races where M Democratic candidates faced M Republican candidates, and their measure of the vote advantage is based on the combined vote share of all copartisan candidates given varying combinations of incumbency within each party's group of candidates. These conditions deviate from the MMD context of Japanese elections, where each voter casts a single vote to fill M seats, and where few races featured the same number of LDP candidates competing against the same number of JSP candidates. Most races also featured competition from additional parties, making it difficult to apply the same party vote share model. More important, the focus on two-party vote share is less relevant to Japanese MMDs, where most of an LDP candidate's competition for votes was against copartisan candidates or LDP-affiliated independent candidates seeking to get the support of conservative voters.

Hirano and Snyder (2009) also focus on fully contested free-for-all races in US state legislative elections but employ pairwise comparisons between incumbents and new candidates from the same party in the same race. For example, in a two-seat district, a voter might choose between two Democrats, an incumbent and a newcomer, and two Republicans (of varying combinations). If all voters choose a "straight ticket" party vote (both votes given to the two copartisan candidates), the result should be that the two Democrats get the same share of the vote. Thus, an incumbent Democrat's greater share of the vote over his or her copartisan running mate can be interpreted as a measure of the incumbency advantage. This is a clever and innovative solution for testing the incumbency advantage in two-member state legislative MMDs in the US but is less adaptable to Japanese MMD elections, where M ranged in most cases from three to five, and the number of copartisan and opposition party candidates varied considerably.

Two other studies focus on the electoral vulnerability of MMD incumbents. Carey, Niemi, and Powell (2000) argue that the outcome-denominated measure of electoral success is more appropriate for MMD elections, although their primary focus is comparing incumbency reelection probabilities between "traditional" SMD races, "post" MMD contests (which essentially function like SMDs), and free-for-all MMD elections. They find that incumbents in both types of MMD races are more vulnerable to defeat than their counterparts in SMD races. Further evidence of the electoral vulnerability of incumbents under MMD is suggested by Ariga (2015), who employs an RD design using Japanese elections from 1958 to 1993 to show that marginal winners did no better than marginal losers in the next election. Ariga's study moves our knowledge about the incumbency advantage in MMD systems beyond the context of US state-level legislative elections; yet because of the methodology employed and its focus on marginal candidates, it does not paint a complete picture of the incumbency advantage in Japan's MMDs, nor is it particularly useful for studying the realized inherited incumbency advantage in terms of vote shares.

The lack of adaptable models for measuring the incumbency advantage in Japan's preform MMD system makes measuring the inherited incumbency advantage without bias complicated.[4] But we can still draw comparisons between the MMD and SMD systems by considering the concept of a successor versus the concept of a challenger in each system. Consider that, in both MMD and SMD systems, incumbency is often the most relevant source of information for both voters and potential challengers. However, incumbents eventually retire, which produces a race between two (or sometimes more) nonincumbents for the "open" seat. But the informational cue provided by incumbency (or lack thereof) is different in SMD and MMD elections. Under SMD systems, incumbents normally run again and face one (or sometimes more) "challengers." Losing challengers seldom run again, so the challengers usually change each election. But under MMD systems, both the concept of a challenger and that of an open seat require rethinking.

For example, in an MMD with four seats there will be four incumbents after an election. If one decides not to run in the next election, there will be one open seat but also three incumbents running for reelection. In SMD systems, an open seat means not only that the incumbent must be replaced by a new candidate from his or her own party but also that a candidate from the party that lost the last election has a better chance to win because he or she will not be facing an incumbent. Under SMD systems, an open seat is thus primarily a rare opportunity for the party that lost in the last election. Under MMD systems, however, an open seat will primarily be seen as a rare opportunity for candidates from the retiring incumbent's party. Other parties will normally already have an established candidate in the district, perhaps even an incumbent. Thus, a seat vacated by one party is not necessarily seen as "open" to any other party.

Incumbents in MMD elections can be expected to oppose running another copartisan even under the best of circumstances (Reed and Bolland, 1999). Even when the party insists on fielding an additional candidate, incumbents may sometimes work behind the scenes to assure that the new candidate does not pose an electoral threat (either because he or she is of inferior quality or will run in a different area of the district). However, the open seat still presents a rare opportunity for potential candidates from the retiring incumbent's party, and it is common for more than one candidate from the retiree's own party to compete to take his or her place. These are the conditions that best describe the intraparty competition in the conservative camp under MMD elections in Japan.

Next, consider whether a candidate who is running to replace a retiree from his or her own party should be considered a "challenger." In SMD systems, since there is only one nominated candidate from each party, the candidate who replaces a retiring incumbent is clearly a successor, not a challenger, whether or not he or she is a hereditary candidate. In MMD systems, if only one candidate runs to replace one retiree, both from the same party, the new candidate is also a successor and not a challenger. Indeed, many new MMD candidates in Japan were designated as such by the retiree. However, it was also common for more than one candidate to compete to succeed a retiring incumbent. If two candidates compete to succeed a retiree from a party, should one be considered an intraparty challenger if he or she has less claim to being the retiring incumbent's successor?

Building on these theoretical considerations, the approach we will take here for evaluating the inherited incumbency advantage in MMDs is to use the case of the LDP and LDP-affiliated independents and the concept and measurement of jiban. When an LDP incumbent candidate (winner or loser) retired or died, his or her jiban might have become "open territory" for candidates seeking conservative votes. The stronger the exiting candidate, the greater the number of votes made available to potential new entrants. But because jiban (in the concrete form of kōenkai) were organized around an individual candidate, and not the party, retiring incumbents could "transfer" some of the political resources of their established kōenkai to a chosen successor, either kin (a hereditary candidate) or non-kin. Often the inheritance of resources was complete and direct—the kōenkai organization and other resources, including financial resources, were transferred to a successor intact, and the operation of the jiban "machine" kept going. The successor candidate in these cases thus immediately gained an advantage in his or her first election by having an existing, well-developed support organization to mobilize voters.

Other times, a new LDP candidate might de facto inherit all or part of an outgoing incumbent's jiban simply by being the only new LDP candidate to fill the geographic electoral void left by the previous candidate, much as new candidates from a retiring incumbent's party might similarly be considered successors in an SMD system, as previously discussed. In such cases, even if the kōenkai organization were not transferred directly, many of the previous incumbent's supporters would have found themselves drawn into the new candidate's campaign mobilization activities. These new LDP candidates thus also benefited from capturing the votes of the outgoing incumbent's existing jiban.

In contrast, a new candidate who did not inherit any jiban had to build his or her personal vote from scratch to compete against the established jiban of other candidates in the district. Although an election following the retirement of an incumbent may seem like the most opportune time for a new candidate with no established jiban in the district to attempt to enter politics, such an attempt was often made more difficult by the transfer of that incumbent's jiban to another candidate. The designated successor in most cases would get the official nomination of the party, leaving other hopefuls with only two options: either to give up on running in that election, or contest the election as an independent (or even perhaps a candidate of a smaller conservative party) in hopes of defeating one of the LDP's existing candidates, or possibly a weak JSP incumbent. The LDP played a part in encouraging such candidacies, since successful independent candidates in many cases were given ex post nominations by the party and allowed to rejoin the LDP (see Chapter 4), and ambitious faction leaders sometimes supported such candidates in hopes of increasing their share of members in the party (Nemoto, Pekkanen, and Krauss, 2014).

To examine the differences in the inherited incumbency advantage given different forms of succession in the LDP, we will use a variable in JHRED called *Jiban*, which is a unique numerical code representing each candidate's support base in a district. When a candidate retires or dies, a new candidate is coded as a successor to that candidate's jiban (so the *Jiban* code stays the same) in any one of the following cases: (1) only one candidate from the party retired and only one new candidate ran, (2) a newspaper report or some other source named the new candidate as a successor, or (3) the new candidate was a hereditary candidate. In contrast, we can define an "entrepreneurial" candidate as any new candidate who ran against the established jiban in the district without succeeding any retiring LDP (or LDP-affiliated) candidate.

Thankfully, a great deal of variation exists among new LDP and LDP-affiliated candidates with regard to jiban inheritance, which permits the analysis of not only the resource advantages accrued to non-legacy succes-

sors, but also the additional "name brand" advantages enjoyed by hereditary successors or legacy entrepreneurs. For example, sometimes a legacy
candidate inherited a predecessor's jiban following a gap of one or more
elections, during which time a nonrelated candidate occupied the jiban.
In these cases, while the legacy candidate is considered a successor to the
jiban, he or she is not coded as a hereditary successor. He or she might,
however, still possess name recognition above and beyond that which a non-
legacy successor would enjoy, even though both candidates inherited other
resource advantages. A legacy candidate who did not directly inherit any
jiban, whether of a relative or otherwise, might still benefit substantially
from name recognition even without the extra organizational benefit of an
established jiban and kōenkai. Such cases of "legacy entrepreneurs" sometimes occurred when a predecessor served in the House of Councillors or
in a separate district, or when the predecessor stopped running many years
earlier, and his or her established kōenkai were disbanded before the legacy
candidate entered the arena.

Each first-time conservative candidate can thus be categorized as one of
five mutually exclusive types:

1. A non-legacy entrepreneur
2. A legacy entrepreneur
3. A non-legacy successor (oftentimes the secretary of the previous incumbent)
4. A legacy successor to non-kin, that is, a legacy candidate whose immediate
   predecessor was not a family member (usually because of a gap between family
   members with a non-kin candidate running in the jiban in the interim)
5. A hereditary successor who directly succeeded his or her relative

The difference between types 1 and 2, and between type 3 and types 4 and 5,
help shed light on the "name brand" advantages that legacy candidates enjoy
relative to non-legacy candidates. How much better do first-time hereditary
successors and legacy candidates of all succession (and nonsuccession) types
perform electorally than nonrelated successors or nonrelated entrepreneurial
candidates with no established jiban?

Table 5.2 gives the number and percent of winners among each type of
first-time candidates among LDP-nominated candidates and LDP-affiliated
independent candidates from 1958 to 1993. In addition, the table gives the
mean proportion of the Droop quota (the number of votes that would
guarantee victory in a given M-sized district) earned by candidates in each

TABLE 5.2
Success rates of different types of first-time LDP and LDP-affiliated candidates in MMDs

	WINNER		TOTAL	QUOTA PROPORTION
	(*N*)	(%)	(*N*)	(Mean)
LDP-nominated candidates				
(1) Non-legacy entrepreneur	76	44.44	171	.67
(2) Legacy entrepreneur	20	57.14	35	.75
(3) Non-legacy successor	71	57.26	124	.76
(4) Legacy successor to non-kin	39	81.25	48	.89
(5) Hereditary successor	75	76.53	98	.86
Returning candidate	3,263	82.50	3,955	.93
Total (all candidate types)	3,544	79.98	4,431	.91
LDP-affiliated independents				
(1) Non-legacy entrepreneur	31	12.70	244	.40
(2) Legacy entrepreneur	6	24.00	25	.58
(3) Non-legacy successor	11	23.91	46	.55
(4) Legacy successor to non-kin	5	22.73	22	.51
(5) Hereditary successor	6	20.69	29	.46
Returning candidate	92	23.65	389	.49
Total (all candidate types)	151	20.00	755	.47

SOURCE: JHRED.

NOTE: By-election candidates are included. Candidates who secured a seat after the election through list promotion (*kuriage tōsen*) are counted as losing. The definition of first-time candidate excludes individuals who ran for the prewar House of Representatives or in 1946 but does not exclude candidates from the House of Councillors.

group. This is calculated by taking the candidate's actual share of the vote divided by the Droop quota. For example, in an SMD contest, the Droop quota is equal to 50 percent of the valid votes cast (plus one vote to break a tie). In a five-member district, the quota is 16.7 percent of the valid votes. A value for the quota proportion that is greater than one represents a candidate who could not lose the election no matter how the other votes might be distributed among the other challengers in the district. Candidates with a quota proportion value lower than one can still be elected, depending on the number of other candidates competing. For comparison, the win rates and mean quota proportions for returning candidates (including incumbents) are also shown.

The success rates and quota shares for different types of first-time LDP candidates indicate substantial differences in outcomes depending on legacy status. Just 44 percent of non-legacy entrepreneurs (those who did not inherit a jiban) won their first election, compared to 57 percent of legacy entrepreneurs. Among the first-time candidates who did inherit a jiban, non-legacy successors have the same success rate as legacy entrepreneurs, which suggests that the inherited resources of a kōenkai may be comparable in value to name recognition or family connections in the absence of an inherited kōenkai. Among successors with dynastic family ties, however, the success rates are almost as high as the success rates for returning candidates (which include incumbents and former incumbents). The success rate for legacy candidates who inherited a jiban from a non-kin predecessor (type 4) is nominally higher than that of direct hereditary successors; however, many of these legacy successors ran in the same district as their predecessors but with a gap between elections while another candidate held the jiban, so they are similar to hereditary candidates (and the difference between the two groups is not statistically significant). First-time legacy and hereditary successors also capture a higher proportion of the Droop quota, on average, than other types of successors or entrepreneurs.

Election outcomes and quota proportions appear less dependent on legacy or successor status for LDP-affiliated independent candidates, who do not tend to do well as new candidates regardless of succession. In other words, being a legacy candidate may help get votes, but it may not fully compensate for the value of the LDP's official party label. Then again, there were likely reasons such independents were not given the official party nomination in the first place—that is, the lack of nomination may reflect the lower quality of the candidate, and lower quality will obviously be correlated with worse electoral outcomes. We can get a better sense of the electoral advantage of different types of first-time LDP and LDP-affiliated candidates by regressing election outcomes on categorical dummies for each type with a simple OLS regression, controlling for quality and campaign expenditures.

The baseline regression model takes the following form:

$$Y_{it} = \beta_0 + \beta_1 \textit{Legacy entrepreneur}_{it} + \beta_2 \textit{Non-legacy successor}_{it}$$
$$+ \beta_3 \textit{Legacy successor to non-kin}_{it} + \beta_4 \textit{Hereditary successor}_{it} \qquad (5.1)$$
$$+ \beta_5 \textit{LDP nomination}_{it} + \beta_6 \textit{Quality candidate}_{it} + \beta_7 \textit{Expenditures / limit}_{it} + \epsilon_{it},$$

where *Y* represents one of two dependent variables. The first is a binary variable, *Win,* an outcome-denominated measure of electoral success. The second, *Quota Prop.,* is a vote-denominated measure based on the proportion of the Droop quota obtained by the candidate. The first four explanatory variables are dummy variables for each type of conservative first-time candidate, with type 1, non-legacy entrepreneur, used as the baseline for comparison. *LDP nomination* is whether the candidate received the official LDP nomination, rather than running as an independent; *Quality candidate* is a dummy variable measuring whether the candidate had any prior experience in elective office (House of Councillors, local assembly, governor, or mayor); and *Expenditures/limit* is measured as the proportion of the legal limit for campaign expenditures spent by the candidate in the election. These latter two variables are included to partial out any effect of legacy status on electoral outcomes that might operate through experience and campaign war chests.[5]

Figure 5.1 presents the results for each dependent variable. The specifications presented include district fixed effects, year fixed effects, and controls for gender, age, age-squared, and number of candidates running. The results indicate a significantly greater vote share and probability of election for a first-time conservative candidate who has the official nomination of the LDP, but also significantly better election outcomes for a hereditary successor—as well as a legacy successor to non-kin—relative to other types of first-time candidates. Both types of successors are approximately 30 percentage points more likely to win their first election than a non-legacy entrepreneur. Prior elective experience (i.e., being a "quality" candidate) and spending more money in the election both help but cannot fully explain the electoral advantage enjoyed by legacy candidates. Interestingly, a legacy candidate who runs without inheriting a jiban (legacy entrepreneur) enjoys a greater advantage, on average, than a non-legacy candidate who does inherit a jiban (non-legacy successor).

Another way to evaluate the electoral advantages of being a legacy candidate in MMDs is to focus only on the subset of direct successors—types 3 and 5—where a jiban is inherited without any gap and the only distinguishing difference is that the successor in the latter type was kin (excluding for this reason type 4 candidates). This approach allows us to control for factors like the strength of the jiban being succeeded and the number of other new

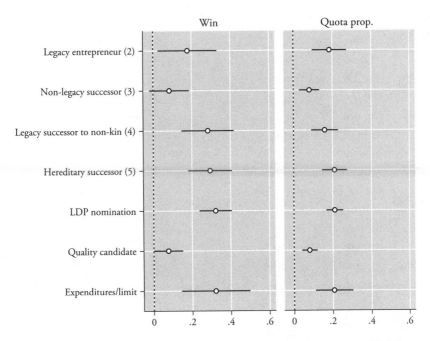

FIGURE 5.1 Electoral advantage of different types of first-time LDP and LDP-affiliated candidates in MMD elections

SOURCE: JHRED.

NOTE: Baseline group is *Non-legacy entrepreneur* (Type 1). *Win* is a dummy variable for winning election. *Quota prop.* is the share of the Droop quota obtained by the candidate. Models estimated with OLS using robust standard errors. Points and bars represent the estimated coefficients (predicted change) and 95 percent confidence intervals. Models include controls for gender, age, age-squared, and the number of candidates running, as well as fixed effects for district and year ($N = 644$). Table A.10 in Appendix A displays the full set of results with and without controls. Plots correspond to results from models 3 and 6 in Table A.10. Candidates who secured a seat after the election through list promotion (*kuriage tōsen*) are counted as losing. The definition of first-time candidate excludes individuals who ran for the prewar House of Representatives or in 1946 but not candidates who previously served in the House of Councillors.

(entrepreneurial) conservative challengers entering the race. For this analysis, we also limit the sample to successor candidates who had the official nomination of the LDP. The results are presented in Figure 5.2, where the first model for each dependent variable includes only a dummy variable indicating whether the first-time candidate was a hereditary successor (the reference group is non-legacy successors). The second model controls for the number of previous jiban wins (standardized), the number of other new conservative candidates who entered the race (including LDP-affiliated independents), and whether the candidate's predecessor won the last election. The second model also controls for candidate quality, expenditures, gender, age,

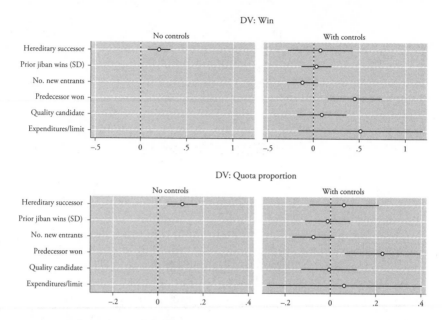

FIGURE 5.2 Electoral advantage of first-time LDP hereditary successors in MMD elections
SOURCE: JHRED.
NOTE: Baseline group is *Non-legacy successor. Win* is a dummy variable for winning election. *Quota prop.* is the share of the Droop quota obtained by the candidate. Models estimated with OLS using robust standard errors. Points and bars represent the estimated coefficients (predicted change) and 95 percent confidence intervals. Models with controls also include controls for gender, age, age-squared, and the total number of candidates running, as well as fixed effects for district and year. Table A.11 in Appendix A displays the full set of results with and without controls. Plots correspond to results from models 1, 3, 4, and 6 in Table A.11. Candidates who secured a seat after the election through list promotion (*kuriage tōsen*) are counted as losing. The definition of first-time candidate excludes individuals who ran for the prewar House of Representatives or in 1946 but not candidates who previously served in the House of Councillors.

age-squared, and the total number of candidates running, as well as including fixed effects for district and year, as in previous analyses. Table A.11 in Appendix A displays the full set of results with and without controls.

On average, hereditary successors in the LDP were roughly 20 percentage points more likely to win than non-legacy successors, and earned 11 percentage points more of the electoral quota. Controlling for the strength of the jiban alone, hereditary successors still tended to do better than non-legacy successors, enjoying a roughly 14-percentage-point higher probability of election (Table A.11). However, the significance of the relationship no longer holds once we control for whether the candidate's predecessor won his or her last election, which is not surprising given the strong correlation between incumbency and hereditary succession documented in Chapter 4. The negative coefficient on *No. of new entrants,* which codes the number of additional new conservatives who ran (min. = 0, max. = 4), suggests that the entry of additional conservatives was a challenge facing first-time LDP candidates of both types of succession. However, hereditary successors do not appear to enjoy a larger "scare-off" effect than non-legacy successors. If anything, hereditary successors are more likely to face intracamp challengers in their first election. While 60 percent of non-legacy successors and 55 percent of hereditary successors faced no competition from other new conservative entrants, only 13 percent of non-legacy successors faced two or more challengers, compared to 20 percent of hereditary successors.

This apparent lack of a "scare-off" effect for hereditary successors may in part be because the retirement of a powerful incumbent—which is correlated with hereditary succession—also increases uncertainty over which new or returning candidates might win over the previous incumbent's voters. This encourages the entry of entrepreneurial candidates who hope to capture a portion of the large bloc of conservative voters made available by the incumbent's exit. The lack of a "scare-off" effect during the MMD period is also noted by Ishibashi and Reed (1992, pp. 375–376), who conjecture that the pattern is perhaps "caused by lieutenants in the kōenkai who feel that their hard work deserves the reward of succession rights and that a relative who has not served a proper political apprenticeship should be defeated at the polls."

THE INHERITED INCUMBENCY ADVANTAGE IN SMD ELECTIONS

The introduction of SMDs in 1994 eliminates many of the challenges to measuring the inherited incumbency advantage, due to the elimination of intraparty competition and the development of a largely two-party system in SMDs—with the LDP and DPJ at the forefront—from the 2000 election until the tumultuous 2012 election. This facilitates an application of the method used by Feinstein (2010) to estimate the inherited incumbency advantage in SMDs without bias. Feinstein's approach builds on previous studies of the incumbency advantage that measure the differential advantage of an incumbent Democratic candidate over a Republican challenger in a SMD race, controlling for other factors that may systematically be related to a higher vote share for the candidate or his or her party (Gelman and King, 1990; Cox and Katz, 1996).

For the Japanese case, the analysis here focuses on the LDP candidate's vote share in the fifty-five open-seat SMD races in the four general elections from 2000 to 2009 in which a new LDP candidate ran (once again, a repeated cross-sectional sample of the data). The sample excludes the chaotic 1996 election where both the NFP and the DPJ competed for the status of main opposition party, as well as the 2012 and 2014 elections, in which two-party competition largely collapsed as the "Third Force" parties attempted to replace the DPJ as the main alternative to the LDP (Reed et al., 2013; Scheiner, Smith, and Thies, 2016). The full regression model takes the following form:

$$Y_{it} = \alpha_t + \beta_1 Dynasty\ difference_{it} + \beta_2 Quality\ difference_{it}$$
$$+ \beta_3 Expenditures\ difference_{it} + \beta_4 LDP\ district\ strength_{it} + \epsilon_{it}, \qquad (5.2)$$

where *Y* is a dependent variable that again takes one of two forms: an outcome-denominated measure *Win* (a dummy variable for winning the SMD seat), or a vote-denominated measure *Vote share*, which is the first-time LDP candidate's share of the top two candidates' vote in district *i* and year *t*. *Dynasty difference* takes the value of 1 if the LDP candidate was a legacy candidate, −1 if the main challenger candidate was a legacy, and 0 if neither candidate (or both candidates) was a legacy;[6] *Quality difference* similarly captures the difference in prior officeholding experience (local legislative office, mayor, governor, House of Councillors, or prior service in the House of Representatives) between the two main candidates; *Expenditures difference* represents the LDP candidate's expenditures as a proportion of the maximum amount allowed minus the corresponding proportion spent by his or her main opponent; *LDP district strength* is the LDP's share of the PR vote in the national tier of the most recent House of Councillors election aggregated to the SMD boundaries. This measure is designed to capture the party's support qua party in that district (i.e., removed from the personal vote of a candidate or his or her predecessor).[7] Finally, *α* represents fixed effects for the year of the election.

Figure 5.3 presents the results. In models 1–3, the dependent variable is the outcome-denominated measure *Win*; models 4–6 use the vote-denominated measure *Vote share*. The first model in each set tests the relationship between *Dynasty difference* and the dependent variable without including any other variables or controls. The second adds controls for quality and expenditures differences. Finally, the third in each set adds the control for party strength (for visual clarity, standardized so that the mean is 0 and standard deviation is 1) and year fixed effects to match the full regression model in Equation 5.2.

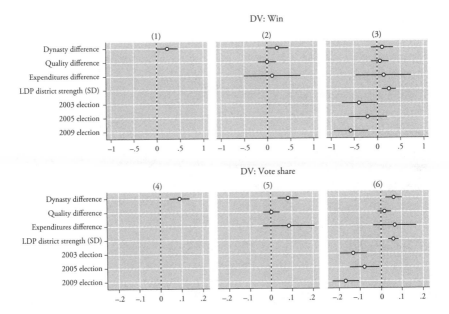

FIGURE 5.3 The inherited incumbency advantage of first-time LDP candidates in SMD elections

SOURCE: JHRED.

NOTE: Dependent variable for top set of results (models 1–3) is a dummy variable for winning election, *Win*. Dependent variable for models 4–6 is the LDP candidate's share of the top two candidates' vote, *Vote share*. Models estimated with OLS using traditional standard errors due to limited sample size ($N = 55$). Points and bars represent the estimated coefficients (predicted change) and 95 percent confidence intervals. Table A.12 in Appendix A displays the full set of results, as well as results for *Hereditary difference* (which counts only hereditary candidates, not all legacy candidates), rather than *Dynasty difference*. Candidates who secured a seat through the PR list ("zombies") are counted as losing.

Although the small number of races means that the estimates should be interpreted with some caution, the results suggest that the inherited incumbency advantage in terms of votes for new LDP legacy candidates is somewhere between 6 and 9 percentage points.[8] This estimate of the inherited incumbency advantage for new legacy candidates is roughly similar in magnitude to the 7 to 10 percentage-point advantage that has been estimated for incumbents in the United States, and is nearly double the 4-percentage-point inherited incumbency advantage Feinstein (2010) estimates for open-seat US races. Moreover, it cannot be explained by differences in the quality of challengers or differences in financial resources. Nor can the vote share advantage be explained by legacy candidates running in districts where the LDP is already popular. These findings suggest, as in the American case, that name recognition, personal connections, or other intangible factors are likely to play the greatest role in explaining the inherited incumbency advantage.

However, it is also worth considering the relationship between legacy ties and the actual outcome of the race. After all, as Gary Jacobson (1987, p. 128) correctly points out with regard to the importance of the incumbency advantage in US congressional elections, "What matters most is winning or losing; the size of the victory or loss is of decidedly secondary importance." The results of the first three regression models using *Win* as the dependent variable indicate that in terms of the "bottom line"—whether or not a new LDP candidate wins or loses the SMD contest—the most important factor is the LDP's party strength in that district. This finding is consistent with the idea that election outcomes in Japan under MMM now hinge predominantly on the popularity of the party rather than the characteristics and popularity of individual candidates (Reed, Scheiner, and Thies, 2012; McElwain, 2012). Under the new SMDs, the "brand name" of the candidate appears to matter less to voters than the party label under which he or she runs. Legacy candidates in the LDP still have a vote advantage over non-legacy opponents, but this advantage may make a difference only when their party is not popular. An implication of this pattern is that the LDP may now have less of an electoral need to rely on legacy candidates.

Survey Evidence: What Do Voters Say They Want?

The preceding analysis provides evidence that legacy candidates, and especially hereditary candidates, do indeed enjoy a considerable inherited incumbency advantage in their first attempt at winning election. It also appears that neither better quality, nor better finances or scare-off of high-quality challengers can fully explain the advantage. This suggests that name recognition or personal connections are key mechanisms behind the advantage.

An additional possible mechanism, however, is that voters in Japan may simply prefer dynasties per se, perhaps because they represent a form of continuity in style of representation, or because voters expect that legacy candidates will be more capable or prepared for office. We can look to both traditional voter surveys and a newer form of survey experiment, conjoint analysis, to explore this possible mechanism.

EVIDENCE FROM TRADITIONAL SURVEYS

A few traditional voter surveys have included questions about dynastic politics. In the run-up to the 2009 House of Representatives election, the

University of Tokyo and *Asahi Shimbun* (UTAS) joint survey asked approximately two thousand voters what they thought about the practice of hereditary succession in candidate selection and whether it ought to be prohibited. Specifically, respondents were asked:

> For the following two positions, A and B, which would you say is closest to your opinion?
>
> A. Hereditary succession for Diet members should be prohibited.
> B. Diet members' children have the freedom to choose their occupation.

Respondents could choose from one of five options: (1) Close to position A; (2) If I must say, closest to A; (3) Can't say either way; (4) If I must say, closest to B; and (5) Closest to B.[9] The results of the survey are shown in Figure 5.4.

Of the 2,085 respondents to the survey, 45 percent answered that they were more of the opinion that Diet members' children have the freedom to choose their occupation (positions 4 and 5). In contrast, 32 percent of respondents felt closer to the position of prohibiting hereditary succession

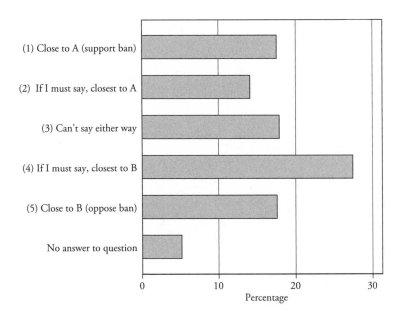

FIGURE 5.4 Voter survey: Should hereditary succession be restricted?
SOURCE: University of Tokyo-Asahi Shimbun (UTAS) 2009 preelection voter survey.
NOTE: Number of respondents = 2,085.

(positions 1 and 2). In a liberal democracy where individuals have the freedom to choose their own desired profession, such a high percentage of voters in favor of prohibiting an entire class of people from politics based on their family relations demonstrates how controversial dynastic politics had become by 2009.

Figure 5.5 shows the results of a similar question embedded in an online survey experiment conducted during the 2016 House of Councillors election. The survey asked 1,717 voting-age citizens whether they approve or disapprove of several common backgrounds of Japanese politicians, including experience in a local assembly or national bureaucrat, and status as a hereditary politician or celebrity (*tarento*—from the English word *talent*). Respondents were asked to select from a five-point scale of (1) approve, (2) weakly approve, (3) indifferent, (4) weakly disapprove, and (5) disapprove. For most backgrounds, the plurality of voters expressed indifference. However, nearly half of all voters responded that they either weakly disap-

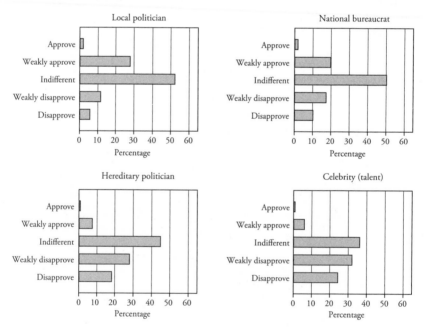

FIGURE 5.5 Voter attitudes toward common candidate backgrounds: Traditional survey results

SOURCE: Online voter survey conducted by the author and Justin Reeves during the House of Councillors election campaign of July 2016 (Reeves and Smith, 2017).

NOTE: Sample = 1,717 voting-age (18+) citizens in Japan.

prove or disapprove of hereditary politicians, a level of disapproval that is only surpassed by voters' opinions of celebrity candidates. On the whole, voters expressed more positive attitudes toward candidates who had local political experience—which is interesting given that legacy candidates are less likely to pass through this channel of recruitment (see Chapter 2).

EVIDENCE FROM A CONJOINT SURVEY EXPERIMENT

An additional method of survey experiment—conjoint analysis—provides strong evidence that Japanese voters do not value dynastic representation in and of itself. Conjoint analysis has been used in marketing research for many years but has only recently been adopted for use in political science (Hainmueller, Hopkins, and Yamamoto, 2014). Recent research has applied conjoint analysis to study a range of preferences, from voters' attitudes toward immigrants and political candidates (e.g., Hainmueller and Hopkins, 2015; Franchino and Zucchini, 2015; Carnes and Lupu, 2016) to parties' policy manifestos (Horiuchi, Smith, and Yamamoto, 2018*b*). The basic design entails juxtaposing two "profiles" (in this case hypothetical politicians) with a randomly ordered set of "attributes," each of which may take on a certain value, or "level." The levels of the attributes are also randomly assigned. Respondents then pick the hypothetical politician that they would prefer most. This design allows for an evaluation of voters' multidimensional preferences for the various attributes, such as dynastic family ties, that make up a politician's overall profile.

Previous studies have used conjoint analysis to evaluate a range of candidate attributes. For example, Jens Hainmueller, Daniel J. Hopkins, and Teppei Yamamoto (2014) focus on eight attributes of hypothetical US presidential candidates and find that voters have strong positive preferences for hypothetical candidates with prior military service and a college degree (from any college but especially from an Ivy League university), and strong negative preferences against evangelical Christians, Mormons, car dealers, and candidates who were sixty-eight or seventy-five years old. Fabio Franchino and Francesco Zucchini (2015) include two personal attributes (level of education and level of income), one attribute related to integrity (whether the candidate had ever been investigated or convicted of corruption) and two attributes related to policy positions on taxation and same-sex marriage rights in Italy. In another recent study, Nicholas Carnes and Noam Lupu (2016) evaluate class bias against candidates in the United Kingdom,

United States, and Argentina, using six attributes with two levels for each—specifically, occupation (business owner versus factory worker), gender (male versus female), education (more versus less), party (two main parties in each country), race (black versus white), and experience (none versus some).

Figure 5.6 displays the results of a conjoint experiment evaluating voter preferences for common candidate attributes in Japan, conducted with Yusaku Horiuchi and Teppei Yamamoto (Horiuchi, Smith, and Yamamoto, 2018*a*). In the experiment, respondents were shown a pair of hypothetical politicians' profiles, each of which featured a random combination of common personal attributes observed among actual Japanese politicians and were then asked to choose the profile they found most desirable for a politician (this exercise was repeated for a total of ten pairwise comparisons per respondent). In addition to party labels for LDP, DPJ, Kōmeitō, and JCP, as well as independent, the profiles included an attribute for "parental political background" (i.e., whether the hypothetical politician's parent also had a career in politics). For this attribute, the possible levels were "a cabinet minister," "a national-level elected politician," "a prefectural assembly member," and "none." The other attributes in the profiles were age, gender, education, former occupation, prior political experience, and hometown.[10] Along with dynastic family ties, many of the attributes included (e.g., local birth, local political experience, celebrity status) are strongly related to the personal vote. The inclusion of these attributes provides the opportunity to investigate whether voters intrinsically value any of these well-known personal-vote-earning attributes per se—detached from the actual politicians who are presumed to benefit from them. In other words, the inclusion of dynastic family ties in this kind of experiment allows us to isolate voters' preferences for dynasties as an abstract concept, without the confounding influence from other attributes, like name recognition, financial resources, and prior experience, that may be correlated with actual legacy candidates and MPs.

The results reveal that Japanese voters do indeed have strong preferences for and against certain personal attributes in politicians. Specifically, voters prefer politicians with prior political experience and politicians who are born in their prefecture, but do not tend to prefer politicians affiliated with one of the major political parties (relative to independents), older politicians (relative to younger politicians), or celebrities (relative to other occupations).

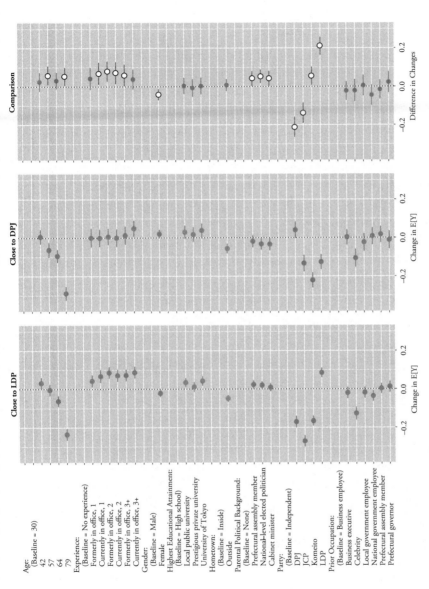

FIGURE 5.6 Voter attitudes toward common candidate backgrounds: Conjoint survey results

SOURCE: Based on conjoint survey results from Horiuchi, Smith, and Yamamoto (2018a).

NOTE: Sample = 2,200 voting-age (20+) citizens in Japan, November–December, 2015. Point estimates represent the average marginal component effect (AMCE) of a given attribute on the respondent's probability of choosing the hypothetical candidate whose profile features that attribute, compared to a profile featuring the baseline attribute. The third panel gives the difference in point estimates between respondents who report being close to the LDP and those who report being close to the DPJ (hollow circles denote differences that are statistically significant at the .05 level).

With regard to dynastic family ties, however, there are no significant effects for any of the parental political backgrounds compared to the baseline level of "none." In other words, the conjoint experiment reveals that Japanese voters are largely indifferent to dynastic ties when this attribute is bundled with other possible attributes that may be more important to voters, or alternatively, when the information about dynastic ties is separated from the specific attributes of the actual legacy politicians (e.g., name recognition, financial resources, personal representational style or reputation).

This finding holds regardless of the priming of different electoral system contexts, and regardless of whether the respondents were assigned to receive priming about the electoral rules in the House of Representatives or House of Councillors. In fact, the only covariate for which there are notably significant differences in preferences for dynastic politicians is the respondent's partisan affiliation. Although the levels of parental political background are insignificant within groups of party supporters, the difference between LDP and DPJ supporters is significant. LDP supporters hold slightly positive preferences for dynastic politicians, whereas DPJ supporters hold slightly negative preferences. This attitude among DPJ supporters may be because dynasties are most prominently linked to the LDP, a fact that the DPJ's campaign in 2009 used to attack the LDP.

Discussion

What have we learned? The results of the empirical analyses presented in this chapter confirm that legacy candidates do indeed perform better in elections than non-legacy candidates. This electoral advantage cannot simply be attributed to support for the LDP as a party, nor can it be attributed to the greater financial resources or higher quality of legacy candidates. The results of the voter surveys also demonstrate that the advantages enjoyed by legacy candidates in Japan are not the result of any intrinsic value placed on dynastic representation by voters. When voters are asked directly and specifically what they think about hereditary politicians, as in the traditional survey questions, their attitudes are generally negative. However, when dynastic ties are bundled with multiple other attributes, as in the conjoint experiment and as they are in real life, voters tend to focus more on party label, experience, age, and local ties. Interestingly, celebrity status is also unpopular in the abstract with voters, regardless of the survey method.

Although it is possible that some voters might positively view specific legacy candidates due to an expectation that their family ties might make them a more capable representative, there is no evidence that voters value dynasties in general as a vehicle for representation. Another way of interpreting these results is with an analogy to American voters' opinions of Congress. Public opinion polls in the United States routinely report that voters hold negative attitudes toward Congress as a whole but tend to view their own representatives and senators in Congress more favorably. Voters might similarly dislike the idea of dynasties in the abstract, but nevertheless believe that their own personal favored son or daughter is of higher quality than most other politicians—a Rockefeller among the Tweeds.

Collectively, the empirical analyses of this chapter point to the value of name recognition and family "brand" in securing electoral success. This conclusion for the prereform MMD period is supported by the difference in vote shares and success rates of hereditary successors compared to non-legacy successors. Both types of successors inherited a kōenkai organization with its financial resources (kaban) and established base of supporters (jiban). However, hereditary successors would have also enjoyed the additional advantage of name recognition (kanban). As we saw in the previous chapter, some hereditary successors even went so far as to change their names so that voters could continue writing the same name on the ballot.

In the postreform SMD period, new legacy candidates in the LDP still do much better than new non-legacy candidates in the LDP, even though all new LDP candidates can now be considered successors to whichever single candidate ran in the previous election under the LDP label. The big difference between the prereform and postreform periods is that what matters most for success since reform may be the particular districts where LDP candidates run: in districts where the LDP is "safe," legacy and non-legacy candidates alike can do well. Of course, legacy candidates are also most likely to emerge in such safe districts. Another consideration is that when the LDP's popularity as a party is low, as in the 2009 election, the additional vote share advantage may be enough to create a "safety buffer" for new legacy candidates where non-legacy candidates might be vulnerable. Such questions will be easier to investigate in the future with the addition of more elections, including additional elections that the LDP loses.

SIX

Promotion
Dynastic Dominance in the Cabinet

> Back in June 1957, Nobusuke Kishi, my grandfather, standing
> right here as prime minister of Japan, began his address by say-
> ing, and I quote, "It is because of our strong belief in demo-
> cratic principles and ideals that Japan associates herself with the
> free nations of the world." Fifty-eight years have passed. Today,
> I am honored to stand here as the first Japanese prime minister
> ever to address your joint meeting.
>
> —*Prime Minister Abe Shinzō, addressing the US Congress on April 29, 2015*

When Prime Minister Abe Shinzō spoke before a joint session of the US
Congress in 2015, he quoted the words of his maternal grandfather, former prime minister Kishi Nobusuke, who addressed an American audience
on the same platform almost six decades earlier. Kishi is most famous for
having to resign in 1960 following the controversial passage of the revised
US-Japan Security Treaty.[1] The year Kishi left office, John F. Kennedy was
elected president of the United States. Fifty-five years later, Kishi's grandson
was prime minister, and the US ambassador in Tokyo was Caroline Kennedy, JFK's daughter.

For Abe, quoting his grandfather's speech was no doubt a matter of great
pride. However, he could have just as easily drawn inspiration from other
members of his family who had previously held influential positions of
power. Kishi's brother Satō Eisaku also served as prime minister from 1964
to 1972 and visited the United States in 1965.[2] Satō was responsible for over-
seeing the return of sovereignty over Okinawa in 1972. Abe's father, Abe
Shintarō, served as minister of agriculture and forestry (1974–1976), chief
cabinet secretary (1977–1978), minister of international trade and industry
(1981–1982), and minister of foreign affairs (1982–1986).[3]

Abe's family history in cabinet is not unique. Indeed, keeping track of dynastic politics at the top levels of power in Japan is enough to make one's head spin. Seven of the ten most recent prime ministers have been legacy MPs, and six had predecessors who also served in cabinet, including Prime Minister Hashimoto Ryūtarō (1996–1998), whose father, Hashimoto Ryōgo, served in the Yoshida and Kishi cabinets in the 1950s—first as minister of health and later as minister of education. Hashimoto was succeeded as prime minister by Obuchi Keizō (1998–2000), whose father, Mitsuhei, served two terms in the House of Representatives but died before he could achieve promotion to a cabinet post.[4] After Obuchi Keizō's death, his daughter Yūko succeeded him in parliament and gained her first cabinet appointment in her third term, at the age of thirty-four.

Prime Minister Koizumi Junichirō (2001–2006) first ran for office in Kanagawa 11th District in 1969, at the age of twenty-seven, after his father, Koizumi Junya, died in office. He lost that election but won three years later in 1972. Junya was minister of state responsible for the defense agency from 1964 to 1965 (prior to the agency obtaining full ministry status) and was the adopted son-in-law of prewar MP Koizumi Matajirō, who also served in cabinet as minister of communications (1929–1931). Before the 2009 general election, Junichirō stepped aside for his twenty-seven-year-old son, Koizumi Shinjirō, who quickly rose to prominence within the party, achieving his first junior ministerial position in 2012. In a July 2017 public opinion survey by *Sankei Shimbun* and FNN News, Koizumi Shinjirō was the third most popular choice for prime minister, behind senior party leaders Abe Shinzō and Ishiba Shigeru.[5]

Prime Minister Fukuda Yasuo (2007–2008) is the son of former prime minister Fukuda Takeo (1976–1978). Takeo's father and older brother both served as mayor of Kanekomachi, a town in Gunma Prefecture. Takeo's younger brother, Fukuda Hiroichi, was a member of the House of Councillors from 1980 to 1992. In 2012, Yasuo retired after his seventh term representing Gunma 3rd District. By that time, the LDP had implemented its reforms requiring most new candidates to apply to an open-recruitment contest in order to get the party nomination. However, Yasuo's eldest son, Fukuda Tatsuo, was the only applicant to the open-recruitment contest, and easily went on to win in the general election.[6] In 2014, he faced only a single challenger from the JCP, and won reelection with 71 percent of the vote.

Prime Minister Asō Tarō (2008–2009) was the grandson of former prime minister Yoshida Shigeru (1946–1947, 1948–1954), whose term in office covered most of the US Occupation, and whose postwar policy of relying on the United States for military security while focusing on economic development would become known as the Yoshida Doctrine (see Samuels, 2007). Asō's great-grandfather Asō Takichi and father, Asō Takakichi, also served in the House of Representatives. His father-in-law was former prime minister Suzuki Zenkō (1980–1982). Suzuki's biological son, Suzuki Shunichi, also served in the House of Representatives and as a cabinet minister in the Koizumi and Abe cabinets.

Hatoyama Yukio, the first prime minister from the DPJ (2009–2010), was first elected to Hokkaido 9th District (originally Hokkaido 4th District) in 1986 as a member of the LDP. He is the son of former minister of foreign affairs and House of Councillors member Hatoyama Iichirō, and grandson of former prime minister Hatoyama Ichirō (1954–1956), who founded the LDP with Yoshida in 1955. His great-grandfather Hatoyama Kazuo was a prewar MP, and his younger brother, Hatoyama Kunio, was a member of the House of Representatives and former cabinet minister in multiple posts. Yoshida Shigeru and Hatoyama Ichirō were rivals prior to the formation of the LDP in 1955, so it is fitting that their respective grandsons, Asō Tarō and Hatoyama Yukio, competed with each other for control of the Diet in the 2009 general election (which the DPJ under Hatoyama ultimately won).

The abundance of legacy MPs in recent cabinets extends beyond the prime ministers. Overall, an astounding 61 percent of all LDP members of the House of Representatives appointed to cabinet since electoral reform in 1994 have been legacy MPs. In Koizumi Junichirō's first reshuffled cabinet (Koizumi 1.1), all twelve of the LDP lower house MPs appointed to ministerial positions were legacy MPs.[7] To illustrate this pattern, the bar graph in Figure 6.1 shows the percentage of legacy MPs among the members of the House of Representatives who were appointed to each cabinet, from the cabinet of Katayama Tetsu (Katayama 1), inaugurated after the 1947 general election, to the second reshuffle of Abe Shinzō's third cabinet in 2016 (Abe 3.2). The line plot in the figure gives the percentage of legacy MPs in the LDP's House of Representatives delegation, beginning with the 1958 election that followed its formation in 1955.[8] In LDP cabinets where the bar is higher than the line, legacy MPs were overrepresented.

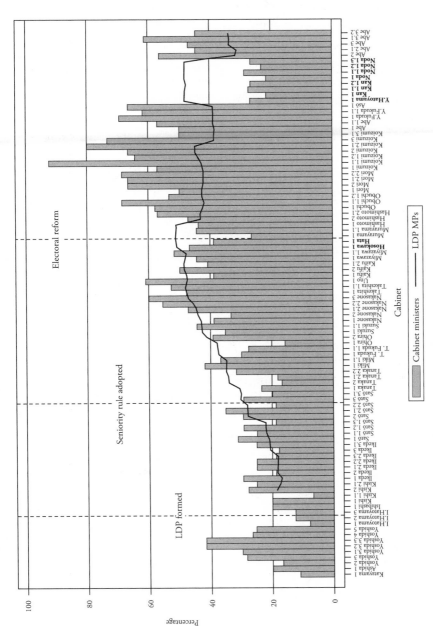

FIGURE 6.1 Percentage of legacy MPs in LDP and cabinet, 1947–2016

SOURCE: JHRED.

NOTE: Only MPs from the House of Representatives are included (i.e., for each cabinet, the denominator for calculating the percentage excludes a small number of members of the House of Councillors or technical ministers, but includes MPs from all governing parties in the case of coalitions).

For reference, three vertical dashed lines mark the time of the LDP's formation (just prior to the third cabinet of Hatoyama Ichirō in 1955), the time at which seniority rule in promotions was introduced as a party norm (i.e., an informal institution) by Satō Eisaku in his third cabinet (Satō and Matsuzaki, 1986), and the time of electoral reform in 1994. Cabinets in which the LDP or its precursor parties (the Liberal Party and the Democratic Party) did not participate are noted by bold cabinet names on the x-axis in Figure 6.1. In the LDP's first period out of government (1993–1994), the eight-party coalition of anti-LDP parties were in power, initially under Prime Minister Hosokawa Morihiro of the JNP and then under Prime Minister Hata Tsutomu of the Renewal Party (both legacy MPs who were previously affiliated with the LDP). The coalition government passed electoral reform in 1994 but fell apart soon after. At that point, the LDP reentered government in coalition with the JSP and New Party Sakigake, with the JSP's leader Murayama Tomiichi serving as prime minister. In 1996, the LDP regained the premiership under Hashimoto but continued to rule in coalition—first with the JSP and Sakigake, and later with the Liberal Party, the New Conservative Party, and Kōmeitō.[9] The latter party has been the LDP's sole coalition partner since 2003. The LDP's second period out of government was from 2009 to 2012, when the DPJ-led coalition held power, first under Prime Minister Hatoyama, then Kan Naoto, and finally Noda Yoshihiko—each serving roughly one year in office.

The high proportion of legacy MPs in cabinet, especially in the LDP-led cabinets of Koizumi, Abe, Fukuda, and Asō, as well as during Abe's second stint as prime minister following the DPJ's defeat in 2012, has resulted in considerable criticism by the media and by the opposition that one seemingly cannot get appointed to the cabinet in recent years without being a member of a powerful political dynasty. Moreover, because Abe (in his first term as prime minister), Fukuda, and Asō all resigned within a year of taking office, dynastic politics were heavily blamed for stale leadership in the face of many of the governance problems plaguing Japan (e.g., Yazaki, 2010).

This chapter evaluates how the inherited incumbency advantage that has been documented in the candidate selection and election stages of a legacy MP's career translates into advantages in the postelectoral stage. The focus is specifically on promotion to cabinet, although the logic should apply generally to all postelectoral legislative and executive posts, including committee chairmanships and high-level party leadership positions.[10] Anecdotal evidence of a legacy advantage in cabinet selection can be found across many democracies. For example, Prime Minister Justin Trudeau of Canada, who came into office in 2015 at the age of forty-three after only two terms in the House of Commons, is the son of long-serving prime minister Pierre Trudeau (1968–1979, 1980–1984). His maternal grandfather, James Sinclair, was also an MP and had served as the minister of fisheries in the 1950s. Former Norwegian prime minister Jens Stoltenberg (2005–2013) is the son of the former minister of defense and minister of foreign affairs Thorvald Stoltenberg. He had served only two years as a substitute (deputy) member of the Storting before being appointed to cabinet at the age of thirty-four in his first full term as an MP. Forty-four percent of the ministers in the 2016 cabinet of Irish prime minister Enda Kenny were legacy MPs, including Kenny, whose father Henry Kenny served in the Dáil for over two decades and as a minister of state (junior minister) for the Department of Finance from 1973 to 1975.

Although the focus in this chapter is ministerial selection in parliamentary democracies like Japan, there is plenty of empirical evidence that members of dynasties are advantaged in reaching executive office in presidential systems as well. The 2016 US presidential primary contest featured Hillary Clinton, Jeb Bush, and Rand Paul—all three of whom were connected by blood or marriage to a previous presidential candidate. The 2012 Republican Party ticket featured Mitt Romney, whose father, George Romney, was a former governor of Michigan and served in cabinet as secretary of housing and urban development. Outside of the United States, dynasties have been notable in recent presidential politics in Argentina (the Perón and Kirchner dynasties), the Philippines (the Aquino and Macapagal dynasties), and South Korea (the Park and Lee dynasties), to name just a few examples. Recent Mexican presidents Felipe Calderón and Enrique Peña Nieto also have close family relations to former politicians. According to a working paper by Timothy Besley and Marta Reynal-Querol (2017), in the past three decades, roughly 15–20 percent of political executives around the world (including in nondemocracies) have been political legacies.

What is it about dynastic family ties that might result in legacy MPs progressing more often or more quickly to the highest positions of power? Are legacy MPs advantaged in terms of reaching the top levels of political office because of intangible interpersonal relations inherited from their predecessors? Or because their family name and electoral strength help them become focal in ministerial selection decisions? Or simply because their electoral advantages make them more likely to reach positions of seniority in the party? Finally, how does the advantage vary under different institutional contexts?

In the early decades of democracy in postwar Japan, legacy MPs—particularly those whose predecessors had previously served in a ministerial position—were overrepresented in most cabinets, but much of this apparent advantage can be attributed to the reappointment of past ministers. During the years from 1970 to 1993 in which seniority rule and factional balancing functioned as informal institutions constraining the appointment choices of LDP prime ministers, ministers were shuffled more regularly, and legacy MPs enjoyed no apparent advantage over their peers. In the years since electoral reform in 1994, however, legacy MPs are again dramatically overrepresented in LDP cabinets. For legacy MPs whose predecessors never served in cabinet themselves, this advantage is still largely due to seniority in the party. Legacy MPs with a family history in the cabinet, in contrast, enjoy a significant advantage in promotion that cannot be explained simply by their seniority. Instead, it is likely that the relatives of former cabinet ministers benefit from internal party networks or other informational advantages within the party.

Ministerial Selection in Parliamentary Democracies

Before investigating the advantages of dynastic family ties in cabinet promotion, it is helpful to briefly review the general literature on ministerial selection in parliamentary democracies like Japan.[11] In parliamentary democracies, the cabinet represents the highest position of political power. From a principal-agent perspective, we can think of voters as principals who elect MPs as their political agents in elections. Once elected, MPs in the legislature become a new set of principals who select a prime minister as *their* agent in the executive, who then goes on to select ministers to serve with him or her in the cabinet. The chain of delegation in ideal-typical parliamentary systems is thus (1) indirect, meaning that voters do not directly select the executive, as they do in presidential systems; (2) singular, meaning that delegation and accountability relationships flow between a single (collective) principal and a single agent; and (3) hierarchical, meaning that cabinet decisions are not subject to checks and balances from outside government agencies, as in many presidential systems (see Strøm, Müller, and Bergman, 2003). Typically, parliament designates the prime minister, and he or she is responsible for appointing other ministers to the various portfolios that collectively make up the cabinet.

Because the cabinet represents the apex of power in parliamentary democracies, a great deal of research has been devoted to understanding how ministerial portfolios (cabinet posts) are allocated to political parties, particularly in the case of coalition governments (e.g., Laver and Shepsle, 1996; Warwick and Druckman, 2001; Bäck, Debus, and Dumont, 2011). This line of research has important implications because the interparty distribution of portfolios in coalition governments can potentially have a significant impact on policy outputs. The question of who gets what in terms of ministerial positions has thus traditionally been answered with a party-level variable, focused on the distribution of cabinet seats *between parties*, rather than the question of which individuals *within parties* receive posts. Similarly, intraparty analyses, including for the case of Japan, tend to focus on the distribution of portfolios across groups within parties, such as factions (e.g., Leiserson, 1968; Mershon, 2001; Ono, 2012).

A smaller but rapidly growing literature investigates the intraparty distribution of portfolios to individual MPs (e.g., Dowding and Dumont, 2009, 2014). Ministerial positions represent significant postelectoral prizes for individual MPs; just as parties and candidates compete for elective office, so too must individual MPs within parties compete with one another for promotion to higher office (Andeweg, 2000; Saalfeld, 2000). Ultimately, moreover, it is the individual MPs appointed to cabinet—not their parties—who are responsible for the day-to-day operation of the ministries, and these individuals may also enjoy considerable discretion and influence over policy outputs (Laver and Shepsle, 1994). This makes it important to investigate and understand not only which party gets which portfolio but also which MP within the party gets the portfolio.

Numerous factors are involved in determining how cabinet posts and other positions of power in parties and parliaments are distributed to individual MPs. Parties and legislatures, like other organizations, are hierarchically structured, such that some members will be promoted to a small number of positions of power in the party, parliament, and government while others will remain on the backbenches, sometimes for their entire careers (Strøm, 1997). Although the prime minister usually holds formal authority to appoint and dismiss cabinet ministers, the choice may be constrained by formal institutions (e.g., constitutional requirements that ministers be sitting MPs) or informal institutions (e.g., seniority rules, norms of factional or regional balancing in appointments). In coalition government situations, the prime minister may also have less control over which individuals are appointed to the portfolios allocated to a coalition partner.

Existing comparative research suggests a relationship between promotion to cabinet and an MP's length of time in parliament (seniority), electoral popularity (under electoral rules that feature a candidate-level preferential vote), level of education, gender, policy preferences, and other less-tangible personal traits. In an early and richly descriptive investigation, Jean Blondel and Jean-Louis Thiébault (1991) focus on the personal characteristics and social backgrounds of Western European ministers who, they find, tend to be older and more highly educated, and to have had longer careers within the party. However, there is considerable variation across countries when it comes to ministers having a background in parliament (versus, for example, experience in extraparliamentary party offices or outside of politics). The ministerial future of an individual legislator can also depend on factors such as his or her electoral strength and favorable relationships to party leaders (Dowding and Dumont, 2009). Some of these factors, such as seniority, can be quantitatively measured. Other factors, such as likability, media savviness, or interpersonal relationships within parties, are intangible. In short, not all MPs seeking a cabinet appointment are created equal.

A number of country-specific studies have investigated the qualities of the individual MPs who achieve ministerial office, taking the pool of MPs (potential appointees) as the data sample, rather than just those who were appointed, as in earlier research. For example, Eoin O'Malley (2006) explores the basis for selecting cabinet ministers in Ireland through interviews with former party leaders and archives of interviews with ministers. He finds that personal characteristics matter for party leaders when choosing ministers. In particular, the prime minister values "talent, loyalty, experience, tenacity, cleanliness (from corruption) and good personal relations" (O'Malley, 2006, p. 329). Other variables that are correlated with promotion include higher levels of education, longer lengths of tenure in parliament, and greater electoral success in the previous general election. Of course, these factors are all also correlated with each other. In Canada, electoral popularity also correlates positively with the likelihood of being selected—on average, cabinet appointees have a margin of victory of 26 percentage points over their runners-up, which compares to 23 percentage points for governing-party MPs who are not appointed (Kerby, 2009). Hence, one common characteristic of those who are appointed to cabinet is that they tend to be ex ante electorally successful.

In the case of Japan, ministerial appointments in LDP cabinets closely adhered to two important norms, beginning from around the time that Prime Minister Satō Eisaku's third cabinet took office in 1970 and continuing up until electoral reform in 1994 (Satō and Matsuzaki, 1986; Pekkanen, Nyblade, and Krauss, 2014). The first norm was the proportional allocation of posts to intraparty factions. Roughly speaking, each faction received a number of cabinet posts in proportion to its strength in the legislative party membership, albeit with some variation (Ono, 2012). Faction leaders would submit a list of names to the prime minister of the members of their factions who were "in line" for a ministerial post, and the prime minister generally obliged. This norm began to break down immediately following electoral reform, and it further deteriorated after Prime Minister Koizumi Junichirō took office in 2001. The second norm was seniority rule for the promotion of individual MPs within those factions. Roughly speaking, each LDP MP had to wait until around the fifth or sixth term before he or she could expect an appointment to cabinet (Satō and Matsuzaki, 1986; Epstein et al., 1997). More senior MPs would often be reappointed to cabinet, but rarely would less senior MPs be given a post. Even then, a cabinet seat was not guaranteed, given the large size of the party and the small number of posts to be distributed. Nevertheless, frequent (almost yearly) reshuffles ensured that many LDP MPs who reached such levels of seniority would eventually get a post at least once.

In a recent quantitative analysis of the MP-level determinants of cabinet promotion in Japan from 1980 to 2008, Robert Pekkanen, Benjamin Nyblade, and Ellis Krauss (2014) argue that the 1994 electoral reform altered the strategies of party leaders in selecting ministers. Since electoral competition under the new MMM system has become less focused on individual candidates (relative to the previous SNTV system), and more centered on the image of the party leader and party platform, prime ministers have an incentive to pay less attention to factional balancing and routine promotion based on seniority. Instead, they appoint more policy experts to serve the party's policy goals and more women to help the party appear more diverse in an effort to appeal to voters. Pekkanen, Nyblade, and Krauss also note the increase in legacy MPs in postreform cabinets (as visible in Figure 6.1), and specifically note an increase in legacy MPs whose predecessors had previously also served in cabinet.[12] They hypothesize that such MPs possess a "national reputation" that may help the party attract support in the increasingly nationally oriented elections of the postreform era.

Although it is not a key part of the analysis of Pekkanen, Nyblade, and Krauss (2014), the authors raise an important distinction between "types" of legacy MPs. More specifically, we can distinguish between *cabinet legacies*, whose predecessors had experience as cabinet ministers, and *non-cabinet legacies*, whose predecessors never advanced beyond the backbenches. Prime Minister Abe is a prominent example of a cabinet legacy—and actually was preceded in cabinet by multiple family members, including two former prime ministers. Prime Minister Obuchi is an example of a non-cabinet legacy, as his father died before being promoted; in contrast, Obuchi's daughter Obuchi Yūko is a cabinet legacy. When she was appointed to Asō Tarō's first cabinet in 2008 at the age of thirty-four, she became the youngest cabinet minister to be appointed in Japan.

It is clear from the aggregate data in Figure 6.1 that legacy MPs have been overrepresented in cabinet, particularly in the postreform era. But what are the sources of this apparent advantage? And how might the advantage differ depending on a legacy MP's family history in cabinet?

The Advantage of Being a Legacy: Further and Faster?

To understand the potential advantage of dynastic ties in securing a seat in cabinet, and how this advantage might differ across cabinet legacies and non-cabinet legacies, it is helpful to first consider the role and preferences of the person who selects members of the cabinet: the prime minister. We can assume that the prime minister will take ministerial selection decisions seriously, and will aim to promote copartisans who will effectively perform their duties in office—those who Michael Laver and Kenneth Shepsle (1994, p. 302) describe as "ministerable." It is important to select competent ministers since the success of the government is dependent, at least in part, on the performance of individual ministers. Ministers are individually responsible for the performance of their respective ministries, but also represent the collective public face of the cabinet. For this reason, the popularity of the party (or parties) in government can be positively or negatively affected by the individual performance and popularity of ministers (Müller and Strøm, 1999; Dewan and Dowding, 2005; Quiroz Flores and Smith, 2011).

From the perspective of individual MPs, a ministerial portfolio is highly desirable. Cabinet positions not only provide the opportunity to influence policy but also come with a number of personal payoffs, including greater public status, more financial compensation, and greater name recognition in subsequent elections (Martin, 2016). However, the demand for a cabinet appointment is typically higher than the supply of available positions. The significant demand for higher office combined with a low supply of positions creates a high-stakes principal-agent selection game for the prime minister. As with party leaders selecting potential candidates for nominations, and with voters selecting candidates to become MPs, the prime minister operates with limited or imperfect information when selecting his or her cabinet ministers.

In making informed choices under limited information, voters often rely on cues and heuristic shortcuts (Popkin, 1991; Lupia and McCubbins, 1998): Does the candidate look like me? Talk like me? Come from my hometown? The prime minister may also rely on such informational shortcuts in selecting his or her cabinet. As party leader, he or she has only limited opportunities to observe and learn about which members of the party would make for good ministers, including at events like party meetings, on the floor of the legislative chamber or in committees, and through public appearances. Such occasions provide would-be ministers with opportunities to make a positive impression on the prime minister. The cabinet selection process can thus be viewed as a game between the prime minister (or party leader in coalition governments) and would-be ministers (MPs) in the party. Would-be ministers need to signal to the prime minister that they have what it takes to be a successful cabinet minister, and thereby contribute positively to the reputations of the prime minister, party, and government.

DIRECT AND INDIRECT EFFECTS OF DYNASTIC FAMILY TIES

How does the inherited incumbency advantage enter into this process? If legacy MPs have an advantage in the cabinet selection game, it is possible that it stems from two potential mechanisms (Smith and Martin, 2017): a direct effect of coming from a dynasty or an indirect effect that operates through the effect of dynastic ties on electoral outcomes. The direct effect includes the intergenerational transmission of political knowledge, connections, and resources, as well as the informational cue of family name and reputation. Political dynasties, like family-run businesses, may persist in part because they retain and internally transfer critical information. Legacy MPs inherit not only electoral and financial resources but also intangible resources such as "specialized knowledge, goodwill, brand (or name) loyalty, and other types of family-specific capital" (Laband and Lentz, 1983, p. 474). All of these factors are also a part of the inherited incumbency advantage in candidate selection and elections that we have already documented.

The inherited incumbency advantage, however, may lead to a second mechanism behind the legacy advantage in cabinet selection that operates through an indirect, mediating effect of dynastic ties. The empirical analysis in the previous chapter documented how new legacy candidates in Japan tend to enjoy an inherited incumbency advantage of up to 9 percentage points, which helps them win their first election. This advantage endures in subsequent elections, helping legacy MPs to reach higher levels of seniority in the party, and often at a younger age (see Chapter 2). Put simply, the inherited incumbency advantage in elections can insulate legacies from competition and help them to achieve greater seniority in their parties. Electoral strength may also signal to party leaders that legacies will be more capable, or at the very least more popular, cabinet ministers.

An alternative view is that weak parties may try to keep electorally powerful members from defecting by rewarding them with cabinet positions. For example, O'Malley (2006) notes that Irish prime ministers need to be cognizant of the personal vote of individual party members and provide those who are electorally popular with sufficient promise of career promotion to avoid defections or leadership challenges (see also Martin, 2014). In both of these views, the relationship between dynastic ties and promotion to cabinet operates via the mediating effect of the electoral advantage. Any legacy advantage in cabinet promotion may therefore at least in part be the result of the greater electoral advantages of legacies, including the ability to reach higher levels of seniority in the party and earn higher vote shares in each election. In other words, legacy MPs may be empirically overrepresented in cabinet simply because of their relative seniority in the party.

The important distinction is that these two mechanisms may not operate in the same way, depending on a legacy candidate's family history in cabinet. While both cabinet legacies and non-cabinet legacies may enjoy significant electoral advantages in their individual local districts, cabinet legacies might be expected to enjoy a larger intraparty "informational advantage" over fellow MPs in gaining promotion from the backbenches to the cabinet. This is because cabinet legacies inherit the knowledge, political resources, high-level connections, and family track record in cabinet that helps them to stand out above their copartisan peers in ministerial selection. Thus, all else equal, we might expect a party leader to select cabinet ministers with an informational advantage in how high-level politics operate. Given the finite number of cabinet positions available for a prime minister to fill, a cabinet legacy may represent a trustworthy and familiar choice. In contrast, non-cabinet legacies may inherit the knowledge, connections, and name recognition to be successful electorally in their local districts, but this knowledge does not necessarily provide the same informational advantage in terms of leadership promotion in the party.

Recall the theoretical discussion from Chapter 3, which assumes that a party will favor the candidate(s) that will provide the highest overall utility in terms of achieving its goals of maximizing policy, office, and votes. The basic logic of this model for candidate selection can be extended to the context of ministerial selection. In this case, rather than a selectorate of party actors choosing a candidate, we can consider a prime minister who is choosing the other members of his or her cabinet. Put simply, the prime minister must balance each of these three goals in ministerial selection decisions. In terms of vote-earning goals, appointing an electorally popular MP to a cabinet position may help bolster support for the cabinet, provided that the minister's popularity in the district is related to qualities that "sell" outside the district as well. As noted, the prime minister may also reward electorally popular MPs to keep them satisfied and prevent defection. In terms of policymaking goals, the most obvious consideration is whether the MP has any experience in the policy area covered by the ministerial position. For example, in appointing a minister of finance, one basic attribute of value to the prime minister may be whether the MP had previously developed policy expertise in financial matters in parliamentary committees, party committees, or through his or her previous career in the outside world. Finally, a prime minister can be expected to value MPs who will serve effectively in the office and not undermine the credibility of the prime minister as the steward of the government. In this case, MPs who had previously served effectively in cabinet without causing any scandals or headaches for the prime minister may be likely targets for reappointment. When it comes to new appointments, however, cabinet legacies may have an advantage in this regard over other MPs. For most MPs, the prime minister has information only about their electoral strength and policy expertise, not about how they might serve in cabinet office. In contrast, the prime minister can infer how a cabinet legacy might perform in office on the basis of what he or she knows about the predecessor's performance.

Previous research with Shane Martin finds that cabinet legacies in Ireland are indeed advantaged in reaching cabinet, even after controlling for seniority and other variables (Smith and Martin, 2017). The probability that a cabinet legacy will get appointed to an Irish cabinet, holding all else equal, is roughly 8 percentage points higher than a non-legacy MP, and 10 percentage points higher than a non-cabinet legacy. The advantage cannot be explained by the strength of the dynasty (i.e., previous wins by family members in the past) or by where cabinet legacies run (i.e., party strongholds). However, being a cabinet legacy in Ireland is correlated with higher levels of education and attendance at elite schools, which hints that network advantages may be part of the mechanism. The Irish electoral system (STV with MMDs) is similar to Japan's prereform SNTV system, so we might expect similar patterns in the Japanese case. In contrast, seniority rule in the later years of the SNTV period may have produced different outcomes. The case of Japan allows us to consider how the legacy advantage in cabinet selection might vary under different institutions.

INSTITUTIONAL CONSIDERATIONS

As with candidate selection (Chapter 4) and elections (Chapter 5), the inherited incumbency advantage in promotion might vary across different institutional contexts. For example, in systems where parties depend upon the electoral popularity of individual MPs for the overall success of the party, party leaders may have incentives to reward electorally popular MPs with cabinet posts to keep them happy and avoid challenges to the party leadership. In such cases, it is possible that both types of legacies will enjoy similar advantages in cabinet selection if they both tend to enjoy similar levels of electoral popularity. When a party's success in elections is based less on the personal attributes of its candidates and more on the party's policies or the party leader's image, then the personal popularity of individual MPs may decrease, and greater weight might be placed on the need for competent policy experts or experienced leaders in office.

Any legacy advantage in ministerial selection, or differences across types of legacy MPs, may also depend on the power of the prime minister or party leader to choose his or her ministers. The power afforded to the prime minister can vary across different countries (O'Malley, 2007), and even over time in the same country, as has been Japan's experience (e.g., Hayao, 1993; Krauss and Pekkanen, 2011; Machidori, 2012; Woodall, 2014). Perhaps most important, the prime minister's choice may be constrained by factors such as strong norms for seniority rule in promotions. The relative contribution of the direct and indirect effects of dynastic ties on cabinet selection may thus vary by the institutional context in which promotion decisions are made.

Scholars have used a number of different junctures at which to divide postwar Japanese cabinets, depending on the research questions being investigated.[13] For the purposes of capturing variation in informal institutions, we shall divide the postwar era into four main institutional periods: (1) the Occupation Era, (2) the Early 1955 System Era, (3) the Seniority Rule Era, and finally, (4) the Postreform Era. These four periods are divided in some cases on the basis of changes that occurred in cabinets that were formed between general elections, and they correspond to the periods delineated by the vertical dashed lines in Figure 6.1. The Occupation Era covers eleven cabinets from 1947 to 1955, three years after the end of the Occupation but prior to the solidification of the 1955 System. In terms of leadership, this period was dominated by Prime Minister Yoshida Shigeru (in office from 1948 to 1954), whose top-down style earned him the nickname "One Man Yoshida" (*wanman Yoshida*). Yoshida was relatively unconstrained in cabinet appointment decisions and may have been more likely to favor legacy MPs of both types. Most cabinets were single-party governments of the Liberal Party or Democratic Party, aside from the first two cabinets (Katayama 1 and Ashida 1), which were coalition governments.

The Early 1955 System Era spans from the third cabinet of Hatoyama Ichirō (I. Hatoyama 3) when the LDP was formed, up until seniority rule and factional balancing were institutionalized as party norms in promotion under the Satō 3 Cabinet. In total, twenty cabinets were formed during this period. Prime ministers still enjoyed relatively free discretion in appointment decisions, often favoring friends and influential members of cooperative factions (Masumi, 1995), and many ministers were able to leapfrog into cabinet prior to reaching their fifth term in the House of Representatives or second term in the House of Councillors (Satō and Matsuzaki, 1986; Kohno, 1997, pp. 97–100). If legacy MPs enjoy an advantage in cabinet selection, they might be most likely to be fast-tracked in this manner.

The Seniority Rule Era covers twenty-seven cabinets during the "heyday" of LDP dominance, from the Satō 3 Cabinet up until the reshuffled first cabinet of Miyazawa Kiichi (Miyazawa 1.1) prior to the 1993 election. This period also includes the two reform cabinets under Hosokawa (Hosokawa 1) and Hata (Hata 1) prior to electoral reform. Cabinet selection in this period largely conformed to the new informal institutions of factional balancing and seniority rule. An appointment to cabinet was a prize that was awarded to an LDP MP after his or her fifth or sixth term. Hence, if legacy MPs (of either type) enjoy any advantage in promotion during this period, it should operate entirely through the greater seniority of legacy MPs.

Finally, the Postreform Era spans thirty-seven cabinets, from the first cabinet in which the LDP reentered government (Murayama 1) through to the second reshuffle of Prime Minister Abe's third cabinet in 2016 (Abe 3.2). In this period, the empirical data (Figure 6.1) show a large overrepresentation of legacy MPs in cabinet. However, it is possible that part of this overrepresentation may still be explained simply by the greater seniority of legacy MPs in the LDP. As so many legacy MPs were recruited as candidates in the late 1980s and early 1990s, they would be at the level of seniority in the 2000s that would normally entitle them to a cabinet post. At the same time, the practice of routine promotion based on seniority has largely ceased since 1993, leaving the effect of seniority uncertain.

Estimating the Advantage in Cabinet Promotion

Estimating the true causal effect of different types of dynastic ties on cabinet selection is a challenge because of the many possible attributes related to quality that may be correlated with being a legacy MP. In addition, legacy status contributes to electoral advantages, which are also likely to increase the probability of cabinet promotion, so any electoral advantages enjoyed by either cabinet legacies or non-cabinet legacies can be considered "posttreatment." The empirical strategy that will be used here is to first estimate the legacy advantage in cabinet selection without controlling for the electoral advantage (operationalized simply as seniority since other variables related to electoral strength, such as vote shares, are not consistent across electoral systems), and then to evaluate whether the estimate of the effect for each type of legacy is changed when this variable and other controls are included. This is the most straightforward way to evaluate whether the electoral advantage has a mediating effect on cabinet appointment but is limited in terms of causal identification of the direct effect because the electoral variables introduce some amount of post-treatment bias (because seniority is also an outcome of legacy status). Nevertheless, this approach allows us to get a sense of the legacy advantage by evaluating whether being a legacy MP is correlated with cabinet promotion, and then how this correlation is affected once we control for an MP's seniority and other observable variables. In addition, we can check whether the relationship between dynastic ties and cabinet promotion has varied across different institutional contexts captured by the four periods previously discussed.

To empirically evaluate the inherited incumbency advantage in ministerial selection, we can merge the JHRED panel dataset with data on all ministerial appointments in each of the ninety-seven cabinets formed between 1947 and 2016. The first cabinet in the resulting panel dataset is the cabinet of Katayama Tetsu (Katayama 1), inaugurated after the 1947 House of Representatives election. The last cabinet is the second reshuffle of the third cabinet of Abe Shinzō (Abe 3.2), inaugurated in August 2016, roughly ten months after the 2014 election. The coding of a cabinet as "new" corresponds to the official designation of cabinets from the Cabinet Office (*Kantei*) and thus includes cabinet reshuffles. Apart from the inclusion of reshuffles, this coding of a cabinet formation opportunity corresponds to conventional definitions of a change in cabinet in the comparative literature (e.g., Müller and Strøm, 2000, p. 12).

The dataset is structured such that the "time" variable is cabinet (in temporal order) rather than election year, and the 46,840 observations are measured at the MP-cabinet level, rather than the candidate-election year level. In other words, for each cabinet, the dataset includes observations for all individuals who were sitting members of the House of Representatives at the time of the cabinet's formation. Individuals who left office midterm due to death or resignation are dropped as observations in cabinets formed after their exit, and individuals who entered office midterm through by-elections are included only if their entry preceded the formation of the cabinet. Because JHRED is based on elections to the House of Representatives, the analysis will exclude ministerial positions that went to members of the House of Councillors (a handful of appointees in each cabinet) or to "technical ministers" from outside the Diet (which are rare in Japan). Prime ministers (who make the appointments) and speakers of the House of Representatives (*giinchō*) who would not be appointed are excluded. All other MPs are included.

Because the vast majority of ministerial positions are allocated to members in the House of Representatives, the structure of the dataset largely captures the pool of MPs that are available for promotion at any given cabinet formation opportunity. This is an important departure from previous analyses that use observations only on ministers to evaluate trends in ministerial personnel decisions (e.g., Ono, 2012; Masuyama and Nyblade, 2014; Woodall, 2014) or that aggregate House of Representatives members into time periods before and after electoral reform (Pekkanen, Nyblade and Krauss, 2014). By including all members in the sample of potential cabinet appointees at each cabinet formation opportunity, we can compare actual appointees to a relevant reference group: other members of the governing party or parties.

The baseline regression model is a linear probability model of the form

$$Y_{ipt} = \alpha_{pt} + \beta_1 \, Non\text{-}cabinet \; legacy_{ipt} + \beta_2 \, Cabinet \; legacy_{ipt} + \epsilon_{ipt}, \qquad (6.1)$$

where *Y* is *Cabinet appointment*, which is a dummy variable for whether an MP *i* from party *p* was appointed to a cabinet formed at time *t*. *Non-cabinet legacy* is a dummy variable equal to 1 if MP *i* was related to any former MP who never served in cabinet, and *Cabinet legacy* is a dummy variable equal to one if a legacy MP's predecessor served in a cabinet position. Party-cabinet fixed effects are represented by α. The baseline comparison group is non-legacy MPs in each party at each cabinet formation time; thus, β_1 estimates the average advantage for non-cabinet legacies over non-legacies, and β_2 estimates the average advantage for cabinet legacies over non-legacies. In a second model, controls are added for *Prior appointment* and seniority, split into categorical dummies for each additional term served, up to ten (MPs with ten or more terms are grouped together). The second model also includes controls for gender and prior service in the House of Councillors, faction fixed effects, region fixed effects, and dummies for method of election: SNTV or FPTP winner, midterm replacement (*kuriage tōsen*), by-election winner, zombie winner, and pure PR list winner.

Figure 6.2 plots the results for both models, splitting the sample of postwar cabinets across the four institutional periods. The results show considerable variation in the legacy advantage across institutional contexts. In the Occupation Era (Period 1, top-left panel), both types of legacy MPs were more likely to get appointed to cabinet, but this relationship is weaker once prior appointments and seniority are taken into account. In the Early 1955 System Era (Period 2, top-right panel), cabinet legacies continue to be more likely to get appointed, but again this relationship is no longer statistically

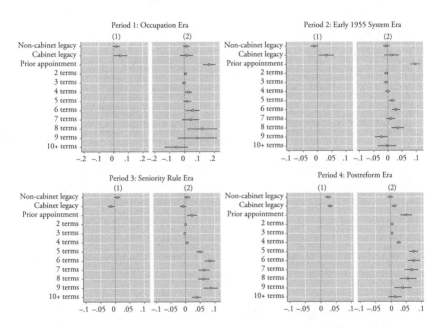

FIGURE 6.2 The legacy advantage in ministerial selection across institutional settings

SOURCE: JHRED.

NOTE: Models estimated with OLS using robust standard errors. Points and bars represent the estimated coefficients (predicted change) and 95 percent confidence intervals. Coefficient scale (x-axis) on top-left plot is larger to accommodate estimates. The dependent variable is a dummy variable for *Cabinet appointment*. Only MPs from the House of Representatives are included. The prime minister and the speaker of the house are excluded from the sample for each cabinet. All models include party-cabinet fixed effects. Model 1 estimations include no other controls. Model 2 estimations include (but do not display in the figure) dummy variables for gender and prior service in the House of Councillors, faction fixed effects, region fixed effects, and dummy variables for method of election: SNTV or FPTP winner, midterm replacement (*kuriage tōsen*; for period 4 these are always from the PR list), by-election winner, zombie winner, and pure PR list winner. Full results are presented in Table A.13 in Appendix A.

significant after controls are added to the model. As expected, neither type of legacy enjoyed an advantage during the Seniority Rule Era (Period 3, bottom-left panel), and the pattern of promotion in an MP's fifth or sixth term is clear from the coefficients in Model 2.

The most interesting pattern emerges in the bottom-right panel of Figure 6.2, which displays the results for the Postreform Era (Period 4). When no controls are included, both non-cabinet legacies and cabinet legacies appear to enjoy a roughly 3-percentage-point advantage over non-legacy MPs when it comes to getting promoted. However, once we control for seniority, it is clear than non-cabinet legacies are not actually advantaged directly—they just happen to be more senior. In other words, the apparent advantage of most legacy MPs in postreform Japan is not a product an increased demand by prime ministers in the new electoral environment but is rather an indirect result of their seniority in the party and their direct advantages in getting reelected. Cabinet legacies, however, still enjoy a small but statistically significant 1-percentage-point advantage in cabinet promotion.

The exact sources of this advantage cannot be pinned down definitively. However, among the different demographic and occupational backgrounds investigated in Table 2.2 in Chapter 2, the patterns for cabinet legacies are more divergent from non-legacy MPs than the patterns for non-cabinet legacies. For example, although both types of legacies tend to enter politics at a similarly young age (forty-three for non-cabinet legacies, forty-two for cabinet legacies), 22 percent of non-cabinet legacies have prior experience in local politics, compared to just 12 percent of cabinet legacies. In addition, 15 percent of non-cabinet legacies were former national bureaucrats, compared to 26 percent of cabinet legacies, and 31 percent served as MP secretaries, compared to 50 percent of cabinet legacies. To the extent that backgrounds in the national bureaucracy or as a political secretary are reflective of qualities that may be valuable in ministerial selection decisions (such as expertise), this difference may help explain the advantage of cabinet legacies. Alternatively, the advantage enjoyed by cabinet legacies could stem from an informational advantage in the party, more connected networks to party leaders, or a better ability to signal desirable qualities to the prime minister.

COMPARATIVE PATTERNS

The Dynasties in Democracies Dataset can be used to explore how well these patterns observed for the case of Japan "travel" to other contexts. Figure 6.3

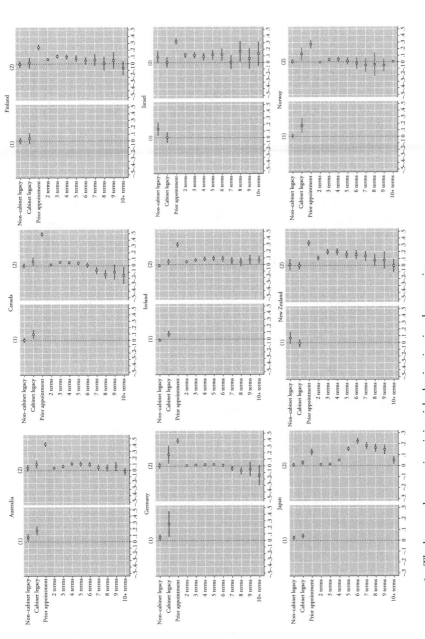

FIGURE 6.3 The legacy advantage in ministerial selection in nine democracies

SOURCE: Dynasties in Democracies Dataset.

NOTE: Models estimated with OLS using robust standard errors. Points and bars represent the estimated coefficients (predicted change) and 95 percent confidence intervals. Coefficient scale (x-axis) for Japan is smaller to better display estimates. Only two Norwegian MPs served 9 terms, and only one served 10 terms. Number of terms for Germany includes only postwar terms. The dependent variable is a dummy variable for *Cabinet appointment*. All models include party-term fixed effects. Model 1 estimations include no other controls. Model 2 controls for *Prior appointment* and seniority. No other control variables are included due to data limitations across cases.

shows the results of a simple replication of the preceding analysis using nine of the country cases from the comparative panel dataset where cabinet promotion information have been coded, for the sample of MPs serving since 1945.[14] In this simplified version of the analysis, the level of observation is MP-term rather than MP-cabinet (including for the case of Japan), and no MPs are excluded from the sample (in other words, prime ministers and speakers are included in all cases). The dependent variable is again *Cabinet appointment*, which now measures whether the MP served in cabinet at any point during the interelectoral legislative term. In model 1, only *Non-cabinet legacy* and *Cabinet legacy* are included as covariates, along with party-term fixed effects as in the baseline specification in Equation 6.1. Model 2 adds controls for *Prior appointment* and seniority (number of terms). The data for Japan are pooled across all institutional periods, as in the other eight cases.

From the comparative data, it is clear that the advantage in cabinet promotion for cabinet legacies is not a phenomenon that is exclusive to Japan. Even in democracies with relatively fewer dynasties, such as Germany and Canada, cabinet legacies are more likely to advance to the highest positions of power than non-cabinet legacies or non-legacy MPs. The three exceptions are Finland, Israel, and New Zealand. In Israel, non-cabinet legacies appear to be more advantaged than cabinet legacies. In Finland and New Zealand, neither type of legacy is significantly more likely to be appointed to cabinet than a non-legacy MP. Whether these differences can be explained by institutional or situational factors in these countries is a puzzle for future research to examine.

Discussion

In parliamentary democracies, effective political power rests with the prime minister and his or her cabinet. Consequently, the question of which parties enter cabinet, as well as the question of which parties acquire control over specific ministries, have been the subject of considerable research. At the end of the day, however, cabinet posts are assigned to individuals rather than simply to political parties. Individual ministers may be loyal agents of their parties (or the coalition agreement), but they may also shirk and pursue a personal agenda according to their own preferences. Despite the vast scholarship on cabinet government, and the potential agency problems that can emerge in the parliamentary chain of delegation (Strøm, 2000), very little research has explored the question of which individuals become cabinet ministers in parliamentary democracies. All too often, existing research has focused on the distribution of cabinet portfolios across parties or factions, ignoring important inequalities in the intraparty distribution of appointments to individual MPs.

This chapter has explored whether MPs who come from political dynasties possess advantages over non-legacy MPs in promotion from the backbench to the cabinet. Such an advantage could exist for two reasons. First, legacy MPs might enjoy an advantage owing to an established family record and reputation in politics, which is part of their inherited incumbency advantage and may signal quality to the prime minister and other party leaders. Alternatively, legacy MPs could be overrepresented in cabinet simply because they are better at getting elected and reelected, and are hence more senior, on average, than their non-legacy peers. In other words, any advantage in promotion for legacy MPs might function directly, through their status, resources, connections, and other intangible qualities, or indirectly, through the effect of those attributes on electoral success.

The empirical findings presented in this chapter indicate important distinctions between types of legacy MPs when it comes to the advantage in promotion to higher office. On the one hand, although both types of legacies enjoy electoral advantages that help them to reach higher levels of seniority, the relatives of former MPs who had themselves previously served in cabinet are decidedly advantaged when it comes to the allocation of a finite number of cabinet posts, even after seniority is taken into account. On the other hand, other legacy MPs are no more likely to get promoted to cabinet than non-legacy MPs at the same level of seniority in the party. The extreme overrepresentation of legacy MPs in recent Japanese cabinets is in large part the product of the more regularized system of seniority and the electoral advantages that help non-cabinet legacies reach these higher levels of seniority in the party. But cabinet legacies continue to enjoy a competitive edge over their peers in getting promoted.

Although the analysis here sheds light on the sources of the legacy advantage in promotion, it does not tell us much about whether legacy MPs—regardless of their family history in cabinet—make for more or less effective ministers than non-legacy MPs. Some critics of dynastic politics in Japan have charged that legacy MPs are ineffective leaders because their privileged and sheltered backgrounds leave them ill prepared to handle the tasks of governance. The apparent advantage of dynasties in ministerial selection thus raises important normative questions. Cabinets are the apex of power in parliamentary systems, and individual cabinet ministers often have the ability to influence policy and administrative outcomes within their own ministries. For democratic theorists and scholars of representative democracy, it is therefore important to understand why ministerial selection appears to favor a small cadre of party members, and whether this apparent bias in who gets selected produces any negative effects on governance. In the next chapter, we explore some of the potential political and economic consequences of dynastic politics for the nature and quality of representation in Japan and other democracies.

SEVEN

The Consequences of Dynastic Politics for Representation

> But it is not so much the absurdity as the evil of hereditary succession which concerns mankind. Did it ensure a race of good and wise men it would have the seal of divine authority, but as it opens a door to the *foolish*, the *wicked*, and the *improper*, it hath in it the nature of oppression. Men who look upon themselves born to reign, and others to obey, soon grow insolent; selected from the rest of mankind, their minds are early poisoned by importance; and the world they act in differs so materially from the world at large, that they have but little opportunity of knowing its true interests, and when they succeed to the government are frequently the most ignorant and unfit of any throughout the dominions.
>
> — *Thomas Paine (1776, p. 30)*

The preceding chapters have documented clear evidence of an inherited incumbency advantage in all three stages of a typical political career: selection, election, and promotion. At the selection and election stages, the collective findings from Japan suggest that a large part of the advantage is the name recognition that legacy candidates enjoy—hence, dynasties are more valuable to parties when their name recognition, and the established family history in politics it signals, serves as a key personal-vote-earning attribute in candidate-centered elections. In the promotion stage, however, district-level name recognition and electoral strength appear less important than the party-level or national-level familiarity that comes from being a member of a dynasty with a prior record in cabinet. However, this latter advantage may also potentially stem from differences in other qualities—such as professional expertise, charisma, and networks—across types of dynasties, and these differences are harder to disentangle.

Understanding the causes of democratic dynasties and the advantages that legacy candidates enjoy in their political careers is a necessary precondition for studying the potential consequences of these advantages. Ultimately, the quality of representation in any democracy depends not only on who is elected but also on how those who are elected behave once in office. In this chapter, we shift the focus to evaluating some of the potential "downstream" effects of the inherited incumbency advantage. What are the political and economic consequences of political dynasties in democracies? And are these consequences positive or negative for the functioning of democracy or the quality of representation? These are important questions to consider if we want to understand the full impact of dynastic politics on democracy.

In her seminal book on the concept of representation, Hanna Pitkin (1967) distinguishes between two types of representation: "standing for" and "acting for." The first type, sometimes also called *descriptive representation*, is associated with the idea that parliament should be a reflection or microcosm of the various demographic groupings in society. In other words, it is important that groups such as women and minorities have some physical presence in parliament (e.g., Phillips, 1995; Mansbridge, 1999). Part of the rationale is that representatives who come from distinct backgrounds will do a better job incorporating the interests of citizens with similar backgrounds into policy outcomes. Indeed, there is a growing body of evidence in support of this claim (e.g., Bratton and Ray, 2002; Chattopadhyay and Duflo, 2004; Svaleryd, 2009). This suggests an important link between descriptive representation and the second type of representation, sometimes called *substantive representation*, which has more to do with whether politicians' actions, through legislation or articulation of positions in parliamentary debates, also serve the interests of those whom they represent.

In the case of dynasties, it is fair to assume that legacy candidates, as with most politicians, do not descriptively represent the electorate in terms of economic and occupational backgrounds. Most politicians, including members of dynasties, come from very privileged family backgrounds and tend to serve in a narrow range of occupations—such as law or business—before entering politics (e.g., Putnam, 1976; Lawless, 2012; Dal Bó et al., 2017). As documented in Chapter 2, legacy MPs in Japan tend to be highly educated and wealthy, although the vast majority are not significantly more educated or wealthy than their non-legacy peers. Non-legacy and legacy MPs alike are more wealthy than most Japanese citizens. The average yearly income for a Diet member in Japan is roughly ¥21 million, whereas the average "salary-man" working for a private company earns just over ¥4 million in a year.[1] On the other hand, legacy MPs tend to enter parliament at a younger age than non-legacy MPs, and also are more likely to be women, which may help to provide better descriptive representation for these groups. When it comes to gender, dynastic succession may be one of the few ways for female candidates to break into politics in systems where women are generally disadvantaged (Jalalzai, 2013; Folke, Rickne, and Smith, 2017). Indeed, many female politicians in Japan and elsewhere first entered politics when their husbands died in office, a process sometimes referred to as a "widow's succession" in the United States (Werner, 1966; Kincaid, 1978).

When it comes to substantive representation, it is not immediately obvious whether a legacy MP should be expected to do objectively better or worse than a non-legacy MP in doing his or her job once in office. One question is whether members of dynasties are of lower or higher quality than other types of politicians. As noted by Timothy Besley (2005, p. 51), the "advantage in name recognition [for legacy candidates] is palpable [but] whether politician quality is transmitted intergenerationally is far from clear." Another question is whether the strong electoral advantages enjoyed by legacy candidates result in fewer incentives to work hard for the interests of the electorate. Although Thomas Paine's critique of hereditary succession in the quote at the head of this chapter was in response to the monarchical rule of King George III, one might wonder whether a similar logic applies to members of democratic dynasties. The connection has at least been raised by the popular media and non-legacy politicians who are critical of the practice. Is it common sense that dynasties might breed poor politicians?

If the demand for legacy candidates in a given country or electoral context is high, then a legacy candidate can be of lower quality (in terms of other attributes related to parties' goals in seeking votes, policy, or office) than a non-legacy candidate and still get selected. Much like how female congress-persons in the United States must outperform their male counterparts to get reelected (Anzia and Berry, 2011), or how female MPs in Germany tend to need more political experience and higher levels of education to obtain desirable extraparliamentary jobs (Geys and Mause, 2014), non-legacy candidates who compete against legacy candidates, either for the party nomination or in a general election, might need to be of higher quality and exhibit higher legislative performance if elected. This means that legacy MPs might be of lower quality in terms of policymaking even if they are of higher quality in terms of electoral strength. If this theoretical logic is true empirically, it may be particularly troubling, since legacy MPs appear to enjoy an advantage over other MPs in progressing from the backbenches to the cabinet, placing them at the pinnacles of political leadership and power. Another possibility is that members of dynasties might use their network connections—as a substitute for skill or talent—to gain advancement in politics.

The idea that democratic dynasties might result in poor outcomes for representation is in keeping with the bulk of the existing research on hereditary leadership succession in family-run firms (e.g., Pérez-González, 2006; Villalonga and Amit, 2006; Bertrand et al., 2008). This literature finds that firms with CEOs who are related to the previous CEO underperform relative to firms where unrelated CEOs are promoted. There is also some evidence from Italy that nepotism in academia damages the quality of a university's teaching and research (Durante, Labartino, and Perotti, 2011). In contrast, there are compelling reasons why members of dynasties in politics might actually provide for qualitatively better representation for their constituents. For example, Glenn R. Parker (1996, p. 88) argues that legacy MPs may be beneficial to the functioning of a legislature, since they will already be familiar with the rules of the game and legislative norms, unlike "amateur" politicians who lack such familiarity. In other words, legacy MPs may be ready to "hit the ground running" on the first day of their legislative careers.

Existing research into whether there is a quality difference among legacy and non-legacy politicians has produced mixed evidence at best. In a study of local-level politicians in Italy, for example, Benny Geys (2017) finds that members of dynasties tend to have lower levels of education—a potential marker of quality—than non-legacy local politicians. But this finding contrasts with the record in Japan (Chapter 2) and in Ireland (Smith and Martin, 2017). One concern might be the appropriate measurement of "quality" across different contexts. In a country with relatively low levels of higher education, years of education may be a reasonable proxy; in other countries, however, it may not (Dal Bó et al., 2017). Moreover, the same network advantages that members of political dynasties are assumed to enjoy in selection decisions may overlap with educational networks or wealth advantages that help them gain access into prestigious universities, even if they might not otherwise gain admission on their own academic merit.

In a similar vein, a common measure of candidate quality in the US literature is prior experience in local-level politics (e.g., Jacobson and Kernell, 1983), but we know that legacy candidates can often "leapfrog" directly into national politics without first gaining experience at the local level (e.g., Dal Bó, Dal Bó, and Snyder, 2009; Feinstein, 2010; Smith and Martin, 2017). By this standard measure, then, legacy candidates might appear to be of lower quality than non-legacy candidates—but this pattern may have few substantive implications for differences in behavior if legacy candidates gain skills and experience through observing their predecessors directly.

It is also unclear whether, and to what extent, markers of quality such as education are connected to the actual legislative behavior of politicians. Some politicians, such as Tanaka Kakuei in Japan or Trygve Bratteli in Norway (neither of whom were legacies), achieved remarkable political success despite having no more than a primary school education. In short, education and other markers of quality may not be good proxies for a politician's performance in office. Although a budding literature is beginning to explore various consequences of dynastic politics, there is very little empirical research into the actual behavior of legacy MPs in office.

There may also be some important economic consequences of dynastic representation, although here again, the existing evidence paints a complex and contradictory picture. In India, Pradeep Chhibber (2013, p. 290) reports that perceptions of the quality of representation are lower among voters who are represented in parliament by parties with dynastic leadership. In the Philippines, districts represented by legacy MPs tend to have higher levels of poverty, lower levels of employment, and greater economic inequality (Mendoza et al., 2012; Tusalem and Pe-Aguirre, 2013). However, it is unclear whether these conditions are the result of poor leadership by legacy politicians, or whether such economic patterns and legacy politicians are both the result of some other common factor, or whether the direction of causality is reversed.

In the case of Japan, Yasushi Asako, Takeshi Iida, Tetsuya Matsubayashi, and Michiko Ueda (2015) find that prefectures represented by a greater number of legacy MPs between 1997 and 2007 had worse economic outcomes (measured as GDP growth at the prefecture level), despite receiving relatively more distributive benefits (measured in terms of fiscal transfers from the central to local governments). The reason, they argue, is that dynastic politicians spend the distributive benefits inefficiently, which suppresses growth (see also Taniguchi, 2008).[2] A very similar pattern is observed in a working paper by Arthur Bragança, Claudio Ferraz, and Juan Rios (2015), who show that when a dynastic politician in Brazil narrowly wins a close election, there is more spending on urban infrastructure, health, and sanitation. Nevertheless, these additional investments do not appear to translate into improved economic outcomes (e.g., local economic growth, quality of public services). The expansion in the size of local governments in Brazil by dynastic politicians thus appears to mostly reflect rent extraction.[3] The findings of these studies thus suggest that dynasties might be correlated with poor economic performance. In contrast, Timothy Besley and Marta Reynal-Querol (2017) present evidence that dynastic leaders may have a positive impact on the rate of economic growth, but only where the leader enjoys significant autonomy in decision making. They rationalize that dynastic leaders will have longer time horizons than other leaders.

Clearly, there may be multiple ways, both direct and indirect, in which dynastic politics can have consequences for socioeconomic outcomes and the quality of representation in a democracy. Yet overall, the mechanisms linking political dynasties and their possible consequences for socioeconomic outcomes remain poorly understood. Moreover, establishing a causal connection between dynasties and their political or economic consequences is a challenge because of the many potentially confounding factors that may be at play. The remainder of this chapter considers three potential consequences of the inherited incumbency advantage for the nature of representation and functioning of democracy. First, what is the relationship between dynastic candidate selection and gender representation? Second, what is the impact of dynastic succession on the representational style of politicians? And finally, what is the relationship between dynastic politics and legislative behavior in parliament?

Dynasties and Gender Representation

Although the descriptive representation of women in democracies around the world has risen considerably over the past several decades, many of the earliest and most prominent female political pioneers first entered public office on the heels of a male relative. An example is Rebecca Felton, the first woman to serve as a US senator, who followed her husband, William Felton, into Congress in 1922.[4] A more recent example from the United States is Hillary Clinton, who, although she may be capable in her own right, owes a large part of her political success to her marriage to former president Bill Clinton. An example from Japan is Nakayama Masa, who became the first female cabinet minister in 1960 when she became the minister of health and welfare under Prime Minister Ikeda Hayato. Her husband, Nakayama Fukuzō, was an MP before her, and two sons and a grandson followed her into politics. Prominent examples from other countries include Indira Gandhi of India, Cristina Fernández de Kirchner of Argentina, Gro Harlem Brundtland of Norway, Corazon Aquino of the Philippines, Yingluck Shinawatra of Thailand, and Park Geun-hye of South Korea. Past research has established this pattern of a dynastic gender bias among presidents and prime ministers (Jalalzai, 2013), in the national legislatures of democracies as diverse as the United States, India, Ireland, and Sweden (Dal Bó, Dal Bó, and Snyder, 2009; Basu, 2016; Smith and Martin, 2017; Folke, Rickne, and Smith, 2017), and among local-level mayors in the Philippines (Labonne, Parsa, and Querubín, 2017).

Why might female politicians be more likely to come from a political dynasty than male politicians? The persistent underrepresentation of women in politics in general has previously been explained by a supply-and-demand model of political recruitment (e.g., Norris and Lovenduski, 1995), similar to the model used in this book to explain the overrepresentation of dynasties in Japan.[5] Existing research in the United States suggests that the greatest factor inhibiting more equal gender representation in politics is the supply of female candidates (e.g., Lawless and Fox, 2010). A large body of work has also shown that women's descriptive representation is higher under PR electoral systems, and when parties or countries adopt gender quotas with placement mandates (e.g., Reynolds, 1999; Krook, 2006). This suggests that institutional differences may generate greater incentives to recruit women—for example, to present a balanced slate of candidates on a party list to voters.[6]

Previous chapters have already documented that an existing family history in politics can be an important supply-side factor influencing the decision to run for office. But it is possible that the size of the effect of this supply-side motivation is greater for women than it is for men. A family history in politics may inspire both men *and* women to run for office, but for those who do not have a family history in politics, an ambition to run may be more prevalent among men than women, thus resulting in a higher ratio of legacy to non-legacy women who seek office, compared to men who seek office. Female relatives of politicians may benefit from having a political role model in their family and will have a greater familiarity with what a life in politics entails, thus removing some of the potential anxiety and uncertainty involved in the decision to enter a political race.

Moreover, when female legacy candidates do seek office, their dynastic ties may help them to overcome vote disadvantages with voters, or informational disadvantages with party elites involved in candidate selection. Although evidence is somewhat mixed, a considerable body of research shows that voters tend to have a negative view of female politicians (e.g., Anzia and Berry, 2011). A negative bias against women among party actors in the selectorate has also been identified in numerous studies (e.g., Niven, 1998; Casas-Arce and Saiz, 2015; Folke and Rickne, 2016). Being part of a political dynasty can lower the considerable barriers to entry for female candidates posed by these biases or other resource inequalities. In candidate-centered systems, for example, party actors involved in candidate selection tend to be less informed about women than men as candidates (e.g., Sanbonmatsu, 2006) and may avoid recruiting or selecting a female candidate if they believe she will be less successful electorally. However, if she is the wife or daughter of a former male politician, the party actors can use the quality and electoral success of the male predecessor as an informational cue for how the female legacy candidate might perform (Folke, Rickne, and Smith, 2017). This idea is similar in spirit to the concept of informational shortcuts in previous work on women's political recruitment (Norris and Lovenduski, 1995) and is also consistent with the general theory of dynastic candidate selection advanced in this book. The difference is that the brand name signal of dynastic family ties may help women disproportionately more than men.[7]

In short, dynastic ties might not only encourage the supply of female candidates where women are otherwise reluctant to come forward as candidates; they might also help such women overcome discrimination and other obstacles that affect women as candidates. Some of this disadvantage may simply be statistical discrimination because fewer women have served in the past, so it is harder for voters and party elites to predict what can be expected from a female candidate. Once enough women have served, however, this discrimination or ignorance about women in politics may begin to decrease, thus decreasing the importance of dynastic family ties for gender representation. Over time, fewer and fewer women will need to depend on dynastic ties to get selected and elected.

The comparative MP-level data in the Dynasties and Democracies Dataset can be used to explore the relationship between gender and dynastic politics in several democracies and across time. To examine whether there is a "dynastic bias" in gender representation, we can compute the ratio of legacy MPs among the women and men in each country, and then take the difference between these two ratios—that is, the proportion of legacy MPs among the women, minus the proportion of legacy MPs among the men:

$$\left(\frac{\text{Number of female legacy MPs}}{\text{Number of all female MPs}} \right) - \left(\frac{\text{Number of male legacy MPs}}{\text{Number of all male MPs}} \right) \quad (7.1)$$

Table 7.1 gives the percentage of legacy MPs among male and female MPs since 1945 in the twelve democracies of the comparative dataset (one observation per MP). The dynastic bias is the difference between the two. In four of the country cases—Finland, Ireland, Japan, and the United States—the difference in dynastic ties between male and female MPs is statistically significant. Each of these countries uses an electoral system (open-list PR, STV, SNTV, or FPTP) in which votes are cast for candidates rather than parties. This suggests that dynastic ties in these contexts may help women disproportionately more than men.

Figure 7.1 illustrates the variation over time by dividing the data into two equal time periods: 1945–1980 and 1981–2016. Here, all MP observations are included for each time period, not just one per individual. When split into two time periods, it is clear that the dynastic bias in gender representation has decreased over time in each of the four democracies just mentioned, as well as in Australia, Canada, Germany, Italy, and New Zealand. The exceptions to the pattern are Israel, Norway, and Switzerland, all of which are places where the bias was already comparatively small. In Japan, the increase in female candidates and MPs since electoral reform has completely erased the dynastic bias in gender representation that existed for most of the postwar period. In recent years, women are less likely to come from a democratic dynasty than their male counterparts in the Diet.

TABLE 7.1

The dynastic bias in gender representation in twelve democracies

Country	Legacy female (% of females)	Legacy male (% of males)	Dynastic bias
Australia	5.00	6.70	−1.70
Canada	5.77	4.56	1.21
Finland	7.37	4.28	3.09[a]
Germany	1.16	1.25	−0.09
Ireland	35.29	20.58	14.71[a]
Israel	8.26	6.45	1.81
Italy	5.73	5.70	0.03
Japan	21.55	15.25	6.30[a]
New Zealand	10.48	7.56	2.92
Norway	7.83	6.74	1.09
Switzerland	4.17	7.07	−2.90
United States	15.62	5.60	10.02[a]
Total	7.62	6.93	0.69

SOURCE: Dynasties in Democracies Dataset.
NOTE: One observation per MP.
[a]Difference significant at $p < .05$.

Another interesting pattern is that the relationship between female legacy MPs and their predecessors tends to change over time. Early female legacy MPs are predominately widows and wives. In later decades, female legacy MPs are more likely to be daughters. In Ireland, for example, a majority of female legacy MPs were widows or wives until the mid-1970s, at which point daughters and nieces became more common. In Japan, until 1980, 82 percent of all female legacy candidates and 77 percent of female legacy MPs were the wives of former MPs (widows in all but one case). Since 1981, only 24 percent of female legacy candidates have been wives, and only half of these were widows (although the widows have been more successful in getting elected). In contrast, 54 percent of female legacy candidates (57 percent of winners) are the daughters of former MPs. Another 16 percent are granddaughters (19 percent of winners). This shift also hints at a possible supply-side change. Widows are often recruited to run in by-elections to succeed their deceased husbands but are soon defeated or replaced by another (male)

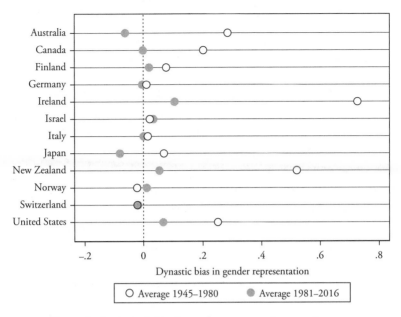

FIGURE 7.1 Change in the dynastic bias in gender representation over time
SOURCE: Dynasties in Democracies Dataset.
NOTE: Includes all MP-level observations for each period.

candidate. Daughters, however, have grown up around politics and may have more personal ambition and motivation to run. However, recent pressure to recruit more women as candidates may also result in more daughters being recruited into running, particularly for the LDP.

Like Father Like Son? Policy Consistency Across Generations

A second important question related to the consequences of dynastic politics is whether members of dynasties maintain similar representational "styles" as their political predecessors. We can think of representational style as the language used and positions articulated when communicating to voters in a district (e.g., Grimmer, 2013). This style is displayed to voters around election time in the form of policy appeals (e.g., calls to enact certain laws), as well as personal appeals (e.g., declarations of personal character or commitment to constituents). Thus, part of a candidate's representational style will be unrelated to his or her party's policy positions, and more related to aspects of his or her personal vote. Another way to think of this concept is

as part of the candidate's "home style" (Fenno, 1978). Dynasties may cultivate distinct styles that represent a family "brand" that transcends the party
"brand," and voters may find this continuity in representational style to be a
positive aspect of dynasties.

We can think about this formally by denoting the representational style
of candidate i as R_i. The exact nature of R_i can vary slightly from election to
election as new issues arise. If a candidate were to simply repeat the same appeals each election, then $R_{it} = R_{it-1}$, where t is a current election, and $t-1$
is the previous election. However, in most cases the difference between R_{it}
and R_{it-1} will take some positive value, $q \in [0,1]$, where $q = 0$ represents a
style that is exactly the same, $q = 1$ represents a style that is completely different, and $0 < q < 1$ represents cases where the style differs somewhat, but
not completely. We might expect that q will be closer to 0 when comparing
the same candidate's representational style across two consecutive elections
than when comparing that candidate's representational style to a different
candidate's representational style.

In the case of Japan, when a candidate retires (or stops running), there
are two basic types of potential successors to his or her jiban, as previously
discussed in detail in Chapter 5: a *kin successor* (i.e., a hereditary candidate)
or a *non-kin successor* (i.e., a secretary or other nonrelative, including legacy
successors to non-kin). Successors can choose their own distinct representational styles, or they can emulate the styles of their predecessors. One possible implication of dynastic candidate selection is that q will be closer to 0
when the retiring candidate is replaced with a kin successor than when he
or she is replaced with a non-kin successor, all else equal. This is because for
kin successors it is more important to maintain the same family "brand" of
representation that has been successful in the past. Non-kin successors may
feel less of an attachment to the personal style of representation developed
by the predecessor.

Legacy candidates may thus represent a continuity in representational
style and policy positions that goes beyond party label alone. A prominent
real-world example is when US President George W. Bush leaned in part on
his family legacy to justify his policy decision to invade Iraq in 2003: "There's
no doubt his hatred is mainly directed at us. There's no doubt he can't stand
us. After all, this is a guy that tried to kill my dad at one time."[8] Another example is Prime Minister Abe Shinzō's frequent invocation of the memory of
his grandfather, former prime minister Kishi Nobusuke, in framing his po-

litical philosophy. One of Abe's key policy goals has been the revision of the Japanese Constitution, which was one of his grandfather's unfulfilled policy wishes. Prime Minister Hatoyama Yukio similarly adopted his grandfather Ichirō's philosophy of "fraternity" (*yūai*) in politics (Itoh, 2003, p. 219).

To get a sense of whether there is continuity in representational style within dynasties, we can compare the candidate election manifestos (*senkyo kōhō*) of predecessors and different types of successors (kin or non-kin) within the same jiban from 1986 to 2009, using the dataset of manifestos created by Amy Catalinac (2016). Following the work of Justin Grimmer (2013), who looks at press releases of US members of Congress, we can reason that the representational styles of politicians should be observable in material produced for the purpose of communicating with voters between and during election campaigns. Unlike politicians in the United States, however, candidates for office in Japan are afforded relatively few means to communicate with voters during campaigns.[9] Candidate election manifestos are one of the most important means for communicating policy goals and priorities to voters, and are widely consumed—an average of 40 percent of voters report having read candidate manifestos in the days leading up to an election (Catalinac, 2016).

Following existing work in comparisons of similarity across text documents (e.g., Moser and Reeves, 2014), we can use a metric called the Hellinger distance to measure the difference in the probability distributions of topics in the text of the candidate manifestos. The Hellinger distance has a minimum of 0 and a maximum of 1, with 0 indicating that two manifestos exhibit identical distributions over topics and 1 indicating that they exhibit very different distributions over topics. It is thus the empirical analog to the theoretical difference q discussed earlier. Figure 7.2 shows kernel density plots of the Hellinger distance for the three types of candidates in the sample: a candidate running again, a non-kin successor running for the first time, and a kin successor running for the first time. The sample is restricted to LDP candidates and LDP-affiliated independents. The left panel of Figure 7.2 shows the plots for the preform SNTV candidates, and the right panel shows the plots for the postreform FPTP candidates.

The mean Hellinger distance for candidates who are themselves running again is .67 in the preform period and .73 in the postreform period. For kin successors, the mean is .75 in the preform period and .80 in the postreform period. For non-kin successors, the mean is .80 in the prereform

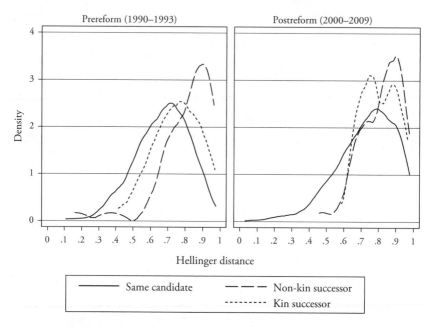

FIGURE 7.2 Similarity of candidate manifestos for different types of succession, 1986–2009
SOURCE: JHRED and candidate manifesto data from Catalinac (2016).
NOTE: The figure shows kernel density plots of the Hellinger distance measuring the similarity of a candidate's manifesto to the manifesto of the candidate who ran in the same jiban in the immediately previous election. Prereform: kin successors (N = 31), non-kin successors (N = 37), candidates who are themselves running again (N = 595). Postreform: kin successors (N = 35), non-kin successors (N = 174), candidates who are themselves running again (N = 902). The first year of data in each period, 1986 and 1996, is excluded as it is the comparison group for the following year.

period and .81 in the postreform period. In other words, these results appear to show some evidence that, relative to non-kin successors, kin successors adopt representational styles that are more similar to their predecessors, and that styles from election to election are less stable in general in the postreform era—although the differences between the types of successors fall short of being statistically significant given the small sample size in each group. The pattern of less stability in representational styles in the postreform period makes sense given that campaign issues have become more focused on the party's policy platform than on personalistic appeals (McElwain, 2012; Catalinac, 2016) and given that the LDP's party platform tends to shift from one election to the next.

These empirical findings, though rudimentary, suggest that there may be some amount of intergenerational transmission of representational style within family dynasties, or that legacy candidates might try to maintain the family brand when they inherit a jiban from a predecessor, perhaps to maximize their potential inherited incumbency advantage in the election.

Do-Nothing Dynasties? Legislative Behavior of Legacy MPs

Finally, it is also possible to explore whether legacy MPs behave differently than non-legacy MPs once in office. Legacy candidates may be comparatively more comfortable and familiar with the policymaking process and able to start work on their first day in office with minimal training or socialization (Parker, 1996). As noted in the introduction to this book, the experiences of non-legacy candidates and legacy candidates might be compared to first-generation college students (i.e., students whose parents did not go to university) and students whose families have a history of sending their children to university. First-generation college students tend to underperform relative to other students, at least initially, even controlling for IQ and high school grades (Terenzini et al., 1996). Legacy MPs might similarly perform better in office, at least initially, than non-legacy MPs.

Measures of legislative activity include committee attendance, number of parliamentary questions and private member bills submitted, and number of speeches given on the floor of the chamber or in committee. Speeches can be particularly useful for gauging parliamentary activity. Because plenary time in all legislatures is scarce, the number of parliamentary speeches given by an individual MP reflects in part the priorities of the MP's party in allocating time as a resource (Proksch and Slapin, 2012) but may also capture some form of initiative on the part of individual MPs. Moreover, party leaders may be more likely to allocate speaking time to members who they consider most competent. In a study of speeches made in the Swedish Riksdag (parliament), Hanna Bäck, Marc Debus, and Jochen Müller (2014) analyze differences in speaking patterns across gender. They find that women tend to speak less often on the floor, and when they do, it is less often about "hard" policy issues like economics, foreign affairs, and defense—in line with gender differences in cabinet portfolios (Reynolds, 1999). Are there similar differences in legislative activity across legacy and non-legacy MPs?

To evaluate the relationship between dynastic ties and legislative behavior, we can examine data on plenary and committee speeches spoken by LDP MPs, collected from the Diet record and made publicly available by Sugawara Taku. The data are available up to the 45th House of Representatives (elected in 2009). To create a symmetrical window in each institutional setting, the prereform sample will be limited to the five elections prior to reform. Table 7.2 shows the average number of speeches spoken by LDP MPs, and the average number of characters (*moji*) in those speeches, per legislative term, split by legacy status and institutional period. Attendance in committees is also included. Legacy status is divided into cabinet legacies and non-cabinet legacies to evaluate whether there are any differences between the two types of legacy MPs.

The aggregate data for the prereform period suggest that there were few meaningful differences between different types of MPs in terms of legislative activity. In the postreform period, however, both cabinet legacies and non-cabinet legacies have been more active, on average, in plenary sessions. The same cannot be said for activity in committees. Non-cabinet legacies speak less in committees than do non-legacies. However, these averages do not take into account that legacy MPs of both types are more likely to be senior in the party and more likely to occupy leadership roles, which come with frequent speaking opportunities. To estimate the differences in speaking behavior

TABLE 7.2

Legislative activity of LDP MPs, 1980–2009

	NON-LEGACY		NON-CABINET LEGACY		CABINET LEGACY	
	Mean	Max	Mean	Max	Mean	Max
Prereform (1980–1993)						
Plenary speeches	3	147	3	80	3	174
Length (in characters)	5,953	411,510	4,825	318,846	4,286	254,961
Committees attended	73	286	75	311	84	300
Committee speeches	3	23	3	17	4	23
Length (in characters)	13,050	150,365	9,160	97,793	16,033	110,790
Postreform (1996–2009)						
Plenary speeches	2	260	5	220	5	233
Length (in characters)	3,657	310,383	9,512	422,847	11,661	490,727
Committees attended	138	505	103	420	122	549
Committee speeches	7	72	5	61	6	54
Length (in characters)	13,050	150,365	9,160	97,793	16,033	110,790

SOURCE: JHRED and data from Sugawara Taku's (archived) website (http://sugawarataku.net).

controlling for these factors, we can use a negative binomial regression, with the number of characters in speeches in plenary sessions as the dependent variable (a negative binomial regression is appropriate because of the large proportion of MPs who do not speak at all in the Diet in any given session).

The results of this analysis are presented in Table A.14 in Appendix A. Controls are included for number of terms and its squared term, gender, and whether the MP served as a cabinet minister, junior minister, or speaker of the House of Representatives during the term. Term fixed effects are also included. Finally, the sample is split into prereform and postreform periods to evaluate whether patterns are distinct in the two institutional contexts. In the prereform period, there is no significant difference in the speaking behavior of MPs across legacy status. Seniority and cabinet appointment are positively associated with speaking, while being a woman is negatively associated with speaking, in line with previous findings from Sweden (although it should be noted that there were few female LDP MPs during this period). In the postreform period, gender is no longer significant, and there is an increased role for junior ministers in plenary speech. This reflects administrative reforms in 2001 that introduced a new and more active role for junior ministers.

Nevertheless, even controlling for these factors, the results indicate that legacy MPs are slightly more active than non-legacy MPs in the postreform period, and the effect is entirely driven by cabinet legacies. The predicted length of speeches per legislative term for a male LDP backbencher (i.e., not a cabinet minister, junior minister, or the Speaker) with the average number of terms (four) is 1,538 characters for non-legacy MPs, 1,593 characters for non-cabinet legacies, and 2,404 characters for cabinet legacies. These patterns do not hold if the number of characters in committee speeches is used as the dependent variable rather than the number of characters in floor speeches (Table A.15 in Appendix A). This is somewhat surprising given that much of the action in Japanese legislative politics occurs in the Budget Committee of the Diet. The difference between floor and committee speech patterns may indicate that cabinet legacies play a greater role on the "public stage" of politics—plenary debate—while other members play equally important roles in parliamentary committees, where the real work happens. More work is needed to investigate whether these patterns are consistent across other democracies or whether the content of speech differs across legacy and non-legacy MPs.

Discussion

The empirical analyses in this chapter have only begun to scratch the surface of the potential effects of dynastic politics for the nature of representation in Japan and other democracies.

One question for future research is whether there is any correlation between dynastic politics and corruption. Eric Chang and Miriam Golden (2006) find evidence in Italy that the incentives to cultivate a personal vote may be linked to higher levels in corruption and money politics because of the pressure to promote oneself electorally and the burden this places on candidates for amassing financial resources (sometimes illegally). It could be the case that the personal advantages in name recognition and inherited resources that legacy candidates possess over non-legacy candidates insulate them from needing to resort to corrupt practices in order to get elected. While non-legacy politicians may feel stronger pressure to engage in illegal fundraising to amass the personal resources necessary to be competitive in personalized elections, legacy politicians may exhibit comparatively lower levels of such corruption. In contrast, Benjamin Nyblade and Steven Reed (2008) note that there are actually two types of political corruption: illegal acts for material gain (looting) and illegal acts for electoral gain (cheating). They find in Japan that political experience and electoral security increase the probability of looting but that electoral insecurity combined with intraparty competition increases the probability of cheating. Therefore, we might expect that when legacy politicians do engage in illegal acts, it will more likely be of the looting variety.

A second question is whether Japan's low levels of gender representation are related to its high number of dynasties. There has been an increase in female candidates in recent years, but if most women are recruited to run in unsafe districts, they might not last more than one term in office. Moreover, if most of the safe districts are being held continuously by male members of political dynasties, it may continue to hamper gender representation in the long run. Legacy women who inherit a seat may be among the few female MPs with "staying power," which can also have an impact on the supply of capable female MPs for higher positions in the cabinet and party leadership. Looking beyond Japan, more work needs to be done to understand how institutional differences—including electoral systems, but also candidate selection procedures and gender quotas—affect the relationship between gender and dynasties.

Finally, a third question is whether different types of legacy candidates are more or less likely to introduce innovative new policies. A case could be made that legacy MPs in the prereform period might have brought a fresh view to politics, as many did not envision a career in politics but were instead brought in at the request of kōenkai or faction leaders. They were not, in this regard, traditional politicians. Since the electoral reform, the legacy candidates who emerge are more likely to self-select into politics and might thus represent a narrower range of viewpoints and experiences than the legacy candidates of the past. It is possible, therefore, that the new order may actually represent less diversity among legacy candidates, even as it has ushered in more diversity among all candidates.

Further explorations into these and other potential outcomes will be necessary to fully understand the consequences of dynastic politics for democracy. The phenomenon of democratic dynasties represents a form of elite self-perpetuation that transcends generations and may prevent meaningful political change. As Vilfredo Pareto (1901, p. 36) argues, "The history of man is the history of the continuous replacement of certain elites: as one ascends, another declines." Electoral competition in modern democracies should theoretically provide for a regular circulation of political leaders and ensure that those in power remain responsive to the demands of the electorate. But if the new generation of politicians tends to emerge from among the children of the previous generation, this circulation might have less substantive meaning, and political change may be only nominal in nature. Rather than an elite transformation, we might simply get old wine in new bottles.

However, the continuity in representation and opportunities for political socialization that are embodied within dynasties might sometimes be a positive aspect for representative stability within democracies. Much depends on the personal qualities of the actual legacy candidates who emerge to contest elections. The true consequences of dynastic politics are thus nuanced, and may include both positive and negative effects.

EIGHT

Conclusion
Family Fiefdoms and Party Politics

> *Legacy:*
> (noun) an amount of money or property left to someone in a
> will; a thing handed down by a predecessor.
> (adjective – *computing*) denoting software or hardware that
> has been superseded but is difficult to replace because of its
> wide use.
>
> —*New Oxford American Dictionary*

In defending and promoting the new form of democracy that would prevail under the US Constitution, the authors of the *Federalist Papers* wanted to assuage concerns that the few in power would be elevated above the many, to the ruin of the people. "Who are to be the electors of the federal representatives? Not the rich, more than the poor; not the learned, more than the ignorant; not the haughty heirs of distinguished names, more than the humble sons of obscurity and unpropitious fortune." And: "Who are to be the objects of popular choice? Every citizen whose merit may recommend him to the esteem and confidence of his country. No qualification of wealth, of birth, of religious faith, or of civil profession is permitted to fetter the judgement or disappoint the inclination of the people."[1] These ideas form part of the basic foundations of our understanding of participatory democracy and political opportunity in modern representative democracies.

And yet, even 230 years later, if we look around the democratic legislatures of the world and ask, "Who gets elected?" all too often the answer is this: "The rich, more than the poor; the learned, more than the ignorant; the haughty heirs of distinguished names, more than the humble sons of obscurity and unpropitious fortune," and often those whose only qualifications appear to be their birth into a particular family. The phenomenon of democratic dynasties is thus a manifestation of the potential narrowing of the political class that can occur within democracies, and one that tends to stand in particular relief when considering that modern democracy was created in opposition to the perceived evils of hereditary rule. But the mechanics underlying the formation and persistence of dynasties in democracy are more complex than simply an elite dominance of the political process. Moreover, the consequences of dynastic politics for the quality of representation are far from obvious.

This book has explored the causes and the consequences of political dynasties in democracies through a close examination of the case of Japan. Where possible, comparative data have been used to put Japan's experience in perspective and draw broader conclusions. The persistence of dynasties in a developed democracy like Japan is a puzzle, as the historical experience of most other developed democracies has been a gradual decline in dynasties over time. Japan's experience for most of its postwar history was exactly the opposite—a dramatic growth in democratic dynasties over time—leaving many observers to wonder whether Japanese politics were becoming dominated by an ever-narrowing political class. The large number of dynasties in Japan, particularly within the Liberal Democratic Party, situates it at the extreme end of cross-national and cross-party variation in dynastic politics.

The theoretical explanation this book offers for why we observe such variation in dynastic politics across democracies and parties focuses on the institutional factors that affect supply and demand in candidate selection. On the supply side of candidate selection, potential legacy candidates will be more likely to want to run for office if their predecessors have served longer tenures, allowing them greater time to be socialized into a life of politics. In addition, potential legacy candidates will be more likely to want to run if the family already has a history of multiple generations in politics. These factors might also help to explain why female candidates who emerge, particularly in earlier elections in a democracy, are more likely to be legacy candidates. When such legacy candidates choose to run, parties may have few reasons to reject them. However, we should expect the supply-side incentives to be relatively universal across countries and parties. The fact that there is variation across country and party cases suggests that demand-side incentives in candidate selection can differ according to institutional context.

The core argument is that legacy candidates—especially those who directly and immediately succeed their political predecessors in the same district as hereditary candidates—enjoy an inherited incumbency advantage in all three stages of a typical political career: selection, election, and promotion. But although all democracies are likely to feature some amount of dynastic politics, particularly in the early years following democratization, certain institutional features can facilitate and even encourage the formation of dynasties by increasing the electoral value of the inherited incumbency advantage to parties. The demand-side rationale for dynasties encompasses the interaction between the inherited incumbency advantage of a potential legacy candidate and factors that increase or decrease its potential value to party actors. Of the possible demand-side factors, the institutions of the electoral system and candidate selection process within parties are arguably the most important variables for explaining patterns in dynastic recruitment, at least in the case of Japan. Other factors, such as population size, years of democracy, level of economic development, political culture, and others, may also play some role in dynastic politics, and this role may vary across countries.

In candidate-centered elections, the inherited incumbency advantage translates into an electoral advantage for a legacy candidate over his or her competitors. Party leaders, knowing this advantage to exist, are likely to give a legacy candidate the nomination when he or she wants it, but they may also actively recruit other legacy candidates to run. However, this recruitment strategy may sometimes pose a trade-off for party leaders if the individual electoral strength of legacy candidates allows them to diverge from the party's preferred legislative or policy priorities. The result may be a party that is weak or dominated by the local concerns of the party's decentralized stakeholders. When elections are more party centered, the inherited incumbency advantage is less relevant for electoral success, and parties may in turn be more likely to seek out candidates who better suit their party goals at the national level, even if those candidates might have a weaker local base or less name recognition.

Party nomination decisions can also be influenced by the nature of the decision-making process in candidate selection and the pool of available would-be candidates. The extent to which party leaders can achieve their goals in candidate selection will depend not only on the supply of candidates who feature the attributes they desire but also on their ability to control which candidates ultimately get the nomination. More inclusive candidate eligibility requirements provide party actors with greater choice, which will lower demand for dynasties as an expedient source of candidates. At the same time, more centralized selection processes give party leaders the power they need to holistically determine their party personnel strategies.

The case of Japan is useful for evaluating the empirical truth of this explanation, not only because there have been so many dynasties (providing enough of a sample size for statistical analysis) but also because the 1994 electoral reform and subsequent party reforms in the LDP have provided institutional change within an otherwise stable, single-country environment. In other words, electoral and party reforms have made Japan into a natural test case for evaluating the relationship between political institutions and dynastic politics. The empirical evidence from Japan reveals that institutions can indeed have a significant influence on the phenomenon of dynastic politics in democracies but that the response to newly introduced institutional incentives will be partly conditioned by path dependence and the preexisting preferences and practices of party elites.

This final chapter draws together the key conclusions of the book and considers the lessons that Japan's experience with dynastic politics might hold for other democracies. Overall, the findings in this book suggest important implications for institutional design, particularly in developing democracies, such as India, the Philippines, and Indonesia, where dynasties have been viewed as a growing problem in recent years, but also in developed democracies like the Republic of Ireland, where politics is still in many ways a family affair. When electoral and party institutions create excess demand for dynasties and similar types of candidates with high personal name recognition (e.g., celebrities, whose national name recognition may even trump that of high-profile legacy candidates), it may crowd out other types of candidates and potentially pose problems for party discipline and cohesion. The key challenge is how to transform party organizations from decentralized cadres of local notables into coherent vehicles for programmatic policies.

Dynasties and Democracy in Japan

What does Japan's experience with dynastic politics teach us about the development and functioning of democracy in Japan more generally? The SNTV electoral system used from 1947 to 1993 to elect members of the House of Representatives resulted in intense intraparty competition, particularly within the dominant LDP. Because LDP candidates could not campaign on the basis of their party label and the policies for which it stood, they resorted to campaigning predominantly on the basis of their personal attributes and behavior. Each candidate worked hard to cultivate his or her own personal support base (their jiban) through the construction and maintenance of kōenkai, which functioned as personal support organizations for mobilizing voters in elections.

From its beginning, the candidate selection process in the LDP was largely decentralized to the kōenkai of outgoing candidates. When an LDP candidate retired or died, it was an ideal solution for the kōenkai to turn to a family member as a successor who would be most suited to maintain the existing support of his or her predecessor. This incentive often resulted in the recruitment of family members who did not have a preexisting desire to run. These hereditary candidates would typically go on to easily win the subsequent election and would then continue to represent the kōenkai and other constituents in much the same fashion as the previous incumbent. Previous studies of dynastic politics in Japan have emphasized the important electoral advantages of inheriting a kōenkai in SNTV elections where an established support base, name recognition, and financial resources (the three "ban") were paramount to success, and often far more important than party label or policies. Apart from the proliferation of political dynasties, however, this pattern of electoral politics in the 1955 System also resulted in unsustainable levels of corruption, pork-barrel spending, and rampant factional politics within the LDP.

The culmination of these dysfunctional features of the 1955 System was the 1993 general election, when voter dissatisfaction and party defections toppled the LDP from its majority-party status and ushered in electoral reform. The new MMM system was designed to encourage Westminster-style politics in Japan: party-centered election campaigns, with two strong, cohesive parties that alternate regularly in government. Intraparty competition was eliminated, dramatically reducing the candidate-centered nature of elections and increasing the importance of party image and national policy platforms in campaigning and voting. The LDP and other parties responded by paying more attention to their collective policy platforms and by choosing candidates who better represented what the party hoped to stand for in elections. This latter shift is exemplified by the adoption of the new open-recruitment system, which has expanded the pool of potential candidates and placed greater control in the hands of party leaders involved in candidate selection.

The substantive chapters of this book present a number of empirical findings about the effects of these reforms on dynastic politics, but these effects also speak to the broader changes to democracy in Japan over the past two and a half decades. First, the results of the analysis of candidate selection in Chapter 4 demonstrate that legacy candidates are more likely to emerge following the exit of long-serving incumbent MPs, and when their families have an existing, multigeneration connection to politics. This empirical regularity suggests that a large part of explaining the emergence of a dynasty rests with supply-side factors. However, the case of Japan has revealed important variation in demand-side factors as well. The incentives for political parties to recruit legacy candidates are lower when personal-vote-earning attributes, like the name recognition inherent in dynasties, are less salient to voters in elections. Following electoral reform, the name recognition inherent in dynastic ties is no longer as important to the LDP's chances of winning an election. Moreover, nominating too many dynasties can even become a liability for the party's national image.

The process for selecting candidates has also become more centralized in response to the new electoral environment, and the LDP no longer seeks out legacy and hereditary candidates to succeed weaker outgoing incumbents, opting instead to nominate a more diverse range of candidates that includes more women. As a result, the overall share of new legacy candidates has dropped from an average of nearly 50 percent in the last years of the pre-reform period, to a level—at around 10 percent in recent elections—that is rapidly approaching that of Westminster democracies like the United Kingdom and Canada, as well as most other advanced industrialized democracies. The analysis of the postreform MMM system also reveals significant differences in dynastic candidate selection across electoral tiers—FPTP versus PR—in the new mixed electoral system. Legacy candidates are much less likely to be nominated in the PR tier, where voters cast their ballots solely on the basis of party considerations.

The investigation in Chapter 5 of the inherited incumbency advantage enjoyed by legacy candidates in elections also reveals important changes in Japan that go beyond the theme of dynastic politics. In both the prereform and postreform periods, first-time LDP candidates who inherited a jiban were more successful than their non-legacy counterparts—in many cases despite facing more competition. However, it is important to keep in mind that because of the effect of the electoral reform on selection decisions— with fewer "low quality" legacy candidates getting selected—the electoral success of legacy candidates across the two periods cannot be easily compared. Among the weaker legacy candidates who have run, many as independents after being denied the LDP's official nomination, the electoral advantage in the postreform period appears to have declined. The most important factor in determining success in the new SMDs may be running in a party stronghold, precisely where legacy candidates are most likely to emerge. This finding speaks to the general trend in Japan toward more party-dominant campaigns and elections.

The electoral advantages enjoyed by legacy candidates may help them to win multiple elections and advance to higher levels of seniority in the party. However, the analysis in Chapter 6 shows that cabinet legacies may also enjoy an additional advantage in getting promoted to cabinet. The exact causal mechanisms are not clear, but the advantage of cabinet legacies in promotion may have something to do with informational advantages within the party. The effect has been most prominent in the past two decades since electoral reform, as prime ministers have enjoyed more discretion in appointment decisions. The past few cabinets of LDP prime ministers have been remarkably dynastic in composition, with roughly 60 percent of membership having ties to past MPs. As turnover in the party reduces the number of senior members who are legacies, this pattern may begin to subside. However, the comparative record in other democracies implies that this pattern goes beyond institutional factors at the electoral or candidate-selection stages of an MP's career.

The political and economic consequences of dynastic politics are another concern that hint at issues of broader importance to Japan's political development. In 2017, Japan ranked 164th in the world's legislatures in terms of gender representation.[2] The results of the analyses in Chapter 7 suggest that dynasties may function as a useful back channel to gender representation. However, it is important to keep in mind that institutional contexts that encourage the formation of dynasties—candidate-centered electoral rules and decentralized candidate selection—may also be associated with worse gender representation. Reforming such institutions to strengthen parties might be expected to decrease the number of dynasties *and* increase the number of women in politics. This appears to be the pattern in Japan, with women increasing in representation and dynasties decreasing—and a gray area where the effect is canceled out, namely, female legacy candidates. However, the new female legacy candidates are more likely to be daughters than widows, which suggests that many of them are selecting into candidacy with a vision of a career in politics. This is a dramatic shift from most of the postwar period.

The results from Chapter 7 also suggest that part of the allure of dynasties may be the continuity in representational style that legacy candidates offer to voters. However, since electoral reform, this continuity in representational style and policy appeals across candidates in elections has lessened, as the party and its platform has taken on the important role of structuring policy alternatives for voters. With the introduction of party manifestos in 2003, candidates in the LDP and other parties can now point to specific policy positions of the party without the need to differentiate themselves with their own policy prescriptions. In other words, the representational continuity previously provided by dynasties may be superseded by the development of strong programmatic parties. Whether this development helps to create strong and enduring ideologies and affiliations in the electorate is a different question. Japan's weak and ever-shifting opposition parties make it difficult to imagine strong party affiliations taking hold in the near future, at least on the center left of the political spectrum.

Finally, although most legacy MPs are not discernibly different from other politicians in terms of legislative behavior, cabinet legacies do appear to be slightly more active in floor speeches in the Diet. In the postreform period, party leaders have begun to exercise more control over speaking time and are also more accountable—leaving less of the parliamentary speaking and explanations of policies to bureaucrats, and placing the responsibility instead on the shoulders of cabinet ministers, junior ministers, and other party leaders. The small edge that backbench cabinet legacies still have in speaking time may reflect their better quality, or it may reflect a strategy of party leaders grooming these individuals as future party leaders. This appears to be the case with some individuals, like Koizumi Shinjirō, but may apply to others as well. To the extent that parliamentary speaking time and ability is a positive trait in an MP, it is encouraging that Japan's newest legacy MPs in recent years have been more likely to be of the type that participates more.

Will Japan continue to move in the direction it is headed? In 2016, four by-elections were held to replace incumbent House of Representatives MPs who died or left office. The outcomes of these by-elections hint that the situation described in this book—of change mediated by path dependence—still predominates. The first two by-elections took place in April. In Hokkaido 5th District, a by-election was needed after Machimura Nobutaka died of a stroke. Machimura was an eleven-term LDP MP, former faction leader, and former speaker of the House of Representatives. It should not be surprising that his son-in-law, Wada Yoshiaki, sought and won the nomination and then the election. In Kyoto 3rd District, a by-election was needed to replace the two-term LDP MP Miyazaki Kensuke. Miyazaki was once married to Katō Ayuko, daughter of LDP veteran Katō Kōichi. He later divorced Katō and married another LDP MP, Kaneko Megumi, whose father was a local mayor. In this case, Miyazaki was too young to have any child old enough to succeed him, and moreover, the scandal-tainted name had little value to the LDP. In the end, the party decided not to nominate a candidate at all, and the Democratic Party candidate, Izumi Kenta, easily won the seat. Izumi was a "zombie" incumbent who resigned his list seat to run for the SMD seat.

The two other by-elections took place in October. In Tokyo 10th District, a by-election was needed after incumbent LDP MP Koike Yuriko resigned her seat to run (successfully) for governor of Tokyo as an independent. The LDP nominated an incumbent PR list winner (not a zombie), Wakasa Masaru, who resigned his PR seat and went on to win the SMD election. Meanwhile, in Fukuoka 6th District, two conservative candidates sought the LDP nomination to replace thirteen-term former cabinet minister Hatoyama Kunio, following his death earlier in the year. Given the Hatoyama family's long history in politics (Kunio and his brother, former prime minister Hatoyama Yukio, were fourth-generation MPs), it is not surprising that the top contender was Kunio's son, Jirō. Jirō faced competition for the nomination from Kurauchi Ken, the son of the chairman of the local prefectural branch of the LDP, prefectural assemblyman Kurauchi Isao. In other words, it was a competition between a national dynasty versus a local dynasty. The LDP leadership could not decide which candidate to nominate, so it let them both run as independents. When it became clear that Hatoyama Jirō had won, the party quickly granted him an ex post nomination.

To the casual observer of Japanese politics, the cases of Wada and Hatoyama might seem to suggest that the LDP is still stuck in its old ways. In contrast, this pattern is exactly what should be expected given the theory proposed in this book. Both Wada and Hatoyama were the relatives of long-serving, powerful incumbents from existing dynasties and both had strong supply-side motivations to run. When such candidates do come forward, the LDP has little reason to deny them the nomination, unless—as in Hatoyama's case—there is additional competition for the nomination and it is unclear which potential candidate will bring in more votes. As fewer and fewer LDP incumbents reach such long tenures, the supply of such legacy hopefuls should continue to decrease.

The word "legacy" is not often used as an adjective, as it has been used in the terminology throughout this book. When it is used as adjective, the definition given by the *New Oxford American Dictionary* pertains to computing: "denoting software or hardware that has been superseded but is difficult to replace because of its wide use." This definition may seem like an appropriate characterization of political legacies in Japan as well—at least for now. When parties are strengthened, dynastic recruitment is a practice that we should expect to be superseded by other patterns in recruitment— but it is difficult to replace because of its wide use and the path dependence of preexisting dynasties with legacy hopefuls waiting in the wings.

Lessons for Other Democracies

Japan's experience with dynastic politics has important implications for institutional design, particularly in developing democracies where dynasties have been viewed as a growing problem in recent years. Dynasties have been a notable feature of Indian democracy, for example, especially if one considers family ties to politicians across local, state, and national levels of politics. Part of the reason, according to Kanchan Chandra (2016), is that political office in India is financially attractive, especially compared to the relatively low standard of living for most citizens. This suggests a supply-side rationale that is economic in nature. However, Chandra also argues that parties will have greater demand for dynasties in districts where the party is organizationally weak at the local level and needs to keep potential defectors in the fold. If a legacy candidate has any kind of embedded support in the district, he or she may be able to run as an independent or from another party and threaten the party's ability to win the seat. This description of the Indian case jibes with the narrative of the prereform LDP in this book, although without the added incentives for dynastic candidate selection produced by intraparty competition in multimember districts. Institutional reforms that strengthen party organization at the local level may help to undercut this tendency toward dynastic politics in India.

Not all institutional reforms will have the intended or expected effects, however. Pablo Querubín (2011) shows that the imposition of term limits in the Philippines after the 1986 People Power Revolution paradoxically led to the proliferation of dynasties. The term-limited politicians simply got their family members to run in their place as they ran for another office, thereby establishing family control over multiple offices at once.[3] In a related working paper, Julien Labonne, Sahar Parsa, and Pablo Querubín (2017) find that term limits for mayors in the Philippines led to a sharp increase in female mayors taking over. However, 70 percent of the new female mayors were members of dynasties. In other words, the previous male elite, forced out of office by term limits, simply installed their relatives in their place, and many of these were female relatives. The problem of dynasties has grown so severe that the Philippine Congress has recently debated a law that would prohibit family members from simultaneously holding public office.[4] It is unclear whether the controversial actions of the current president of the Philippines, Rodrigo Duterte—such as advocating for the extrajudicial killings of drug dealers, and bad-mouthing the leaders of other countries—should be attributed to his background as a non-legacy "outsider." One might view his erratic behavior as proof that dynasties provide more stable and responsible leadership; however, his rise to power might not have occurred were it not for public dissatisfaction with inept leadership and governance under previous leaders, most of whom came from established dynasties.

In Indonesia, legislators succeeded in passing a law against dynasties. The law prohibited any candidate with blood or marital ties to the incumbent (regional leader) from running for governor, district head, or mayor (or deputy positions). This law was in response to an increase in dynasties following decentralization in the late 1990s. Many of the most prominent dynasties controlled multiple levels of government in Indonesia's regions, and several prominent dynastic politicians have been convicted on corruption charges and sent to jail. However, the Constitutional Court voided the law in 2015 on the basis that it violated basic constitutional rights of members of dynasties to run for office (unlike the party-level norm adopted by Japan's DPJ, as parties are private organizations that may adopt whatever rules they choose for candidate eligibility).[5] Prabowo Subianto, the son-in-law of Indonesia's former dictator, Suharto, ran in the 2014 presidential election but was defeated by Joko Widodo, a popular governor of Jakarta who does not come from a political dynasty. Prabowo initially declared victory for himself but later withdrew from the count, essentially conceding the election.[6]

Dynasties have also garnered much attention in the Republic of Ireland, where in recent years roughly a quarter of all MPs, and more than 40 percent of cabinet ministers, have had a family history in the Dáil (Smith and Martin, 2017). In 2016, there was some speculation that Prime Minister Enda Kenny would retire before the next general election (he did retire as prime minister in 2017, but a new election was not held). His twenty-three-year-old daughter, Aoibhinn Kenny, was seen within the local Fine Gael organization as the favorite to succeed him, suggesting that dynasties may continue to dominate Irish politics into the near future.[7] The Irish perhaps have the most to learn from the Japanese experience, as the STV electoral system used to elect members of the Dáil is very similar to Japan's prereform SNTV system (Chapter 3). One way to strengthen parties and decrease the prevalence of dynasties would be to introduce an FPTP or AV system with SMDs. The experience of Japan's LDP, viewed through the lens of dynastic politics, sheds important light on the possibilities and challenges involved in such institutional reforms.

Future Directions

The hope is that this book, and the questions that remain unanswered in it, will encourage the continued study of political dynasties as a research agenda in political science and other fields. Democratic dynasties are just one thread in the wider fabric of political representation in modern democracies, but pulling on this thread can potentially unravel important insights into the functioning and outcomes of political processes. More data need to be collected, and the two motivating research questions of this book—why dynasties, and so what?—should be tackled using additional theoretical perspectives and methodological tools.

One worthwhile pursuit is to look at the patterns in dynasties across levels of government—national, regional, and local—and how networks and family connections across these levels affect career paths and electoral and policy outcomes (e.g., Cruz, Labonne, and Querubín, 2017). This book has focused on relationships between national-level politicians, but political families tend to have a much wider reach than simply national politics. For example, although the percentage of dynasties in the US House of Representatives and Senate has been less than 10 percent since the 1920s, the percentage has been as high as 50 percent if relationships to local and state-level politicians are included (Clubok, Wilensky, and Berghorn, 1969). Similarly, if relationships to state-level politicians and failed candidates are included, India's Lok Sabha has been, on average, 24 percent dynastic in recent years (Chandra, 2016). Such relationships may be more consequential in federal systems, but the existing data and research are sparse.

Even in Japan, many candidates for the House of Representatives who have been treated as non-legacy candidates for the purpose of the analyses in this book nevertheless have ties to local politicians. Between 1947 and 2014, there were 600 individual candidates who were related to a previously elected or appointed national-level politician (and so count as legacy candidates). However, if known ties to failed candidates are included, this number increases to 619 individuals, and if known ties to local politicians are also included, the number increases to 721 individuals. These figures, as well as the statistics from other countries, likely undercount many individuals whose local ties were not reported in newspapers or other media, which poses a considerable measurement challenge for researchers. Nevertheless, future research that incorporates such ties is likely to reap rich rewards for the study of families in politics.

A second promising direction for future research is to look into the historical development of political dynasties in democracies, particularly following episodes of institutional change (e.g., Cirone and Velasco Rivera, 2017; Velasco Rivera, 2017). Early elections in many democracies were characterized by decentralized competition of local notables, with only loose party affiliations and fluid party systems. In much of Western Europe, the introduction of PR to replace SMD elections in the early 1900s generated a shift toward more party-centered elections and simultaneously strengthened the control of party leaders over their members (Duverger, 1954; Schröder and Manow, 2014; Cox, Fiva, and Smith, 2018). Similar transitions toward stronger parties occurred in the United States and elsewhere under different conditions. In other words, the changes that have played out in Japan over the past three decades may be similar to the evolution of politics at an earlier time in other democracies. The increased availability of digitized historical data on candidates and MPs in several longtime democracies provides an opportunity to examine the transition from family fiefdoms to party politics in different environments and time periods.

There is every reason to believe that such future research endeavors will greatly advance our understanding of modern representative democracy and how institutional choices influence its development.

Appendix A

Detailed breakdown of legacy candidates by party, 1947–2014

	LEGACY		TOTAL
	(N)	(%)	(N)
LDP, Democratic Liberal, Liberal	2,395	27.65	8,661
LDP-affiliated independent	185	19.19	964
JSP, Leftist JSP, SDP	191	5.65	3,382
JSP-affiliated independent	3	4.00	75
Kōmeitō	41	4.32	950
Kōmeitō-affiliated independent	0	0.00	8
DSP, Rightist JSP	89	8.53	1,043
DSP-affiliated independent	5	13.51	37
JCP	12	0.28	4,234
JCP-affiliated independent	0	0.00	22
DPJ	239	13.12	1,822
DPJ-affiliated independent	4	10.26	39
Democratic (1947, 1954), Reform (1952)	88	7.20	1,222
National Cooperative Party	6	3.31	181
Hatoyama Liberals	4	4.08	98
New Liberal Club	32	29.36	109
New Party Sakigake	10	32.26	31
Japan New Party	7	12.50	56
Renewal Party	17	24.29	70
New Frontier Party	51	14.13	361
Ozawa Liberals	9	11.69	77
Liberal Alliance	4	1.85	216
Social Democratic League	11	36.67	30
Labor-Farmer Party	4	4.82	83
Conservative Party	5	16.67	30
People's New Party	5	13.89	36
New Party Japan	0	0.00	17
New Party Daichi	1	7.14	14
Your Party	12	14.29	84
Japan Restoration/Innovation Party	28	10.94	256
Tomorrow Party of Japan	18	12.77	141
Party for Future Generations	6	12.50	48
Other independents, minor parties	55	1.75	3,148
Total	3,537	12.84	27,545

SOURCE: JHRED.

NOTE: All candidate observations included.

Detailed breakdown of legacy MPs by party, 1947–2014

	LEGACY		TOTAL
	(N)	(%)	(N)
LDP, Democratic Liberal, Liberal	2,042	32.59	6,265
LDP-affiliated independent	65	30.66	212
JSP, Leftist JSP, SDP	153	7.58	2,019
JSP-affiliated independent	1	6.25	16
Kōmeitō	37	5.76	642
Kōmeitō-affiliated independent	0	0.00	7
DSP, Rightist JSP	56	11.16	502
DSP-affiliated independent	2	18.18	11
JCP	4	1.05	380
JCP-affiliated independent	0	0.00	8
DPJ	168	18.01	933
DPJ-affiliated independent	3	33.33	9
Democratic (1947, 1954), Reform (1952)	65	12.08	538
National Cooperative Party	5	10.87	46
Hatoyama Liberals	1	3.13	32
New Liberal Club	23	48.94	47
New Party Sakigake	7	46.67	15
Japan New Party	1	20.00	5
Renewal Party	16	28.57	56
New Frontier Party	32	20.25	158
Ozawa Liberals	6	26.09	23
Liberal Alliance	0	0.00	2
Social Democratic League	9	45.00	20
Labor-Farmer Party	4	20.00	20
Conservative Party	2	18.18	11
People's New Party	2	25.00	8
New Party Japan	0	0.00	2
New Party Daichi	1	20.00	5
Your Party	9	39.13	23
Japan Restoration/Innovation Party	19	19.59	97
Tomorrow Party of Japan	3	27.27	11
Party for Future Generations	2	100.00	2
Other independents, minor parties	17	10.69	159
Total	2,755	22.43	12,284

SOURCE: JHRED.

NOTE: All MP observations included.

TABLE A.3

Legacy and hereditary candidates in each party or camp, 1947–1993

	LEGACY		HEREDITARY		TOTAL
	(*N*)	(%)	(*N*)	(%)	(*N*)
Conservatives (camp)	354	13.87	149	5.84	**2,552**
LDP	181	37.47	100	20.70	483
LDP-affiliated independent	77	20.81	29	7.84	370
NLC	5	14.29	4	11.43	35
Others	91	5.47	16	0.96	1,664
Socialists (camp)	62	4.78	27	2.08	**1,296**
JSP	29	7.16	14	3.46	405
DSP	14	7.65	7	3.83	183
Others	19	2.68	6	0.85	708
Kōmeitō	5	2.69	0	0	**186**
JCP	3	0.39	0	0	**779**
Minor party/independent	4	0.32	1	0.08	**1,257**
Total	428	7.05	177	2.92	**6,070**

SOURCE: JHRED.

NOTE: One observation per candidate. Party label is whatever the candidate used in his or her first election attempt between 1947 and 1993. By-election candidates are included, as are candidates who previously served in the House of Councillors. For the conservative and socialist camps, "Others" include the precursor parties to the LDP (the Liberals and Democrats) and pre-1958 JSP (including Leftist and Rightist Socialists). Kōmeitō group includes one party-affiliated independent (Kusakawa Shōzō). JCP group includes thirty-seven independents or candidates from minor communist-ideology parties. All other minor party and independent candidates whose camp could not be identified are grouped with "minor party/independent." Bold entries in the far-right column sum to the total number of candidates (*N* = 6,070).

TABLE A.4

Predicting dynastic succession in the LDP, 1958–1990

	(1)	(2)	(3)	(4)	(5)	(6)
DV: Precede candidate						
Incumbent	0.326				0.178	0.175
	(0.036)				(0.046)	(0.048)
Prior wins		0.038			0.024	0.024
		(0.004)			(0.005)	(0.007)
Existing dynasty			0.308		0.245	0.227
			(0.051)		(0.050)	(0.054)
Death				0.308	0.134	0.123
				(0.048)	(0.056)	(0.059)
Constant	0.159	0.114	0.252	0.242	0.036	0.308
	(0.020)	(0.023)	(0.019)	(0.019)	(0.020)	(0.434)
R^2	0.124	0.105	0.064	0.073	0.216	0.247
DV: Precede MP						
Incumbent	0.287				0.152	0.155
	(0.035)				(0.043)	(0.045)
Prior wins		0.036			0.023	0.024
		(0.004)			(0.005)	(0.007)
Existing dynasty			0.342		0.286	0.281
			(0.051)		(0.049)	(0.053)
Death				0.259	0.099	0.086
				(0.048)	(0.054)	(0.056)
Constant	0.130	0.080	0.200	0.206	0.005	0.492
	(0.018)	(0.021)	(0.018)	(0.018)	(0.019)	(0.417)
R^2	0.106	0.102	0.088	0.057	0.217	0.255

(*continued*)

TABLE A.4 (CONTINUED)

	(1)	(2)	(3)	(4)	(5)	(6)
DV: Bequeath						
Incumbent	0.293				0.174	0.159
	(0.032)				(0.041)	(0.042)
Prior wins		0.029			0.016	0.014
		(0.004)			(0.004)	(0.006)
Existing dynasty			0.175		0.119	0.109
			(0.048)		(0.045)	(0.048)
Death				0.291	0.144	0.146
				(0.046)	(0.055)	(0.057)
Constant	0.064	0.048	0.165	0.135	−0.015	0.207
	(0.013)	(0.018)	(0.016)	(0.015)	(0.016)	(0.413)
R^2	0.135	0.085	0.028	0.088	0.190	0.225

NOTE: Robust standard errors in parentheses. All models estimated as linear probability models using ordinary least squares. Results are consistent when estimated using logit or probit. Level of observation is each candidate in the final election before no longer running (N = 625). The dependent variable for the top rows is a dummy variable for whether the candidate preceded a family member as a candidate; dependent variable for the middle rows is a dummy variable for whether the candidate preceded a family member as a candidate who also won; the dependent variable for the bottom rows is a dummy variable for whether the candidate was immediately succeeded by a family member as a candidate in the same district. Coefficient values in Figure 4.2 are based on the results for model 6, which includes controls for gender, age, age-squared, four categorical dummies for population density (rural, semirural, semiurban, urban), categorical dummies for district magnitude, and fixed effects for region and year (not shown).

TABLE A.5

Number of applicants and approved candidates in official DPJ open-recruitment contests

Open-recruitment round	Applicants (N)	APPROVED		WOMEN	
		(N)	(%)	(N)	(%)
March 1999	564	94	16.7	—	—
August 1999 (women only)	56	37	66.1	56	100
April 2002	416	46	11.1	41	9.9
February 2004	713	81	11.4	94	13.2
February 2005[a]	231	—	—	14	6.1
May 2006	1,314	164	12.5	168	12.8
November 2009	1,982	208	10.5	394	19.9
Total	5,276	630	11.9	767	14.5

SOURCE: DPJ Election Strategy Committee.

[a]The number of approved candidates in 2005 is not available since that round of open recruitment was for specific SMD races. Similarly, the number of applicants and approved candidates is not available for the four district-level open-recruitment contests held in 2012.

TABLE A.6

Number of applicants and districts for official LDP open-recruitment contests

Open-recruitment round	Applicants (N)	Districts (N)
2004 (Saitama 8th District by-election)	81	1
2004	296	20
2005 (preelection emergency round)	868	26
2006	299	8
2007	89	4
2008	25	2
2009 (preelection round)	60	3
2009 (postelection, Shizuoka 3rd District)	0	1
2010	546	53
2011	51	6
Total	2,315	124

SOURCE: LDP Election Strategy Committee.

NOTE: Includes some open-recruitment contests, such as for Shizuoka 3rd District in 2009, in which no applicants applied or the process failed to produce a candidate. For this reason, the total number of districts is higher than the number of open-recruitment candidates who ultimately ran for election.

TABLE A.7
Number and percentage of legacy candidates, 1976–2014

	ALL PARTIES			LDP CANDIDATES			DPJ CANDIDATES		
Year	Legacy (N)	Total (N)	Legacy (%)	Legacy (N)	Total (N)	Legacy (%)	Legacy (N)	Total (N)	Legacy (%)
All candidates									
1976	162	904	17.92	115	322	35.71			
1979	175	891	19.64	126	322	39.13			
1980	169	842	20.07	131	312	41.99			
1983	186	848	21.93	142	338	42.01			
1986	192	838	22.91	144	322	44.72			
1990	213	957	22.26	156	336	46.43			
1993	206	955	21.57	133	285	46.67			
1996	219	1,545	14.17	126	364	34.62	24	168	14.29
2000	197	1,450	13.59	128	346	36.99	35	270	12.96
2003	186	1,179	15.78	129	341	37.83	41	282	14.54
2005	188	1,151	16.33	122	351	34.76	44	306	14.38
2009	186	1,388	13.40	120	329	36.47	44	331	13.29
2012	167	1,510	11.06	95	339	28.02	28	267	10.49
2014	156	1,191	13.10	100	353	28.33	23	198	11.62

First-time candidates

1976	32	260	12.31	16	36	44.44			
1979	27	202	13.37	17	41	41.46			
1980	6	82	7.32	6	11	54.55			
1983	22	207	10.63	13	39	33.33			
1986	23	168	13.69	14	34	41.18			
1990	46	315	14.60	21	39	53.85			
1993	24	321	7.48	13	30	43.33			
1996	35	840	4.17	12	123	9.76	6	87	6.90
2000	24	652	3.68	12	46	26.09	5	106	4.72
2003	26	446	5.83	18	63	28.57	4	85	4.71
2005	22	329	6.69	16	88	18.18	4	59	6.78
2009	19	676	2.81	3	31	9.68	9	113	7.96
2012	23	719	3.20	11	135	8.15	0	42	0.00
2014	13	269	4.83	6	36	16.67	2	36	5.56

SOURCE: JHRED.

NOTE: Includes both SMD and pure PR list candidates in the postreform period. By-election candidates are included, grouped with the previous general election. First-time candidates exclude former members of the House of Councillors who switched chambers. Numbers and percentages for LDP and DPJ do not include affiliated independents.

TABLE A.8

First-time legacy and hereditary candidates in each party, 1996–2014

	LEGACY		HEREDITARY		TOTAL
	(N)	(%)	(N)	(%)	(N)
LDP	78	14.94	44	8.43	522
LDP-affiliated independent	18	20.45	11	12.50	88
DPJ	30	5.68	7	1.33	528
NFP	12	7.64	4	2.55	157
Kōmeitō	0	0.00	0	0.00	113
JCP	0	0.00	0	0.00	1,157
SDP	1	0.56	1	0.56	180
Ozawa's Liberal Party	1	2.94	0	0.00	34
Liberal Alliance	1	0.57	1	0.57	174
People's New Party	0	0.00	0	0.00	17
Your Party	6	9.52	0	0.00	63
JRP/JIP	5	3.50	2	1.40	143
TPJ	2	4.76	0	0.00	42
Party for Future Generations	0	0.00	0	0.00	16
New Party Daichi	1	14.29	0	0.00	7
Happiness Realization Party	1	0.26	0	0.00	380
Other minor party/independent	6	1.94	2	0.65	310
Total	162	4.12	72	1.83	3,931

SOURCE: JHRED.

NOTE: One observation for each candidate. By-election candidates are included. Members of the House of Councillors who switched chambers are excluded. Party label is whatever the candidate used in his or her first election. Apart from LDP-affiliated independents, party-affiliated independents are grouped with "minor party/independent." All legacy candidates in this category ran as independents. The two cases of hereditary candidates in this category were independents Tokuda Takeshi (2005, endorsed by the DPJ but later joined Liberal Alliance and LDP) and Gotōda Yayoi (2014, daughter of former DPJ MP Tanaka Keishū).

TABLE A.9

Predicting dynastic succession in the LDP, 1993–2012

	(1)	(2)	(3)	(4)	(5)	(6)
DV: Precede candidate						
Incumbent (SMD)	0.385				0.153	0.149
	(0.059)				(0.066)	(0.070)
Incumbent (zombie)	0.243				0.128	0.129
	(0.124)				(0.118)	(0.127)
Prior wins		0.051			0.035	0.019
		(0.006)			(0.007)	(0.010)
Existing dynasty			0.232		0.116	0.142
			(0.058)		(0.054)	(0.054)
Death				0.502	0.309	0.329
				(0.091)	(0.099)	(0.096)
Constant	0.132	0.051	0.180	0.201	0.010	0.209
	(0.022)	(0.023)	(0.025)	(0.023)	(0.020)	(0.348)
R^2	0.155	0.228	0.057	0.102	0.311	0.376
DV: Precede MP						
Incumbent (SMD)	0.359				0.134	0.131
	(0.058)				(0.065)	(0.069)
Incumbent (zombie)	0.201				0.091	0.095
	(0.118)				(0.115)	(0.120)
Prior wins		0.048			0.034	0.014
		(0.006)			(0.007)	(0.010)
Existing dynasty			0.196		0.085	0.109
			(0.056)		(0.052)	(0.050)
Death				0.495	0.316	0.336
				(0.094)	(0.101)	(0.098)
Constant	0.111	0.032	0.159	0.172	−0.002	0.457
	(0.021)	(0.021)	(0.023)	(0.022)	(0.018)	(0.333)
R^2	0.147	0.222	0.045	0.109	0.302	0.381

(*continued*)

TABLE A.9 (CONTINUED)

	(1)	(2)	(3)	(4)	(5)	(6)
DV: Bequeath						
Incumbent (SMD)	0.383				0.214	0.232
	(0.057)				(0.065)	(0.069)
Incumbent (zombie)	0.123				0.058	0.087
	(0.099)				(0.099)	(0.100)
Prior wins		0.039			0.021	0.012
		(0.006)			(0.007)	(0.010)
Existing dynasty			0.166		0.074	0.090
			(0.052)		(0.047)	(0.048)
Death				0.503	0.320	0.332
				(0.095)	(0.104)	(0.101)
Constant	0.064	0.023	0.122	0.127	−0.015	0.226
	(0.016)	(0.019)	(0.021)	(0.019)	(0.016)	(0.307)
R^2	0.196	0.172	0.039	0.135	0.307	0.357

NOTE: Robust standard errors in parentheses. All models estimated as linear probability models using ordinary least squares. Results are consistent when estimated using logit or probit. Level of observation is each candidate in the final election before no longer running in an FPTP district ($N = 335$). The dependent variable for the top rows is a dummy variable for whether the candidate preceded a family member as a candidate; the dependent variable for the middle rows is a dummy variable for whether the candidate preceded a family member as a candidate who also won; the dependent variable for the bottom rows is a dummy variable for whether the candidate was immediately succeeded by a family member as a candidate in the same district. Coefficient values in Figure 4.8 are based on the results for model 6, which includes controls for gender, age, age-squared, four categorical dummies for population density (rural, semirural, semi-urban, urban), and fixed effects for region and year (not shown).

TABLE A.IO

OLS regression estimates of the electoral advantage of different types of first-time LDP and LDP-affiliated candidates in MMDs, 1958–1993

	WIN			QUOTA PROPORTION		
	(1)	(2)	(3)	(4)	(5)	(6)
Legacy entrepreneur	0.112	0.191	0.179	0.114	0.189	0.185
	(0.064)	(0.066)	(0.077)	(0.035)	(0.036)	(0.045)
Non-legacy successor	0.106	0.084	0.084	0.100	0.060	0.081
	(0.044)	(0.046)	(0.053)	(0.023)	(0.024)	(0.026)
Legacy successor to non-kin	0.269	0.279	0.283	0.182	0.148	0.159
	(0.055)	(0.062)	(0.069)	(0.030)	(0.033)	(0.035)
Hereditary successor	0.246	0.286	0.294	0.161	0.176	0.210
	(0.046)	(0.053)	(0.058)	(0.028)	(0.030)	(0.033)
LDP nomination	0.372	0.350	0.322	0.278	0.255	0.210
	(0.032)	(0.036)	(0.043)	(0.019)	(0.020)	(0.022)
Quality candidate			0.076			0.079
			(0.038)			(0.020)
Expenditures/limit			0.321			0.206
			(0.090)			(0.049)
Constant	0.105	0.228	0.008	0.398	0.606	0.678
	(0.021)	(0.359)	(0.430)	(0.014)	(0.228)	(0.281)
N	842	842	644	842	842	644
R^2	0.228	0.404	0.477	0.326	0.517	0.602
District FE	No	Yes	Yes	No	Yes	Yes
Year FE	No	Yes	Yes	No	Yes	Yes
Controls	No	Yes	Yes	No	Yes	Yes

SOURCE: JHRED.

NOTE: Robust standard errors in parentheses. All models estimated using ordinary least squares. Baseline group is *Non-legacy entrepreneur*. Dependent variable for models 1–3 is a dummy variable for winning election. Dependent variable for models 4–6 is the share of the Droop quota obtained by the candidate. Controls in models 2–3 and 5–6 include gender, age, age-squared, whether the election was a by-election (dropped in models 3 and 6 due to lack of data on expenditures), and the number of candidates running. Models 2–3 and 5–6 include district and year fixed effects. Candidates who secured a seat after the election through list promotion (*kuriage tōsen*) are counted as losing. The definition of first-time candidate excludes individuals who ran for the prewar House of Representatives or in 1946 but not candidates from the House of Councillors.

TABLE A.II

OLS regression estimates of the electoral advantage of first-time LDP hereditary successors in MMDs, 1958–1993

	WIN			QUOTA PROPORTION		
	(1)	(2)	(3)	(4)	(5)	(6)
Hereditary successor	0.196	0.140	0.072	0.107	0.075	0.059
	(0.062)	(0.064)	(0.177)	(0.034)	(0.032)	(0.077)
No. of prior jiban wins		0.024	0.007		0.016	−0.003
		(0.008)	(0.020)		(0.004)	(0.012)
No. of other new conservative entrants		−0.012	−0.121		−0.047	−0.076
		(0.036)	(0.084)		(0.019)	(0.047)
Predecessor won last race			0.451			0.230
			(0.147)			(0.083)
Quality candidate			0.091			−0.005
			(0.134)			(0.062)
Expenditures/limit			0.513			0.061
			(0.338)			(0.172)
Constant	0.569	0.442	0.474	0.757	0.691	1.386
	(0.045)	(0.066)	(1.238)	(0.020)	(0.031)	(0.594)
N	221	221	177	221	221	177
R^2	0.042	0.079	0.773	0.046	0.130	0.738
District FE	No	No	Yes	No	No	Yes
Year FE	No	No	Yes	No	No	Yes
Controls	No	No	Yes	No	No	Yes

SOURCE: JHRED.

NOTE: Robust standard errors in parentheses. All models estimated using ordinary least squares. Baseline group is *Non-legacy successor*. Dependent variable for models 1–3 is a dummy variable for winning election. Dependent variable for models 4–6 is the share of the Droop quota obtained by the candidate. Controls in models 3 and 6 include gender, age, age-squared, whether or not the election was a by-election, and the number of candidates running. Models 3 and 6 include district and year fixed effects. Candidates who secured a seat after the election through list promotion (*kuriage tōsen*) are counted as losing. The definition of first-time candidate excludes individuals who ran for the prewar House of Representatives or in 1946 but not candidates from the House of Councillors.

TABLE A.12

OLS regression estimates of the electoral advantage of first-time LDP legacy candidates in SMDs, 2000–2009

	WIN			VOTE SHARE		
	(1)	(2)	(3)	(4)	(5)	(6)
Dynasty difference	0.231	0.219	0.108	0.091	0.083	0.061
	(0.115)	(0.123)	(0.116)	(0.023)	(0.025)	(0.020)
Quality difference		0.003	0.061		0.003	0.016
		(0.098)	(0.091)		(0.020)	(0.016)
Expenditures difference		0.110	0.138		0.086	0.066
		(0.305)	(0.297)		(0.061)	(0.051)
LDP district strength			3.178			0.757
			(0.969)			(0.166)
2003 election			−0.391			−0.132
			(0.186)			(0.032)
2005 election			−0.208			−0.079
			(0.201)			(0.034)
2009 election			−0.576			−0.169
			(0.185)			(0.032)
Constant	0.470	0.461	−0.193	0.483	0.476	0.347
	(0.076)	(0.085)	(0.282)	(0.015)	(0.017)	(0.048)
N	55	55	55	55	55	55
R^2	0.071	0.073	0.331	0.224	0.254	0.605

(*continued*)

TABLE A.12 (CONTINUED)

	WIN			VOTE SHARE		
	(1)	(2)	(3)	(4)	(5)	(6)
Hereditary difference	0.271	0.272	0.109	0.096	0.088	0.050
	(0.132)	(0.146)	(0.137)	(0.027)	(0.030)	(0.025)
Quality difference		0.032	0.071		0.011	0.020
		(0.101)	(0.094)		(0.021)	(0.017)
Expenditures difference		0.078	0.150		0.083	0.082
		(0.309)	(0.299)		(0.063)	(0.054)
LDP district strength			3.174			0.774
			(0.980)			(0.176)
2003 election			−0.369			−0.120
			(0.186)			(0.033)
2005 election			−0.194			−0.072
			(0.202)			(0.036)
2009 election			−0.565			−0.165
			(0.187)			(0.034)
Constant	0.462	0.460	−0.201	0.483	0.478	0.339
	(0.077)	(0.085)	(0.282)	(0.016)	(0.017)	(0.051)
N	55	55	55	55	55	55
R^2	0.074	0.078	0.328	0.186	0.222	0.564

SOURCE: JHRED.

NOTE: Standard errors in parentheses. All models estimated using ordinary least squares. Top set of models uses *Dynasty difference*; bottom set uses *Hereditary difference*. Dependent variable for models 1–3 is a dummy variable for winning election. Dependent variable for models 4–6 is the LDP candidate's share of the top two candidates' vote.

TABLE A.13

OLS regression estimates of the legacy advantage in ministerial selection across different institutional periods, 1947–2016

	PERIOD 1		PERIOD 2		PERIOD 3		PERIOD 4	
	(1)	(2)	(1)	(2)	(1)	(2)	(1)	(2)
Non-cabinet legacy	0.021	0.014	−0.011	−0.005	0.009	0.008	0.025	−0.001
	(0.012)	(0.011)	(0.006)	(0.006)	(0.005)	(0.005)	(0.005)	(0.005)
Cabinet legacy	0.048	0.015	0.031	0.014	−0.013	−0.007	0.032	0.012
	(0.025)	(0.023)	(0.014)	(0.014)	(0.006)	(0.006)	(0.005)	(0.004)
Prior appointment		0.168		0.098		0.023		0.051
		(0.022)		(0.010)		(0.009)		(0.010)
2 terms		0.008		−0.005		0.001		0.005
		(0.005)		(0.004)		(0.002)		(0.002)
3 terms		−0.002		−0.006		−0.002		0.005
		(0.007)		(0.004)		(0.002)		(0.002)
4 terms		0.027		−0.001		0.006		0.027
		(0.012)		(0.005)		(0.003)		(0.004)
5 terms		0.019		0.015		0.049		0.075
		(0.014)		(0.006)		(0.006)		(0.007)
6 terms		0.054		0.029		0.083		0.075
		(0.025)		(0.007)		(0.009)		(0.010)
7 terms		0.039		0.010		0.064		0.068
		(0.030)		(0.008)		(0.010)		(0.011)
8 terms		0.119		0.036		0.062		0.056
		(0.052)		(0.012)		(0.010)		(0.014)
9 terms		0.085		−0.024		0.086		0.039
		(0.067)		(0.011)		(0.013)		(0.015)

(continued)

TABLE A.13 (CONTINUED)

	PERIOD 1		PERIOD 2		PERIOD 3		PERIOD 4	
	(1)	(2)	(1)	(2)	(1)	(2)	(1)	(2)
10+ terms		-0.055		-0.004		0.038		0.013
		(0.040)		(0.017)		(0.008)		(0.011)
Female		-0.008		0.001		0.004		0.014
		(0.005)		(0.008)		(0.003)		(0.004)
Prior HoC MP		-0.005		0.004		0.025		0.010
		(0.031)		(0.012)		(0.009)		(0.008)
Midterm (*kuriage*) win		-0.008		-0.036		0.002		-0.004
		(0.012)		(0.011)		(0.011)		(0.005)
By-election win		-0.013		0.002		-0.002		0.009
		(0.014)		(0.008)		(0.008)		(0.005)
Zombie win								-0.008
								(0.002)
Pure PR win								-0.018
								(0.003)
Constant	0.026	0.017	0.032	-0.005	0.036	-0.002	0.022	0.012
	(0.002)	(0.010)	(0.002)	(0.009)	(0.002)	(0.008)	(0.001)	(0.007)
N	5,071	5,071	9,240	9,240	14,476	14,476	17,858	17,858
R²	0.031	0.128	0.030	0.083	0.035	0.073	0.031	0.086
Party-cabinet FE	Yes	Yes	Yes	Yes	Yes	Yes	Yes	Yes
Controls	No	Yes	No	Yes	No	Yes	No	Yes

SOURCE: JHRED.

NOTE: Robust standard errors in parentheses. All models estimated using ordinary least squares. Dependent variable is a dummy variable for *Cabinet appointment*. Only MPs from the House of Representatives are included. The prime minister and the speaker of the house (*gimchō*) are excluded from the sample for each cabinet. All models include party-cabinet fixed effects. Estimations in model 1 for each period include no other controls. Estimations in model 2 include dummy variables for gender and prior service in the House of Councillors, faction fixed effects, region fixed effects, and dummies for method of election: SNTV or FPTP winner (baseline), midterm replacement (*kuriage tōsen*; for period 4 these are akin to zombie winners who enter midterm), by-election winner, zombie winner, and pure PR list winner.

TABLE A.14

Negative binomial regression estimates of length of speeches spoken on the floor

	PREREFORM (1980–1993)		POSTREFORM (1996–2009)	
	(1)	(2)	(3)	(4)
Legacy (combined)	−0.062		0.338	
	(0.103)		(0.108)	
Non-cabinet legacy		−0.083		0.035
		(0.137)		(0.169)
Cabinet legacy		−0.044		0.446
		(0.117)		(0.120)
Number of terms	0.307	0.308	0.521	0.537
	(0.070)	(0.070)	(0.057)	(0.058)
(Number of terms)^2	−0.014	−0.014	−0.028	−0.029
	(0.005)	(0.005)	(0.004)	(0.004)
Female	−26.098	−27.548	0.117	0.099
	(1.017)	(1.018)	(0.230)	(0.227)
Cabinet minister	1.886	1.887	2.187	2.155
	(0.163)	(0.163)	(0.174)	(0.172)
Junior minister	−0.268	−0.263	0.580	0.592
	(0.147)	(0.148)	(0.146)	(0.146)
Speaker	3.997	3.994	4.911	4.878
	(0.487)	(0.486)	(0.331)	(0.301)
Constant	6.290	6.287	5.790	5.765
	(0.238)	(0.237)	(0.226)	(0.227)
N	1,333	1,333	1,161	1,161
Log-pseudolikelihood	−7,428	−7,428	−7,062	−7,061

SOURCE: JHRED and data from Sugawara Taku's (archived) website: http://sugawarataku.net.

NOTE: Dependent variable is number of characters in speeches spoken by LDP MPs in plenary sessions (*hon kaigi*). Estimates are negative binomial regression coefficients. Models include term fixed effects (not shown). In models 1 and 3, the two types of legacy MPs are pooled together; in models 2 and 4, they are disaggregated into non-cabinet legacies and cabinet legacies. Robust standard errors in parentheses.

TABLE A.15

Negative binomial regression estimates of length of speeches spoken in committees

	PREREFORM (1980–1993)		POSTREFORM (1996–2009)	
	(1)	(2)	(3)	(4)
Legacy (combined)	0.061		0.095	
	(0.102)		(0.079)	
Non-cabinet legacy		−0.002		−0.094
		(0.144)		(0.129)
Cabinet legacy		0.106		0.167
		(0.110)		(0.090)
Number of terms	−0.132	−0.131	−0.129	−0.126
	(0.058)	(0.058)	(0.069)	(0.068)
(Number of terms)^2	−0.015	−0.015	−0.012	−0.012
	(0.005)	(0.005)	(0.007)	(0.007)
Female	−0.222	−0.249	0.020	0.032
	(0.161)	(0.166)	(0.142)	(0.143)
Cabinet minister	−0.295	−0.301	−0.209	−0.232
	(0.183)	(0.183)	(0.154)	(0.150)
Junior minister	−0.327	−0.326	−0.221	−0.202
	(0.094)	(0.094)	(0.089)	(0.089)
Speaker	−25.033	−25.008	−24.181	−24.179
	(0.601)	(0.598)	(0.617)	(0.612)
Constant	9.831	9.825	10.732	10.733
	(0.153)	(0.154)	(0.121)	(0.120)
N	1,333	1,333	1,161	1,161
Log-pseudolikelihood	−10,480	−10,480	−11,489	−11,488

SOURCE: JHRED and data from Sugawara Taku's (archived) website: http://sugawarataku.net.

NOTE: Dependent variable is the number of characters in speeches spoken by LDP MPs in committees (*iinkai*). Estimates are negative binomial regression coefficients. Models include term fixed effects (not shown). In models 1 and 3, the two types of legacy MPs are pooled together; in models 2 and 4, they are disaggregated into non-cabinet legacies and cabinet legacies. Robust standard errors in parentheses.

Appendix B

Dynasties in Democracies Dataset

The Dynasties in Democracies Dataset contains 134,803 observations for the members of parliament (MPs) of twelve countries, basic background information on gender and age when available, information on appointments to cabinet for parliamentary democracies, and information on each MP's membership in a political dynasty. For some country cases, MP observations commence with the first parliament. For other country cases, observations are limited to post–World War II parliaments. However, any dynastic ties to pre–World War II politicians are coded, as are ties to politicians in proto-parliaments and preindependence parliaments. Junior MPs are those who have family members who served in parliament (either chamber in the case of bicameral systems), the cabinet or presidency, or proto-parliaments, and served prior to the MP's own service. By-election winners are generally included, grouped with the previous general election. Primary sources and relevant notes are provided for each country here. In most cases, primary data sources were supplemented with additional information obtained from online candidate websites and Wikipedia biographies.

Australia: *Time Period:* 1901 (1st House of Representatives) to 2013 (44th House of Representatives); 44 sessions. *Data Sources:* (1) ParlInfo Archive (online); (2) *Australian Dictionary of Biography* (online); (3) Lumb, Martin. 2012. *Parliamentary Relations: Political Families in the Commonwealth Parliament.* Commonwealth of Australia Parliamentary Library.

Canada: *Time Period:* 1867 (1st House of Commons) to 2015 (42nd House of Commons); 42 sessions. *Data Sources:* (1) ParlInfo Archive (online).

Finland: *Time Period:* 1907 (1st Eduskunta) to 2011 (36th Eduskunta); 36 sessions. *Data Sources:* (1) Archive of the Eduskunta (online). *Special Notes:* MPs whose relatives served in the Privy Council or Diet of the Grand Duchy before Finnish independence are coded as junior.

(West) Germany: *Time Period:* 1949 (1st Bundestag) to 2013 (18th Bundestag); 18 sessions. *Data Sources:* (1) Archive of the Bundestag (online); (2) Rudolf Vierhaus and Ludolf Herbst, 2002, *Biographisches Handbuch der Mitglieder des Deutschen Bundestages 1949–2001* [Biographical Dictionary of Members of the German Bundestag, 1949–2001], bilingual ed. (K. G. Saur Verlag). *Special Notes:* Data are for West Germany until reunification. MPs whose relatives served in the Prussian parliament, Weimar Republic, East German parliament, and so on, are coded as junior. Other nobility who did not have any close relatives in national-level political office are not coded as junior.

Ireland: *Time Period:* 1918 (1st Dáil) to 2016 (32nd Dáil); 32 sessions. *Data Sources:* (1) Elections Ireland (online); (2) Houses of the Oireachtas Archive (online); (3) Michael Gallagher, ed., 1993, *Irish Elections 1922–44: Results and Analysis* (Dublin: PSAI Press). (4) Michael Gallagher, ed., 2009, *Irish Elections 1948–1977: Results and Analysis* (New York: Routledge and Political Studies Association of Ireland); (5) *Nealon's Guide*, various years, 1973–2011; (6) *Magill Book*, various years, 1982–1987; (7) *Irish Dictionary of Biography* (online); (8) Irish Election Literature (online).

Israel: *Time Period:* 1949 (1st Knesset) to 2015 (20th Knesset); 20 sessions. *Data Sources:* (1) Archive of the Knesset (online).

Italy: *Time Period:* 1946 (Constituent Assembly) to 2013 (17th Legislature); 18 sessions. *Data Sources:* (1) Archive of the Chamber of Deputies (online); (2) Maurizio Cotta and Luca Verzichelli, 1993, *PARLIT46_92* (Centre for the Study of Political Change (CIRCaP), Università degli Studi di Siena); (3) Danilo Chirico and Raffaele Lupoli, 2008, *Onorevoli figli di: I parenti, i portaborse, le lobby istantanea del nuovo parlamento* (Rome: Rinascita edizioni). *Special Notes*: MPs whose relatives served during the Kingdom of Italy (Regno d'Italia), in the National Council (Consulta Nazionale), or in the Senate are coded as junior.

Japan: *Time Period*: 1947 (23rd House of Representatives) to 2014 (47th House of Representatives); 25 sessions. *Data Sources*: JHRED.

New Zealand: *Time Period*: 1853 (1st House of Representatives) to 2014 (51st House of Representatives); 51 sessions. *Data Sources*: (1) New Zealand parliamentary library data archives (online); (2) *Encyclopedia of New Zealand* (online); (3) *New Zealand History* (online).

Norway: *Time Period*: 1945 (142nd Storting) to 2013 (160th Storting); 18 sessions. *Data Sources*: (1) Storting Archive of Biographies (online); (2) Norwegian Social Science Data (NSD) Archive.

Switzerland: *Time Period*: 1848 (1st Federal Assembly) to 2011 (49th Federal Assembly); 49 sessions. *Data Sources*: (1) Swiss Parliament Archives (online); (2) *Historical Dictionary of Switzerland* (online); (3) *Biographie-Portal* (online). *Special Notes*: The Swiss Federal Assembly has two chambers: the National Council (lower chamber) and the Council of States (upper chamber). The Council of States is excluded from statistics presented in this book. The executive is called the Federal Council.

United States: *Time Period*: 1788 (1st Congress) to 2016 (115th Congress); 115 sessions. *Data Sources*: (1) ICPSR Study No. 7803; (2) Replication data from Ernesto Dal Bó, Pedro Dal Bó, and Jason Snyder, 2009, "Political Dynasties," *Review of Economic Studies* 76(1): 115–142; (3) *Biographical Directory of the United States Congress* (online). *Special Notes*: Individuals whose relatives served in the Continental Congress or in the presidency or vice presidency are coded as junior. Senate terms are divided into two-year periods to overlap with House terms.

Japanese House of Representatives Elections Dataset (JHRED)

This panel dataset includes every single candidate who ran in any general election or by-election for the Japanese House of Representatives from 1947 to 2014. The dataset includes a total of 27,545 observations (i.e., election candidacies), for 10,060 unique individuals, across 25 general elections. From 1947 to 1993, candidates competed for votes in multimember districts (MMDs) under the single nontransferable vote (SNTV) electoral system. Since electoral reform in 1994, candidates in the mixed-member majoritarian (MMM) system compete in one of 300 (reduced to 295 in 2014) single-member districts (SMDs) based on first-past-the-post (FPTP) rules, on a party list in one of eleven regional closed-list proportional representation (PR) blocs, or dual listed in both tiers.

The dataset is based on three separate datasets (MMD, SMD, and PR) originally collected by Steven R. Reed, and then updated, expanded, and cleaned by the author. The basic candidate information and electoral results were compiled from *Asahi Shimbun, Yomiuri Shimbun, Mainichi Shimbun,* and other newspaper records, as well as official election statistics from the Japanese Ministry of Internal Affairs and Communications. Some candidate background information was compiled from yearly almanacs such as *Seikan Yōran, Seiji Handbook, Kokkai Binran,* candidate website profiles, *Za Senkyo,* and Wikipedia. Other sources vary for specific variables or groups of variables. Special thanks are owed to Yusaku Horiuchi, Kuniaki Nemoto, Amy Catalinac, and Petter Lindgren for their help in cleaning the data, and to Yusaku Horiuchi, Ko Maeda, Masaru Kohno, Benjamin Nyblade, Gary Cox, Matthew Carlson, and Mike Thies for providing some of the data for specific variables or years. Finally, Shiro Kuriwaki, Anthony Volk, and Eric Xiao provided very helpful research assistance.

List of Interviews

TABLE B.I

Interviews with Japanese politicians and party organization personnel

Name	Description	Party	Legacy?	Date	Lang.
LDP Staff "A"	Party staff; male	LDP	N/A	May 31, 2011	J
				Mar. 14, 2013	J
LDP MP "A"	HR (rookie); male	LDP	Yes	Jun. 14, 2011	E
LDP MP "B"	HR (veteran); male	LDP	Yes	Feb. 1, 2010	J
Fukuda Tatsuo	HR (1); male	LDP	Yes	Mar. 15, 2013	J
Inoguchi Kuniko	HC (1); HR (1); female	LDP	No	May 11, 2011	E
Kōno Tarō	HR (5); male	LDP	Yes	Jun. 1, 2011	E
Murai Hideki	HR (1); male	LDP	No	Mar. 14, 2013	J
Ōno Yoshinori	HR (8); male	LDP	Yes	Apr. 22, 2011	E
Sekō Hiroshige	HC (3); male	LDP	Yes	Jun. 9, 2011	J
Shibayama Masahiko	HR (3); male	LDP	No	Jun. 7, 2011	E
Shiozaki Yasuhiro	HR (6); male	LDP	Yes	Jun. 30, 2011	E
Tsuji Kiyoto	HR (1); male	LDP	No	Mar. 11, 2013	E
Tsushima Jun	HR (1); male	LDP	Yes	Mar. 15, 2013	J
Tsushima Yūji	HR (11); male	LDP	Yes	Jun. 14, 2011	E
				Jun. 17, 2011	E
DPJ Staff "A"	Party staff; male	DPJ	N/A	Jun. 15, 2011	E
DPJ Staff "B"	Party staff; male	DPJ	N/A	Jun. 15, 2011	J
DPJ MP "A"	HR (rookie); female	DPJ	No	May 27, 2011	E
Kondō Yōsuke	HR (3); male	DPJ	Yes	May 26, 2011	J
Nakabayashi Mieko	HR (1); female	DPJ	No	Jun. 7, 2011	E
Ōizumi Hiroko	HR (1); female	DPJ	No	Jun. 15, 2011	E
Ōta Akihiro	HR (5); male	Kōmeitō	No	Jun. 21, 2011	J
Shirahama Kazuyoshi	HC (4); male	Kōmeitō	No	May 31, 2011	J
Takagi Yōsuke	HR (5); male	Kōmeitō	No	June 8, 2011	J
Tōyama Kiyohiko	HR (1); HC (2); male	Kōmeitō	No	Jun. 29, 2011	E
				Mar. 11, 2013	E
Baba Nobuyuki	HR (1); male	JRP	No	Mar. 13, 2013	J
Ueno Hiroshi	HR (1); HC (1); male	JRP	Yes	Mar. 13, 2013	J
Asao Keiichirō	HR (2); HC (2); male	Your Party	Yes	Mar. 13, 2013	E
Mitani Hidehiro	HR (1); male	Your Party	No	Mar. 12, 2013	J

NOTE: Interviewees who requested anonymity are given letters in place of names. HR = House of Representatives; HC = House of Councillors. Number of terms in parentheses (broad categories of "rookie" and "veteran" used for anonymous MPs to protect their identities). DPJ = Democratic Party of Japan; JRP = Japan Restoration Party; LDP = Liberal Democratic Party. Language of interview: E = English, J = Japanese.

Notes

Chapter 1

1. Japanese names throughout this book are written in the order of surname before given name, apart from authors of publications in English. The same rule applies for Korean and Chinese names where used. Japanese words are romanized primarily according to the modified Hepburn system, with exceptions including common words, newspaper names, and place-names such as Tokyo.

2. Kristof, Nicholas D. "Mr. 'Cold Pizza' earns respect in Japan with deft tinkering." *New York Times*, April 1, 1999.

3. The DPJ rebranded itself as simply the Democratic Party (Minshintō) on March 27, 2016. The timeline and data covered in this book includes four by-elections held in 2016 after this rebranding.

4. There are a few additional studies of dynasties in nondemocratic contexts, such as North Korea (Monday, 2011) and the Middle East (McMillan, 2013). In the People's Republic of China, President Xi Jinping and other prominent "princelings" (the children or grandchildren of senior communist officials) have also attracted scholarly attention (e.g., Shih, Adolph, and Liu, 2012).

5. Hess (1966, p. 1) uses the term "People's Dukes," citing its use by Stewart Alsop in a newspaper article about Ted Kennedy, "What made Teddy run?" *Saturday Evening Post*, October 27, 1962.

6. For reasons of data availability, this definition excludes relationships to local-level politicians, although these may be important in some contexts, such as federal systems.

7. The percentage of legacy MPs in India would be higher if the definition were expanded to include relationships to local-level politicians. The percentage would also be higher if ties to members of the upper chamber (Rajya Sabha) were included,

but these ties are not delineated in the data compiled by Chandra, Bohlken, and Chauchard (2014).

8. For example, the group of Icelandic MPs elected in 2013 contained fourteen legacy MPs (22 percent). This is in part a result of a change in the party system. Fifteen parties contested the 2013 election, in contrast to seven in 2009, and five of the new parties won seats. But in raw numbers, the change was only a decrease of two members from the previous parliament elected in 2009, which was 25 percent legacy MPs. Prominent Icelandic legacy MPs include former finance minister Árni M. Mathiesen, whose father, Matthías Á. Mathiesen, also once held that post; Independence Party leader Bjarni Benediktsson, whose great-uncle with the same name served as prime minister from 1963 to 1970; and the first female prime minister, Jóhanna Sigurdardóttir of the Social Democratic Alliance (in office from 2009 to 2013), whose father, Sigurdur Ingimundarson, was an MP from 1959 to 1971. Former prime minister Sigmundur Davíd Gunnlaugsson, who resigned in April 2016 following the revelation that he was connected (through his wife) to secret offshore companies he had not disclosed, is also a legacy MP (his father, Gunnlaugur M. Sigmundsson, had previously served one term in parliament from 1995 to 1999).

9. In most of Western Europe, the involvement in politics of the hereditary aristocracy in particular declined steadily from the late 1800s to the point at which their influence over present-day politics is negligible (Rush, 2000). Several recent studies explore the impact of franchise extension and other institutional changes on dynastic politics in early historical periods (e.g., Berlinski, Dewan, and Van Coppenolle, 2014; Velasco Rivera, 2017; Cirone and Velasco Rivera, 2017).

10. Mitt Romney's father, George Romney, was governor of Michigan and unsuccessfully sought the Republican nomination for president in 1968. However, he also served as secretary of housing and urban development in the cabinet of President Richard Nixon, making him a legacy candidate by the definition used in this book.

11. The Public Offices Election Law stipulates minor restrictions on suffrage and eligibility with regard to citizenship, age, mental incompetence, and prior criminal offenses.

12. Other early and influential works in the elite dominance literature include Pareto (1901), Mosca (1939), Mills (1956), and Putnam (1976).

13. Hatoyama Yasuko was the daughter of Bridgestone founder Ishibashi Shōjirō. The name Ishibashi means "stone bridge."

14. Regression-discontinuity-based studies of the incumbency advantage have blossomed since Lee (2008). Examples of studies in the US context include Fowler and Hall (2014), Hall and Snyder (2015), and Eggers et al. (2015). Similar designs applied to comparative cases include Redmond and Regan (2015), Golden and Picci (2015), and Fiva and Smith (2018).

15. Additional studies of dynasties in Japan include Usui and Colignon (2004), North (2005), and Asako et al. (2015) in English, and Ichikawa (1990), Matsuzaki (1991), Uesugi (2009), Inaida (2009), Iida, Matsubayashi and Ueda (2010), and Fukumoto and Nakagawa (2013) in Japanese.

16. Indeed, empirical studies on the power-treatment effect in different democracies have produced different results (Dal Bó, Dal Bó, and Snyder, 2009; Rossi, 2017; Querubín, 2016; van Coppenolle, 2017; Fiva and Smith, 2018).

17. A clear example of an exogenously imposed institutional change in Japan includes the set of democratic reforms imposed by the US Occupation following Japan's defeat in World War II (Dower, 1999). In contrast, examples of endogenous institutional change in Japan include the many revisions to the Public Offices Election Law that reduced the length of campaigns, restricted campaigning activities, and increased in the cost of the election deposit for candidates. These regulations were enacted over time by incumbent MPs whose personal electoral prospects were improved by constructing such barriers to competition (McElwain, 2008; Harada and Smith, 2014).

18. This assumes that parties are not organized "personalistically" in the sense that individual families dominate the leadership of the party. In such cases, centralized control over nominations may very much favor the members of the leaders' families, at least in top positions (Chhibber, 2013).

19. Krauss and Pekkanen (2011, p. 30) define kōenkai as "permanent formal-membership organizations, or overlapping sets or networks of organizations, devoted to supporting an individual politician," which are "heavily involved in electoral mobilization."

20. In Japan, a candidate fitting the definition used in this book for a legacy candidate is often referred to as a *nisei* (second-generation) candidate. However, dynasties can extend beyond two generations, so the more general term is preferred. The definition given in this book for a hereditary candidate generally corresponds to the Japanese term *seshū*; however, exact definitions vary in the existing literature.

21. During the ninety-one meetings of the Diet's Special Committee on Political Reform held between January 22, 1993, and December 9, 1994, the topic of hereditary candidates was mentioned in passing just ten times, and never as the primary argument for reform.

22. Quoted in *Asahi Shimbun*, April 4, 2009.

23. Wagner, John. "Martin O'Malley: Presidency not 'some crown' to be passed between two families." *Washington Post*, March 29, 2015.

24. Ferrarella, Luigi and Giuseppe Guastella. "Houses, a Porsche, and degrees on the list of hand-outs to the Bossi family." *Corriere della Sera*, April 5, 2012.

25. In the 2013 House of Councillors election, legacy candidates made up roughly 6 percent of candidates but 16 percent of winners.

Chapter 2

1. Some comparative work has made significant progress in collecting ties to local politicians. See, for example, van Liefferinge and Steyvers (2009), Chandra, Bohlken and Chauchard (2014), Querubín (2016), Geys (2017), Folke, Persson, and Rickne (2017), and Bragança, Ferraz and Rios (2015). For the case of Japan, there are 600 individuals who were related to a previously elected or appointed national-level politician (and so count as legacy candidates). If known ties to failed candidates are included, this number increases to 619 individuals. If known ties to local politicians are also included, the number increases to 721 individuals but likely undercounts many individuals whose local ties were not reported in newspapers or other media (particularly in earlier years in the data).

2. Studies of dynasties in the US context include Hess (1966), Clubok, Wilensky, and Berghorn (1969), Laband and Lentz (1985), Dal Bó, Dal Bó, and Snyder (2009), and Feinstein (2010).

3. In the Senate (not shown in Figure 2.1), the highest proportion of legacy members, 23 percent, occurred twice—first after the 1878 election and again after the 1916 election. Levels of dynastic politics in the Senate are higher than in the House of Representatives, but with fluctuations. The 115th Congress elected in 2016 included five legacy members in the Senate (5 percent), the lowest since 1792.

4. Department of Information Services, House of Commons Library. "Current MPs related to other current or former Members of the House of Commons." Document SN/PC/04809, February 21, 2014.

5. Stanley, Tim. "Euan Blair for Parliament? Labour is more inbred than the North Korean politburo." *Telegraph*, April 14, 2014. See also Savage, Michael. "Blair's son shuns chance to run for MP." *The Times*, January 1, 2015. The speculation is that Blair may wait until 2020 to make his entry into politics.

6. Cohen, Tobi. "Chow opens up on Layton's final moments, vows not to seek NDP leadership." *Postmedia News*, September 6, 2011.

7. The membership of the Five Star Movement is relatively young and new to politics. One member of the Chamber of Deputies, Cristian Iannuzzi, is the son of Senator Ivana Simeoni; however, they were both elected in the 2013 elections, so neither counts as a legacy MP. Another Five Star Movement MP, Azzurra Cancelleri, has a brother who is active in local politics in Sicily.

8. A mosaic plot is a type of stacked bar chart that is useful for visualizing the two-way distribution of two categorical variables in a single plot. The mosaic plots in this book were made in Stata with the *spineplot* package (Cox, 2008).

9. The number of seats held by the New Liberal Club between 1976 and 1986 (forty-nine) includes two affiliated independents: Hatoyama Kunio (legacy) and Ōhara Ichizō (non-legacy). Other legacy MPs in the party included Kōno Yōhei, Tagawa Seiichi, Nishioka Takeo, Kobayashi Masami, and Yamaguchi Toshio.

10. Sir Francis Galton (1886) noted the tendency of regression toward the mean in height across generations. Similar arguments about the talent and skills of the heirs to wealth were later made by the Scottish American industrialist Andrew Carnegie (1889).

11. This explanation is hard to test given the difficulty in measuring quality. During the SNTV era (1947–1993), however, the average tenure in office of candidates who directly preceded a son-in-law was seven terms, the same as for those who preceded a son. Thus, at least as far as length of tenure goes, predecessor quality is equivalent.

12. In total, there were 463 families who supplied two or more members as candidates between 1947 and 2014, and of those families, 373 were successful in forming a democratic dynasty. Note that determining the "boundaries" of different families can be a challenge because of intermarriage and overlapping branches of family trees. In cases of intermarriage between two dynasties, Table 2.1 reflects only the relationship to the individual who married into the family, not all other relationships connected through that marriage (which are counted in the other dynasty). Some legacy candidates would actually count as having succeeded a larger number of relatives if such distant relatives were to be included. The numbers of generations given in Table 2.1 may thus be less precise when there have been multiple politicians in the dynasty.

13. The scandal was not simply that he had an affair with the geisha, but that he was stingy in providing financial support for her services (West, 2008).

14. The exception is legacy MPs whose relatives previously served in cabinet. Such cabinet legacies tend to have higher levels of education than other legacy MPs and non-legacy MPs. This distinction between types of legacy MPs is explored in Chapter 6.

15. Information on the educational backgrounds of MPs elected in 2014 is from the replication data for Horiuchi, Smith, and Yamamoto (2018a).

16. Tokugawa Tsunenari (2009, p. 117), the eighteenth head of the Tokugawa lineage, explains how the education system reinforced the rigid occupational structure of Tokugawa Japan: "Each child would use a textbook suited to his father's occupation, to which he was expected to succeed in the future. There were around seven thousand different textbooks in Tokugawa Japan."

17. Imperial appointees to the House of Peers included personal appointments at the discretion of the emperor, representatives of the highest taxpayers, and representatives from the Imperial Academy.

18. These elected members of the House of Representatives attempted to introduce increased popular rights and party-based cabinet politics, but were blocked by oligarchs who controlled the House of Peers and the Privy Council. Their efforts were made all the more difficult because the parties during this period—including the two main parties in the House of Representatives, the Seiyūkai and the

Kenseikai—were internally divided and unstable. Nevertheless, the period of time between the end of the Russo-Japanese War in 1905 and the assassination of Prime Minister Inukai Tsuyoshi and subsequent fall of the Seiyūkai party cabinet in 1932 is generally referred to as the period of Taishō Democracy (named after Emperor Taishō, who succeeded Emperor Meiji in 1912 and ruled until 1926), as it seemed as though the development of party politics was beginning to give greater democratic voice to the common man.

19. Wallace, Bruce. "Japan's dynasty politics losing favor among the public." *Los Angeles Times*, January 22, 2008.

20. A useful statistic is the odds ratio. If greater than 1 for any particular occupation, it indicates a level of occupational inheritance, and larger odds ratios indicate a greater association between father's and son's occupations. In the 2005 wave of the SSM, the odds ratio for engineering professions is roughly 6; for teaching, it is 10; for farming, 13; for medicine, 27; for military, 166; and for priests, it is 1,234. Unfortunately, there are not enough politicians among the SSM survey respondents to compute similar odds ratios for politics.

Chapter 3

1. Arguments along these lines have been made by Pradeep Chhibber (2013) and Kanchan Chandra (2016) to explain the prevalence of dynasties in India; however, both authors also consider the weakness of party organizations to be an important factor. See also Ziegfeld (2016).

2. Recent research using Swedish register data connecting adoptees to biological and adoptive parents suggests that part of the supply-side effect may be attributed to "pre-birth" factors such as genes, in addition to "post-birth" factors such as socialization (Oskarsson, Dawes, and Lindgren, 2017).

3. Wheeler, Dennis. "Dan Lipinski aims to step into his dad's big shoes." *Star Newspapers* (Chicago South), August 19, 2004.

4. More formally, let $X = (x_1, x_2, x_3, \ldots x_k)$ be the set of attributes possessed by a potential candidate. Party leaders will favor the potential candidate whose set of attributes X maximizes the party's expected utility function $EU = P(X)V(X)$, where $P(X) \in [0, 1]$ represents the probability that the candidate will win the election given his or her set of attributes X; and $V(X) \in [0, 1]$ represents the value to the party of that candidate, given that he or she will have those attributes. This setup clearly illustrates the potential trade-off that might result from a given combination of attributes X. The numerical range for $V(X)$ is set to $[0, 1]$ for simplicity, but one might also allow for it to take on higher values, or even be negative. A possible extension of this model might also consider the material cost C of finding different types of candidates, $EU = P(X)V(X) - C(X)$, but here we will keep things simple.

5. This assumption could be relaxed to expand the concept of the inherited incumbency advantage to include non-kin successors, such as political secretaries or protégés. In this case, a non-kin successor may have a positive value accruing from inherited resources or connections, but not from name recognition, genes, or other benefits of family relations.

6. Alternatively, a cabinet legacy may be better at signaling to party leaders that he or she is capable of handling government office, most obviously if the performance of his or her predecessor in higher office had been strong (Smith and Martin, 2017). The postelectoral advantages of cabinet legacies in terms of promotion are explored in Chapter 6.

7. Italian deputies were eligible for a state-provided pension after two terms. As many of the PCI's candidates were also employees of the party organization, this reduced the financial burden on the party.

8. Interview with Sekō Hiroshige in Tokyo, June 9, 2011 (in Japanese).

9. Switzerland switched from a two-round system in SMDs to a mostly open-list PR system in 1919, although SMDs still exist in the five smallest cantons.

10. Fifty-four of the sixty-three seats in the Icelandic Althingi are allocated using the d'Hondt method in six or seven districts with ten to eleven seats each. The remaining nine seats are supplementary seats added to particular districts in order to give each party a total number of seats in proportion to its share of the national vote (but a party must win at least 5 percent of the national vote to be eligible for a supplementary seat). A reform in 2000 increased the value of optional candidate preference votes; however, in practice the system has largely functioned like closed-list PR. In Norway, 150 of 169 seats are proportionally allocated to parties within districts using the Modified Sainte Laguë method. The remaining nineteen seats, one from each district, are allocated as adjustment seats to parties that receive at least 4 percent of the national vote. As in Iceland, voters in Norway are allowed to reorder the candidates on party lists, or cross candidates' names off the list, but for these changes to be enacted over half of the party's voters have to make the same change. This has never happened, so the system is essentially closed-list PR. Italy's PR system from 2006 to 2013 included a majoritarian seat bonus to whichever electoral list or coalition won the most votes.

11. For Germany and Italy, the number of terms served represents only the terms served in postwar parliaments because prewar observations are not available. Thus, the estimated relationship may be somewhat biased.

12. The longest serving MP in the entire comparative dataset is US Democratic Party representative John Dingell Jr., who served thirty terms and was succeeded in office by his wife, Debbie Dingell. John Dingell Jr. himself succeeded his father, John Dingell Sr. Together, the Dingells have served more than eighty years in Congress. In the subsample of MPs who stopped running between 1945 and 2000,

the longest serving MP is US Representative Jamie Lloyd Whitten (twenty-seven terms). The longest serving Japanese MP in the dataset (and subsample) is Ozaki Yukio (twenty-five terms), followed by Nakasone Yasuhiro and Hara Kenzaburō (twenty terms each).

13. The slope of the predicted relationship between *Senior* and *Number of terms* also tends to be flatter for existing legacy MPs, which suggests that length of tenure matters little within existing dynasties. However, the confidence intervals in country cases with fewer legacy MPs are wide and overlapping.

Chapter 4

1. Interviews with Tsushima Yūji in Tokyo, June 14 and 17, 2011 (in English).

2. Interview with Tsushima Jun in Tokyo, March 15, 2013 (in Japanese).

3. Voters had two to three votes depending on the magnitude of the district, which ranged from four to fourteen seats.

4. The five largest parties after the 1946 election were the conservative Liberal Party, the short-lived Progressive Party (also conservative in nature despite its name), the JSP, the JCP, and the leftist Cooperative Party (also ephemeral). However, twenty-eight other minor parties also won seats, as well as eighty-one independents.

5. The Amami Islands elected a single MP from 1953 to 1990, when the district became part of Kagoshima 1st District. Eight other districts at some elections returned two MPs. Hokkaido 1st District elected six MPs from 1986 to 1993, as did Fukuoka 1st District in 1993. For the House of Councillors, which replaced the prewar House of Peers, lawmakers chose a mixed system combining a prefecture-based tier using SNTV to elect 150 members (with magnitude varying by prefecture), and a national tier using SNTV to elect one hundred members in a single, nationwide district. The system for the national tier was changed to closed-list PR in 1983 and again to open-list PR in 2001.

6. The JCP ran multiple candidates in a few districts in early elections, and in the five-member Kyoto district where the party was strong. The DSP ran two candidates in only two districts in the first election after its founding in 1960.

7. The number of ex post nominations is based on data in the *Asahi Shimbun* 1996 House of Representatives Election CD-ROM.

8. Based on data in Richardson (1991) and surveys conducted by the Association for Promoting Fair Elections (Akarui Senkyo Suishin Kyōkai). The survey results are not broken down by party affiliation of respondents—it is likely that the salience of candidate over party would have been even higher among LDP supporters.

9. The percentage of MP secretaries among LDP candidates increased from around 10 percent to around 40 percent by the early 1990s. The percentage of lo-

cal assembly members climbed from 20 percent in the 1960s to over 30 percent in the late 1990s. Former national bureaucrats declined from 30 percent of candidates throughout the 1960s and 1970s to around 20 percent in the 1990s and 2000s.

10. Dōmei and Sōhyō eventually merged in 1989-1990 to form the Japanese Trade Union Confederation (Rengō).

11. An additional Kōmeitō legacy candidate was Hōjō Hiroshi, who served one term in the House of Councillors, and later became president of Sōka Gakkai. His uncle Hōjō Shunpachi served in the prewar House of Peers and two terms in the postwar House of Councillors. House of Councillors MP Ishikawa Hirotaka is the son-in-law of former House of Councillors MP Kazama Hisashi. Another House of Councillors MP, Taniai Masaaki, was preceded in politics by his mother and grandfather, who both served in local assemblies.

12. Another confirmed legacy candidate in the JCP, Kikunami Hiroshi, served one term in the House of Councillors from 1992 to 1998. His father, Kikunami Katsumi, had been elected to one term in the House of Representatives for Tokyo 6th District in 1949, before being purged in 1950 by the Occupation (part of the "red purge" during the so-called Reverse Course strategy following the onset of the Cold War).

13. Only 5 percent of hereditary candidates did not share the same surname as their predecessor. In comparison, 28 percent of non-hereditary legacy candidates did not share the same surname as a predecessor.

14. Hatoyama Kunio later moved to Fukuoka 6th District after resigning his seat to run unsuccessfully for governor of Tokyo in 1999. He continued to win elections in his new district until he died in office in 2016. His second-born son, Hatoyama Jirō, already a local mayor in Fukuoka Prefecture, succeeded him in the by-election following his death. His first-born son, Hatoyama Tarō, is a local politician in Tokyo who failed to win a seat in the 2017 House of Representatives election running as a candidate for the Party of Hope.

15. *Asahi Shimbun*, December 9, 1983.

16. In another case, Shimamura Ichirō of Tokyo 10th District retired prior to the 1976 election. He was also opposed to the idea of hereditary succession, and did not want his son, Yoshinobu, to succeed him. Instead, he supported the candidacy of his secretary, Udagawa Yoshio. However, Shimamura's kōenkai rallied around Yoshinobu, who was given the official LDP nomination and eked out a victory in the election. Udagawa ran as an independent and lost. Udagawa was later elected to the Tokyo Prefectural Assembly, and finally to the House of Representatives as an independent in the 2000 election (*Mainichi Shimbun*, October 24, 2003).

17. *Asahi Shimbun*, June 27, 1986, and July 7, 1986.

18. Two other candidates adopted the names of their fathers prior to running: Yamamura Shinjirō of Chiba 2nd District and Chizaki Usaburō in Hokkaido 1st

District. In these cases, the name change had been a family tradition for ten and two previous generations, respectively, and was related to business succession as well.

19. There were five such simultaneous father-son candidacies in 1996, but Kōno Tarō was the only son to win. Unlike many hereditary candidates, he decided to officially disband his father's former kōenkai and form a new organization of his own. Nevertheless, he was running in a district that included part of his father's jiban and former supporters.

20. Interview with Kōno Tarō in Tokyo, June 1, 2011 (in English).

21. This insight is similar to Oscar Wilde's quip in *The Picture of Dorian Gray* that "there is only one thing in the world worse than being talked about and that is not being talked about."

22. Martín Rossi (2017) notes similar patterns among female politicians in Argentina and whether they keep their maiden names or adopt the names of their husbands. Many female legacy candidates opt for whichever name is associated with their political predecessor (i.e., father or husband).

23. JHRED includes a variable, *Jiban*, which is a unique code designed to capture a candidate's support base within a district. Whenever a candidate inherits another candidate's support base, the jiban code stays the same. A jiban is considered to be inherited by a new candidate in any of the following cases: (1) only one candidate from the party retires and only one new candidate from the party runs; (2) a newspaper or some other source names the new candidate as a successor (newspaper or case study accounts supersede any other information); or (3) a new candidate is related to a retiring candidate, that is, a hereditary candidate. The jiban code changes when a candidate changes camps (but not parties within the same camp). There are very few of these cases, but changing camps usually changes a candidate's vote substantially, indicating that the support base has indeed changed. The jiban code also changes whenever district lines are redrawn because the geographic support base in the district changes. However, for the purposes of coding hereditary candidates in 1996, candidates only need to have run in the same geographic area. This exception does not affect any of the regression analyses, which exclude the transition year from 1993 to 1996.

24. The data sample includes three candidates who made their last election attempt in a by-election (none was succeeded).

25. The *Death* variable is based primarily on Diet records of eulogies given on the Diet floor. In Japan, it is customary to eulogize a Diet member when he or she dies in office, so official Diet records contain such events in the agenda notes. *Asahi Shimbun* obituaries and official biographies provided further data for former incumbent candidates who intended to run again after losing but passed away prior to the election. The 129 deaths recorded in the sample include nine nonincumbents; in these cases, the assumption is that the candidate was still serving as the

local party branch representative (*shibuchō*), and could have been a candidate again in the future.

26. Of the 122 cases of direct succession, twenty-two of the successors first ran as LDP-affiliated independents, and two each ran as New Liberal Club and Renewal Party candidates. The results of the analysis presented in Figure 4.2 and Table A.4 in Appendix A are robust to the recoding of *Bequeath* to include only successions with the same party label (i.e., the coefficients and *p*-values change only slightly). The results are also consistent if LDP-affiliated independents are included in the sample along with LDP candidates (total $N = 904$).

27. On the advantages and limitations of linear probability models with binary dependent variables, see Horrace and Oaxaca (2006).

28. In the first election under this system in 1996, there were 200 seats in the PR tier. This number was reduced before the 2000 election. The number of SMDs was reduced to 295 in 2014. The number of seats in each tier was reduced again for the 2017 election.

29. Since 2005, the LDP has restricted candidates over the age of seventy-three from being dual listed, in an attempt to rejuvenate the party by forcing older incumbents to retire if they cannot win their SMD outright. Even with this restriction, 94 percent of LDP candidates and 99 percent of DPJ candidates typically run in both tiers.

30. In the 2000 election, seven Kōmeitō candidates were dual-listed at the same rank (with the *sekihairitsu* provision used to determine postelection rank). Since then, no Kōmeitō candidate has been dual listed. Apart from the 2009 election, when nearly 40 percent of its candidates were dual listed, the JCP has dual listed approximately 10 percent or fewer of its candidates. In contrast to the LDP and DPJ, which usually put dual-listed candidates at rank 1 or 2, dual-listed JCP candidates, though generally equally ranked, are ranked below the party's top candidates on the list.

31. In early postreform elections, safe list positions were frequently negotiated to resolve disputes in the LDP where there was more than one incumbent in a new SMD after redistricting (Di Virgilio and Reed, 2011), but these problems have largely disappeared, and safe list positions have become more and more of a rarity in the past few elections, as party competition has increased and dual-listed SMD candidates have opposed the presence of a sure-winner above them on the list.

32. Interview with Inoguchi Kuniko, Tokyo, May 11, 2011 (in English).

33. Interview with Kōno Tarō, Tokyo, June 1, 2011 (in English). Most of the kōenkai members he inherited from his father were elderly, so Kōno sought in particular to recruit younger members into his new kōenkai.

34. Both Hatoyama brothers were originally members of the LDP, with Kunio first getting his start in the LDP splinter party New Liberal Club. Kan was first

elected as a member of the SDL. Hatoyama Yukio joined Sakigake in 1993 prior to the election, and Kan joined in 1994 after the dissolution of the SDL. Hatoyama Kunio ran as an independent in 1993.

35. For a detailed discussion of Ozawa Ichirō's prominent role in Japanese politics over the past four decades, see Mulgan (2014). For detailed accounts of the DPJ's formation and time in government, see Uekami and Tsutsumi (2011), Kushida and Lipscy (2013), and Maeda and Tsutsumi (2015).

36. For example, in the 1996 election, the LDP won 169 SMD seats with a total SMD vote share of 38.6 percent. The NFP won 96 SMD seats with 28 percent of the total SMD vote, while the DPJ won 17 seats with 10.6 percent of the SMD vote. A single, unified opposition party with the same vote shares could have potentially secured 158 SMD seats to the LDP's 127. Similar coordination failures occurred in the 2012 and 2014 House of Representatives elections, again to the LDP's benefit (Reed et al., 2013; Scheiner, Smith, and Thies, 2016).

37. For its part, the JSP (renamed the Social Democratic Party, SDP) struggled to elect even a handful of candidates to either house of the Diet after the reform, though it was briefly part of the DPJ-led coalition government from 2009-2010.

38. Although the party was out of government briefly from 1993 to 1994, and did not reclaim the post of prime minister until 1996, it was always the largest party.

39. *Kōbo* could more literally be translated as "public recruitment."

40. These women were Yamaguchi Shizue in Tokyo 6th District, Mikami Hideko in Tokyo 4th District, Sakamura Aonami in Gunma 2nd District, Takahashi Chihiro in Niigata 1st District, Abe Reiko in Osaka 3rd District, Hamada Makiko in Saitama 2nd District, and Noda Seiko in Gifu 1st District. Yamaguchi and Abe were the only two non-legacy candidates. Yamaguchi's father, Yamaguchi Shigehiko, was elected to the House of Councillors in 1953, after her first election in 1946. Of the female candidates who ran between 1976 and 1993, only Noda and Yamaguchi were successfully elected, although Takahashi had won a seat in 1972 that was formerly held by her husband before his death.

41. Parties are eligible to receive funds if they have five or more Diet members (either chamber), or at least one Diet member and exceeded two percent of the vote share for parties in the previous election. The law provides for a yearly fund of ¥250 per citizen to be allocated proportionally to parties based on their Diet membership and vote share in the most recent election. For the past several years, this has been around ¥30 billion. The JCP opposes the system on the principle that citizens must donate to parties they oppose, so it abstains from receiving any public funds.

42. Interview with senior LDP staff member in Tokyo, May 31, 2011 (in Japanese).

43. Interview with Asao Keiichirō in Tokyo, March 13, 2013 (in English).

44. Interview with a senior staff member of the DPJ Election Strategy Committee in Tokyo, June 15, 2011 (in Japanese).

45. Detailed data on the DPJ's open-recruitment contests can be found in Table A.5 in Appendix A.

46. To be eligible for the DPJ's open-recruitment process, would-be candidates are required to have held Japanese citizenship for at least twenty-five years. In the 2009 round of open recruitment, the theme for the application essay was "Politics After the Change in Government: What I Want to Tackle."

47. Interview with Sekō Hiroshige in Tokyo, June 9, 2011 (in Japanese).

48. The female applicant, economist Satō Yukari, was later also nominated to run in the 2005 general election.

49. Interview with Shibayama Masahiko in Tokyo, June 7, 2011 (in English). The interview committee consisted of Abe (then secretary general), Sekō, and Shiozaki, as well as Deputy Secretary General Kyūma Fumio, Internal Affairs Bureau Chief Machimura Nobutaka, Secretary General for the House of Councillors Aoki Mikio, and Saitama 9th District incumbent MP Ōno Matsushige, who also served as the party's prefectural branch leader (Sekō, 2006, pp. 22–23). All six candidates were interviewed together over the course of about an hour, with each candidate getting about ten minutes to make his or her case for selection.

50. Detailed data on the LDP's open-recruitment contests can be found in Table A.6 in Appendix A.

51. Interview with Inoguchi Kuniko in Tokyo, May 11, 2011 (in English).

52. Interviews with DPJ MP "A" in Tokyo, May 27, 2011 (in English), Nakabayashi Mieko in Tokyo, June 7, 2011 (in English), and Ōizumi Hiroko in Tokyo, June 15, 2011 (in English).

53. Interview with senior LDP staff member in Tokyo, May 31, 2011 (in Japanese).

54. Several months prior to the 2012 election, Ozawa and several of his followers in the DPJ defected from the party over the issue of raising the consumption tax and internal power struggles between Ozawa and other DPJ leaders.

55. One legacy candidate, former minister of education Moriyama Mayumi (widow of Tochigi 1st District MP Moriyama Kinji), resigned her position in the House of Councillors to run on the House of Representatives Kita Kanto PR list in 1996. She is not counted as a "first-time" candidate. Three of the other legacy candidates—Ōishi Hidemasa on the Tokai PR list in 1996, Katō Katsunobu on the Chugoku PR list in 2000, and Nakayama Kazuo on the Kita Kanto PR list in 2003—ran in the election directly after the retirement of their predecessor but were compelled to first run as pure PR candidates before running in their predecessor's SMD, so they do not count as hereditary candidates. Ōishi was ranked fourth on

the party's list and won a seat in 1996. However, he failed to get the party's official nomination in Shizuoka 2nd District in 2000 and ran instead as an independent (and lost). Katō was ranked seventh on the list in 1996 and was not elected, but was promoted to third on the list in 2000 and won. In 2009, he swapped with the SMD incumbent, Murata Yoshitaka, in Okayama 5th District as part of a so-called Costa Rica agreement (Reed and Shimizu, 2009) between candidates whose prereform jiban were divided by the new SMDs. Nakayama was given a hopeless thirty-second-place rank on the PR list in Kita Kanto in 2003. In 2005, he ran as an independent in his father's old Ibaraki 3rd District and lost to the LDP incumbent, Hanashi Yasuhiro, a third-generation legacy MP. Hasegawa Michio, the son of former House of Councillors MP Hasegawa Shin, ran on the Hokuriku Shinetsu PR list in 2003 but was ranked twenty-third and was not elected. Sekiya Taira, son of House of Councillors MP Sekiya Katsutsugu, won the 2005 open-recruitment contest to be listed on the party's Shikoku PR list after the dual-listed SMD candidates but ended up one position short of getting elected. Neither Hasegawa nor Sekiya attempted another election.

56. One was Yamahana Ikuo in Tokyo 22nd District. His father and grandfather were both JSP MPs. Another, Tanabu Masayo in Aomori 1st District, was the daughter of six-term MP Tanabu Masami, formerly of the LDP, Renewal Party, and NFP, before joining the DPJ. Brothers Ishihara Shinichirō and Ishihara Yōzaburō both attempted to succeed their father, Ishihara Kentarō, in Fukushima 1st District. Shinichirō tried first, in 2003 and 2005, failing in both attempts. Yōzaburō took over the jiban in 2009 and won election in the DPJ's landslide, only to be soundly defeated in 2012. The final hereditary candidate, Okajima Kazumasa in Chiba 3rd District, succeeded his father, Liberal Party MP Okajima Masayuki, after the latter's death in 2002 and the merger of the Liberal Party and DPJ in 2003.

57. *Asahi Shimbun*, April 4, 2009.

58. *Asahi Shimbun*, September 29, 2008.

59. In a similar survey of candidates as well as voters conducted by *Asahi Shimbun* in cooperation with the University of Tokyo, 64 percent of all candidates were in favor of restricting hereditary succession. In contrast, only 32 percent of voters thought that it was a problem.

60. Suga served as secretary to Okonogi Hikosaburō in Kanagawa 1st District for eleven years, before being elected to the Yokohama City Council in 1988. In 1991, Okonogi passed away, leaving an opening for Suga to run for the open seat. However, Okonogi's son, Hachirō, decided to run and was given the nomination over Suga. Suga had to wait until the district lines were redrawn in 1996 and he could run in neighboring Kanagawa 2nd District instead. *Asahi Shimbun*, June 12, 2009.

61. *Asahi Shimbun*, May 22, 2009, and June 6, 2009.

62. This variable was coded on the basis of whether the MP's secretary had the same family name as the MP. It is possible that it overlooks some family secretaries with different last names or erroneously counts some unrelated secretaries with the same last name.

63. *Asahi Shimbun*, October 1, 2009.

64. Interviews with Tsushima Yūji, June 14 and 17, 2011 (in English), and Tsushima Jun, March 15, 2013 (in Japanese).

65. Yokoyama won with 101,290 votes to Tsushima's 68,910 and Masuta's 35,283. The combined total of Tsushima's and Masuta's votes, 104,193, would have been enough to defeat Yokoyama.

66. Ironically, although the DPJ put the LDP on the defensive about dynastic politics, the DPJ itself nominated six new legacy (not hereditary, as promised) candidates in SMDs in 2009. Moreover, it nominated an additional four new legacy candidates as pure PR candidates, despite having never nominated a pure PR legacy candidate in previous years.

67. *Yomiuri Shimbun*, November 23, 2012.

68. Itō later won a seat through the Tokyo PR list in 2017, under the Party of Hope label. Three other new candidates for the JRP and four new candidates for Your Party also had legacy ties. The TPJ nominated two new legacy candidates with close ties to Ozawa in Iwate Prefecture: Tasso Yōko, the wife of Iwate Governor Tasso Takuya, in Iwate 1st District, and Satō Naomi, daughter of former Liberal Party MP Sugawara Kijūrō, in Iwate 3rd District. New Party Daichi nominated party leader Suzuki Muneo's daughter, Takako, in Hokkaido 7th District. Suzuki, who had been the personal secretary of Nakagawa Ichirō and rebelled when Nakagawa's kōenkai rallied behind Nakagawa's son Shōichi in 1983, apparently had a change of heart about the practice of dynastic politics.

69. *Nikkan Gendai*, February 11, 2016. Miyazaki Kensuke is not coded as a legacy candidate, as his brief marital connection to the Katō family was severed before he attempted to enter politics. He later married fellow MP Kaneko Megumi, only to resign from the Diet in 2016 after it was revealed he cheated on her while she was pregnant with their first child.

70. *Sankei Shimbun*, November 20, 2014.

71. Interview with Ōno Yoshinori in Tokyo, April 22, 2011 (in English).

72. Table A.9 in Appendix A replicates the results of the prereform analysis for predicting dynastic succession using only the postreform data. The results indicate that incumbency and longer tenures still increase the probability of hereditary succession. Controlling for other variables, an SMD incumbent who leaves office is roughly 23 percentage points more likely than a losing candidate to be directly followed by a relative. Winning a seat through the PR list as a zombie has a positive

but statistically insignificant relationship, as does an increasing number of prior wins, and coming from an existing dynasty. Death in office has become more important, with an estimated 33-percentage-point increase in the probability of direct hereditary succession.

73. The coding of *Bequeath* includes hereditary successions from LDP candidates to legacy successors who did not receive the party nomination or ran from another conservative party. Many of these candidates, such as Tsushima Jun, nevertheless went on to win the official nomination in a later election, so including them makes sense, and also fully captures the supply of aspiring legacy candidates. If *Bequeath* is recoded to include only cases where the successor was given the official LDP nomination, the patterns are roughly equivalent to those in Figure 4.9 and Figure 4.10.

74. *Asahi Shimbun*, June 29, 2011.

75. Family ties are inferred from common surnames, unless additional information is available.

76. This by-election and other by-elections held after 2014 are not included in the main analyses in this book since other candidates who ran in 2014 could not yet be considered as having exited politics. The 2017 general election took place after this book was already in production.

Chapter 5

1. *Kahoku Shinpō* newspaper, July 1, 2014.

2. Katō Ayuko's first husband, fellow MP Miyazaki Kensuke, adopted the Katō name, but they later divorced (see Chapter 4). After remarrying, she continued to use the Katō name for her public activities.

3. Interview with Ōno Yoshinori in Tokyo, April 22, 2011 (in English).

4. Smith and Martin (2017) evaluate the vote advantages of legacy candidates in Ireland's MMD system but focus more on comparing the advantages of legacy candidates whose predecessors served in cabinet (*cabinet legacies*) to other legacy and non-legacy candidates.

5. Unfortunately, expenditures data are only available for general elections from 1960 onward, so the sample used for this specification is slightly smaller than the full sample (see Table A.10 in Appendix A).

6. A new non-legacy LDP candidate faced off against a legacy candidate from the opposition in only three races. In twenty-one races, the LDP newcomer was a legacy candidate, and the remaining twenty-nine races, neither candidate was a legacy.

7. The PR vote in the national tier for the previous House of Councillors election is unrelated to the support for a candidate running in the SMD tier of the House of Representatives, unlike the party's vote share in the PR tier of the

House of Representatives, which may be influenced by "contamination effects" from popular SMD candidates. The national tier of the House of Councillors uses open-list PR since 2001, which means that the measure is partially influenced by the popularity of candidates in that tier. However, these candidates tend to represent interest groups with cross-cutting support, rather than geographically concentrated support, so the risk that any particular SMD features a biased value of party support is low. The mean is 31 percent (standard deviation of 8 percentage points). Because detailed polling data from each SMD are not available, it the best possible measure of the party's latent support.

8. Restricting the analysis only to direct hereditary successors, the estimate in model 6 drops to 5 percentage points (see Table A.12 in Appendix A).

9. Of the 2,085 respondents, 109 did not respond to this question.

10. In the actual conjoint tables, *Incumbency* (newcomer, formerly in office, currently in office) and *Number of wins* (1, 2, 3+) were separate attributes. For the analysis, these attributes are combined as *Experience*.

Chapter 6

1. On the controversy surrounding the revision, see Masumi (1995). The full name of the treaty is the Treaty of Mutual Cooperation and Security between the United States and Japan. It is often abbreviated in Japan as *Anpō*. Kishi's successor as prime minister, Ikeda Hayato, focused on the less controversial goal of economic growth, leading to Japan's "economic miracle."

2. Kishi and Satō were biological brothers. Their father was from the Kishi family, but adopted his wife's surname at marriage to preserve the Satō family line, which lacked a male heir. When Kishi was a child, he went to live with his father's older brother and became his adopted son and heir, taking the Kishi name in the process (Kishi himself was the second son).

3. Abe Shintarō was married to Kishi's daughter. His father (Abe Shinzō's paternal grandfather) was Abe Kan, who served in the prewar House of Representatives. Abe Shinzō's biological younger brother, Kishi Nobuo, was adopted by his mother's eldest brother, becoming the heir to the Kishi name, and subsequently followed his brother into politics.

4. Obuchi suffered a stroke in 2000 and was replaced by Mori Yoshirō, who served until 2001. Mori's father and grandfather both served in local politics but never transitioned into national politics. Mori's son, Yūki, also served in local politics before his sudden death in 2011; his nephew-in-law, Okada Naoki, was later elected to the House of Councillors.

5. Reported in English in *Japan Times*, July 25, 2017. The original results appeared online at https://www.fnn-news.com/yoron/inquiry170724.html.

6. Interview with Fukuda Tatsuo in Tokyo, March 15, 2013 (in Japanese).

7. The only other lower house MP appointed to the Koizumi 1.1 cabinet, Kōmeitō MP Sakaguchi Chikara, was not a legacy. The Koizumi 1.1 cabinet also included three non-MP "technical" ministers, one of whom, Takenaka Heizō, later won a seat in the House of Councillors, as well as three sitting House of Councillors MPs. The father of one of the House of Councillors MPs, Kōnoike Yoshitada, served in local politics.

8. Party affiliation is based on affiliation at the time of the general election and does not take into account midterm party switches.

9. For a detailed description of cabinets over time, see Woodall (2014).

10. On the distribution of parliamentary and PARC committee posts in Japan and the LDP, see Pekkanen, Krauss, and Nyblade (2006) and Fujimura (2015).

11. The following sections are loosely based on parts of previous research with Shane Martin (Smith and Martin, 2017).

12. Naoko Taniguchi (2008) notes that legacies in Japan were overrepresented in cabinet as early as 1996, even controlling for seniority. A similar overrepresentation of cabinet legacies has been documented in historical data from the United Kingdom (van Coppenolle, 2017) and Ireland (Smith and Martin, 2017).

13. Machidori Satoshi (2012), for example, divides the postwar era into five periods based on the prime minister's power relations vis-à-vis parliament: (1) 1945–1955, (2) 1955–1960, (3) 1960–1973, (4) 1973–1989, and (5) 1989–2012. The first period covers the Occupation and its immediate aftermath. The second period covers the formation of the LDP up until the political crisis of the US-Japan Security Treaty renewal in 1960. The third period is notable for Prime Minister Ikeda Hayato's policy focus on rapid economic growth and the entry of the DSP and Kōmeitō as new parties. The fourth period saw a gradual weakening of the LDP's one-party dominance, as well as the routinization of internal party norms. Finally, the fifth period is characterized by divided control of the Diet, coalition governments, and alternation in power. Brian Woodall (2014) also divides the postwar years into five periods: (1) 1946–1955, (2) 1955–1972, (3) 1972–1993, (4) 1993–2006, and (5) 2006–2013. The first period is dominated initially by ex-bureaucrats and only later by prewar party politicians. The second period covers the emergence of the 1955 System, in which leadership in the cabinet was divided across rival factions controlled by both career politicians and former bureaucrats, but policy decision making was increasingly shared with the bureaucratic elite. The third period was dominated by career politicians who relied on the bureaucracy and exercised little strategic choice in policy decisions. Finally, the fourth and fifth periods represent two stages characterized by nominally increased powers of the prime minister and cabinet vis-à-vis the bureaucracy but policy gridlock due to coalition governments, divided government, and a number of ineffective leaders.

14. Switzerland and the United States are excluded because they are not parliamentary democracies. Italy is excluded because the dataset lacks complete information on the exact family relations for many MPs (because this information is absent in the original data source), so cabinet legacies cannot be distinguished from non-cabinet legacies.

Chapter 7

1. Brasor, Philip and Masako Tsubuku. "Politicians' pay: Even more than you think." *Japan Times* online, December 13, 2011.

2. Another recent study finds a positive correlation between LDP legacy candidates and the proportion of the preelection candidate manifesto devoted to pork-barrel policies in postreform elections from 1996 to 2009 (Muraoka, 2017). It is not clear whether this correlation can be attributed to the fact, as documented in Chapter 4, that postreform legacy candidates are qualitatively different from their prereform counterparts, or whether they tend to run in more rural districts postreform. Additional inconclusive evidence of pork-oriented behavior among legacy candidates has been documented for the case of Brazil (Ames, 1995).

3. There is also some mixed evidence that family members of currently serving politicians might benefit economically from their political connections (Gagliarducci and Manacorda, 2016; Folke, Persson, and Rickne, 2017).

4. The first woman to serve in the US House of Representatives was Jeannette Rankin, who was elected to serve Montana in 1916. She was not a legacy candidate to Congress, but had relatives in other public offices. Her brother, Wellington Rankin, was active in the Republican Party and would later become the attorney general of Montana and an associate justice of the Montana Supreme Court.

5. Alternative theoretical frameworks include the "feminist institutionalism" approach (e.g., Krook and MacKay, 2011) and approaches based on the political economy of labor markets (Iversen and Rosenbluth, 2010).

6. Folke, Rickne, and Smith (2017) explore the impact of the introduction of a zipper quota (mandatory alternation of men and women on the party list) across all local elections by the Swedish Social Democratic Party (SAP) in 1994. The introduction of the quota led to a quantitatively small but positive increase in the recruitment of female legacy candidates. However, the effect was only temporary, with recruitment patterns returning to the pre-quota status quo within two elections.

7. Another explanation for the dynastic gender bias is that male elites might recruit female members of their families into office to serve as "proxies" for their own power, or placeholders for future male relatives (e.g., Schwindt-Bayer, 2011; Jalalzai, 2013; Ban and Rao, 2008). This explanation may have more of a role in developing democracies or early female recruitment following enfranchisement.

8. Moran, Terry. "Is Bush's Iraq stance rooted in revenge?" *ABC News* (online), March 18, 2002.

9. Catalinac (2016) notes that among the campaign materials that are permitted under Japan's restrictive campaign laws, those that are conducive to offering policy views are the candidate election manifesto, newspaper advertisements, campaign postcards, campaign flyers, radio and television policy broadcasts, and campaign speeches. Other activities that are not conducive to offering policy views include campaign posters and name chanting—in which candidates drive around their district or position themselves in front of train stations repeating their names from loudspeakers.

Chapter 8

1. These passages are from *The Federalist Papers*, no. 57, believed to have been written by either Alexander Hamilton or James Madison.

2. Ranking is based on the "women in national parliaments" data compiled by the Inter-Parliamentary Union (www.ipu.org), as of July 1, 2017.

3. The 2014 abolition of term limits in Mexico might provide an opportunity to explore the effect of term limits on dynastic recruitment in a before-and-after design similar to the one employed in this book.

4. Trajano, Julius Cesar I. and Yoes C. Kenawas. "Political dynasties in Indonesia and the Philippines." *East Asia Forum*, February 13, 2013.

5. "'Political dynasties legalized' as court allows leaders' relatives to run for office." *Jakarta Globe*, July 8, 2015.

6. "Jokowi and Prabowo both claim victory in early Indonesian election results." *The Guardian*, July 9, 2014.

7. Ryan, Philip. "Fight for Kenny's seat is more than a two-horse race." *Independent* (online edition), August 7, 2016.

References

Adams, Julia. 2005. *The Familial State: Ruling Families and Merchant Capitalism in Early Modern Europe.* Ithaca, NY: Cornell University Press.

Akirav, Osnat. 2010. "Candidate Selection in a Crowded Parliament: The Israeli Knesset, 1988–2006." *Journal of Legislative Studies* 16(1):96–120.

Alt, James, Ethan Bueno de Mesquita, and Shanna Rose. 2011. "Disentangling Accountability and Competence in Elections: Evidence from U.S. Term Limits." *Journal of Politics* 73(1):171–186.

Ames, Barry. 1995. "Electoral Strategy under Open-List Proportional Representation." *American Journal of Political Science* 39(2):406–433.

Amundsen, Inge. 2016. "Democratic Dynasties? Internal Party Democracy in Bangladesh." *Party Politics* 22(1):49–58.

Andeweg, Rudy B. 2000. "Ministers as Double Agents? The Delegation Process Between Cabinet and Ministers." *European Journal of Political Research* 37(3):377–395.

Ansolabehere, Stephen, James M. Snyder Jr., and Charles I. Stewart. 2000. "Old Voters, New Voters, and the Personal Vote: Using Redistricting to Measure the Incumbency Advantage." *American Journal of Political Science* 44(1):17–34.

Anzia, Sarah F. and Christopher R. Berry. 2011. "The Jackie (and Jill) Robinson Effect: Why Do Congresswomen Outperform Congressmen?" *American Journal of Political Science* 55(3):478–493.

Ariga, Kenichi. 2015. "Incumbency Disadvantage under Electoral Rules with Intraparty Competition: Evidence from Japan." *Journal of Politics* 77(3):874–887.

Ariga, Kenichi, Yusaku Horiuchi, Roland Mansilla, and Michio Umeda. 2016. "No Sorting, No Advantage: Regression Discontinuity Estimates of Incumbency Advantage in Japan." *Electoral Studies* 43:21–31.

Asako, Yasushi, Takeshi Iida, Tetsuya Matsubayashi, and Michiko Ueda. 2015. "Dynastic Politicians: Theory and Evidence from Japan." *Japanese Journal of Political Science* 16(1):5–32.

Asano, Masahiko. 2006. *Shimin Shakai ni Okeru Seido Kaikaku: Senkyo Seido to Kōhosha Rikurūto* [System reform at the level of civil society: Electoral system and candidate recruitment]. Tokyo: Keiō Gijuku Daigaku Shuppansha.

Bäck, Hanna, Marc Debus, and Patrick Dumont. 2011. "Who Gets What in Coalition Governments? Predictors of Portfolio Allocation in Parliamentary Democracies." *European Journal of Political Research* 50(4):441–478.

Bäck, Hanna, Marc Debus, and Jochen Müller. 2014. "Who Takes the Parliamentary Floor? The Role of Gender in Speech-making in the Swedish *Riksdag*." *Political Research Quarterly* 67(3):504–518.

Ban, Radu and Vijayendra Rao. 2008. "Tokenism or Agency? The Impact of Women's Reservations on Village Democracies in South India." *Economic Development and Cultural Change* 56(3):501–530.

Basu, Amrita. 2016. Women, Dynasties, and Democracy in India. In *Democratic Dynasties: State, Party, and Family in Contemporary Indian Politics*, ed. Kanchan Chandra. Cambridge: Cambridge University Press, pp. 127–160.

Batto, Nathan F. 2015. "Fewer Rungs, More Political Families: Legacy Candidates in Taiwan Elections." Paper presented at the 2015 Annual Meeting of the American Political Science Association, San Francisco, CA.

Benedict, Ruth. 1946. *The Chrysanthemum and the Sword: Patterns of Japanese Culture*. New York: Routledge & Kegan Paul.

Berlinski, Samuel, Torun Dewan, and Brenda Van Coppenolle. 2014. "Franchise Extension and the British Aristocracy." *Legislative Studies Quarterly* 39(4):531–558.

Bertrand, Marianne, Simon Johnson, Krislert Samphantharak, and Antoinette Schoar. 2008. "Mixing Family with Business: A Study of Thai Business Groups and the Families Behind Them." *Journal of Financial Economics* 88(3):466–498.

Besley, Timothy. 2005. "Political Selection." *Journal of Economic Perspectives, American Economic Association* 19(3):43–60.

Besley, Timothy and Anne Case. 1995. "Does Electoral Accountability Affect Economic Policy Choices? Evidence from Gubernatorial Term Limits." *Quarterly Journal of Economics* 110(3):769–798.

Besley, Timothy and Marta Reynal-Querol. 2017. "The Logic of Hereditary Rule: Theory and Evidence." Unpublished manuscript.

Bestor, Theodore C. 2004. *Tsukiji: The Fish Market at the Center of the World*. Berkeley: University of California Press.

Blau, Peter M. and Otis Dudley Duncan. 1967. *The American Occupational Structure*. New York: John Wiley and Sons.

Blondel, Jean and Jean-Louis Thiébault. 1991. *The Profession of Government Minister in Western Europe*. Basingstoke, UK: Palgrave Macmillan.

Bohlken, Anjali Thomas. 2016. Dynasty and "Paths to Power." In *Democratic Dynasties: State, Party, and Family in Contemporary Indian Politics*, ed. Kanchan Chandra. Cambridge: Cambridge University Press, pp. 223–249.

Bragança, Arthur, Claudio Ferraz, and Juan Rios. 2015. "Political Dynasties and the Quality of Government." Unpublished manuscript.

Bratton, Kathleen A. and Leonard P. Ray. 2002. "Descriptive Representation, Policy Outcomes, and Municipal Day-Care Coverage in Norway." *American Journal of Political Science* 46(2):428–437.

Brownlee, Jason. 2007. "Hereditary Succession in Modern Autocracies." *World Politics* 59(4):595–628.

Burden, Barry C. and David C. Kimball. 2004. *Why Americans Split Their Tickets: Campaigns, Competition and Divided Government*. Ann Arbor: University of Michigan Press.

Cain, Bruce E., John A. Ferejohn, and Morris P. Fiorina. 1987. *The Personal Vote: Constituency Service and Electoral Independence*. Cambridge, MA: Harvard University Press.

Calonico, Sebastian, Matias D. Cattaneo, and Rocío Titiunik. 2014. "Robust Data-driven Inference in the Regression-Discontinuity Design." *Stata Journal* 14(4):909–946.

Camp, Roderic A. 1982. "Family Relationships in Mexican Politics: A Preliminary View." *Journal of Politics* 44(3):848–862.

Carey, John M. 1996. *Term Limits and Legislative Representation*. Cambridge: Cambridge University Press.

Carey, John M. 2009. *Legislative Voting and Accountability*. Cambridge: Cambridge University Press.

Carey, John M., Richard G. Niemi, and Lynda W. Powell. 2000. "Incumbency and the Probability of Reelection in State Legislative Elections." *Journal of Politics* 62(3):671–700.

Carey, John M. and Matthew S. Shugart. 1995. "Incentives to Cultivate a Personal Vote: A Rank Ordering of Electoral Formulas." *Electoral Studies* 14(4):417–440.

Carlson, Matthew. 2007. *Money Politics in Japan: New Rules, Old Practices*. Boulder, CO: Lynne Rienner Publishers.

Carnegie, Andrew. 1889. "Wealth." *North American Review* 148(391):653–664.

Carnes, Nicholas and Noam Lupu. 2016. "Do Voters Dislike Working-Class Candidates? Voter Biases and the Descriptive Underrepresentation of the Working Class." *American Political Science Review* 110(4):832–844.

Carty, R. Kenneth and William Cross. 2010. Political Parties and the Practice of Brokerage Politics. In *The Oxford Handbook of Canadian Politics*, ed. John C. Courtney and David E. Smith. Oxford: Oxford University Press, pp. 191–207.

Casas-Arce, Pablo and Albert Saiz. 2015. "Women and Power: Unpopular, Unwilling, or Held Back?" *Journal of Political Economy* 123(3):641–669.

Catalinac, Amy. 2016. *Electoral Reform and National Security in Japan: From Pork to Foreign Policy.* Cambridge: Cambridge University Press.

Caughey, Devin and Jasjeet S. Sekhon. 2011. "Elections and the Regression Discontinuity Design: Lessons from Close U.S. House Races, 1942–2008." *Political Analysis* 19(4):385–408.

Chandra, Kanchan. 2016. Democratic Dynasties: State, Party, and Family in Contemporary Indian Politics. In *Democratic Dynasties: State, Party, and Family in Contemporary Indian Politics*, ed. Kanchan Chandra. Cambridge: Cambridge University Press, pp. 10–50.

Chandra, Kanchan, Anjali Bohlken, and Simon Chauchard. 2014. "Dataset on Dynasticism in the Indian Parliament." Provided by the authors.

Chang, Eric C. C. and Miriam Golden. 2006. "Electoral Systems, District Magnitude, and Corruption." *British Journal of Political Science* 37(1):115–137.

Chattopadhyay, Raghabendra and Esther Duflo. 2004. "Women as Policy Makers: Evidence from a Randomized Policy Experiment in India." *Econometrica* 72(5):1409–1443.

Chhibber, Pradeep. 2013. "Dynastic Parties: Organization, Finance and Impact." *Party Politics* 19(2):277–295.

Chirico, Danilo and Raffaele Lupoli. 2008. *Onorevoli Figli di: I Parenti, i Portaborse, le Lobby Istantanea del Nuovo Parlamento* [Honorable children of . . . : The relatives, assistants, and instant lobbyists of the new parliament]. Rome: Rinascita edizioni.

Christensen, Raymond V. 1994. "Electoral Reform in Japan: How It Was Enacted and Changes It May Bring." *Asian Survey* 34(7):589–605.

Cirone, Alexandra and Carlos Velasco Rivera. 2017. "Electoral Reform and Dynastic Politics: Evidence from the French Third Republic." Unpublished manuscript.

Clark, Gregory. 2014. *The Son Also Rises: Surnames and the History of Social Mobility.* Princeton, NJ: Princeton University Press.

Clubok, Alfred B., Norman M. Wilensky, and Forrest J. Berghorn. 1969. "Family Relationships, Congressional Recruitment, and Political Modernization." *Journal of Politics* 31(4):1035–1062.

Colomer, Josep M. 2005. "It's Parties That Choose Electoral Systems (or, Duverger's Laws Upside Down)." *Political Studies* 53(1):1–51.

Cotta, Maurizio and Luca Verzichelli. 1993. *PARLIT46_92.* Centre for the Study of Political Change (CIRCaP), Università degli Studi di Siena.

Cowhey, Peter F. and Mathew D. McCubbins. 1995. Conclusion. In *Structure and Policy in Japan and the United States*, ed. Peter F. Cowhey and Mathew D. McCubbins. Cambridge: Cambridge University Press, pp. 253–260.

Cox, Gary W. 1994. "Strategic Voting Equilibria under the Single Nontransferable Vote." *American Political Science Review* 88(3):608–621.

Cox, Gary W., Jon H. Fiva, and Daniel M. Smith. 2018. "Parties, Legislators, and the Origins of Proportional Representation." *Comparative Political Studies.* DOI:10.1177/0010414018762369.

Cox, Gary W. and Jonathan N. Katz. 1996. "Why Did the Incumbency Advantage in U.S. House Elections Grow?" *American Journal of Political Science* 40(2):478–497.

Cox, Gary W. and Scott Morgenstern. 1995. "The Incumbency Advantage in Multimember Districts: Evidence from the U.S. States." *Legislative Studies Quarterly* 20(3):329–349.

Cox, Nicholas J. 2008. "Speaking Stata: Spineplots and Their Kin." *Stata Journal* 8(1):105–121.

Crisp, Brian F., Kathryn M. Jensen, and Yael Shomer. 2007. "Magnitude and Vote Seeking." *Electoral Studies* 26(1):727–734.

Cruz, Cesi, Julien Labonne, and Pablo Querubín. 2017. "Politician Family Networks and Electoral Outcomes: Evidence from the Philippines." *American Economic Review* 107(10):3006–3037.

Curtis, Gerald L. 1971. *Election Campaigning, Japanese Style.* New York: Columbia University Press.

Curtis, Gerald L. 1979. The Opposition. In *A Season of Voting: Japanese Elections of 1976 and 1977*, ed. Herbert Passin. Washington, DC: American Enterprise Institute, pp. 43–80.

Curtis, Gerald L. 1988. *The Japanese Way of Politics.* New York: Columbia University Press.

Dal Bó, Ernesto, Pedro Dal Bó, and Jason Snyder. 2009. "Political Dynasties." *Review of Economic Studies* 76(1):115–142.

Dal Bó, Ernesto, Frederico Finan, Olle Folke, Torsten Persson, and Johanna Rickne. 2017. "Who Becomes a Politician?" *Quarterly Journal of Economics* 132(4):1877–1914.

Dewan, Torun and Keith Dowding. 2005. "The Corrective Effect of Ministerial Resignations on Government Popularity." *American Journal of Political Science* 49(1):46–56.

Di Virgilio, Aldo and Steven R. Reed. 2011. Nominating Candidates Under New Rules in Italy and Japan: You Cannot Bargain with Resources You Do Not Have. In *A Natural Experiment on Electoral Law Reform: Evaluating the Long Run Consequences of 1990s Electoral Reform in Italy and Japan*, ed. Daniela Giannetti and Bernard Grofman. New York: Springer-Verlag, pp. 59–73.

Dowding, Keith and Patrick Dumont, eds. 2009. *The Selection of Ministers in Europe: Hiring and Firing.* New York: Routledge.

Dowding, Keith and Patrick Dumont, eds. 2014. *The Selection of Ministers Around the World: A Comparative Study.* London: Routledge.

Dower, John W. 1999. *Embracing Defeat: Japan in the Wake of World War II.* New York: W. W. Norton and Company.

Droop, Henry Richmond. 1881. "On Methods of Electing Representatives." *Journal of the Statistical Society of London* 44(2):141–196.

Durante, Ruben, Giovanna Labartino, and Roberto Perotti. 2011. "Academic Dynasties: Decentralization and Familism in the Italian Academia." NBER Working Paper No. 17572.

Duverger, Maurice. 1954. *Political Parties: Their Organization and Activity in the Modern State.* New York: John Wiley.

Eggers, Andrew C., Anthony Fowler, Jens Hainmueller, Andrew B. Hall, and James M. Snyder Jr. 2015. "On the Validity of the Regression Discontinuity Design for Estimating Electoral Effects: New Evidence from Over 40,000 Close Races." *American Journal of Political Science* 59(1):259–274.

Ehrenhalt, Alan. 1991. *The United States of Ambition: Politicians, Power, and the Pursuit of Office.* New York: Times Books.

Ehrhardt, George, Axel Klein, Levi McLaughlin, and Steven R. Reed, eds. 2014. *Kōmeitō: Politics and Religion in Japan.* Berkeley: Institute of East Asian Studies, University of California, Berkeley.

Epstein, David, David Brady, Sadafumi Kawato, and Sharyn O'Halloran. 1997. "A Comparative Approach to Legislative Organization: Careerism and Seniority in the United States and Japan." *American Journal of Political Science* 41(3):965–998.

Epstein, Leon D. 1980. *Political Parties in Western Democracies.* New Brunswick, NJ: Transaction Publishers.

Erickson, Lynda and R. K. Carty. 1991. "Parties and Candidate Selection in the 1988 Canadian General Election." *Canadian Journal of Political Science* 24(2):331–349.

Erikson, Robert S. 1971. "The Advantage of Incumbency in Congressional Elections." *Polity* 3(3):395–405.

Erikson, Robert S. and Rocío Titiunik. 2015. "Using Regression Discontinuity to Uncover the Personal Incumbency Advantage." *Quarterly Journal of Political Science* 10(1):101–119.

Faas, Thorsten. 2003. "To Defect or Not to Defect? National, Institutional and Party Group Pressures on MEPs and Their Consequences for Party Group Cohesion in the European Parliament." *European Journal of Political Research* 42(6):841–866.

Fallon, Johnny. 2011. *Dynasties: Irish Political Families.* Dublin: New Island.

Fearon, James D. 1999. Electoral Accountability and the Control of Politicians: Selecting Good Types versus Sanctioning Poor Performance. In *Democracy, Accountability, and Representation,* ed. Adam Przeworski, Susan C. Stokes, and Bernard Manin. Cambridge: Cambridge University Press, pp. 55–97.

Feinstein, Brian D. 2010. "The Dynasty Advantage: Family Ties in Congressional Elections." *Legislative Studies Quarterly* 25(4):571–598.

Fenno, Richard F. 1978. *Home Style: House Members in their Districts.* Boston: Little, Brown.

Ferraz, Claudio and Frederico Finan. 2011. "Electoral Accountability and Corruption: Evidence from the Audits of Local Governments." *American Economic Review* 101(4):1274–1311.

Fiva, Jon H. and Daniel M. Smith. 2018. "Political Dynasties and the Incumbency Advantage in Party-Centered Environments." *American Political Science Review.* DOI:10.1017/S0003055418000047.

Folke, Olle, Torsten Persson, and Johanna Rickne. 2017. "Dynastic Political Rents? Economic Benefits to Relatives of Top Politicians." *Economic Journal* 127(605):F495–F517.

Folke, Olle and Johanna Rickne. 2016. "The Glass Ceiling in Politics: Formalization and Empirical Tests." *Comparative Political Studies* 49(5):567–599.

Folke, Olle, Johanna Rickne, and Daniel M. Smith. 2017. "Gender and Dynastic Political Recruitment." Unpublished manuscript.

Fowler, Anthony and Andrew B. Hall. 2014. "Disentangling the Personal and Partisan Incumbency Advantages: Evidence from Close Elections and Term Limits." *Quarterly Journal of Political Science* 9(4):501–531.

Fowler, Linda L. and Robert D. McClure. 1989. *Political Ambition: Who Decides to Run for Congress.* New Haven, CT: Yale University Press.

Franchino, Fabio and Francesco Zucchini. 2015. "Voting in a Multi-dimensional Space: A Conjoint Analysis Employing Valence and Ideology Attributes of Candidates." *Political Science Research and Methods* 3(2):221–241.

Fujimura, Naofumi. 2015. "The Influence of Electoral Institutions on Legislative Representation: Evidence from Japan's Single Non-Transferable Vote and Single-Member District Systems." *Party Politics* 21(2):209–221.

Fukui, Haruhiro. 1997. Japan. In *Passages to Power: Legislative Recruitment in Advanced Democracies*, ed. Pippa Norris. Cambridge: Cambridge University Press, pp. 98–113.

Fukumoto, Kentarō and Kaoru Nakagawa. 2013. "Tokuhyō no Keishō no Tai Suru Seshū no Kōka: Seitō Tōhyō, Kōhosha Tōhyō no Hikaku" [The effect of the hereditary inheritance of votes: A comparison of party and personal votes]. *Senkyo Kenkyū* 29(2):118–128.

Gagliarducci, Stefano and Marco Manacorda. 2016. "Politics in the Family: Nepotism and the Hiring Decisions of Italian Firms." Institute for the Study of Labor (IZA) Discussion Paper No. 9841.

Gallagher, Michael. 1988*a*. Introduction. In *Candidate Selection in Comparative Perspective: The Secret Garden of Politics*, ed. Michael Gallagher and Michael Marsh. London: Sage Publications, pp. 1–19.

Gallagher, Michael. 1988*b*. Ireland: The Increasing Role of Centre. In *Candidate Selection in Comparative Perspective: The Secret Garden of Politics*, ed. Michael Gallagher and Michael Marsh. London: Sage Publications, pp. 119–144.

Gallagher, Michael, ed. 1993. *Irish Elections 1922–44: Results and Analysis*. Dublin: PSAI Press.

Gallagher, Michael. 2003. Ireland: Party Loyalists with a Personal Base. In *The Political Class in Advanced Democracies*, ed. Jens Borchert and Jürgen Zeiss. Oxford: Oxford University Press, pp. 187–202.

Gallagher, Michael, ed. 2009. *Irish Elections 1948–1977: Results and Analysis*. New York: Routledge, Political Studies Association of Ireland.

Galton, Francis. 1886. "Regression Towards Mediocrity in Hereditary Stature." *Journal of the Anthropological Institute* 15:246–263.

Gaunder, Alisa. 2013. The DPJ and Women: The Limited Impact of the 2009 Alternation of Power on Policy and Governance. In *Japan Under the DPJ: The Politics of Transition and Governance*, ed. Kenji E. Kushida and Phillip Y. Lipscy. Stanford, CA: Walter H. Shorenstein Asia-Pacific Research Center, pp. 305–330.

Gelman, Andrew and Gary King. 1990. "Estimating Incumbency Advantage Without Bias." *American Journal of Political Science* 34(4):1142–1164.

Geys, Benny. 2017. "Political Dynasties, Electoral Institutions and Politicians' Human Capital." *Economic Journal* 127(605):F474–F494.

Geys, Benny and Karsten Mause. 2014. "Are Female Legislators Different? Exploring Sex Differences in German MPs' Outside Interests." *Parliamentary Affairs* 67(4):841–865.

Gidengil, Elisabeth. 2010. Challenge and Change: Elections and Voting. In *The Oxford Handbook of Canadian Politics*, ed. John C. Courtney and David E. Smith. Oxford: Oxford University Press, pp. 226–243.

Gluck, Carol. 1985. *Japan's Modern Myths: Ideology in the Late Meiji Period*. Princeton, NJ: Princeton University Press.

Golden, Miriam A. and Lucio Picci. 2015. "Incumbency Effects Under Proportional Representation: Leaders and Backbenchers in the Postwar Italian Chamber of Deputies." *Legislative Studies Quarterly* 40(4):509–538.

Gordon, Sanford C., Gregory A. Huber, and Dimitri Landa. 2007. "Challenger Entry and Voter Learning." *American Political Science Review* 101(2):303–320.

Grimmer, Justin. 2013. *Representational Style: What Legislators Say and Why It Matters*. Cambridge: Cambridge University Press.

Grofman, Bernard. 2005. "Comparisons Among Electoral Systems: Distinguishing Between Localism and Candidate-Centered Politics." *Electoral Studies* 24(1):735–740.

Hainmueller, Jens and Daniel J. Hopkins. 2015. "The Hidden American Immigration Consensus: A Conjoint Analysis of Attitudes toward Immigrants." *American Journal of Political Science* 59(3):529–548.

Hainmueller, Jens, Daniel J. Hopkins, and Teppei Yamamoto. 2014. "Causal Inference in Conjoint Analysis: Understanding Multi-dimensional Preferences via Stated Preference Experiments." *Political Analysis* 22(1):1–30.

Hall, Andrew B. and James M. Snyder Jr. 2015. "How Much of the Incumbency Advantage Is Due to Scare-Off?" *Political Science Research and Methods* 3(3):493–514.

Hall, Peter A. and Rosemary C. R. Taylor. 1996. "Political Science and the Three New Institutionalisms." *Political Studies* 44(5):936–957.

Harada, Masataka and Daniel M. Smith. 2014. "You Have to Pay to Play: Candidate and Party Responses to the High Cost of Elections in Japan." *Electoral Studies* 36(1):51–64.

Hayao, Kenji. 1993. *The Japanese Prime Minister and Public Policy*. Pittsburgh: University of Pittsburgh Press.

Hazan, Reuven Y. and Gideon Rahat. 2010. *Democracy Within Parties: Candidate Selection Methods and Their Political Consequences*. Oxford: Oxford University Press.

Hess, Stephen. 1966. *America's Political Dynasties: From Adams to Kennedy*. Garden City, NY: Doubleday.

Hirano, Shigeo. 2006. "Electoral Institutions, Hometowns, and Favored Minorities: Evidence from Japanese Electoral Reforms." *World Politics* 59(1):51–82.

Hirano, Shigeo and James M. Snyder Jr. 2009. "Using Multimember District Elections to Estimate the Sources of the Incumbency Advantage." *American Journal of Political Science* 53(2):292–306.

Hix, Simon. 2004. "Electoral Institutions and Legislative Behavior: Explaining Voting Defection in the European Parliament." *World Politics* 56(2):194–223.

Horiuchi, Yusaku, Daniel M. Smith, and Teppei Yamamoto. 2018a. "Identifying Voter Preferences for Politicians' Personal Attributes: A Conjoint Experiment in Japan." *Political Science Research and Methods,* forthcoming.

Horiuchi, Yusaku, Daniel M. Smith, and Teppei Yamamoto. 2018b. "Measuring Voters' Multidimensional Policy Preferences with Conjoint Analysis: Application to Japan's 2014 Election." *Political Analysis*. DOI:10.1017/pan.2018.2.

Horrace, William C. and Ronald L. Oaxaca. 2006. "Results on the Bias and Inconsistency of Ordinary Least Squares for the Linear Probability Model." *Economics Letters* 90(3):321–327.

Hrebenar, Ronald J. 1992. The Kōmeitō: Party of "Buddhist Democracy." In *The Japanese Party System*, ed. Ronald J. Hrebenar. Boulder, CO: Westview Press, pp. 151–183.

Ichikawa, Taichi. 1990. *'Seshū' Daigishi no Kenkyū* [Study of hereditary Diet members]. Tokyo: Nihon Keizai Shimbunsha.

Igarashi, Akio. 1986. "Seijika Nisei: Mezase Nagatachō Ichibanchi" [Second-generation politicians: Aiming for number one, Nagatacho]. *Ushio,* pp. 110–137.

Iida, Takeshi, Tetsuya Matsubayashi, and Michiko Ueda. 2010. "Seshū Giin no Jisshō Bunseki" [Empirical analysis of dynastic legislators]. *Senkyo Kenkyū* 26(2):139–153.

Iijima, Isao. 2006. *Koizumi Kantei Hiroku* [Secrets of the Koizumi administration]. Tokyo: Nihon Keizai Shimbunsha.

Ike, Nobutaka. 1957. *Japanese Politics: An Introductory Survey.* New York: Alfred A. Knopf.

Inaida, Shigeru. 2009. *Seshū Giin: Kōzō to Mondai-ten* [Hereditary Diet members: Structure and problems]. Tokyo: Kōdansha.

Ishibashi, Michihiro and Steven R. Reed. 1992. "Second-Generation Diet Members and Democracy in Japan: Hereditary Seats." *Asian Survey* 32(4):366–379.

Ishida, Hiroshi. 1993. *Social Mobility in Contemporary Japan: Educational Credentials, Class and the Labor Market in a Cross-national Perspective.* Stanford, CA: Stanford University Press.

Ishikawa, Masumi and Michisada Hirose. 1989. *Jimintō: Chōki Shihai no Kōzō* [LDP: The structure of long-term rule]. Tokyo: Iwanami Shoten.

Isoda, Michifumi. 1998. "Daimyō Kashin dan no Tsūkon Kōzō." *Shakai Keizai Shigaku* 63(5):599–628.

Itoh, Mayumi. 2003. *The Hatoyama Dynasty: Japanese Political Leadership Through the Generations.* New York: Palgrave Macmillan.

Iversen, Torben and Frances Rosenbluth. 2010. *Women, Work, and Politics: The Political Economy of Gender Inequality.* New Haven, CT: Yale University Press.

Iwai, Tomoaki. 1990. *Seiji Shikin no Kenkyū: Rieki Yūdō no Nihon-teki Seiji Fūdo* [Study of political funds: Japanese political culture of influence peddling]. Tokyo: Nihon Keizai Shimbunsha.

Jacobson, Gary C. 1987. "The Marginals Never Vanished: Incumbency and Competition in Elections to the U.S. House of Representatives." *American Journal of Political Science* 31(1):126–141.

Jacobson, Gary C. 1989. "Strategic Politicians and the Dynamics of U.S. House Elections, 1946–86." *American Political Science Review* 83(3):773–793.

Jacobson, Gary C. 2001. *The Politics of Congressional Elections.* 5th ed. Boston: Allyn and Bacon.

Jacobson, Gary C. and Samuel Kernell. 1983. *Strategy and Choice in Congressional Elections.* New Haven, CT: Yale University Press.

Jalalzai, Farida. 2013. *Shattered, Cracked, or Firmly Intact? Women and the Executive Glass Ceiling Worldwide.* Oxford: Oxford University Press.

Jewell, Malcolm E. and David Breaux. 1988. "The Effect of Incumbency on State Legislative Elections." *Legislative Studies Quarterly* 13(4):495–514.

Johnson, Joel W. and Jessica S. Wallack. 2012. "Electoral Systems and the Personal Vote." Harvard Dataverse, V1. http://hdl.handle.net/1902.1/17901.

Kato, Junko and Yuto Kannon. 2008. "Coalition Governments, Party Switching, and the Rise and Decline of Parties: Changing Japanese Party Politics since 1993." *Japanese Journal of Political Science* 9(3):341–365.

Katz, Richard S. and Peter Mair. 1995. "Changing Models of Party Organization and Party Democracy: The Emergence of the Cartel Party." *Party Politics* 1(1):5–28.

Kawato, Sadafumi. 2000. "Strategic Contexts of the Vote on Political Reform Bills." *Japanese Journal of Political Science* 1(1):23–51.

Kawato, Sadafumi. 2002. The Study of Japan's Medium-Sized District System. In *Legislatures: Comparative Perspectives on Representative Assemblies*, ed. Gerhard Loewenberg, Peverill Squire, and D. Roderick Kiewiet. Ann Arbor: University of Michigan Press, pp. 178–198.

Keefer, Philip and Stuti Khemani. 2009. "When Do Legislators Pass on Pork? The Role of Political Parties in Determining Legislator Effort." *American Political Science Review* 103(1):99–112.

Kerby, Matthew. 2009. "Worth the Wait: Determinants of Ministerial Appointment in Canada, 1935–2008." *Canadian Journal of Political Science* 42(3):593–611.

Kincaid, Diane D. 1978. "Over His Dead Body: A Positive Perspective on Widows in the U.S. Congress." *Western Political Quarterly* 31(1):96–104.

Kirchheimer, Otto. 1966. The Transformation of West European Party Systems. In *Political Parties and Political Development*, ed. Joseph LaPalombara and Myron Weiner. Princeton, NJ: Princeton University Press, pp. 177–200.

Kitaoka, Shinichi. 1985. Jiyū Minshutō [The Liberal Democratic Party]. In *Gendai Nihon no Seiji Kōzō* [The structure of contemporary Japanese politics], ed. Jirō Kamishima. Kyoto: Hōritsu Bunkasha, pp. 25–141.

Kohno, Masaru. 1997. *Japan's Postwar Party Politics.* Princeton, NJ: Princeton University Press.

Kostadinova, Tatiana. 2007. "Ethnic and Women's Representation Under Mixed Election Systems." *Electoral Studies* 26(2):418–431.

Krauss, Ellis, Kuniaki Nemoto, and Robert Pekkanen. 2012. "Reverse Contamination: Burning and Building Bridges in Mixed-Member Systems." *Comparative Political Studies* 45(6):747–773.

Krauss, Ellis S. and Robert J. Pekkanen. 2011. *The Rise and Fall of Japan's LDP: Political Organizations as Historical Institutions.* Ithaca, NY: Cornell University Press.

Krook, Mona Lena. 2006. "Reforming Representation: The Diffusion of Candidate Gender Quotas Worldwide." *Politics & Gender* 2(3):303–327.

Krook, Mona Lena and Fiona MacKay, eds. 2011. *Gender, Politics, and Institutions: Towards a Feminist Institutionalism.* New York: Palgrave.

Kushida, Kenji E. and Phillip Y. Lipscy, eds. 2013. *Japan Under the DPJ: The Politics of Transition and Governance.* Stanford, CA: Walter H. Shorenstein Asia-Pacific Research Center.

Laband, David N. and Bernard F. Lentz. 1983. "Like Father, Like Son: Toward an Economic Theory of Occupational Following." *Southern Economic Journal* 50(2):474–493.

Laband, David N. and Bernard F. Lentz. 1985. "Favorite Sons: Intergenerational Wealth Transfers Among Politicians." *Economic Inquiry* 23(3):395–414.

Labonne, Julien, Sahar Parsa, and Pablo Querubín. 2017. "Political Dynasties, Term Limits and Female Political Empowerment: Evidence from the Philippines." Unpublished manuscript.

Lam, Peng Er. 1996. "The Japanese Communist Party: Organization and Resilience in the Midst of Adversity." *Pacific Affairs* 69(3):361–379.

Lancaster, Thomas D. and W. David Patterson. 1990. "Comparative Pork Barrel Politics: Perceptions from the West German Bundestag." *Comparative Political Studies* 22(4):458–477.

Laver, Michael and Kenneth A. Shepsle. 1996. *Making and Breaking Governments.* Cambridge: Cambridge University Press.

Laver, Michael and Kenneth A. Shepsle, eds. 1994. *Cabinet Ministers and Parliamentary Government.* Cambridge: Cambridge University Press.

Lawless, Jennifer L. 2012. *Becoming a Candidate: Political Ambition and the Decision to Run for Office.* Cambridge: Cambridge University Press.

Lawless, Jennifer L. and Richard L. Fox. 2010. *It Still Takes a Candidate: Why Women Don't Run for Office.* Cambridge: Cambridge University Press.

Lee, David S. 2008. "Randomized Experiments from Non-Random Selection in U.S. House Elections." *Journal of Econometrics* 142(2):675–697.

Leiserson, Michael. 1968. "Factions and Coalitions in One-Party Japan: An Interpretation Based on the Theory of Games." *American Political Science Review* 62(3):770–787.

Levitt, Steven D. and Catherine D. Wolfram. 1997. "Decomposing the Sources of Incumbency Advantage in the U.S. House." *Legislative Studies Quarterly* 22(1):45–60.

Lipset, Seymour Martin and Stein Rokkan. 1967. *Party Systems and Voter Alignments: Cross-National Perspectives.* Toronto: Free Press.

Lumb, Martin. 2012. "Parliamentary Relations: Political Families in the Commonwealth Parliament." Commonwealth of Australia Parliamentary Library.

Lundell, Krister. 2004. "Determinants of Candidate Selection: Degree of Centralization in Comparative Perspective." *Party Politics* 10(1):25–47.

Lupia, Arthur and Mathew D. McCubbins. 1998. *The Democratic Dilemma: Can Citizens Learn What They Need to Know?* Cambridge: Cambridge University Press.

Machidori, Satoshi. 2012. *Shushō Seiji no Seido Bunseki: Gendai Nihon Seiji no Kenryoku Kiban Keisei* [The Japanese premiership: An institutional analysis of the power relations]. Tokyo: Chikura Shobō.

Machlachlan, Patricia L. 2006. "Storming the Castle: The Battle for Postal Reform in Japan." *Social Science Japan Journal* 9(1):1–18.

Maeda, Ko. 2009. Has the Electoral System Reform Made Japanese Elections Party-Centered? In *Political Change in Japan: Electoral Behavior, Party Realignment, and the Koizumi Reforms*, ed. Steven R. Reed, Kenneth Mori McElwain, and Kay Shimizu. Stanford, CA: Walter H. Shorenstein Asia-Pacific Research Center, pp. 47–66.

Maeda, Yukio and Hidenori Tsutsumi, eds. 2015. *Tōchi no Jōken: Minshutō ni Miru seiken unei to tōnai tōchi* [Party government and party governance: The case of the Democratic Party of Japan]. Tokyo: Chikura Shobō.

Mahoney, James and Kathleen Thelen. 2009. A Theory of Gradual Institutional Change. In *Explaining Institutional Change: Ambiguity, Agency, and Power*, ed. James Mahoney and Kathleen Thelen. Cambridge: Cambridge University Press, pp. 1–37.

Mair, Peter, Wolfgang C. Müller, and Fritz Plasser. 2004. Introduction: Electoral Challenges and Party Responses. In *Political Parties and Electoral Change: Party Responses to Electoral Markets*, ed. Peter Mair, Wolfgang C. Müller, and Fritz Plasser. London: Sage Publications, pp. 1–19.

Manow, Philip. 2015. *Mixed Rules, Mixed Strategies: Candidates and Parties in Germany's Electoral System*. Colchester, UK: ECPR Press.

Mansbridge, Jane. 1999. "Should Blacks Represent Blacks and Women Represent Women? A Contingent 'Yes.'" *Journal of Politics* 61(3):628–657.

Marangoni, Francesco and Filippo Tronconi. 2011. "When Territory Matters: Parliamentary Profiles and Legislative Behaviour in Italy (1987–2008)." *Journal of Legislative Studies* 17(4):415–434.

March, James G. and Johan P. Olsen. 1984. "The New Institutionalism: Organizational Factors in Political Life." *American Political Science Review* 78(3):734–749.

Marsh, Michael. 2007. "Candidates or Parties? Objects of Electoral Choice in Ireland." *Party Politics* 13(4):500–527.

Martin, Shane. 2014. "Why Electoral Systems Don't Always Matter: The Impact of 'Mega-Seats' on Legislative Behaviour in Ireland." *Party Politics* 20(3):467–479.

Martin, Shane. 2016. "Policy, Office, *and* Votes: The Electoral Value of Ministerial Office." *British Journal of Political Science* 46(2):281–296.

Mason, Richard H. P. 1969. *Japan's First General Election, 1890.* Cambridge: Cambridge University Press.

Masumi, Junnosuke. 1995. *Contemporary Politics in Japan.* Berkeley: University of California Press.

Masuyama, Mikitaka and Benjamin Nyblade. 2014. Ministerial Selection and Deselection in Japan. In *The Selection of Ministers Around the World: A Comparative Study,* ed. Keith Dowding and Patrick Dumont. New York: Routledge, pp. 61–83.

Matsuzaki, Tetsuhisa. 1991. *Nihon-gata Demokurashī no Gyakusetsu: 2-sei Giin ha Naze Umareru no ka.* Tokyo: Tōjusha.

Mayhew, David R. 1974. "Congressional Elections: The Case of the Vanishing Marginals." *Polity* 6(3):295–317.

McCubbins, Mathew D. and Frances M. Rosenbluth. 1995. Party Provision for Personal Politics: Dividing the Vote in Japan. In *Structure and Policy in Japan and the United States,* ed. Peter F. Cowhey and Mathew D. McCubbins. Cambridge: Cambridge University Press, pp. 35–55.

McElwain, Kenneth Mori. 2008. "Manipulating Electoral Rules to Manufacture Single Party Dominance." *American Journal of Political Science* 52(1):32–47.

McElwain, Kenneth Mori. 2012. "The Nationalization of Japanese Elections." *Journal of East Asian Studies* 12(3):323–350.

McKean, Margaret and Ethan Scheiner. 2000. "Japan's New Electoral System: La Plus ça Change . . ." *Electoral Studies* 19(1):447–477.

McMillan, M. E. 2013. *Fathers and Sons: The Rise and Fall of Political Dynasty in the Middle East.* New York: Palgrave Macmillan.

Mehrotra, Vikas, Randall Morck, Jungwook Shim, and Yupana Wiwattanakantang. 2013. "Adoptive Expectations: Rising Sons in Japanese Family Firms." *Journal of Financial Economics* 108(3):840–854.

Mendoza, Ronald U., Edsel L. Beja Jr., Victor S. Venida, and David B. Yap. 2012. "Inequality in Democracy: Insights from an Empirical Analysis of Political Dynasties in the 15th Philippine Congress." *Philippine Political Science Journal* 33(2):132–145.

Mershon, Carol. 2001. "Contending Models of Portfolio Allocation and Office Payoffs to Party Factions: Italy, 1963–79." *American Journal of Political Science* 45(2):277–293.

Michels, Robert. 1915. *Political Parties: A Sociological Study of the Oligarchical Tendencies of Modern Democracy.* New York: Hearst's International Library.

Mills, C. W. 1956. *The Power Elite.* Oxford: Oxford University Press.

Monday, Chris. 2011. "Family Rule as the Highest Stage of Communism." *Asian Survey* 51(5):812–843.

Mosca, Gaetano. 1939. *The Ruling Class (Elementi di Scienza Politica)*. New York: McGraw-Hill Book Co.

Moser, Robert G. and Ethan Scheiner. 2012. *Electoral Systems and Political Context: How the Effects of Rules Vary Across New and Established Democracies*. Cambridge: Cambridge University Press.

Moser, Scott and Andrew Reeves. 2014. "Taking the Leap: Voting, Rhetoric, and the Determinants of Electoral Reform." *Legislative Studies Quarterly* 39(4):467–502.

Mulgan, Aurelia George. 2014. *Ozawa Ichirō and Japanese Politics: Old Versus New*. London: Routledge.

Müller, Wolfgang C. 2000. "Political Parties in Parliamentary Democracies: Making Delegation and Accountability Work." *European Journal of Political Research* 37(3):309–333.

Müller, Wolfgang C. and Kaare Strøm. 2000. Coalition Governance in Western Europe: An Introduction. In *Coalition Governments in Western Europe*, ed. Wolfgang C. Müller and Kaare Strøm. Oxford: Oxford University Press, pp. 1–31.

Müller, Wolfgang C. and Kaare Strøm, eds. 1999. *Policy, Office, or Votes? How Political Parties in Western Europe Make Hard Decisions*. Cambridge: Cambridge University Press.

Müller, Wolfgang C. and Ulrich Sieberer. 2006. Party Law. In *Handbook of Party Politics*, ed. Richard S. Katz and William J. Crotty. London: Sage Publications, pp. 435–445.

Muraoka, Taishi. 2017. "Political Dynasties and Particularistic Campaigns." *Political Research Quarterly*. DOI:10.1177/1065912917745163.

Nakane, Chie. 1970. *Japanese Society*. Berkeley: University of California Press.

Nemoto, Kuniaki, Robert Pekkanen, and Ellis Krauss. 2014. "Over-Nominating Candidates, Undermining the Party: The Collective Action Problem Under SNTV in Japan." *Party Politics* 20(5):740–750.

Neumann, Sigmund. 1956. Towards a Comparative Study of Political Parties. In *Modern Political Parties*, ed. Sigmund Neumann. Chicago: University of Chicago Press, pp. 395–421.

Niven, David. 1998. "Party Elites and Women Candidates: The Shape of Bias." *Women & Politics* 19(2):57–80.

Nonaka, Naoto. 1995. *Jimintō Seikenka no Seiji Eriito: Shinseidoron ni yoru Nichi-Futsu hikaku* [Political elites under the LDP government]. Tokyo: Tokyo Daigaku Shuppankai.

Norris, Pippa. 1997. Introduction: Theories of Recruitment. In *Passages to Power: Legislative Recruitment in Advanced Democracies*, ed. Pippa Norris. Cambridge: Cambridge University Press, pp. 1–14.

Norris, Pippa and Joni Lovenduski. 1995. *Political Recruitment: Gender, Race and Class in the British Parliament*. Cambridge: Cambridge University Press.

North, Christopher Titus. 2005. "From Technocracy to Aristocracy: The Changing Career Paths of Japanese Politicians." *Journal of East Asian Studies* 5(2):239–272.

North, Douglass C. 1990. *Institutions, Institutional Change and Economic Performance*. Cambridge: Cambridge University Press.

Nyblade, Benjamin and Steven R. Reed. 2008. "Who Cheats? Who Loots? Political Competition and Corruption in Japan, 1947–1993." *American Journal of Political Science* 52(4):926–941.

Olson, Mancur. 1993. "Dictatorship, Democracy, and Development." *American Political Science Review* 87(3):567–576.

O'Malley, Eoin. 2006. "Ministerial Selection in Ireland: Limited Choice in a Political Village." *Irish Political Studies* 21(3):319–336.

O'Malley, Eoin. 2007. "The Power of Prime Ministers: Results of an Expert Survey." *International Political Science Review* 28(1):7–27.

Ono, Yoshikuni. 2012. "Portfolio Allocation as Leadership Strategy: Intraparty Bargaining in Japan." *American Journal of Political Science* 56(3):553–567.

Oskarsson, Sven, Christopher T. Dawes, and Karl-Oskar Lindgren. 2017. "It Runs in the Family: A Study of Political Candidacy Among Swedish Adoptees." *Political Behavior*. DOI:10.1007/s11109-017-9429-1.

Otake, Hideo. 1996. "Forces for Political Reform: The Liberal Democratic Party's Young Reformers and Ozawa Ichiro." *Journal of Japanese Studies* 22(2):269–294.

Otake, Hideo. 1998. *How Electoral Reform Boomeranged: Continuity in Japanese Campaigning Style*. Tokyo: Japan Center for International Exchange.

Ozawa, Ichirō (translated by Louisa Rubinfein). 1994. *Blueprint for a New Japan: The Rethinking of a Nation*. Tokyo: Kōdansha International.

Paine, Thomas. 1776 [1856]. *Common Sense*. Boston: J. P. Mendum.

Pareto, Vilfredo. 1901. *The Rise and Fall of the Elites*. New York: Arno Press.

Park, Cheol Hee. 1998. The Enduring Campaign Networks of Tokyo's Shitamachi District. In *How Electoral Reform Boomeranged: Continuity in Japanese Campaigning Style*, ed. Hideo Otake. Tokyo: Japan Center for International Exchange, pp. 59–96.

Parker, Glenn R. 1996. *Congress and the Rent-Seeking Society*. Ann Arbor: University of Michigan Press.

Patrikios, Stratos and Michalis Chatzikonstantinou. 2015. "Dynastic Politics: Family Ties in the Greek Parliament, 2000–12." *South European Society and Politics* 20(1):93–111.

Pekkanen, Robert, Ellis S. Krauss, and Benjamin Nyblade. 2006. "Electoral Incentives in Mixed Member Systems: Party, Posts, and Zombie Politicians in Japan." *American Political Science Review* 100(2):183–193.

Pekkanen, Robert J., Benjamin Nyblade, and Ellis S. Krauss. 2014. "The Logic of Ministerial Selection: Electoral System and Cabinet Appointments in Japan." *Social Science Japan Journal* 17(1):3–22.

Pérez-González, Francisco. 2006. "Inherited Control and Firm Performance." *American Economic Review* 96(5):1559–1588.

Phillips, Anne. 1995. *The Politics of Presence.* Oxford: Clarendon Press.

Pierson, Paul. 2004. *Politics in Time: History, Institutions, and Social Analysis.* Princeton, NJ: Princeton University Press.

Pitkin, Hanna F. 1967. *The Concept of Representation.* Berkeley: University of California Press.

Poguntke, Thomas, Susan E. Scarrow, Paul D. Webb, Elin H. Allern, Nicholas Aylott, Ingrid van Biezen, Enrico Calossi, Marina Costa Lobo, William P. Cross, Kris Deschouwer, Zsolt Enyedi, Elodie Fabre, David M. Farrell, Anika Gauja, Eugenio Pizzimenti, Petr Kopecký, Ruud Koole, Wolfgang C. Müller, Karina Kosiara-Pedersen, Gideon Rahat, Aleks Szczerbiak, Emilie van Haute, and Tània Verge. 2016. "Party Rules, Party Resources and the Politics of Parliamentary Democracies." *Party Politics* 22(6):661–678.

Popkin, Samuel. 1991. *The Reasoning Voter: Communication and Persuasion in Presidential Campaigns.* Chicago: University of Chicago Press.

Pratt, Edward E. 1999. *Japan's Protoindustrial Elite: The Economic Foundations of the Gōnō.* Cambridge, MA: Harvard University Press.

Proksch, Sven-Oliver and Jonathan B. Slapin. 2012. "Institutional Foundations of Legislative Speech." *American Journal of Political Science* 56(3):520–537.

Putnam, Robert D. 1976. *The Comparative Study of Political Elites.* Englewood Cliffs, NJ: Prentice-Hall.

Querubín, Pablo. 2011. "Political Reform and Elite Persistence: Term Limits and Political Dynasties in the Philippines." Unpublished manuscript.

Querubín, Pablo. 2016. "Family and Politics: Dynastic Persistence in the Philippines." *Quarterly Journal of Political Science* 11(2):151–181.

Quigley, Harold S. 1932. *Japanese Government and Politics.* New York: Century Co.

Quiroz Flores, Alejandro and Alastair Smith. 2011. "Leader Survival and Cabinet Change." *Economics and Politics* 23(3):345–366.

Rahat, Gideon. 2007. "Candidate Selection: The Choice Before the Choice." *Journal of Democracy* 18(1):157–170.

Ramseyer, J. Mark and Frances M. Rosenbluth. 1993. *Japan's Political Marketplace.* Cambridge, MA: Harvard University Press.

Ramseyer, J. Mark and Frances M. Rosenbluth. 1995. *The Politics of Oligarchy: Institutional Choice in Imperial Japan.* Cambridge: Cambridge University Press.

Ranney, Austin. 1981. Candidate Selection. In *Democracy at the Polls: A Comparative Study of Competitive National Elections*, ed. David Butler, Howard R. Penniman, and Austin Ranney. Washington, DC: American Enterprise Institute for Public Policy Research, pp. 75–106.

Redmond, Paul and John Regan. 2015. "Incumbency Advantage in a Proportional Electoral System: A Regression Discontinuity Analysis of Irish Elections." *European Journal of Political Economy* 38:244–256.

Reed, Steven R. 1990. "Structure and Behaviour: Extending Duverger's Law to the Japanese Case." *British Journal of Political Science* 20(3):335–356.

Reed, Steven R. 2009. "Party Strategy or Candidate Strategy: How Did the LDP Run the Right Number of Candidates in Japan's Multi-Member Districts?" *Party Politics* 15(3):295–314.

Reed, Steven R. and John M. Bolland. 1999. The Fragmentation Effect of SNTV in Japan. In *Elections in Japan, Korea, and Taiwan under the Single Non-Transferable Vote: The Comparative Study of an Embedded Institutions*, ed. Bernard Grofman, Sung-Chull Lee, Edwin A. Winkler, and Brian Woodall. Ann Arbor: University of Michigan Press, pp. 211–226.

Reed, Steven R. and Ethan Scheiner. 2003. "Electoral Incentives and Policy Preferences: Mixed Motives Behind Party Defections in Japan." *British Journal of Political Science* 33(3):469–490.

Reed, Steven R., Ethan Scheiner, Daniel M. Smith, and Michael F. Thies. 2013. The 2012 Election Results: The LDP Wins Big by Default. In *Japan Decides 2012: The Japanese General Election*, ed. Robert Pekkanen, Steven R. Reed, and Ethan Scheiner. New York: Palgrave Macmillan, pp. 34–46.

Reed, Steven R., Ethan Scheiner, and Michael F. Thies. 2012. "The End of LDP Dominance and the Rise of Party-Oriented Politics in Japan." *Journal of Japanese Studies* 38(2):353–376.

Reed, Steven R. and Kay Shimizu. 2009. Avoiding a Two-Party System: The Liberal Democratic Party Versus Duverger's Law. In *Political Change in Japan: Electoral Behavior, Party Realignment, and the Koizumi Reforms*, ed. Steven R. Reed, Kenneth Mori McElwain, and Kay Shimizu. Stanford, CA: Walter H. Shorenstein Asia-Pacific Research Center, pp. 29–46.

Reed, Steven R., Kenneth Mori McElwain, and Kay Shimizu, eds. 2009. *Political Change in Japan: Electoral Behavior, Party Realignment, and the Koizumi Reforms.* Stanford, CA: Walter H. Shorenstein Asia-Pacific Research Center.

Reeves, Justin F. and Daniel M. Smith. 2017. "Getting to Know Her: Information and Gender Bias in Preferential Voting Systems." Unpublished manuscript.

Reynolds, Andrew. 1999. "Women in the Legislatures and Executives of the World: Knocking at the Highest Glass Ceiling." *World Politics* 51(4):547–572.

Richardson, Bradley M. 1991. Voting Behavior in Comparative Perspective. In *The Japanese Voter*, ed. Scott C. Flanagan, Shinsaku Kohei, Ichiro Miyake, Bradley M. Richardson, and Joji Watanuki. New Haven, CT: Yale University Press, pp. 3–46.

Riker, William. 1962. *The Theory of Political Coalitions*. New Haven, CT: Yale University Press.

Rosenbluth, Frances McCall and Michael F. Thies. 2010. *Japan Transformed: Political Change and Economic Restructuring*. Princeton, NJ: Princeton University Press.

Rossi, Martín A. 2017. "Self-Perpetuation of Political Power." *Economic Journal* 127(605):F455–F473.

Rush, Michael. 2000. The Decline of the Nobility. In *Democratic Representation in Europe: Diversity, Change, and Convergence*, ed. Maurizio Cotta and Heinrich Best. Oxford: Oxford University Press, pp. 29–50.

Saalfeld, Thomas. 2000. "Members of Parliament and Governments in Western Europe: Agency Relations and Problems of Oversight." *European Journal of Political Research* 37(3):353–376.

Saito, Takuji. 2008. "Family Firms and Firm Performance: Evidence from Japan." *Journal of the Japanese and International Economies* 22(1):620–646.

Samuels, Richard J. 2007. *Securing Japan: Tokyo's Grand Strategy and the Future of East Asia*. Ithaca, NY: Cornell University Press.

Sanbonmatsu, Kira. 2006. *Where Women Run: Gender and Party in the American States*. Ann Arbor: University of Michigan Press.

Satō, Seizaburō and Tetsuhisa Matsuzaki. 1986. *Jimintō Seiken* [LDP rule]. Tokyo: Chūō Kōronsha.

Schattschneider, E. E. 1942. *Party Government*. New York: Rinehart & Co.

Scheiner, Ethan. 2006. *Democracy Without Competition in Japan: Opposition Failure in a One-Party Dominant State*. Cambridge: Cambridge University Press.

Scheiner, Ethan, Daniel M. Smith, and Michael F. Thies. 2016. The 2014 Japanese Election Results: The Opposition Cooperates, but Fails to Inspire. In *Japan Decides 2014: The Japanese General Election*, ed. Robert J. Pekkanen, Steven R. Reed, and Ethan Scheiner. New York: Palgrave Macmillan, pp. 22–38.

Schlesinger, Joseph A. 1975. "The Primary Goals of Political Parties: A Clarification of Positive Theory." *American Political Science Review* 69(1):840–849.

Schoppa, Leonard J., ed. 2011. *The Evolution of Japan's Party System: Politics and Policy in an Era of Institutional Change*. Toronto: University of Toronto Press.

Schröder, Valentin and Philip Manow. 2014. "Elektorale Koordination, Legislative Kohäsion und der Aufstieg der Modernen Massenpartei: Die Grenzen des Mehrheitswahlrechts im Deutschen Kaiserreich, 1890–1918" [Electoral coordination, legislative cohesion, and the rise of the modern mass party: The limits of majoritarian representation in Germany, 1890–1918]. *Politische Vierteljahresschrift* 55(3):518–554.

Schwindt-Bayer, Leslie A. 2011. "Women Who Win: Social Backgrounds, Paths to Power, and Political Ambition in Latin American Legislatures." *Politics & Gender* 7(1):1–33.

Seawright, Jason. 2016. *Multi-Method Social Science: Combining Qualitative and Quantitative Tools.* Cambridge: Cambridge University Press.

Sekō, Hiroshige. 2006. *Jimintō Kaizō Purojekuto 650 Nichi* [LDP reform project: 650 days]. Tokyo: Shinchōsa.

Shih, Victor, Christopher Adolph, and Mingxing Liu. 2012. "Getting Ahead in the Communist Party: Explaining the Advancement of Central Committee Members in China." *American Political Science Review* 106(1):166–187.

Shinoda, Tomohito. 2013. *Contemporary Japanese Politics: Institutional Changes and Power Shifts.* New York: Columbia University Press.

Shiratori, Rei. 1988. Japan: Localism, Factionalism, Personalism. In *Candidate Selection in Comparative Perspective: The Secret Garden of Politics,* ed. Michael Gallagher and Michael Marsh. London: Sage Publications, pp. 169–189.

Shomer, Yael. 2009. "Candidate Selection Procedures, Seniority, and Vote-Seeking Behavior." *Comparative Political Studies* 42(7):945–970.

Shomer, Yael. 2014. "What Affects Candidate Selection Processes? A Cross-National Examination." *Party Politics* 20(4):533–546.

Shugart, Matthew Soberg. 2001. "Electoral 'Efficiency' and the Move to Mixed-Member Systems." *Electoral Studies* 20(1):173–193.

Shugart, Matthew Soberg and Martin P. Wattenberg. 2001. Mixed-Member Electoral Systems: A Definition and Typology. In *Mixed-Member Electoral Systems: The Best of Both Worlds?*, ed. Matthew Søberg Shugart and Martin P. Wattenberg. Oxford: Oxford University Press, pp. 1–24.

Shugart, Matthew Søberg, Melody Ellis Valdini, and Kati Suominen. 2005. "Looking for Locals: Voter Information Demands and Personal Vote-Earning Attributes of Legislators Under Proportional Representation." *American Journal of Political Science* 49(2):437–449.

Siavelis, Peter M. and Scott Morgenstern. 2008. Political Recruitment and Candidate Selection in Latin America: A Framework for Analysis. In *Pathways to Power: Political Recruitment and Candidate Selection in Latin America,* ed. Peter M. Siavelis and Scott Morgenstern. University Park: Pennsylvania State University Press, pp. 3–37.

Sieberer, Ulrich. 2010. "Behavioral Consequences of Mixed Electoral Systems: Deviating Voting Behavior of District and List MPs in the German Bundestag." *Electoral Studies* 29(1):484–496.

Smith, Daniel M. 2013. Candidate Recruitment for the 2012 Election: New Parties, New Methods . . . Same Old Pool of Candidates? In *Japan Decides 2012:*

The Japanese General Election, ed. Robert Pekkanen, Steven R. Reed, and Ethan Scheiner. New York: Palgrave Macmillan, pp. 101–122.

Smith, Daniel M. 2014. Party Ideals and Practical Constraints in Kōmeitō Candidate Nominations. In *Kōmeitō: Politics and Religion in Japan*, ed. George Ehrhardt, Axel Klein, Levi McLaughlin, and Steven R. Reed. Berkeley: Institute of East Asian Studies at the University of California, Berkeley, pp. 139–162.

Smith, Daniel M. 2016. Candidates in the 2014 Election: Better Coordination and Higher Candidate Quality. In *Japan Decides 2014: The Japanese General Election*, ed. Robert J. Pekkanen, Steven R. Reed, and Ethan Scheiner. New York: Palgrave Macmillan, pp. 118–133.

Smith, Daniel M. and Shane Martin. 2017. "Political Dynasties and the Selection of Cabinet Ministers." *Legislative Studies Quarterly* 42(1):131–165.

Smith, Daniel M., Robert J. Pekkanen, and Ellis S. Krauss. 2013. Building a Party: Candidate Recruitment in the Democratic Party of Japan, 1996–2012. In *Japan Under the DPJ: The Politics of Transition and Governance*, ed. Kenji E. Kushida and Phillip Y. Lipscy. Stanford, CA: Walter H. Shorenstein Asia-Pacific Research Center, pp. 157–190.

Smith, Daniel M. and Hidenori Tsutsumi. 2016. "Candidate Selection Methods and Policy Cohesion in Parties: The Impact of Open Recruitment in Japan." *Party Politics* 22(3):339–353.

Stockwin, J. A. A. 1992. The Japan Socialist Party: Resurgence After Long Decline. In *The Japanese Party System*, ed. Ronald J. Hrebenar. Boulder, CO: Westview Press, pp. 81–115.

Stratmann, Thomas and Martin Baur. 2002. "Plurality Rule, Proportional Representation, and the German Bundestag: How Incentives to Pork-Barrel Differ Across Electoral Systems." *American Journal of Political Science* 46(3):506–514.

Streeck, Wolfgang and Kathleen Thelen. 2005. *Beyond Continuity: Institutional Change in Advanced Political Economies*. Oxford: Oxford University Press.

Strøm, Kaare. 1990. "A Behavioral Theory of Competitive Political Parties." *American Journal of Political Science* 34(2):565–598.

Strøm, Kaare. 1997. "Rules, Reasons, and Routines: Legislative Roles in Parliamentary Democracies." *Journal of Legislative Studies* 3(1):155–174.

Strøm, Kaare. 2000. "Delegation and Accountability in Parliamentary Democracies." *European Journal of Political Research* 37(3):261–290.

Strøm, Kaare and Wolfgang C. Müller. 1999. Political Parties and Hard Choices. In *Policy, Office, or Votes? How Political Parties in Western Europe Make Hard Decisions*, ed. Wolfgang C. Müller and Kaare Strøm. Cambridge: Cambridge University Press, pp. 1–35.

Strøm, Kaare, Wolfgang C. Müller, and Torbjörn Bergman, eds. 2003. *Delegation and Accountability in Parliamentary Democracies.* Oxford: Oxford University Press.

Svaleryd, Helena. 2009. "Women's Representation and Public Spending." *European Journal of Political Economy* 25(2):186–198.

Taniguchi, Naoko. 2008. Keeping It in the Family: Hereditary Politics and Democracy in Japan. In *Democratic Reform in Japan: Assessing the Impact,* ed. Sherry L. Martin and Gill Steel. Boulder, CO: Lynne Rienner Publishers, pp. 65–80.

Tatebayashi, Masahiko. 2004. *Giin Kōdō no Seiji Keizaigaku: Jimintō Shihai no Seido Bunseki* [The political economy of Diet member behavior: A system analysis of LDP rule]. Tokyo: Yuhikakusha.

Tavits, Margit. 2009. "The Making of Mavericks: Local Loyalties and Party Defection." *Comparative Political Studies* 42(6):793–815.

Tavits, Margit. 2010. "Effect of Local Ties on Electoral Success and Parliamentary Behaviour: The Case of Estonia." *Party Politics* 16(2):215–235.

Terenzini, Patrick T., Leonard Springer, Patricia M. Yaeger, Ernest T. Pascarella, and Amaury Nora. 1996. "First-Generation College Students: Characteristics, Experiences, and Cognitive Development." *Research in Higher Education* 37(1):1–22.

Thananithichot, Stithorn and Wichuda Satidporn. 2016. "Political Dynasties in Thailand: The Recent Picture After the 2011 General Election." *Asian Studies Review* 40(3):340–359.

Thayer, Nathaniel B. 1969. *How the Conservatives Rule Japan.* Princeton, NJ: Princeton University Press.

Thistlethwaite, Donald L. and Donald T. Campbell. 1960. "Regression-Discontinuity Analysis: An Alternative to the Ex Post Facto Experiment." *Journal of Educational Psychology* 51(6):309–317.

Tokugawa, Tsunenari. 2009. *The Edo Inheritance.* Tokyo: International House of Japan.

Totman, Conrad. 1981. *Japan Before Perry: A Short History.* Berkeley: University of California Press.

Tsutsumi, Hidenori. 2012. "Kohōsha Sentei Katei no Kaihō to Seitō Soshiki" [Opening up the candidate selection process and party organization]. *Senkyo Kenkyū* 28(1):5–20.

Tsutsumi, Hidenori and Takayoshi Uekami. 2011. Minshutō no Seisaku: Keizokusei to Henka [DPJ policies: Continuity and change]. In *Minshutō no Soshiki to Seisaku* [DPJ organization and policy], ed. Takayoshi Uekami and Hidenori Tsutsumi. Tokyo: Tōyō Keizai Shinpōsha, pp. 225–253.

Tusalem, Rollin F. and Jeffrey J. Pe-Aguirre. 2013. "The Effect of Political Dynasties on Effective Democratic Governance: Evidence from the Philippines." *Asian Politics & Policy* 5(3):359–386.

Uekami, Takayoshi and Hidenori Tsutsumi. 2011. Minshutō no Kessei Katei, Soshiki to Seisaku [DPJ formation, organization, and policy]. In *Minshutō no Soshiki to Seisaku: Kettō kara Seiken Kōtai made* [The organization and policies of the DPJ: From formation to acquisition of power], ed. Takayoshi Uekami and Hidenori Tsutsumi. Tokyo: Tōyō Keizai Shinpōsha, pp. 1–28.

Uesugi, Takashi. 2009. *Seshū Giin no Karakuri* [The mechanics of hereditary Diet members]. Tokyo: Bungei Shunjū.

Usui, Chikako and Richard A. Colignon. 2004. "Continuity and Change in Paths to High Political Office: Ex-Bureaucrats and Hereditary Politicians in Japan." *Asian Business & Management* 3(4):395–416.

van Coppenolle, Brenda. 2017. "Political Dynasties in the UK House of Commons: The Null Effect of Narrow Electoral Selection." *Legislative Studies Quarterly* 42(3):449–475.

van Liefferinge, Hilde and Kristof Steyvers. 2009. "Family Matters? Degrees of Family Politicization in Political Recruitment and Career Start of Mayors in Belgium." *Acta Politica* 44(2):125–149.

Velasco Rivera, Carlos. 2017. "Political Dynasties and Party Strength: Evidence from Victorian Britain." Unpublished manuscript.

Vierhaus, Rudolf and Ludolf Herbst. 2002. *Biographisches Handbuch der Mitglieder des Deutschen Bundestages 1949–2001/Biographical Dictionary of Members of the German Bundestag 1949–2001*. Bilingual ed. Munich: K. G. Saur Verlag.

Vilas, Carlos M. 1992. "Family Affairs: Class, Lineage and Politics in Contemporary Nicaragua." *Journal of Latin American Studies* 24(2):309–341.

Villalonga, Belen and Raphael Amit. 2006. "How Do Family Ownership, Management, and Control Affect Firm Value?" *Journal of Financial Economics* 80(2):385–417.

Warwick, Paul V. and James N. Druckman. 2001. "Portfolio Salience and the Proportionality of Payoffs in Coalition Governments." *British Journal of Political Science* 31(4):627–649.

Weiner, Robert. 2011. The Evolution of the DPJ: Two Steps Forward, One Step Back. In *The Evolution of Japan's Party System: Politics and Policy in an Era of Institutional Change*, ed. Leonard J. Schoppa. Toronto: University of Toronto Press, pp. 63–98.

Werner, Emmy E. 1966. "Women in Congress: 1917–1964." *Western Political Quarterly* 19(1):16–30.

Wertman, Douglas A. 1988. Italy: Local Involvement, Central Control. In *Candidate Selection in Comparative Perspective: The Secret Garden of Politics*, ed. Michael Gallagher and Michael Marsh. London: Sage Publications, pp. 145–168.

West, Mark D. 2008. *Secrets, Sex, and Spectacle: The Rules of Scandal in Japan and the United States*. Chicago: University of Chicago Press.

White, Linda E. 2014. Challenging the Heteronormative Family in the Koseki: Surname, Legitimacy and Unmarried Mothers. In *Japan's Household Registration System and Citizenship: Koseki, Identification and Documentation*, ed. David Chapman and Karl Jakob Krogness. London: Routledge, pp. 239–256.

Wittman, Donald A. 1973. "Parties as Utility Maximizers." *American Political Science Review* 67(2):490–498.

Woodall, Brian. 2014. *Growing Democracy in Japan: The Parliamentary Cabinet System since 1868*. Lexington: University Press of Kentucky.

Worley, Matthew, ed. 2009. *The Foundations of the British Labour Party: Identities, Cultures and Perspectives, 1900–39*. New York: Routledge.

Yazaki, Eiji, ed. 2010. *Seiken Kōtai, saa Tsugi ha Seshū Seijika Kōtai!* [Change in government, next change in hereditary politicians!]. Tokyo: Honnoki.

Yoshino, M. Y. 1968. *Japan's Managerial System: Tradition and Innovation*. Cambridge, MA: MIT Press.

Ziegfeld, Adam. 2016. Dynasticism Across Indian Political Parties. In *Democratic Dynasties: State, Party, and Family in Contemporary Indian Politics*, ed. Kanchan Chandra. Cambridge: Cambridge University Press, pp. 97–126.

Index

Page numbers followed by "f" or "t" indicate material in figures or tables.

Finland, 37, 41–42, 48, 88, 99, 104. *See also*
Dynasties in Democracies Dataset
first-time candidates: age of, 2; effects of
reform on, 161–162 (161f, 162f), 170;
former positions of, 149–150; importance of name recognition for, 134;
LDP's age limit for, 156–157; under
MMD, 187–189 (188t); second-generation, 173; success of by type, 197–205
(198t, 201f, 202f, 205f), 285t–287t; success rates of, 189, 191
formal institutions, defined, 14
Forsius, Merikukka, 48
Fox, Richard, 78
FPTP (first-past-the-post) system, 22–23;
in Japan, 25; legacy candidates decreasing, 117; maximizing short-term votes
in, 83; MMM tier, 179
Fukuda Hiroichi, 215
Fukuda Takeo, 215
Fukuda Tatsuo, 167, 215
Fukuda Yasuo, 23, 164, 167, 215
Fukui Haruhiro, 144
Fukumoto Kentarō, 191
future research, 269–271

Gallagher, Michael, 98
Galton, Sir Francis, 303n10
Gandhi, Indira, 245
Gandhi, Rahul, 4
Gandhi, Sonia, 4
Gelman, Andrew, 192
gender: and dynasties, 244–249 (248t);
female candidates rare in LDP, 2; positive effects from dynasties, 31; quotas
bringing in more women, 96; "widow's
succession," 31, 57, 61, 248; women
must outperform to win, 27
General Council of Trade Unions of Japan
(Sōhyō), 123
generational turnover, reforms encouraging, 156
geographic dispersion of dynasties, 59–61
(60f)
George III, 241
Germany, 5 (5f), 45, 71, 99, 104. *See also*
Dynasties in Democracies Dataset

Gestrin, Christina, 48
Geys, Benny, 64
Golden, Miriam, 256
Gore, Al, 6, 40
Gore, Albert Sr., 40
Graham, Kennedy, 47
Granvik, Nils-Anders, 48
Greece, 4, 5f, 104
Grimmer, Justin, 251
Gunnlaugsson, Sigmundur Davíd, 300n8
Guttenberg, Karl-Theodor zu, 45

Hainmueller, Jens, 209
Hara Kenzaburō, 306n12
Hashimoto Ryōgo, 215
Hashimoto Ryūtarō, 23, 215, 218
Hashimoto Tōru, 157
Hata Tsutomu, 145, 148, 168, 218; cabinet
of, 230
Hata Yūichirō, 168
Hatoyama Hideo, 129
Hatoyama Ichirō, 118, 126, 129–130, 216,
218, 229
Hatoyama Iichirō, 129, 216
Hatoyama Jirō, 266, 307n14
Hatoyama Kazuo, 129, 216
Hatoyama Kunio, 9, 129–130, 145, 216,
266, 307n14, 309–310n34
Hatoyama Tarō, xvii, 307n14
Hatoyama Yasuko, 300n13
Hatoyama Yukio, 9, 23, 129–130, 145, 148,
216, 251, 266–267, 310n34
Hazan, Reuven, 19, 97
Hellinger distance, 251–252 (252f)
Henare, Raymond, 47
hereditary candidates: defined, 21–22; in
LDP, 22, 166; voter surveys regarding,
184, 206–212 (207f, 208f, 211f). *See also*
legacy candidates
hereditary leadership in family-run firms,
242
hereditary rule in Japan, 69–70
Herzog, Chaim, 43
Herzog, Isaac, 43, 49
Hess, Stephen, 4, 9, 40–41, 55, 89–90,
299n5
hierarchy, vertical, 71–72

Failed Democratization in Prewar Japan: Breakdown of a Hybrid Regime
Harukata Takenaka (2014)

New Challenges for Maturing Democracies in Korea and Taiwan
Edited by Larry Diamond and Gi-Wook Shin (2014)

Spending Without Taxation: FILP and the Politics of Public Finance in Japan
Gene Park (2011)

The Institutional Imperative: The Politics of Equitable Development in Southeast Asia
Erik Martinez Kuhonta (2011)

One Alliance, Two Lenses: U.S.-Korea Relations in a New Era
Gi-Wook Shin (2010)

Collective Resistance in China: Why Popular Protests Succeed or Fail
Yongshun Cai (2010)

The Chinese Cultural Revolution as History
Edited by Joseph W. Esherick, Paul G. Pickowicz, and Andrew G. Walder (2006)

Ethnic Nationalism in Korea: Genealogy, Politics, and Legacy
Gi-Wook Shin (2006)

Prospects for Peace in South Asia
Edited by Rafiq Dossani and Henry S. Rowen (2005)